"A visionary in his field."

- ELIZABETH MARIE ANNE SPRAGGINS (FORMERLY ALURA JENSON)

"The coolest cat you could ever meet. Unshakable and honest, which is rare in the adult world."

- NICKI HUNTER, AVN HALL OF FAME PERFORMER

"Irreplaceable and sorely missed."

- JULIA ANN, HALL OF FAME ADULT PERFORMER

"A sexy porn god. With the best cock."

- HAILEY YOUNG, WORLD RENOWNED FILTH BUCKET

"A maestro of the industry, a visionary whose artistic tapestry is woven with threads of profound professionalism and boundless creativity."

- SUNNY LANE, AVN HALL OF FAME PERFORMER, SUNNYLANELIVE.COM

"Vic Lagina has the biggest balls in the business. He always put amazing energy on set."

- MARKUS DUPREE, MALE PERFORMER OF THE YEAR, 2018

"A free spirit in the industry, who never left anything on the table and claimed that a facial was the only acceptable cumshot."

- JOHNNY SINS, MALE PERFORMER AND MEME EVERYWHERE

"Vic Lagina was the man who not just let, but encouraged me to destroy an entire set and light it on fire."

- JAMES DEEN, MALE PERFORMER OF THE YEAR 2009, 2013

"Tall, dark and handsome as well as friendly, fun and kind. Something you don't expect while in the makeup chair on a porn set. Like the bartender at the strip club, he was the one you want, but not the one you got."

- SARA JAY, AVN HALL OF FAME PERFORMER

"Vic Lagina was no bullshit."

- CHARLES DERA AKA KARL TOUGHLOVE

"I loved Vic Lagina the moment I met him. I was extremely horny and couldn't wait to attack my co-stars which Vic appreciated. He loved my antics and crazy ways. He was always respectful and a dear friend."

- AVA DEVINE, AVN BEST ORAL SEX SCENE, 2005 AND HOWARD STERN'S WORLD BIGGEST WHORE CONTESTANT (RUNNER UP)

"No BS kinda guy, always a good time. I always looked forward to seeing him on set. He had such a huge role in building Brazzers."

- TOMMY GUNN, AVN HALL OF FAMER, AVN MALE PERFORMER OF THE YEAR, 2007

"His original ideas took us to do unusual scenes where pornography was not the main focus. Vic had a special touch or vision to make everything more entertaining."

- RAMÓN NOMAR, AVN HALL OF FAMER

"My grounding force in a sea of chaos, a friend I knew I would walk through many lives with, while learning and laughing along the way."

- THE REAL LISA ANN

"A book waiting to happen."

- NIKKI, EX-PERFORMER AND LOVE INTEREST

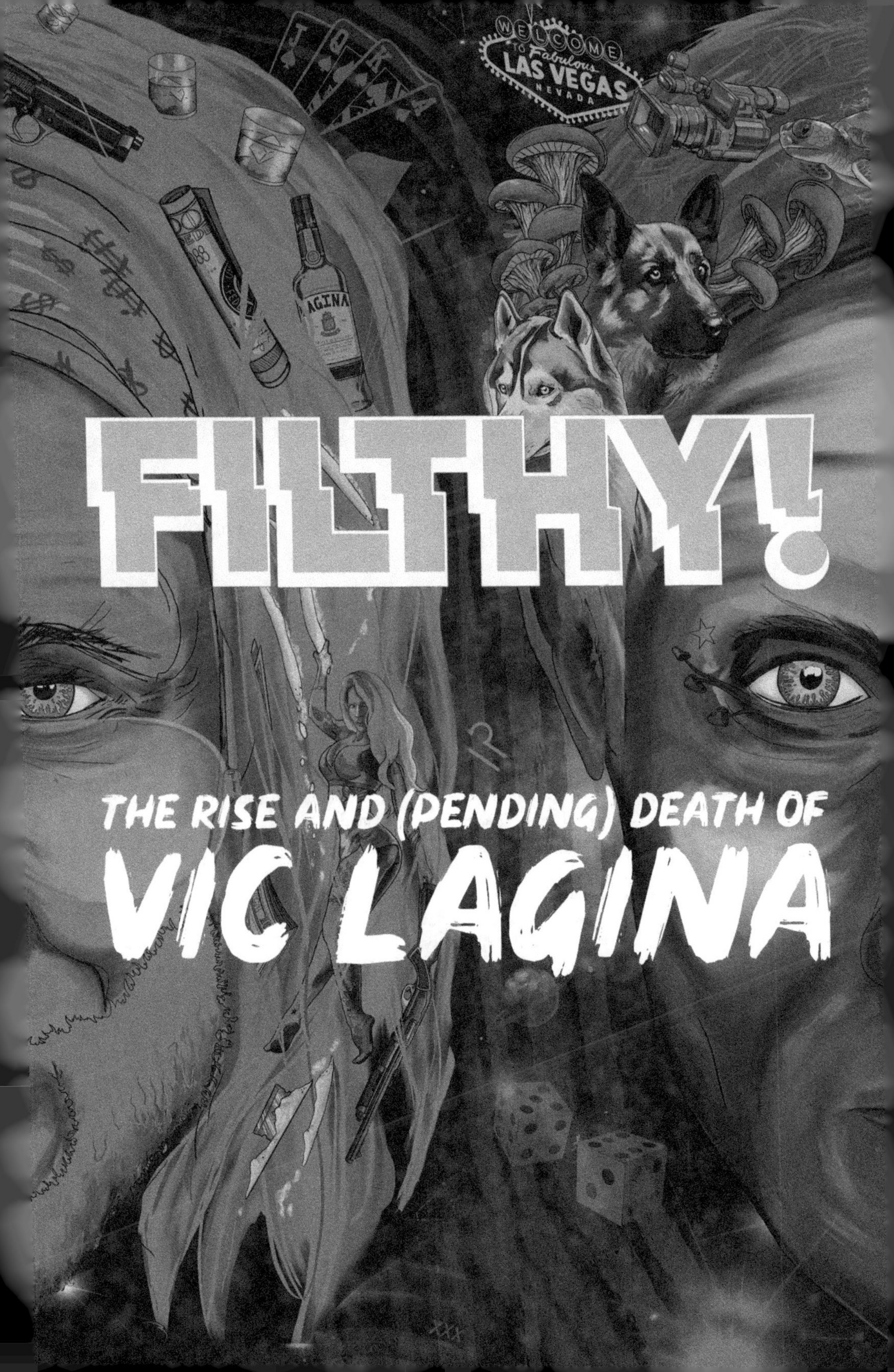

FILTHY!

THE RISE AND (PENDING) DEATH OF VIC LAGINA

Filthy! The Rise and (Pending) Death of Vic Lagina

Tweet Vic @viclagina OZ @zpaceball

Cover Art: Breze Schmitz www.brezeart.com
Book Design: Paul-Hawkins.com

ISBN: 979-8-9891981-0-8 (Paperback)
ISBN: 979-8-9891981-1-5 (eBook)

This book is dedicated to my mother. While I am certain she'd be proud of the man I evolved into, I often wonder what she'd think of the man I was. My guess is she'd be somewhat repulsed.

CONTENTS

> Autobiography is only to be trusted when it reveals something disgraceful. A man who gives a good account of himself is probably lying, since any life when viewed from the inside is simply a series of defeats.
>
> - GEORGE ORWELL

AUTHOR'S FOREWORD

What you're about to read started out in 2015 as a journal. I needed to get everything which had transpired during my career as a pornographer out of my head. Cocaine was starting to lose her grasp while I was trying to keep another one of my dysfunctional relationships together. After spending a month recalling and writing about my previous forty-one years on Spaceship Earth, it became a cathartic exercise acknowledging what a shit show my life had become. Although I was still chest-deep in the porn industry, I started turning corners. The focus became making better life decisions to ensure a soft landing whenever I left the adult industry. This is where I am now. In my quest for financial stability, I made shitty people very wealthy. I wrestle with this daily.

Every few years I added and updated, not knowing when the story of Vic Lagina would end. Until it did. For over eight more years, I added chapters and side topics, but I never revised. I cringe knowing the fucked-up headspace I was in. It was all ego, rationalization, and shallowness. There was an anger and a mean-spiritedness toward my colleagues. However, my intention was to write a raw and brutally honest story. I did not want to soften my many rough edges. I struggled with the idea of releasing a memoir. Who's going to care? Who the fuck am I?

With no scientific backing, I feel my remaining time is limited. Even though I am pushing fifty at the time of this writing, I am keeping it together. Blood tests look great. Cardiac score is perfect. I don't have to get another colonoscopy for ten years. I exercise every day and have zero stressors because I no longer work. I chill all day. Professional bum. Yet, I don't think I am long for this world/simulation. It's not a death wish. I love waking up every day to see what's going to happen next. Still, anything can happen.

So, I made a full push in the summer and fall of 2022 to transform the journal into a manuscript. If I did pass, release instructions were in place and I would not have to be around for the reaction. Instead, I didn't die and I found a wave of support and encouragement from family, friends, and strangers to tell my story. Turns out, people want to hear about my bizarre existence. This was the real reason, and not financial stability, for my two-decade sentence in the porn industry. With no more ties to or cares for the porn industry, my mouth is unbound.

When I finished the "final" draft of this manuscript in October of 2022, I thought the process of publishing would take a matter of months. Way off. First, it went to Hauser, a lawyer friend, who corrected grammar and strongly suggested what I should omit from my opus.

From there, it went to Ed, another one of my lawyer friends who wanted to help shape the crude piece of granite I presented to him. Ed hates the word "that." He has declared jihad on "that." However, when a lawyer is graciously giving his time for no cost because he believes in you and the project, you accept their generosity and cut out most of the "thats." I sneaked a few in to make him twitchy. Lawyers are the Word Gestapo, so he helped me pare down the unnecessary details and be more succinct with the narrative. For THAT, I thank him. He suggested I have a literary editor do another pass to help me in ways he could not. Enter Kush.

I have known this dude for over twenty-five years, but we fell out of touch when the Blonde Phenom and I (you will meet her shortly) left Los Angeles for Miami where I began my full descent into Pornlandia. We reconnected during the pandemic and I spilled the beans on where the fuck I had been the past twenty years. He thought it was hilarious. Plus, he had a Masters in Literature, so naturally I felt comfortable with him. Kush taught me how to write with authority. Me, Ed, and Kush sliced and diced the raw slab of beef from 170,000 words to 130,000 words to prepare the delicious feast you are about to devour.

In May of 2023, the 'final' edit was ready for publishing lawyers. I settled on one and paid her a small fortune to tell me how to best cover my ass. This process took another four months.

My legal dream team weighed all contents while I pushed back on not suppressing what I had to say. I did not want this book to be castrated. There are footnotes within on what I acquiesced to and why, but for the most part, this is the manuscript I turned in.

I did not take any decision lightly on how people and events should be portrayed. Accuracy and brutal honesty was the goal. Certain candid discussions regarding my sexual relations with porn stars were included for the sole reason of showcasing the bizarre and awkward. Some I felt obligated to protect. Others, not so much. It will be easy to discern who and why. Some names and details were changed for legal or personal reasons. All of this happened. It is what I saw and can recollect. Specific people are called out on their bullshit. I chose to save others from embarrassment while painting a vivid picture of the things this smut producer encountered.

If you are reading this and I am still wandering the earth, I was wrong and I made it long enough to see it get published and bear the wrath it may ensue. I can't be afraid of whatever comes next.

FAR OUT, MAN.

Fear is a powerful thing, it's got a lot of firepower. Make fear a tailwind instead of a headwind.

- JIMMY IOVINE

I liken my time in the porn industry to the scene from "The Shawshank Redemption" in which Andy Dufresne escapes from Shawshank Prison. I crawled through hundreds of yards of shit-ridden foulness and came out clean on the other side. Hopefully toward the end of the journey, you can appreciate this metaphor. You may need to shower after. Here's an honest, true, and factual assessment of the porn industry, and my life in it. People will hate me for this.

I don't give a fuck what anybody thinks.

When you're a racehorse, the reason they put blinders on these things is because if you look at the horse on the left or the right, you're going to miss a step. That's why the horses have blinders on. And that's what people should have. When you're running after something, you should not look left or right – what does this person think, what does that person think?

No. *Go*.

- JIMMY IOVINE (AKA VIC LAGINA'S SPIRIT ANIMAL)

VL, 7/27/23

P.S. This book was written organically. No AI bullshit.

THE AUTHOR WISHES TO THANK

A lot of wonderful people helped me over the years. I am grateful for having such a strong support group. Many within the porn/sex worker community aren't afforded that luxury.

Dawt, Bubs, Peps, Q, Poop (RIP), Porker, LeBewlski... you sick bastards took me in. Allowed the lone wolf to enter the pack. You let me rope onto your ridiculous caravan. Welcomed me to participate in your shenanigans. If it wasn't for you assholes, I wouldn't be here. Seriously. You kept me on the better side of the fence. Thank you. I love you all and you're all responsible for scattering the fuckin' ashes.

To my father, brother, and their wives, I know my nonsense caused a toll. For that, I am eternally sorry. We all have karma to sort out which makes little sense to us at the time. The good news is, I finally got my shit together. I don't anticipate any further surprises. But you never know with me.

To Jackie, the fact we are still great friends despite all of the horrible shit we did to each other gives me hope that forgiveness is possible. I love you.

To Merlyn, Maddie, Jess, Xander, smAshly, Andrew, Julie, Frazier, Emily, Lady Bubs, Meg, Will, Heady, Kali, and all of you sparkly beautiful people I have forgotten, your spirit is what makes this world a better place.

To Lisa Ann, who has been a true and sincere friend in an industry of mass insincerity. Thank you for all of your help over the years.

To those who made their way to my sets and helped us achieve the objective, this book is dedicated to you.

To the male talent who helped anchor and execute the *fakockta* concepts being sent down to us, I sing specific praises in the pages within.

To those who missed their flights, who brought their bad baggage to set, who phoned in their performances, who shamelessly wasted my time... this book is also dedicated to you. For without your nonsense, I may very well have forgotten you.

Mark Spiegler, who represents all the agents that helped bail us out at 7 a.m. over the years, thank you. I am not sorry I sought out meaningful relationships with women from your roster. Your girls just wanted to hang out, man, and well, The Dude Abides. I also forgive you for ignoring my request for a quote in this book. I understand you are still suckling the teat of Mindgeek and want to keep the waters calm.

Howard Stern. You have been a voice of reason in insane times. Thank you for taking my calls and influencing my compass in this world.

Sal Governale. Thank you for being one of my biggest advocates.

JD Harmeyer. Uh. I enjoyed our times and whatever.

Moses. You delivered me to The Promised Land.

Hauser. A lawyer and friend. One of the Original Five from Jew Camp. I love that the world gifted you back to me at the most fortuitous time. For a minute, I was content to turn into Homer Simpson. You showed me there was potential with this book and a purpose beyond Vic Lagina.

Edward. Another lawyer and friend. Not from Jew Camp. You have been a voice of reason and my motivator. You pushed me to dig deep to get this story out. Thank you for helping me tame this beast of a manuscript. Who knows what happens next?

Kush. My editor. I am glad the University of Miami was not a complete waste of time. I love it when life reconnects an old bridge. Because of you, I have a book I feel comfortable birthing to the world. If Ed was my midwife, you were my OB/GYN.

Mansef/Manwin/Mindgeek. This story could not have happened without you. Thank you for keeping me employed for the better part of sixteen years.

The Senator. Yet another lawyer. Another of the Original Five of Jew Camp. My other brother. While I didn't listen to a lot of your advice, you kept me somewhat sensible when I was in sixth gear, heading at warp speed to my destination. The world needs to know that he created 'Vic Lagina'.

AND NOW SOME LEGALESE ADVISED BY MY LAWYERS:

> *This book is a memoir. It reflects the author's present recollections of experiences over time and some individuals' recollections may differ. Some names and characteristics have been changed, some events have been compressed or reimagined, and some dialogue has been recreated. This memoir is not intended to be a record of fact, nor a condemnation or judgment of any other individuals, but a telling of the author's experiences in the context of this life story.*

Alright. Enough of the legal speak. It's time to get Filthy!

PROLOGUE
9/29/11 - LAGINALAND

"YEAH FUCK ME IN MY ASS HARD, PLEASE. UH UGHHHH! YEAH!!! UGHHHHH!!!" As soon as these words left Diana Prince's lips as she was getting pile-driven rectally, I was fairly certain this was the exact moment my neighbors called the police.

As 'research' for this segment, I dug this shoot out of my antiquated hard drives to review for accuracy and fairness. It took place almost eleven years ago on September 29, 2011. It was the day I held a massive orgy in my backyard, broadcasted live on the internet. The title of the production? *Brazzers Live 17: Poolside Pounding.*

Before I went back to the tape, I could only recollect that Nicole Aniston participated in this show. That would mean that somehow, I blocked out from memory the woman who not only took one penis in her ass in my pool but also took two men inside her at once in said pool. One would think that I would remember such a detail, but that's what happens when you have produced somewhere around 3,800 scenes during a twenty-year porn career. Details such as names, faces, who took an underwater DP (double penetration) in your pool, get lost in the haze.

The Cast:

Nicole Aniston, a popular blonde-haired, blue-eyed beauty who easily could be confused for a swimsuit model, is co-hosting this show. This means she will have a radio in her ear so she can relay my direction (which is mostly coming from Alex at the head office at Manwin, talking to me via instant messenger from Montreal) to my cameramen and the other performers. Technically, she was only hired to have vaginal sex with the three male performers. Separately, not all at once.

Samantha Saint, a tall, blonde, green-eyed bombshell who could easily be a runway model. She will be co-hosting with Nicole and she too will be hearing my voice incessantly in her ear. Like Nicole, she was hired to have vaginal sex with all the male performers at some point during the show, but her duties are mainly as co-host.

The heavy lifting falls onto the following people:

Charisma Cappelli, who has been booked to do everything, which is one of the lures of the live shows. Live shows were marketed to the members as an 'anything goes'-type atmosphere and her reps negotiated that she take her first double penetration ever on live television, which will be marketed by Manwin accordingly after the show and during replays. Charisma is short with highlighted brown hair and large augmented breasts.

Diana Prince, a leggy brunette who also signed on to do everything. She is our designated 'filth bucket.' While that is not a title one normally self-applies, she wears the label proudly.

Brandy Aniston, no relation to Nicole, another brunette who also was booked to do, you guessed it: everything.

Aside from their physical attributes, I never really delved into getting to know much about female talent or their stories. Whatever I witnessed while directing a scene was it, except on the rare occasion when I spent hours with a female performer on our time.

While the last three performers have a very challenging day ahead of them, the real heavy lifting falls upon the male talent.

John Strong, a Russian-born performer who has become a staple in live productions due to his ability to keep his dick hard under the most difficult and challenging productions, such as a live show. John is always hungry and asking my production assistants to take him somewhere to eat, which my company paid for.

Marco Banderas, a Spanish performer with limited English abilities and a rumored bionic dick, also known as an internal penis pump. (As told to me by a top-level performer, while on her knees ready to give Marco a blowjob, she saw him pushing something around his grundle/nifkin/taint, and heard inflating noises while he coughed trying to suppress said noises.) Regardless of whether it's rumor or fact, the guy's abilities made him legendary and perfect for live shows and gonzo scenes... but very little else due to his limited acting range. He is also skilled in being able to pop (ejaculate) multiple times during a live show. He chews and smacks gum incessantly (which he sticks to furniture or the ground when he's finished) while showcasing his mouthful of veneers.

Tommy Gunn, a Jersey native and porn veteran who is always in search of love. It's no wonder after he creampies (ejaculates inside of) Nicole during the show, he falls hard for her. He's a good guy who sometimes can't get out of his own way. He believes 9/11 was an inside job and that chemtrails are deliberate means used to calm the masses.

Solid woodsmen were booked repeatedly and spent a lot of time lounging while their female counterparts spent most of their time in hair and makeup. As such, knowing the men's personalities was the byproduct.

Live shows are what made my crew indispensable and what separated us from other crews. Once we found our groove on the third live show, they became weekly events for all the brands owned by what was then called Manwin. (Over the course of my tenure, the parent company I worked for changed their name from Mansef to Manwin to Mindgeek in less than eight years.) While I am not sure if the shows were ever profitable, they were events that differentiated Manwin from the competition. With *Brazzers Live* being the flagship show, skimping on male talent was not an option. While you could save money on male talent on lesser live shows I produced like Wicked or Mofos, it was always a risk in booking a shaky performer due to the pressure and stressful nature of the format. If their dick was not hard and ready shortly into showtime, the members would torch and ridicule them with relentless comments live on the screen for him to see. As much as this would bum me out, it did give me ammunition for 'I told you so' on the next booking. My live show liaison Alex trusted my judgment and we always booked the strongest performers for *Brazzers Live.* Although I met him a handful of times in person, unless he was standing in front of me, I would not be able to describe him to you. He was words on a screen and an occasional voice on the phone. He was a big advocate of me and my crew and was very easy to work with.

Although we start broadcasting at 4 p.m., all talent land in Vegas from LA around 10 a.m. The first order of business is to get everyone signed in, fill out releases, copy current IDs, and record performers on camera signing the paperwork and stating they were not impaired with drugs or alcohol at the present time. With that completed, I gather my crew of Pete, Moe, Ethan, Toad, and Huggy, and all eight performers into my corner office, where they spread out amongst the couches and chairs. The point of all of this was to go around and have every performer verbally express their 'do's and don'ts' list for everyone to hear. Anything can happen during a live show, so this was the only logical option I knew to prevent anyone from crossing anyone else's boundaries. It worked, most of the time. Sometimes people "forgot." Sometimes their English was "not so good." Sometimes performers would say they weren't into something but then decided in the heat of the moment to go for it. My general rule was to have open and honest conversations with performers, with hopes that they would verbalize their discontent on the spot. It wasn't a perfect system, but it was the only one that made sense to me. Communication is and was everything.

Questions to the women would be, "Do you like to be choked? Do you like to be slapped? Do you squirt? Is there anyone you don't want to interact with?" Yes, these were sometimes uncomfortable conversations to have, especially if you have two talent in the same show who disliked one another. The head office encouraged rough sex ("but not too rough"), so we booked talent who said they were genuinely into rough sex. There were no surprises since the talent and their agents received all of the information via email the week before but if anything fell through the cracks, which it did with certain agents, we'd address it in the morning meeting.

In today's case, there were no major issues to be addressed, thankfully. Once we wrapped the meeting, the five female performers would head into hair and makeup where they would languish for a few hours. The anal girls would also start 'the ritual': prepping their buttholes with butt plugs and enemas. This also meant they could not eat all day, so they would keep their blood sugar raised by eating candy until after we wrapped.

I had been operating out of my leased sixteen thousand square foot Licensed Adult Production studio in Las Vegas for over two years. This was the seventeenth live show for Brazzers, and up until that point, we shot everything at the studio, with concepts and elaborate sets that sometimes pushed the boundaries of good taste. *Brazzers Live 15: The Three Little Pigs (versus the Big Bad Wolves)*, which we shot a few months prior comes to mind. However, the powers that be wanted to end the summer by changing it up with a pool party. This meant finding a suitable house with a warm pool, and an owner who would allow a massive orgy in said pool, where we were able to do internet tests days beforehand so there would not be any connection issues on the day. Easy, right? They had been pushing to pull this show off in August, a concept that I squashed. While this was only my sixth summer since landing in Vegas, I knew how hot it could be in August with temperatures sometimes hitting one hundred and ten degrees. The quickest way to achieve a porn mutiny is to ask eight performers to fuck in the scorching heat, so we booted it as close to October as possible. Still, this was our first remote live show and there were a lot of glitches occurring and we needed to run more tests.

Soon it became clear the only feasible option for the location was my house, *LaginaLand*. I had stopped shooting porn there in 2007, so I felt enough time had passed where I could pull off a shoot that would last less than two hours. It's not like I hadn't shot hardcore scenes by my pool in the past (Lisa Ann with Johnny Sins, and Lichelle Marie with Marco Banderas come to mind), but this was going to be next level, with eight participants in a massive orgy. Still, it was the best option and provided I took some safety measures by obstructing views with tarps and drowning out fuck noises with royalty-free music, I was willing to take the risk. By the time we were to go live, school would be out and any school buses with kids on the road that could see into my backyard would be long gone. I had to worry about my neighbors, but with the safeguards in place, I felt that the risk had been mitigated.

While the girls are in makeup, my crew loads up gear and makes their way to my house. Jetta and Joker, my German shepherds, will no doubt have to stay inside during the show, but I'm still concerned about barking and dog noises. While the crew unloads cases, the dogs sniff everyone and everything before settling down close to me. Set up will take a few hours, from hooking up the monitor so our hosts can read the member comments to running cables to the A and B cameras into the encoders, which will convert the high-definition signal and broadcast us live to the internet. Toad and Ethan set up a blue tarp so one neighbor couldn't see anything. My other neighbor's view is blocked by hibiscus trees that divide the property line alongside the dividing wall. We rented wicker furniture for this show. Once the 'set' is built and all cameras connected, Moe, who is stationed in my casita with the encoders, started running tests for Alex in the head office. From there, we fine-tune and tweak the set until everyone up in headquarters was happy. Now we wait for the girls to arrive from hair and makeup.

I transformed into a stress monster a few hours before showtime, pacing and scowling. I was the mad conductor on this crazy train who needed to make sure all pieces were in place well before showtime. As my cocaine addiction got worse in the coming months, this intensity became magnified in the next thirty live shows I produced. My crew knew and they gave me a wide berth. I wanted every show to be amazing to keep the gig going. Keeping the bosses happy meant lasting prosperity. I was over-leveraged as it was, so I had to keep hitting home runs or otherwise face imminent financial implosion. The heat wasn't helping my demeanor. Back then, I was clean-shaven with short hair. Even in shorts, tank top, and Phillies visor, I was sweating and irritable and did my best to internalize it. Keeping everyone else cool and comfortable, mostly the performers, was essential. Otherwise, they would not be at their most relaxed to perform extreme sex acts live on the internet.

BE COOL, DUDE.

Once the ladies arrive via the caravan of my makeup artist and my PA Ethan, they set up in my two spare bedrooms that house makeup, wardrobe, and suitcases, much like they did when I was shooting at home in 2006 and 2007.

"Ladies, don't leave any panties or stockings out. Joker's a pervert. He'll eat them."

The ladies giggle. "No, seriously. He ate a stocking once and could not pass it.

It was hanging out of his butthole and I had to put a plastic bag on my hand to pull it out. I felt like a clown performing a trick as it was never-ending."

NICE, DUDE. THAT'LL PUT THEM AT EASE.

Awkward comes easy to me. Always has.

We go over the wardrobe purchased and assigned by the head office. The ladies start in bikinis for the pre-show where they will talk to the members and tease them by playing with each other. Once we get out of pre-show, there is a quick change for the wet T-shirt portion, but otherwise, it's pretty simple. In previous shows, it wasn't uncommon for the head office to ask for a major costume change with only a five-minute break in between segments. I bring my hosts Nicole and Samantha together and we discuss the sequence of events. Shows like this start slowly and then build. It's supposed to be a marathon mentality, but given the live nature and the adrenaline, sometimes performers start in fifth gear as to throw down the gauntlet.

Reaffirmation in the form of member applause was and still is a thing. Sometimes co-stars decided to try and match their competitors. Sometimes they let them race by, dumbfounded by what they were witnessing. Bragging rights existed, especially on the Brazzers Forum. It could be chaos. My job was to control that chaos and manage liability. That is why I got paid the big bucks. It wasn't because I was a great producer, director, or shooter. It was because I set up an operation that was above board and run like a business. It was intended to be a safe haven in porn production for my crew, my performers, the company funding this endeavor, and for me.

While I had layers of safeguards in place to shield me from liability, I was the boots on the ground for the company. Their "front line commander." If anything were to happen on my set, they would be scrutinized, but I would be the one they could potentially hang out to dry. That comes at a cost and this is what some of my previous employees who complained I was getting paid much more than them never grasped. While it may look like they were doing the heavy lifting (they were), I was keeping an eye on the details eighteen hours a day, making sure the magic happened and they had a safe space to work. I wasn't doing it for charity.

I joked with Alex about perhaps faking a raid by the police at the end of the show. Oh, the irony. The idea was for us to hire some actors and things would get physical: slapping on handcuffs, altercations, performers screaming. And then we cut the camera. I wanted to fuck with the members for being demanding, unsatisfied little shits. Never happy and always wanting more. Plus, the idea cracked me up in an Andy Kauffman kind of way. Ultimately, we decided against it as it was already going to be a complicated day, with them wanting us to capture underwater sex as well. This required a third camera with waterproof casing wired to the encoders, which would be fully immersed during the entire show. We hired an operator, Mark, out of LA. He had enough tanks to stay underwater for the entire two-hour show. The complicated part would be capturing those sex acts since sex and water do not mix well. Requests from the head office and the negotiated talent rate required Diana to do anal and double penetration in the pool. Ideally, they wanted pool anal and double penetrations for Brandy and Charisma as well, but I told them to taper their expectations. We would try valiantly, but success hinged on circumstances. So far though, everything was working.

It was general practice to run tech rehearsals about an hour before showtime. I reminded Samantha and Nicole to always be talking to members and to camera. Based on Samantha's eye contact, I could tell she was hanging on every word. Nicole looked like she was zoning out with her big beautiful blue eyes glossing over at some point during the discussion. The most important aspect of the show is 'Member Interaction.' Members want to hear their names called out while performers make eye contact with the camera. They will contest it's not live. Nicole and Samantha's job is to show them otherwise by saying their comments in real-time. I tell Brandy, Charisma, and Diana to do their part as well when it came to doing 'shoutouts.' Most if not all performers found this aspect very annoying. They wanted to fuck, get paid, and go home, and that was an ethos I could get behind. I wanted all of this gear and these people out of my house so I could go 'home' to my dogs.

During most shows, I would be in the control room of the studio next to Moe and IT Brent or Pete and Marcos who eventually ran the tri-caster during live events. There was a need, so they took it upon themselves to learn the system to make additional money. In this case, my station was a few feet away where I was tethered to remote monitors that displayed the camera feeds, the member chat, but mostly to Alex via Skype on my laptop. He would tell me what he wanted and then I would tell my crew and performers what to focus on or what sex acts to engage in. That was the chain of command, with who knows who telling Alex what to do up in the headquarters in Montreal.

I had separate walkies for speaking to my crew and hosts, but in today's case, due to my close proximity to the action, there was no need. I would tell Huggy and Toad, Cameras A and B, what I needed and they would whisper it to the talent.

This was Porn Whisper Down The Lane, so live shows tended to have a circus-like atmosphere filled with brief confusion before understanding what the actual direction was.

There would be times when I had to make my presence known if camera wasn't conveying my directions properly. This tended to be when there wasn't action going on all the camera feeds at the same time or if I sensed a talent's line was being crossed. We were trained in compliance, so I had to be sure all of the talents' verbal boundaries communicated in the earlier meeting were heeded by all parties at all times. If they weren't, I gave them a warning, and if it happened again, they were off the show. Somehow that never happened. The only times performers missed a show were when they were impaired.

After our third dry run, my feeling is we're all on the same page. The men have been waiting all day. Even though I fed them earlier and they have been lounging around, waiting for showtime, they seem eager to fuck. Each male has his own routine to be ready when I need him to be. Viagra and Cialis were common, but for men advancing in years such as Marco, John, and Tommy, other methods were required.

I already covered Marco and his alleged machinery, but with Tommy and John, I cannot say for certain. There is a product called Caverject which is administered via a needle into the shaft of the penis which results in erections lasting a few hours. I can imagine this being a method for them and a few other male performers I've worked with over the years. I give the male talent the nod, telling them "dick's up in thirty minutes." Any solid male performer worth their weight always asked me to give them a proper heads up so they know exactly when to be ready.

By this point, I am sweating with anticipation. The buzz in the air seems positive. The ladies are in good spirits and that's contagious. Just as it can be if one goes in the opposite direction. When one domino falls, the next are likely to tumble. There is a window of opportunity to thread the needle and the moment is almost upon us. Then, one of our camera feeds gets static, with five minutes to go before showtime. Moe, Ethan, and Pete frantically run a new cable into Huggy's Sony EX-1, which doesn't do the trick.

It's not the cable. Moe runs back to the casita while I am being told that. The chat room is already open for the members but we have to delay the show by fifteen minutes while they reboot the system.

"Fifteen minutes? Fuck off!" I blurt out, putting everyone on edge.

TAKE 'ER EASY, DUDE.

"Sorry ladies, short delay. Everyone stay in position."

I message Alex for updates while running the scenarios of what a fifteen-minute delay could mean. Even though sunset was still three hours away, now was a time when the sun would perfectly backlight the action rather than become too harsh as it moved west. The men already administered their regimens, so the clock was ticking in the boner department. Plus, the longer we waited, and the more the voices in my backyard continued to bellow, I would be at risk of getting shut down. After an agonizing fifteen minutes, Moe got the system up and running with no visible static. Technical glitches seemed to always materialize before start time. Clearly, I forgot to say my prayers to Testiclese, my porn god, before those days began.

Brandy announces to everyone, "I only want to do anal in and by the pool."

She is concerned she is not fully clean. She then apologizes to me and my pool filter.

"Don't worry about it" I tell her. "My pool guy will shock the water tomorrow." From there, everyone with a penis jokes that they are now going to jerk off in my pool. Porn humor.

"We have water-based lube so we can fuck them in the pool?" Tommy asks.

Valid question, but I was not sure any amount of lube would help fucking vaginally in the pool, much less anally. "We have all kinds of lube," I tell him, "Oil-based, silicone-based, and water-based." Ethan hides all bottles behind pillows, within reach of the action. It would have helped if people noticed, but tension was high, sexual and otherwise.

"Two minutes people! Toad, get into position."

"I am! I put my camera down a second ago and am in position," he whines back to me.

The footage tells another story as he set the camera down while it was rolling a few minutes prior. I tell them to cue Nicole, who is standing in my beach entry in a blue bikini, looking amazing, while the men hang in the background like vultures. Toad continues to talk to Nicole, even as Huggy counts down from "three, two, one" before telling her "go."

Nicole starts the show with, "Hi guys, I am Nicole Aniston and we are live here today on a very, very hot day in Sin City, Las Vegas, Nevada at the Lagina Compound and I have my girlfriend Savannah, excuse me, Samantha ready to announce the really hot chicks we have today for ya. Samantha?"

Nothing like we had rehearsed, but whatever, the train has left the station!

Toad continues to shoot Nicole and the men in the pool. Marco makes his way toward Nicole, chomping his gum and showing his teeth.

Samantha introduces the ladies while talking to the members. She is excellent in maintaining eye contact and her green eyes are piercing in the natural light. Somewhere there are many men with one hand typing at a computer while they furiously jerk their lubed-up cocks with the other.

Joker barks during the action, his face pressed to the window watching the action from inside, much like the members through the screen with their demands: Lick nipples! Play with your feet! Brandy, stick your finger in Diana's ass! How do I get my girlfriend to let me do anal on her?

Brandy takes over by telling him it needs to be worked up to and gradual. "Your ass has the capacity to open up wider than your vagina. I promise you that. There are penises in this business I can fit in my ass that I can't fit in my vagina. I promise you that's a fact."

Free anatomy lessons apparently are also included in your Brazzers membership.

"Slide a finger in Brandy's ass!" demands a member as Charisma complies. As the girls play with each other, I gauge that, while loud, the noise is still at a respectable level. The members are demanding more, so Samantha is cued to throw it to the five-minute intermission so we can get the orgy underway.

The ladies throw on their white T-shirts and make final preparations for sex, which entails a quick butt check to make sure everything is neat and tidy. If not, my cameramen will make adjustments on the fly. Intermission winds down and Samantha brings us back in a similar fashion as Nicole did, only smoother. She throws it to Camera B where Nicole and the ladies are lined up for their wet T-shirt contest. Tommy takes control of the hose and slowly sprays boobs.

Members are encouraged to vote on the first poll question, *Who has the best wet tits*? Samantha wins. Her reward? Fluffing all the men to get them ready for sex.

SHE'S SO HOT. I CAN'T BELIEVE SHE DOES THIS ON CAMERA.
HOW LUCKY WE ARE.

"BRING OUT THE COCKS!!!" Brandy screams, making me wince at her volume and what that potentially means so early in the show. If my neighbor heard it while relaxing by his pool with his wife, it could be a problem.

The next poll question? *Should the girls get fucked now? Yes or no?* Given the monsters were chomping at the bit for double anal during the pre-show, the question is a formality. The orgy commences vaginally with Brandy, Charisma, and Diana taking the brunt, while Samantha inserts herself into the action wherever she can. I see Nicole, who likely is happy she is not at the center of the sex attention and is without partners, so I instruct her to read the message board and talk to the members.

SHE SOUNDS LIKE A CASHIER AT WALMART.

"Tell her to speak into the camera and not at the monitor as she is reading." Huggy conveys the message as best he can but Nicole continues to do it in the same way.

By this point, the underwater camera is being grossly under-utilized, only capturing stylistic but unusable underwater footage of the action above the surface. It is cool in a *Boogie Nights* kind of way, but in this production, we need to see the penis going into the mouth or vagina.

Cue the next poll question: *What do you want to see now? Underwater BJ's, underwater titty-fucking, or underwater fucking?* No matter.

The poll was manipulated to make *underwater BJ's* the winner because we specifically negotiated with Charisma to handle this portion. More than likely, the rest of the performers chose to keep their heads above water to save their hair and makeup. Charisma was a performer who did not give a shit about any of that and wanted to stand out. She takes a big breath, submerges herself, and gives our underwater rig its first usable content.

Meanwhile, after having been fucked vaginally for five minutes and decreeing anal was only to be done in the pool, Brandy decides to try anal on the couch with John while we are still in the vaginal phase of the show. At the same time, Diana starts getting pounded anally by the side of the pool.

WARP SPEED ENGAGED, CAPTAIN LAGINA.

While we are clearly getting ahead of ourselves, I doubt anyone is going to care. This is why we are here. Brandy keeps looking up at Huggy to make sure there is no doody present and he keeps the camera focused on her face while inspecting the penetration point to reassure her that in fact, there is no doody. Anal sex resumes while Brandy presses her hand on John's right leg if he goes too deep or fast. This tactic is known as 'The Heisman.'

Next poll question: *Which girl shall be the first to take it in the ass?*

Oops. Not to be outdone by Diana and Brandy, Charisma makes her way over to the couch so Marco can also fuck her ass, where he finds no Heisman nor push back. Charisma, like Diana, is already in fifth gear.

The masses get more adventurous, demanding an underwater creampie. We are finally in Nicole Aniston's wheelhouse. While facials aren't her thing, as displayed with closed eyes and mouth while male talent did their deed, she seemed to enjoy creampies. Tommy releases after patiently waiting for the go ahead from the head office to proceed with the underwater creampie. Nicole gets a genuine look of pleasure and joy during this moment. Mark captures it underwater as Tommy's little fishies float in the salt water of my pool.

WHILE THIS MIGHT NOT BE THE FIRST UNDERWATER CREAMPIE IN PORN HISTORY, IT MUST BE THE FIRST DONE LIVE ON THE INTERNET. WELL DONE.

Next poll question: *What do you want to see now?*

Winning Answer: Girls lined up with pile driver anal!

Duty bound, the girls line up on the smalls of their backs, legs in the air while John, Tommy, and Marco fuck in a downward motion into their anuses. It is a big ask, but not as big as what the members are demanding: Double anal! Triple anal!

We're only twenty-five minutes into the show when Diana screams, "Oh god fuck me in my ass hard please. Yessssss!! Ughhhh! Yeah! Goddammit feels so good!" while grabbing John's hand and placing it on her throat so he can choke her. In porn, this was the proper protocol to show compliance officers who would review this footage that she was encouraging this behavior from her co-star. Otherwise, it would be flagged and possibly deemed un-releasable unless edited. Still, we are now broaching level-red noise volume and I pray to Testiclese we make it through the rest of the show without incident.

At this point, Tommy came once (in Nicole) and Marco came twice, first on Nicole's face while receiving a blow job in the opening minutes of the show, then almost inside Charisma underwater, before pulling out and ejecting his swimmers.

The sixth poll question is *Who should get DP'd first?* Winner, by fix or otherwise, is Diana.

Having done anal in the first ten minutes and in pile driver, Diana's asshole looks puffy and resembles raw meat, but this does not affect her intensity. When John and Tommy both enter her, she screams to them and my neighborhood, "Oh god I want you to split me in half! Yeah! Oh god I love both of these dicks in me!'" Shortly after, Brandy starts her DP and screams, "I need another dick!" Tommy jumps in and while Huggy captures a great angle of penetration in both holes *and* Brandy's face, I tell Huggy, "zoom in a little so you can frame out Tommy's asshole. Members are complaining."

As Ringmaster, when the energy wanes, as it does around this time, I have to keep it going for the duration of the show. We still have fifteen minutes. Poll question seven: *Which girl should go Air Tight first?* Irrelevant, since Diana is already in position getting DP'd by Marco and Tommy, so we send John in to insert his penis into her mouth, thus making Diana 'Air Tight.' Get it? Now, we are officially done with poll questions and in free-for-all mode.

How else can we top this while maximizing our underwater camera? Charisma already handled underwater vaginal sex with Marcos. Diana did underwater anal with Tommy, who forgot the water-based lube was placed behind a couch pillow and searched for it during the chaos. Still, she managed a good three minutes of underwater anal, which explains the puffiness of her anus.

The only thing remaining was an underwater DP, which Diana immediately volunteered for.

WHAT A SOLDIER. I MEAN, FILTH BUCKET.

This is an easier request to give than to pull off. Tommy and John try docking successfully outside of the water but we need the penetration to be *under* the water. After a few repeated attempts, they are successful, for five seconds of footage. Frustrated, John walks off, and having not had sex with Nicole yet with the show winding down, he grabs her and starts having sex with her, first in doggie followed by brief cowgirl, all while she and everyone else are yelling at him and her to make it over for the group facial.

Nicole successfully dodged as much boy/girl sex as possible, having clocked in a total of six minutes of actual vaginal penetration.

She accumulated two creampies between Tommy and Marco (his third pop of the day), took one facial from Marco, and was now about to receive on her face whatever the men had left in their systems. She avoids Marco's fourth pop, but receives the brunt of John's first and only delivery, which Diana and Brandy clean off with their tongues. Given this will be Tommy's second pop of the show, he uses Samantha's vagina to achieve liftoff.

BRILLIANT. THAT'S WHAT I WOULD DO.

After a few minutes in doggie, he achieves climax all over Samantha, Charisma, Diana, and Brandy. While the heavy lifting is done, we are not finished. The plan is for all performers to jump in the pool so Mark can capture them entering the water. Instead, Toad inexplicably tells them to go into the hot tub which was to happen *after* the pool.

NICE WORK, SHITHEAD.

I yell out the proper instructions and the performers enter the pool. They get cold and jump into the hot tub, effectively starting the post show.

While sex is encouraged during the post-show, everyone seems to be fucked out. Well, everyone other than the Bionic Man, Marco Banderas, who is ready for pop number five.

"That's enough for you! Jesus! Put that thing in a cage for god's sakes!" Nicole tells him.

FUCKING POETRY.

They reminisce about the show, highlighting their favorite parts. It is here that Charisma tells Porn World this was her first DP. The girls cheer and congratulate her. We also had another first: at minute fifty of the extravaganza, Diana took her first double vag, ever!

While her eyes rolled back into her head, Marco and John both entered her vagina as the ladies looked on in awe. "That's some real freaky shit," Samantha deadpanned to camera, her eyes still popping in the natural light. Nicole adds she was happy we provided them with "five hot, not crazy chicks."

There had been crazy moments in Live Show History which prompted this remark. Like when Jynx Maze almost put a heel through Jennifer White's skull during a post-show. While Marco still hopes to have more sex, the girls promote *Brazzers Live 18* coming next month before saying goodbye to the camera and we end the live feed and get the replay ready for broadcast.

WE MADE IT.

As usual, the talent rush to the showers and get their belongings while my crew breaks down equipment and tarps. Earlier in the day I wrote checks for all performers while also having them fill out a W-9. While my crew gets paid bi-weekly through payroll, performers always received same day pay from me as an independent contractor. Talent checks exceed eleven grand for the day with Charisma making the most and Marco the least. Factoring in crew, travel, furniture, food, drinks, props, equipment rentals or purchases, and underwater camera rental, the show cost over twenty-one thousand dollars.

A typical month would see Manwin wiring a quarter of a million dollars to cover that month's production costs. We were averaging twenty-five shoots a month before the inevitable squeeze that would follow in the coming years. I never concerned myself with their profitability since it had zero to do with me. I assumed the work constantly being ordered was a sign I was doing things right.

As I am handing the checks to Huggy so he can sign out the talent, Joker and Jetta are barking madly and running toward my side gate where they hear voices trying to get someone's attention. I tell my crew to continue striking and go out to find three of Las Vegas' finest along with their cruisers parked in front of my house.

"Can I help you, officers?"

"We received a complaint from one of your neighbors about excessive profanity in your backyard. Can you come out front to speak with us?"

"Certainly, sir. Be right there."

I make my way back through the house and announce, "Cops are here. Everyone stay put and out of sight." Given the day is complete, it does not seem to jostle anyone. I open my garage door to the three cops standing in my driveway.

THEY ALWAYS SEND MULTIPLE COPS ON CALLS LIKE THESE. WHY IS THAT?

I hit the button to close the garage door and jump over the sensors, keeping the inside of my house out of sight from prying eyes.

"Excessive profanity you say?" I quip.

"You throwing a party or something?"

"Yes. A party that got out of hand a few times. But it's over now."

"Do you own this house?" one of them asks.

"Yes, sir." I hand him my ID and he talks into his shoulder radio.

"I have to tell you, officer, my neighbors can be a pain in the butt sometimes. This isn't the first time they have done this. I am truly sorry you had to come out here for nothing."

A few years prior, the cops came by looking for an illegal brothel. I had become numb to the scrutiny, but knew the basics: if you are polite and white, this should be over shortly. As long as they are not Anti-Semites and can't sniff the Jew on me, that is.

"I just want to let you know the call did not come from any of these houses here," he says, pointing to my neighbor's houses in my cul-de-sac.

AH RALPH, YOU CHOAD.

My face tightens.

"Ah yes, that guy put a note on my door asking me to keep my dogs inside, during the day, because they bark too much. Very irritable that one." The officer who was holding my ID returns it, getting the all-clear from headquarters that I am a model citizen.

Filthy pornographer notwithstanding, I pay all my taxes, abide most laws that aren't drug related, and have never seen the inside of a jail cell.

"Thank you for your time, we'll get out of your hair. But please be mindful to keep your parties from getting out of control. This is a family town." He winks and they all head back to their cruisers. This won't be the last time I see badges, but this is the playbook I would always stick to.

LIVE TO SHOOT ANOTHER DAY...

A few days later, I left Ralph a voicemail berating and mocking him for being unneighborly. A few years later, I would attempt to buy his home to shoot porn. But this would be the last live orgy at my house. It wasn't even the craziest live show I ever directed.

That title goes to a show a few months later: *Brazzers: How Hard Can You Give It?*

Watching it now over a decade later, so far removed from the business, it is hard to ignore how much things have changed. Producing a scene like that today with names of that caliber would be nearly impossible. The only female talent I remembered from that day was Nicole Aniston, and in today's world, she would command a fortune to shoot an orgy like that and most likely would decline.

I totally forgot about Diana Prince. If you were to ask me if I ever shot her, I would have said no, even though she did an underwater double penetration in my pool. That's how far removed I could be, and based on the sheer volume of content we were outputting at the time, isn't it forgivable that I completely forgot such a thing?

Samantha and Nicole were anomalies in the business being *that* beautiful while taking several dicks on camera. This is what made them superstars. Nicole would be the first to tell you she was a "terrible porn star" based on how vanilla and disinterested she was at times. Nicole's sex switch would turn on after I called "action." Soon as she heard "cut," she would go back to being her goofy, lovable self.

Live shows would start calming down once the third ownership took over, but we produced them until 2017. There was talk in early 2020 about reviving them, but COVID hit and everything changed. I'm getting ahead of myself. To make things easier and cheaper on the company, I allowed Tommy and Nicole to crash in my guest bedrooms since we were shooting again the following day. It would have been nice to have a few drinks with Nicole later that night to see where things could go, but my girlfriend Jackie insisted on staying the night, thereby laying her claim. Only six months into this relationship and it was already getting annoying. Again.

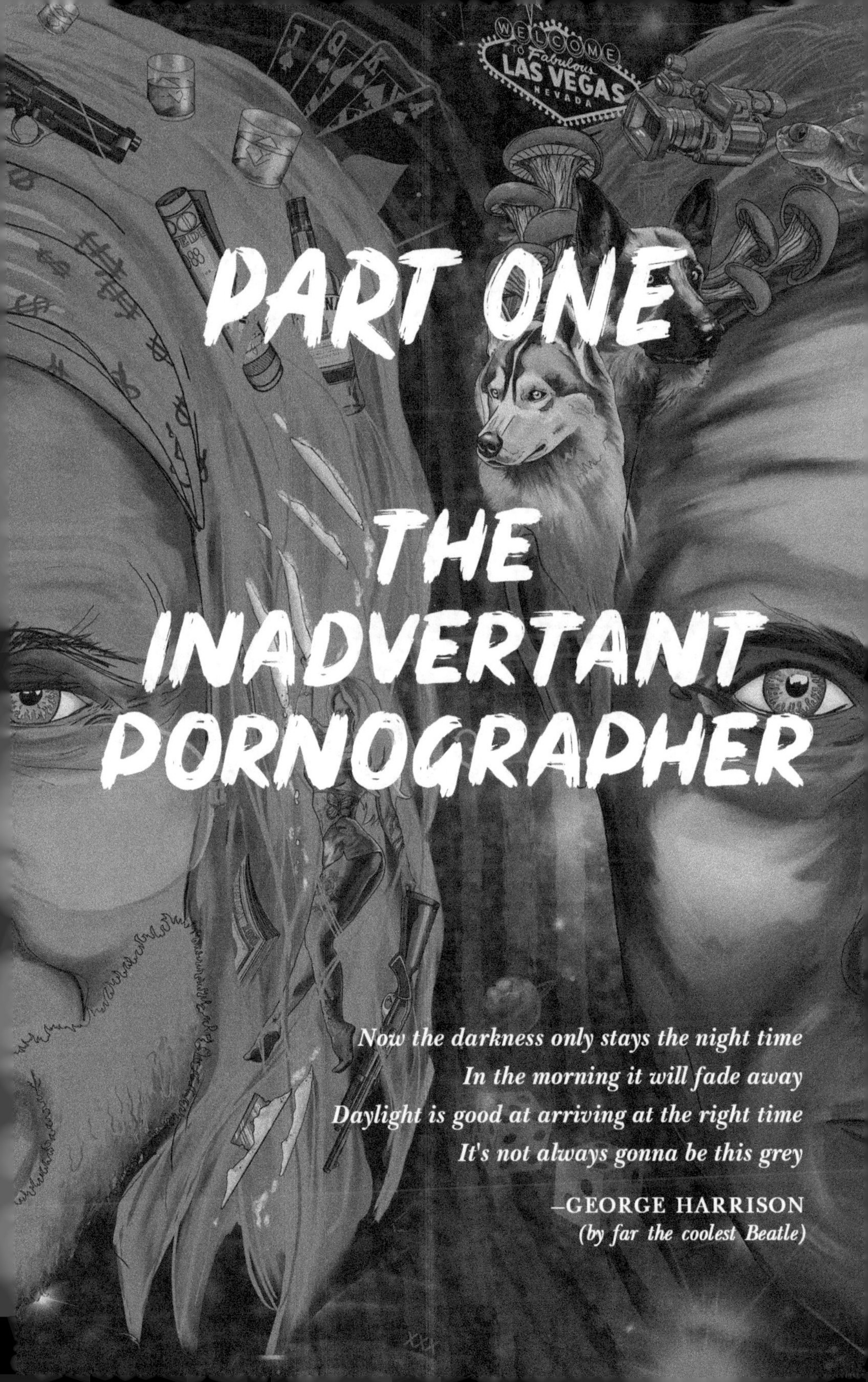

PART ONE

THE INADVERTANT PORNOGRAPHER

Now the darkness only stays the night time
In the morning it will fade away
Daylight is good at arriving at the right time
It's not always gonna be this grey

–GEORGE HARRISON
(by far the coolest Beatle)

Robin Quivers: "Who in the world is Vic Lagina?"

Howard Stern: "Vic Lagina is a very famous porn director, Robin. How dare you? It's like saying 'who's Usher'?"

- THE HOWARD STERN SHOW, 25TH AUGUST 2016

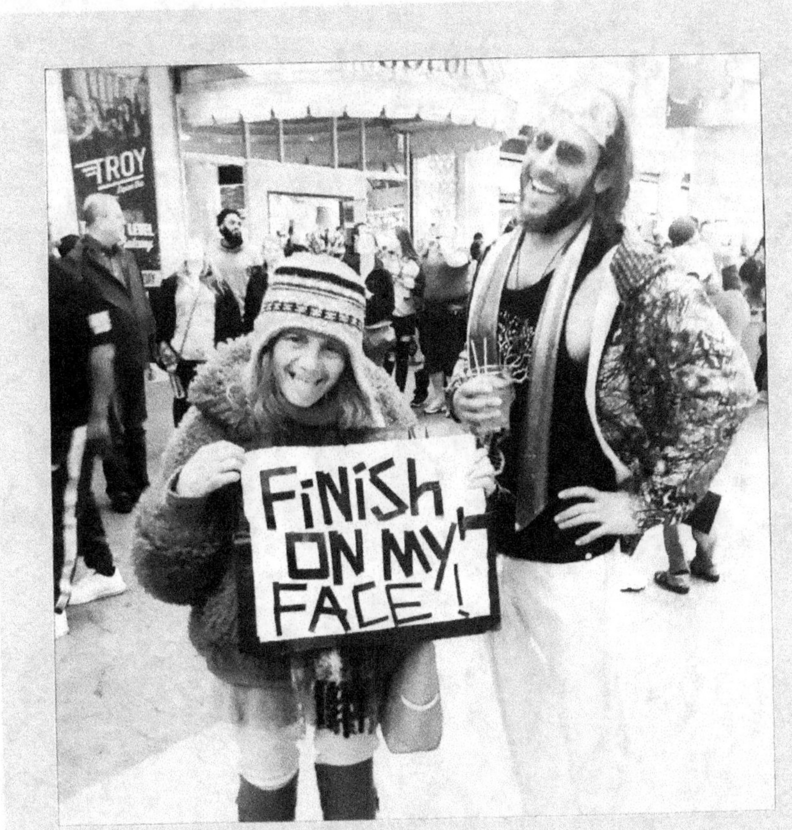

SEE? FACIAL UNICORNS EXIST!

1 IN THE BEGINNING…

My rise in the porn world was as fast as it was unexpected. I have benefitted financially from this as well as taken my lumps. During my time in that world, notoriety took a back seat to longevity.

Years ago, if you were to try and read up on me on the internet, you would find very little. The truth is, I helped grow the largest porn company in the world and at one point was the busiest pornographer almost no one ever heard of.

For me, routine is everything. I woke up at 4 a.m. every morning, made a smoothie and worked out at home before heading to my studio at 7 a.m. to supply the world with online filth. I was the first one at work and the last one to leave.

At the end of each day, I love nothing more than to come home to my pack of dogs and my bachelor freedom. These are *my* babies, the only kind I wish to have. I prefer dogs over people. My home life is peaceful and tranquil, but it wasn't always this way.

The real me is a peace-loving hippie who likes to drop acid and swim with sea turtles in Maui. A recluse who doesn't want to bother or be bothered. I give everyone a fair shake and allow them enough rope to hang themselves. I treat others with respect and consideration of their time. Being transparent and not fucking anyone over is paramount. I am a believer in karma and the laws of attraction.

So who am I? Where did I come from? What led me here? Who the fuck is Vic Lagina?

My life began in 1973 outside of Philadelphia. My parents were Jewish liberals. I had an older brother and a dog and we lived in a modest house in the suburbs. I stubbornly went to Hebrew school in order to have a Bar Mitzvah. Then sleep-away Jew camp in the Poconos. In school, the non-Jews made fun of me for being the only Jew in class.

"Don't marry a *shiksa!*"

These were the words my great-grandmother Rose bestowed onto me as a child. Ironically, they seemed to have the opposite effect on me throughout my life. I was all about the *shiksas*. Perhaps that is because I was the sole Jew in my class amongst all the *goyim,* while I attended Hebrew School once a week in the Jewish area of the Main Line of Philadelphia. I already was uncomfortable in my own skin, and seeing these Jewish kids every week only seemed to make it worse. I had a difficult time assimilating with them, even if we came from the same tribe.

Things got better every summer though when my parents sent me away to camp in the Poconos for eight weeks so they could have their *shtup* time. As a kid, I always thought how hard it must have been for them to send their kids away, but it's clear as day to me now that this was all about them. Even though the food was terrible, the bunks were graffiti-marked sweat boxes with inadequate bathroom floor drainage we children were expected to clean, it was heaven. Each year would pass by, but from mid-June to mid-August, I would reunite with my fellow Tribesmen. Even though we were vastly different in personality and geography, living under the same roof, we were forced to develop brother-like relationships. Still, my interactions with the Jewish girls were nothing but awkward.

My parents instilled the basics in me: work hard at school, don't smoke, treat others as you want to be treated, and if you are going to do anything, do it to the best of your abilities.

There is nothing unique about my upbringing except where it leads. I was an A/B student, awkward looking with oversized feet, crooked teeth, and lips too big for my face, which earned me the nickname 'N*****lips.' I didn't have many friends, was neither popular nor an exceptional athlete, girls did not notice me, and I didn't have many interests except for TV, video games, and movies. I was a loner and a brat to my peers and my parents.

Because I lacked confidence, my parents had a tough time raising me. My brother was the popular and confident 'good' kid, while I often got into trouble. One of the many reasons why I have chosen not to reproduce is because my offspring will balance the Karma of how big of a headache I was to my parents tenfold onto me.

Around nine years old, I remember finding my dad's *Playboy* and *Penthouse* magazines and was fascinated (and frightened) by the female form. Why does this one have hair and this one doesn't? Why is this one meaty while this one isn't? Why are these two girls kissing?

If I put on my Freud cap for a second, were those magazines the first step in a series of many which led me here? I would like to think my decisions were based on financial reasons, not psychological. It's debatable.

I never had the birds and the bees talk with my father. He allowed the public school system to do the work, so a lot of what I learned was in tenth grade sex education class. I also received a stellar education from the likes of Larry Flynt and Al Goldstein (RIP, gentlemen) which was littered in the filthy magazines our counselors had at summer camp.

When I was fifteen, my mother died.

As far back as I remember, she had been dealing with a debilitating condition known as Alpha-1 antitrypsin deficiency. It affects either the lungs or the liver, in her case the latter. She could not drink alcohol and had to adjust her diet to limit sodium, otherwise she would retain massive amounts of fluid.

I am a carrier of the gene, but am not affected by it, another good reason for me not to reproduce. The summer she died, I was in Israel like a stereotypical Jew teenager. The last time I saw her alive was the day I left on the birthright trip. My hand flat on the glass window of the departing bus where she placed hers over mine and we 'touched'.

After I left, she wasn't feeling well and went to the hospital. Over a three-week period, her body shut down. My parents decided I should remain in the dark about it because I was six thousand miles away. Blissfully in the dark. No one told me about her decline until the last minute. As she was knocking on death's door, I got the phone call from my father. Twenty-four hours later she was gone.

I rushed back for the funeral and tried to make sense of it all, as best as a fifteen-year-old could. I was lucky my last memory of her was through the bus window. My older brother experienced everything first hand. He saw the life drain from the beautiful and caring woman who was my mother.

My brother left for college a few months later and now I was alone with my father at home. Although he was mourning the woman he deeply loved, my father kept it together and focused on my well-being. I had been closer to my mother, so perhaps this was her way of bringing us together. At

My college years are mostly bad memories of trying to fit in. The first few years were rough after recently losing my mother. For comfort, I followed my brother to Syracuse and into a fraternity. I had emotional meltdowns, which as a frat member made me more of a target than a brother. Into my Junior and Senior years, I came into my own and stood up for myself. While no longer a pussy, I still didn't belong in a fraternity. At least not the one I was in. I was more of a creative while they were more about partying, gambling, working out, and banging chicks. Well, I didn't gamble. Still, there were good times I'm now able to acknowledge instead of blocking it all out. The dickheads in the fraternity toughened me up for the trials later in life. It's worth noting former president of CNN, Chris Licht, was my frat brother, proving a media titan and a successful pornographer came from the same place.

the same time, through all the sadness and turmoil, something else happened. I became a man. Not just mentally, but physically.

I filled into those oversized feet with a six-foot-three frame and broad shoulders. My braces came off and the crooked teeth were no longer. Those lips which drew me so much personal anguish? It became quite apparent females like full, supple lips during make out sessions.

The girls who shunned me now started to take notice. It was a crucial time in my life to have a positive female role model. Someone to inform and instruct on how a budding man should treat women. I didn't have one.

I had Nali. She was my one female friend but her objectivity was clouded by her crush on me. The feelings weren't mutual. She was more like my sexual training guide. She was my first make out partner, gave me my first blowjob, and ultimately took my virginity.

THANKS, NALI.

It didn't take long for me to get labeled a player and womanizer. With raging hormones and a desire to hunt and conquer, I hooked up as often as I could. Little changed after graduation and into college.

I followed my brother to Syracuse where I suffered through four brutal winters and received my BS in TV and Film Production. My college memories aren't exactly favorable. It was also four drunken years filled with a lot of bad decisions.

With girls, I always had the same conundrum. If a girl was interested in dating me, I was only interested in fucking them. If I had a legitimate interest, my approach never worked. If I liked a girl, I would tell her in a lot of corny and awkward ways, like how I thought nice guys talked.

NICE GUYS FINISH LAST. WE KNOW THAT NOW.

Eventually, I figured out a winning combination: aloof and disinterested. While the drunken idiots aggressively threw down their rap, I kept my distance and watched them punch themselves out. My move was to give the occasional eye contact, smile, and slide in toward the end of the night. It worked like a charm.

I had mastered the first part of the equation: getting the girl.

The second part I would battle the rest of life: what to do once I got them.

After graduation I vowed to never live in cold weather again, setting my sights for Los Angeles and film school. The plan went awry when I didn't get accepted into USC.

So instead I went the other direction, ending up in South Florida. The University of Miami accepted me into their MFA Film Production program and I got my first job: production assistant for a production company specializing in corporate and commercial videos.

Having one degree in film is useless. Having two is pointless, unless you want to teach. I applied and at twenty-four the soon-to-be Vic Lagina was a college professor.

How does this make any sense? A twenty-four year-old with very little real world experience can teach on a college level, based on having six years of higher education and little else? It mattered little at the time. Even though my bank account balance was laughable, I came off as a successful professional, which women were attracted to.

During my college professor phase I had my first real relationship: Doctor Blow.

PAGING DOCTOR BLOW! DOCTOR BLOW!
YOU ARE NEEDED IN THE TRAUMA WARD!

Doctor Blow was the first of the three highly-dysfunctional relationships which helped define my love life. Had she not been a disaster, Vic Lagina would have never been born.

I met Doctor Blow at a bar, using the same smile-and-hang-back technique which worked for me in the past. She was pretty, four years older than me, and a doctor.

A JEWISH DOCTOR. JACKPOT, RIGHT?

I could already hear the *kvelling* from my Dad that I finally set aside my *shiksa*-loving ways and dated within my tribe. When my mother died, I abandoned any and all Jewish beliefs and deemed all religions hokey superstitions created to control people and allay the fear of death. That said, I was never attracted to Jewish women. Maybe because I dealt with them and became annoyed by them during my Jewish summer camp getaways and in college. They seemed whiny. Demanding. Controlling. Costly. And probably would murder you in a divorce when they hired a better lawyer than yours with your own money. No thank you.

Initially, there was plenty to like about Doctor Blow. She was way more successful than me, more experienced, and her hair color turned me on. I had a ginger in college during a mostly unmemorable one-night stand, but I remembered the red bush and it stuck with me.

Doctor Blow and I lasted a little over a year. It was tumultuous mainly because she had a severe cocaine problem.

You would be amazed at how many doctors, working in high-pressure environments such as trauma centers, are cokeheads. Between the emotional highs and lows which come with being an addict and a female, I never knew which way was up with her. She was older, so I deemed her wiser.

I learned a lot about addiction during that relationship and developed an extreme hatred of blow. Ironic considering my future life choices.

A few hours after the millennium turned, we broke up.

A few days later, I met the girl who would be indirectly responsible for my entering the world of porn.

GOODBYE DOCTOR BLOW. HELLO JOY.

2 LAYING THE FOUNDATION

A few days after Y2K and the Doctor Blow breakup, the production company I was working for sent me to Jamaica to produce a video at an all-inclusive resort. We brought down male and female models, one of whom was... let's call her Joy. She resembled Jaime Pressly's character on *My Name Is Earl*. She was a freckly blonde with blue eyes from the South with the accent to match.

It didn't take long for me to seduce her. She wanted to take it slow, so when we hooked up the first night we didn't have sex. I guess slow in the South means twenty-four hours.

Joy was getting out of a bad relationship and setting her sights on LA, which I found intriguing. Miami was comfortable, but unfulfilling. The teaching part was tolerable, but corporate production left much to be desired. In my spare time I wrote scripts for movies and TV shows and shot short films with my own money. I wanted to break into the mainstream and South Florida is not the place to achieve that kind of success.

As dysfunctional relationship number two heated up, I began plotting my big move to Tinseltown.

During those seven months, Joy moved to LA, but kept returning to Miami to spend time with me. All the warning signs were there. Regardless, I was blind to them.

It's obvious now I was reliant on the comfort of a relationship, so I had no problem jumping into another one so quickly. On the plus side, Joy was super-hot and a great fuck. So even with proper guidance I still wouldn't have listened.

I was deep in the clutches of 'Good Pussy Addiction,' a self-diagnosed condition I would not tame until later in life.

G.P.A. is akin to drug addiction and the afflicted are affected in similar ways. The addict does not care about logic or reason. All they care about is getting high. Same goes for someone blinded by great sex with a partner who is easy on the eyes. Good judgment and reasoning vanish because spectacular sex is an easy crutch to lean on.

It's been several years since I relapsed. Good decision-making has put good pussy in the back seat. Once an addict, always an addict, but my progress is holding.

Joy and I drove cross-country in August of 2000 and the trip alone was our very brief honeymoon phase. A phase that lasted about eight hours into our arrival in Southern California.

Joy lived in a studio apartment in West Hollywood. I was going to share with her four hundred square feet of living space. Plus, she had a cat. I love all animals, but I am allergic to cats. As long as it doesn't get worse than allergies, I told myself I could make this work.

The first night in LA, Joy dropped her bombshell: her father murdered her mom when she was eight and he was still in jail.

DADDY ISSUES HAVE ALWAYS BEEN OUR FORTE.

My gut told me this was a huge mistake. Did I get in my truck and hightail it back to Miami? Nope. I mean, it's not her fault for having a murderous father, right? And look, she got herself a degree in Marine Biology on her own and was making something of herself. That's a good thing, right? Yes, assuming you don't allow your past to dictate your future. Joy had an unrealistic sense of entitlement, the delusion the universe owed her something for all of her bad life experiences.

A few months later, her truck got repossessed. Something about how her ex-boyfriend was the one who got the truck under her name because his credit was shit and he stopped making payments. Joy was once again a victim. Now, we had to share my truck to make ends meet.

Finding work in LA was not easy. There were plenty of assistant jobs and internships, but at twenty-seven, I had taught at the college level and had been a producer and editor on corporate videos. At least partial dues paid, right?

WRONG! NO ONE GIVES A FUCK.

Absent pure luck or connections there is only one way to start in LA: at the bottom. My ego would not allow me to take a few steps back.

Had I humbled myself, my life could have taken a very different turn and I would not have ended up where I am. Instead, I flew back to Miami for extended periods of time to do commercial work and Joy continued working as a SAG extra. It was a time of struggle and living hand-to-mouth. There was barely enough money to buy eggs. I developed more projects for TV and film and took meetings with any executives who gave me the time, only to get rejected. I was naïve, thinking the material alone would be strong enough to give me my first break.

Not only was the material not good and from a nobody, it's not the way Hollywood worked. Names drew interest, so I worked on developing relationships with published authors, one of whom was a *NY Times* Best Seller who had one of his projects go to a studio bidding war. He allowed me to shop his smaller projects as his manager. We came close to a few deals, but nothing materialized. I was funding this dream on my credit cards and the debt was mounting.

Then Joy decided she no longer wished to work as an extra, she wanted to be a White Female Rapper.

In 2002, Eminem was huge. He sold millions of records, was the star of a successful film, and won an Oscar for *Lose Yourself*. All of his success raised the question: Where is Feminem?

At the time, there had been no superstar white female rapper. In the rap world, street credibility is paramount. Not only was Eminem a great lyricist with a unique voice, he had legit street cred.

In a bizarre miscalculation, I saw the same in Joy. Yep, I was convinced my girl was going to be Feminem.

Not only did she have the model looks which would be the envy of horny teenagers everywhere, she had life experience. Her mom was murdered, her dad was in prison, and she had a horrific upbringing at the hands of her grandmother, her father's mom nonetheless. This is the pain and trauma great songs are made of.

But none of it mattered if she couldn't rap. I encouraged her to seek out producers who would help her with a cheap demo.

You get what you pay for when you buy cheap tracks from hack producers but I saw what I hoped to see: she was raw but she was at least competent on the microphone. She channeled her childhood pain into her lyrics. I believed all she needed was a good producer to produce one hit song.

DAMN YOU, GOOD PUSSY ADDICTION!

My skewered logic led me to fund ten-thousand dollars on my credit card for Joy's demo. We found a producer who was a former Crip and we rented a professional recording studio. While Joy sounded all right, the direction of the songs came off more as a white Little Kim talking about rolling blunts and drinking forties, something Joy did neither of. Additionally, this educated girl from the South started developing a 'black affect.' Like she was trying to be accepted by the black people she was around. None of it rang true and it was all very forced. Any professional ears deemed it "whack" and disingenuous. Even when she rapped about her mom's death at the hands of her father, it became evident no one cared and she had no business in the rap game.

I was close to thirty grand in debt with no salvation or platinum record in sight. My girlfriend was not working and was obsessed with a music career which never quite started. I was forced to sell personal belongings, cameras, equipment, and anything else which could fetch money on eBay to survive.

The need to make money led me to a website called *AdultStaffing.com* where a job listing caught my eye.

Ricardo was looking for directors to shoot his adult film. He was a young Mexican with a speech impediment, more like a stutter, who had the dream of becoming a porn producer. When you're desperate any work was good work so I agreed to shoot his porn movie for five hundred bucks.

I bullshitted him and told him I had experience in porn. To Ricardo, I was known as Ned Wood, a name which needed little explanation. No one got the joke. The white lie was acceptable because I surmised you didn't need experience to shoot sex scenes. It all seemed pretty straightforward.

Ricardo had a small budget. After some 'research' he was told by whatever porn advisory board guiding him he needed five scenes, utilizing both hard and softcore footage, to make a full and marketable adult film.

"No problem," I told him. I laid out a plan to shoot most of the scenes in one day, with a back-up day to clean up any mistakes. My plan sounded great to him and we started our very short-lived relationship.

At the time, Jim South was the biggest agent in the porn world and we visited his office in the Valley. The stench of cigarette smoke billowed from every corner. He had Polaroids of his girls, even though this was 2002. The internet existed. Web pages existed. Digital cameras existed. Yet, here we were sifting through fucking Polaroids. Eventually, R-R-Ricardo chose the girls he wanted and we set a production date a few weeks out.

This meeting would set in motion the rest of the tale, the birth of Vic Lagina. Looking back, I still see the humor in how over my head I was and how some of those same performers would resurface later in my career, unbeknownst to them.

We shot in a location owned by Pamela Peaks, complete with a tanning bed. John West was our contact and he was also going to perform in the day's second scene. The first scene was with a couple who left the business not long after. The second girl was a tall manly blonde named Malitia who seemed to have an awkward attraction to me.

The third scene was with Nick Manning and Shay Sights, the latter of whom I shot for Brazzers about seven years later. She didn't remember me because the scene was terrible, despite their rates being the most expensive. Nick insisted on shooting all the hardcore angles first. In the first two scenes, we shot the hard and softcore angles on the fly to keep the day moving and the men had zero dick issues. Nick, however, did. His demands now made sense. He yelled at my cameraman for switching between hard and softcore because he could not stay hard.

"I shoot four hundred scenes a year!" he boasted. "You're playing with fire!"

HOW MANY HAD HALF-CHUB SUSPECT WOOD LIKE THIS ONE, NICK?

Shay apologized for him. The hardcore angles we got had lots of Nick's ball-bag, man-ass, and butthole because he could not open up for camera properly. Nor could he fuck with sustainable rhythm. Slow and boring mixed in with the dumb shit he said during the scene including his usual 'droppin' loads' nonsense. I never shot Nick again after that.

THE DOUCHE ACTUALLY TRADEMARKED THE PHRASE "DROPPIN' LOADS."

Rumor had it he sued the makers of *Hot Tub Time Machine* and *The Howard Stern Show* for trademark infringement when they both used it. I heard he owns a 'Nick Manning' robe he wore on set, which puts him on a higher tier of douchebaggery than I thought existed. During his appearance on Howard Stern, he claimed to have an eight-inch penis, which was an outright lie. Nick is packing a six, maybe, because I know what a real eight looks like.

I CHALLENGE YOU TO A COCK-OFF, NICK! I'LL BRING THE TAPE MEASURE!

Adding inches is what male porn stars and perhaps most of the male population do when they find themselves inadequate and insecure in the dick department. I was asked to book Nick years later during my Brazzers years but refused. Fuck that guy. He should have conducted himself like a professional.

WE PREFER STUDS WHO CAN KEEP THEIR ACTUAL EIGHT-INCH DICKS HARD, DESPITE THE WORK CONDITIONS.

At some point, the stink of crack cocaine filled the air. I knew it was crack because I had been told it smells very similar to a smoking electrical socket. This was the element I now resided in, and it felt pretty gross.

We were only able to shoot four scenes that day, but our last scene was forever memorable. Ricardo was ecstatic because he secured Ron Jeremy for the scene. I was fascinated. Everybody knew who Ron Jeremy was.

Ron rolled in, carrying the large and schticky personality, wearing sweatpants and a loud Hawaiian shirt reeking of Old Spice. He was friendly and cracked jokes as if he were doing standup. We partnered him with a busty blonde named Chantz Fortune and it was the easiest scene of the day. Back then, Ron had the ability to ejaculate on command and he had Chantz count down from twenty. Sure enough, when one hit, so did his semen all over Chantz's face.

In an odd way, I have to commend that kind of body control. Ron ended the day by giving me a lasting memory of him eating cold pizza while naked in the kitchen. I may make it to ninety years of age with no idea of who I am, but I'll remember a naked, sweaty Hedgehog munching down cold pizza in a crack smelling condo. I would encounter Ron several times over the course of my career. I even shot him at my house but he never remembered me, which is fine.

Although I have zero insights into the allegations that plagued him in 2020 and thereafter[1], everything else you may have heard about Ron is true. He carried a plastic bag with his belongings, he loved free stuff, and was notoriously cheap. While he couldn't remember a guy for the life of him, he never forgot a vagina.

We ended the day and made up the fifth scene a few days later with Nikita Denise and John West on another location. I collected my five hundred dollars from Ricardo.

"Filthy" is the best word to describe it. Once the camera started rolling on the first scene, I felt like I stepped over the line. I sensed more was coming since my finances were a disaster. A few days later John called frantic, telling me Nikita's check had bounced and I needed to help fix the situation because he was the one who vouched for Ricardo. He sounded as if the Russian Mafia was ready to break his fingers. Aside from telling him to sort it directly with the Mexican kid who was

1 I would be remiss if I did not acknowledge Ron's later legal troubles. In 2012, he suffered a massive heart attack. I wonder if he wished he left the Earth then, knowing what was coming. As for the rape and sexual assault charges, they are awful. He'll likely never stand trial after being deemed mentally incompetent and will spend his remaining days in a mental hospital.

writing all the checks, I offered no recourse since I also was a work-for-hire. My dealings with Ricardo were limited after and who knows if he ever sold his movie. My guess is no. What I learned is that the porn world is as shady as you would think. It attracted a certain type who, in all likelihood, was failing in life as I was.

My days in LA were waning. I could not keep my head above water and all Joy was doing was standing on my shoulders. I took odd porn jobs off *AdultStaffing* to make ends meet, mostly editing because I had little experience operating a camera.

During my last month in LA, I met someone who would be both my mentor in the porn business as well as the type I strived to not become.

Reed was a successful businessman in his late thirties who lived in Orange County. In the civilian world, he worked for a tech company, had a BMW, and a nice condo close to the beach. He also operated a pay site which specialized in facials not of the esthetician nature.

I drove down there with the intention of running camera and soon found out Reed was also male talent. Let me put it in simpler terms: he paid a few hundred dollars to get his dick sucked while he filmed it POV-style and uploaded it to his website. It was not a complicated business model. Soon he would be moving up from getting blown by the girls to full-on fucking them (if the price was right), which is why he needed a cameraman. Shockingly, the girl did not show up and the trip was mostly wasted. I say "mostly" wasted because I did have an informative conversation with him and he showed me where to find business leads for content producers. The site was *GoFuckYourself.com.*

A month later, I left LA. I had massive credit card debt, no consistent work, and a lazy girlfriend. It pained my ego to accept defeat and be another casualty of LA. I was a wannabe who got chewed up and spit out by a cold, soulless, and uncaring town. I convinced myself and Joy it would only be for a year and both of us would work our asses off, fix our financial situations, and give it another try when we could afford it.

It was a good plan. On paper.

3 BECOMING VIC LAGINA

Before I entered the porn world, I had a discussion with my father about it.

"As long as you don't star in the movies," he said.

My father wound up getting remarried and my brother was now married with one child. I kept my experience in the porn industry to myself, with only Joy and my best friend, The Senator, knowing the sordid details.

Porn has a certain stigma attached to it and I didn't care to be judged. Nor did I care about my job choices being fodder for judgmental people who needed something to talk about. I also believed if it was known I worked in porn, any attempts to go mainstream would be squashed.

My family disliked Joy. They saw all the bad I was not willing to see. After a few testy exchanges between them, my relationship with my father and his wife became so strained we didn't speak for seven months. After the loss of my mother, all I had was my father, but Joy had me convinced he was too involved in my life and I needed to be my own man. After I returned to Miami, I kept him and the rest of the world in the dark about my fledgling business. I told him I stopped shooting porn after leaving LA.

I returned to the corporate production company and worked my ass off. Joy obsessed about her non-existent music career. She still did not have a vehicle, so she smoked weed all day while I supported us. During my slow days, I would scour *GoFuckYourself.com* for job leads and they began to materialize.

I needed a new name. Ned Wood wasn't cutting it and, at the time, I naïvely believed the porn industry was run by the Mafia. Having an Italian-sounding name would make people think twice before fucking with me. I also believed (and still do) porn should not be taken seriously and my name should reflect this. After extensive deliberations and discussions with The Senator, Vic Lagina was born.

The Senator needs the world to know the name was his creation. While true, I brought the motherfucker to life.

South Florida was a training ground for porn stars and producers. Reality Kings and Bang Bros. were already established and there were local girls willing to shoot boy/girl scenes for five hundred dollars. Internet porn was still in its infancy, while DVD features were the big leagues. Had I entered this world any earlier or later, things wouldn't have clicked as they did. Timing was perfect and the geniuses who knew how to make money with internet porn were out there getting started themselves.

I still find it funny when people don't get the joke and try to legitimize it. The variations I typically encounter are Vic LaGeeNuh, Vic Lah-gui-nuh, or just Mr. Lah-gin-uh. If one must formalize I would prefer DOCTOR Lagina. By this point, I think I have seen enough vagina to have an honorary title. It's given me great pleasure to read that my porn name has been voted in some circles as the best porn name of all time.

I landed my first big porn job for some guys in Canada. They needed a variety of scenes shot and I offered my services. Plus, I was willing to undercut any other bidder and offer additional services they wouldn't, including editing and encoding.

The only problem was I didn't have my own gear and aside from knowing the fundamentals of photography and videography, I had never operated a camera. I'd always hired a cameraman and told him what I needed.

However, if I was going to make money at this, I needed to do it all. The Canadian guys wired me twelve grand. Never before had anyone paid me so much money at once, let alone before I shot one frame of video. This was a very different business model than corporate production.

I phased out mainstream work. The dark side took over.

GOOOOOOOOD. GOOOOOOOOD. YOUR ANGER MAKES YOU POWERFUL. NOW FULLY EMBRACE THE POWER OF THE DARK SIDE!

I bought a new video camera, lights, a still camera, and flashes. The camera was a Panasonic DVX-100, the first of its kind that used the digital video tape format and shot at 24 frames per second (like film) as opposed to the normal 29.97 frames per second. It was supposed to give the video content a film feel, but it fell short in that department. I purchased a used 'high tech' four megapixel camera on eBay, along with tungsten balanced lights with soft boxes. I rented a hotel room for a night and shot everything there. Very amateur, very simple, and very cheap. Those lights got hot quickly and at times made porn production in a sweaty Miami hotel room very uncomfortable.

If I were to view anything I shot from this time period I'd cringe, but this is where I sharpened my skills. Those were the trenches where I earned my stripes.

Editing my footage made me a better shooter. I learned in the editing room (my spare bedroom) where I'd made mistakes and knew how to correct them while shooting. I also developed a reputation among content buyers as a hard worker who most importantly did not fuck with their money. Apparently, people took other people's money and gave them nothing in return. It wasn't hard for the cream to rise to the top in this world.

First and foremost, I never shot anything illegal. I've always kept meticulous records noting all performers were over eighteen years old and were doing everything on their own accord. When I entered this world I decided it was important to keep my soul intact. I needed to treat this as a business and any dealings between my performers and I were part of a mutually-beneficial financial transaction. I never wanted a check to bounce or the performers to have a bad experience on set.

I passed on jobs in the gay porn business. Not that I have any problems with the gay business - it's very lucrative, but if I was going to shoot something, I needed to at least be interested. I don't know what gay men like in their porn, so I was the wrong guy to shoot it.

There were some jobs I took on thinking I would be able to handle it. The one that comes to mind was shooting a guy giving his wife an enema in a hotel shower. I could have done without that one, credit card debt notwithstanding.

It had been almost two years since returning to South Florida. I'd been shooting all sorts of porn and my debt had gone down by only three thousand dollars.

This is what happens when you have an entitled girlfriend who is clinging to a pipe dream, but does not care to live the life of a struggling artist. I persuaded her to get a waitressing job to at least help in any capacity, but she got fired.

This was a dark time. I was shooting unfulfilling (sometimes gross) pornography to make money and it wasn't working. The only joy in life was from Jamie, my German shepherd puppy. It seemed this road would go on forever and any creative potential I once fostered was fading on this never-ending path. I was angry and bitter, which is why Joy broke up with me.

Sixteen years after the breakup, when I was looking for daily activities to keep the mind busy when the world shut down, I unearthed a treasure trove of DV tapes during my time with Joy. Remember, she was jobless and obsessed about being a 'Blonde Phenom' and a 'Lyrical Dominatrix,' while I was working two jobs. I always wondered what she was up to back in our shitty Kendall, FL apartment while I was supporting us. This discovery answered all of my questions.

I suppose in preparation for her soon to be exploding rap career, she created video diaries that came off more like 'White Trash Cribs' with her talking and narrating about her journey. She would talk about me, sometimes recording before interacting with me as a set-up. This was all about trying to incite me. One particular clip stands out.

I was moving us from said shitty apartment in Deep South Dade to better digs in a townhouse community in West Palm Beach. I rented a moving truck which she was to drive to our new home, after I loaded all of our possessions, by myself. Slight problem, my jalopy of a vehicle had a serpentine belt that would not stay on its rollers making the trek impossible. I stood over the open hood, greasy, shirtless, sweaty, and frustrated while I used a wrench in an attempt to keep the belt secure. That's when Joy decided to roll camera.

"I'm hungry. All I want is a fuckin' bacon, egg and cheese biscuit!" she whined in her backwoods Southern accent. "That's all I want, can you run to McDonald's please, get me a biscuit!"

While adjusting the belt, I quietly grumble that "me doing that is exactly what got us into this position." She then called me a "grouchy ass" before giving me the news that "no matter where I went next, whether it be McDonald's or church, your thing was going to break off."

As I continued to struggle, she began to lament to camera, "It is not even nine o'clock and it's shaping up to be a great day. This is the day we're supposed to move... see the Budget truck? (Swings camera), fuckin' maintenance man (swings camera again showing me), sweaty ass boyfraaand... "

At this point, I have had it. But I remained calm.

"You know what? Instead of fucking around, why don't you make sure Jamie isn't eating anything."

Jamie was 12 weeks at the time and running amok in the apartment we're about to vacate.

"Jamie ain't eating anything there ain't nothing for her to eat!"

"My shoes are in there."

"Get off the rag! You're just mad because I ain't as mad as you are."

"No, I am mad because I'm fucking doing everything."

"You're not doing everything!"

"I'm the one who loaded everything."

"Ohhhhh! What do you have those muscles for? And I offered to load and what did you say? 'Don't load' because you didn't want me pulling out my back!"

"I'm allowed to be grumpy."

"And I packed everything."

"I'm allowed to be grouchy."

"And I'm allowed to offer you a tampon."

"You don't have to put a fucking magnifying glass on everything."

At that point, I tell her to make herself useful and to pull and hold the wrench so I can adjust the belt. This got her to thankfully stop recording.

Those who I shared the video with commended me for not losing my cool, but more importantly, for not socking her in the mouth. This was never an option. Not my style. Watching later as a more mature man, I was proud of my younger self for keeping it together, despite her intentional agitation.

AHHHHH, JOY. SHE WAS HOT. AND HER VAGINA FELT WONDERFUL. TOO BAD THE REST OF HER WAS GARBAGE.

We wound up making the move successfully without the serpentine belt falling off on the Florida Turnpike. The resentment grew, as did my grouchy demeanor in the subsequent months. She kept the camera rolling through the twenty four hours that was Hurricane Frances and during the remaining six months we were together before she decided that it was time for her to move on. But she left me with a video catalog of her nonsense which reaffirmed my memories of her were not very far off from reality.

2004 was closing, as was our nearly five-year relationship. Part of me rode it out, even though I was miserable, because I still believed her music would drop and I would reap the benefits of investing in her and her career. The sex was now non-existent, but even though she initiated the breakup, I was not willing to let go. Her last night in Florida, instead of spending time with her, I decided to join my *New York Times* best-selling writer friend at a lecture he was going to give at a local film school.

YOU CHOSE... WISELY.

The film school was right up my alley. It was ten minutes away and they needed accredited professors to teach screenwriting. I applied and they were receptive, although I had to tap dance around the nature of the production I was involved in. Corporate production was the cover story and I at least had the experience to be able to lie convincingly about it. After his lecture, I had dinner with my friend and he noticed how dark and negative I had become.

"When I met you, you were full of piss and vinegar. A go-getter ready to take over the world. What happened?"

Joy happened. He had a point though, and it was an eye opener. It was time for a change and I had to let Joy go. So off she went, to the thrill of my family. She moved to Jacksonville to live with her friend using a rental car I paid for. She left her cats (she got another one along the way), but wanted to take Jamie, the dog I found, bought, and loved, saying Jamie was hers. I told her to get settled and we could discuss it at a later time.

When 2004 changed over to 2005, I sat at home, playing *Indiana Jones* on Xbox while drinking cheap red wine. I heard the fireworks at midnight and a new year began. I told myself when I woke up, I would formulate a plan which would get me out of debt by year's end. It only took ten months.

The goal was to make at least five thousand a month shooting porn. Then I could pay my bills and get out of debt. January ended and I hit my goal for the month. Jobs were coming in left and right. My good reputation and word of my work ethic spread to other content buyers. I was hustling every angle. No longer needing to consider Joy and rent hotel rooms, I shot in my rented townhouse instead.

The film school hired me to teach screenwriting at night and it jump started my creative side. I started to paint. I bonded with Jamie and trained with her every day. The dark cloud lifted. There was a light at the end of the tunnel as I made my mark over the next two months. Then Joy resurfaced. She wanted to come home. She said she made a mistake. She was ready to give up her rap career, work for a living, and be a better partner. I still loved her and was open, but I could not ignore the progress I made without her in my life, sucking my soul dry. I visited her in Jacksonville with Jamie for a weekend to take it slow. My friends and family were mortified, convinced I was going to take her back.

OH, YE OF LITTLE FAITH.

We fucked all night the first night and discussed the future. Something was off. She was convinced Eminem had traveled to Jacksonville to meet with her and discuss her music career. She also told me she had a miscarriage.

I spent Sunday morning alone with Jamie on the beach in Jacksonville while I figured out how I was going to end things for good. She seemingly took the news well and I went back to South Florida. While I was nearing home, my engine started to smoke right as my phone rang. It was Joy, in tears, begging me to come back and get her. I told her it wasn't going to happen and we needed to build a better foundation if there was going to be a future.

A few days later, I got a call from one of her friends asking me what was wrong with her. She'd gotten a call from a neighbor alleging Joy came to their house naked and said she was drugged by her friend's boyfriend. She also said her record label was bugging her house and listening in on her conversations. She had to be institutionalized for a short period.

When I spoke with her, the caring and sweet person who wanted to be a better partner turned into a stone-cold bitch. She insisted the people at the hospital said she had been drugged and I turned my back on her. Her friend kicked her out of her house as she caused a rift between her and her boyfriend and she was moving back home to live with her grandmother. She also told me I stole her dog.

"What about your cats? Are you ever going to come get them?"

"Eventually," she said.

I cannot say for certain if she ever was pregnant, let alone with my child. If so, it was the first time the universe spared me from being forever tied to a horrible person but it wouldn't be the last.

The remainder of 2005, I continued to hustle and my debt faded. Being single for the first time in the porn industry had its benefits and I shit where I ate. Girls who I shot frequently and wanted to have sex with me finally got their chance.

I won't lie: it was fun. If you wonder what it's like fucking a porn star, just watch a scene they are in. The noises are the same and so are the positions.

NOTE TO PORN STARS AND PROSTITUTES:
KEEP YOUR VERBAL REPERTOIRE FRESH.

The mistake I made was getting to know them. Before, it was a business transaction. Now, I was swapping fluids and sharing my bed and personal space with them.

To be clear, I never offered work for sex. Never. I'll swear on a stack of Bibles and everything I love to drive this point home. That behavior is disgusting, abhorrent, and it went against everything I promised myself when I got into the game. Getting the girl was never a problem in the past and I wasn't going to use the job for the sexual benefits. This mindset resulted in a lot more sex, going back to the basics of being aloof and disinterested.

Along the way, I started shooting for the group of guys who would form Brazzers. They had heard about me from other content buyers and decided to keep me busy. They had a lot of work for me, but there were not enough girls to shoot in South Florida. Even so, I briefly considered staying in South Florida, but the trifecta of hurricanes Frances, Jeanne, and Wilma sealed my fate. All three passed directly over me and I suffered through the subsequent weeks of having no power, no air conditioning, and living amongst the disarray.

Even though Joy was behind me, I was still living in the house we shared and with all the bad memories. It was time for a change. My hard work had created an unstoppable snowball of a business and I had become The Inadvertent Pornographer. Porn Mecca was the San Fernando Valley, but moving back to the over-populated, over-developed, overly-expensive hellhole known as LA was not an option.

Vic Lagina's School of Porn

Lesson One:
Sign-In/Sign-Out + Recordkeeping

Whenever people ask me to describe a porn shoot, I stress to them it's all quite boring and time consuming before we get to the actual sex act.

The sex act, assuming you hired consummate professionals (see *Lesson Seven: Hiring and Directing Your Talent*), is the fastest and easiest part of the day. Getting there takes patience, diligence, and foresight. Anticipating problems is a skill all producers need sharpened and it was paramount for me given more than eighty percent of the time I was importing talent from out of town.

Once the talent made it into the makeup chair and after greeting them with my usual chipper demeanor, I would ask for their ID's. According to 18 U.S.C. § 2257 and 18 U.S.C. § 2257A, primary producers are required to have two forms of government-issued IDs on record. If your talent has an expired ID, this is not kosher. Talent not having the proper IDs happened on occasion and I would have to ask their agent or a fellow producer to send over a digital scan, otherwise we didn't shoot.

As talent, you have two main jobs: keep your test current and always bring your ID to set! (I'll get into more detail about what else I expected of the talent in *Lesson Seven*).

In addition to having proper, current identification, talent is required to fill out a release form. This grants the company full use of their likeness to be exploited in whatever means desired for whatever fee was negotiated at the time of booking. Many are shocked at how little the talent made.

Things are different today, but during my tenure circa 2002-2020, talent would get paid a one-time fee, ranging from eight hundred to thirty-five hundred dollars depending on the level of the star and the agreed-upon sex act(s). The company would then market their likeness across the internet, driving traffic from their free 'tube' sites to their paid sites, generating sales that dwarfed their production costs.

The release also indemnified the company in the event a performer contracted a sexually-transmitted infection. (Today, all talent is required to have a fresh test within fourteen days of the production date). I was on top of this and made sure test results were current before talent boarded their flight to Vegas. One time I got burned while we were shooting the non-sex intro when a male talent's results came back positive for gonorrhea.

Fortunately, Marcus London was my non-sex actor and he had a current test, so at the approval of the female talent, we swapped and Marcus saved the day. From then on I was inflexible about my testing policy and had my production managers Pete and Ethan bug the shit out of talent and their agents days prior to the shoot. Even though all talent was current on my sets and the testing system was pretty good, it was not one hundred percent foolproof when incubation time is factored. Someone on their fourteenth day could have been exposed to chlamydia or gonorrhea early in their testing cycle and it wouldn't show up on their subsequent test. They may be shooting under a 'clean' test while infecting talent, hence the legal clause, which I doubt is very enforceable. But no matter, everyone signed the release regardless of what it said. Most people did not even read their paperwork.

Then the performers held their IDs next to their faces and I hit the record button.

"Please state your full name for the camera."

"What is your date of birth?"

"Are you aware you are shooting content for *Brazzers.com*?"

"Are you ok with this?"

"Are you under the influence of drugs or alcohol at the present time?"

I went through this process thousands of times. Of course, no one ever affirmed they were drunk or on drugs. After a performer passed out on GHB on one of my sets in 2006, I implemented a drug and alcohol policy during production.

KEEP READING. THAT RIDICULOUS TALE IS TOLD IN ABOUT FIFTEEN PAGES.

After we were wrapped, I had no problem smoking weed with talent. Off set, I would be happy to party with them, but during work hours people needed to keep their shit together. I was less concerned about weed, especially if a performer had a medical marijuana card and later when it was legalized. But alcohol, opioids, or Xanax (ironically all legal) could blur the line of consent or result in belligerent behavior.

At the end of the day, I tucked all releases into a 9x12 envelope labeled with the shoot date, talent, and scene type, and filed them away into a four-drawer filing cabinet. By career's end, I had filled up four of those filing cabinets, sixteen drawers total. 3,792. That's the number of scenes I produced and/or directed for which I have §2257 documentation. If I count the OnlyFans garbage I shot toward the end of the road, we are definitely north of 3,800.

TODAY'S WORD, BOYS AND GIRLS, IS: PROLIFIC.

In addition to having all releases on hand, as a good producer, it's good practice to back up the day's content onto an external hard drive. It amazed me how often the head office would lose photo sets and entire scenes, so I was organized enough to save their asses from themselves. I still have scenes backed up from 2009 (100 TB total) and have copies of the ID's from everyone I ever shot. My work from 2003-2009 is nowhere to be found, aside from various digital video tapes in some of those aforementioned envelopes.

While I have footage of Nick Manning yelling at my cameraman because he could not keep his wood, as well as Ricardo's original scenes from my very first day of porn, a lot of my original work has been lost to technology obsolescence. Once high-definition video became a thing in 2007, all standard definition porn was phased out. It's for the best. I was still learning. Plus, you know the fucktard cameraman who is talking to the talent while you're trying to jerk your Johnson? Well, I was the fucktard for a while until the trends shifted, thankfully. If ever there was a dispute or claim about one of my sets, I can always go to the tape. You can never be too careful while swimming in porn waters. Protect your tushy. On this note:

Even back in my South Florida days, well before Brazzers, when I was operating out of my West Palm Beach townhouse, I did video testimonials at the end of each shoot. My questions then were the same questions I asked on my last Brazzers shoot:

"How did your shoot go?"

"Were you treated okay?"

"Were you asked to do anything you didn't want to do?"

I never had anyone say anything negative during the post interview. If a shoot was going sideways and I had to end it early, we never got to the exit interview. I would reshoot the scene with different talent. Not finishing the scene meant not getting paid. Only talent got the kill fees.

From 2013 onward, I pushed for crew compensation on busted days, usually around half a day's rate. Years later, I started demanding it for myself when we had the occasional mishap. Example:

Don't be like Rob Piper. During a parody where Nikki Benz was playing

Ivanka Trump and Rob was supposed to play Dr. Ben Carson, they were supposed to pork on a couch in a green room before a televised debate.

Rob, I imagine, was going through a rough patch and drank some Four Loko during the day (we don't know when, except it was after his sign-in). We barely got through the intro because Rob could not remember his dialogue. I sensed something was off and when he could not keep his dick hard with Nikki-fucking-Benz during the hardcore stills, we took a break. Nikki was upset because this never happened to her. She felt rejected but was willing to reschedule for a generous kill fee. My crew broke down the lights and set up for tomorrow while Rob was asleep on the couch, dick in hand. We woke him up and took him to the airport and I have not seen him since. A few weeks later, Isiah Maxwell, one of my favorites, rocked the scene with Nikki and all was right in the world. This was the fucktardary I had to manage regularly.

Isiah Maxwell was a great sport over the years. He was cast in our porn parody 'HaMILFton' with Katie Morgan who worked with him diligently to learn the song. Yes, they sang. Somebody in the head office told Isiah his vocals would be auto-tuned, but they never were. "What kind of fucked up shit are you having me do today?" was a typical question when he arrived to set. Isiah is a gem and is crushing it in porn and in life. Bravo.

There are no problems, only solutions. Start with good record-keeping.

4 VIVA LAS VEGAS

Throughout my time in Florida, I helped Reed resell his content to interested buyers. Things seemed to be going well for him. His facials website was profitable and we were shooting for the same customers. All in all, it seemed like we had the potential to be successful business partners. We toyed with the idea of getting property together in Las Vegas after Hurricane Wilma. Plus, Las Vegas has no state income tax and the cost of living is much lower than LA.

For my entire life, I'd rented apartments or houses, which is the equivalent of throwing money out the window. In October, I paid off the remainder of my debt two months ahead of schedule. I could have just as easily kept my overhead low and lived an easy life, but something bigger was brewing, something I could not ignore. It was time to start building for the future. If I was going to get filthy, I wanted something to show for it.

Around this time, an eighteen-year-old blonde entered my life, Meridiana. She was coming to South Florida to shoot her first porn scenes and her handler, Jack Spade, emailed me her photos as she was looking for work. Meridiana was naturally beautiful, with gorgeous green eyes. Eighteen years old and brand new, finding her work was very easy. I was smitten.

Sure, I was enchanted by her beauty, but there was something else: she was sassy, quick-witted, and possessed an intelligence rare in a person her age. Most girls in the business had little to offer on a personal level. After the scene, we said our goodbyes and went about our day. She knew how to play aloof as well.

Reed and I planned a trip to Las Vegas to look for houses. The soon-to-be Brazzers were very happy with my work and revealed to me their grand plans, which entailed making a large monthly production commitment to me upon my arrival in Nevada.

Quick reality check: the only time I spent in Las Vegas was for weekends of debauchery when I lived in LA. I drove through the city a few times when I made cross country trips and always wanted to live there someday, for some unknown reason. I wasn't a big gambler, I couldn't afford it anyway, but something about the place was alluring. Here I was, ready to buy a house in a city I knew very little about. There was a tingling in my plums I could not ignore.

Meridiana made a second visit to South Florida because I had more work for her. She stayed the night after one of her scenes and a romance blossomed. We discussed her coming to Vegas with me.

THIS IS WHY WE ALL NEED A VOICE TO PROTECT US FROM POOR DECISIONS.

The sex was amazing. She recently dropped out of college where she had a softball scholarship to become a stripper in order to defy her parents. Getting into porn was just another way to piss them off. She had a boyfriend who cheated on her as well.

RECIPE FOR AWESOMENESS, FUCK-O!

My birthday is in October and Meridiana was there to celebrate with me. Also joining the party was a male performer I used for all my scenes and a female performer I had sex with on occasion from Orlando.

WHAT IS IN THE FLORIDA WATER THAT BREEDS SO MANY WONDERFUL STRUMPETS?

After a few drinks, we went back to my house where we had a foursome. It wasn't the first time I had sex with two girls at once, but it was the first time there was another dude in the room participating. I was unfazed by it and focused on enjoying the girls. In the midst of the insanity, the guy pulled out because Meridiana's vagina felt too good. He insisted he did not cum inside her. A few days later, Meridiana went back home to the Midwest. We made plans for her to stay with me after Thanksgiving until I was ready to move to Las Vegas. Then, she went silent on me.

A few weeks later, I met Reed in Las Vegas where we took a tour with Brian the real estate guy. I was a little heartbroken about Meridiana. I had so many unanswered questions. Had I known her reasons, I wouldn't have spent so much energy speculating if she went back with her boyfriend, if she got freaked out about the foursome, or if things were moving too fast. I didn't know, which was maddening.

I WASN'T THERE TO PHIL JACKSON YOUR DUMB ASS.

We needed a house with privacy for our productions. Reed's plan was to use this house as a getaway from LA where he would bring in girls to shoot and whatever else. Having ample living space for the both of us was necessary. Most houses we visited were too close to the neighboring houses or did not have the square footage we desired. After a few days of searching, we found the Goldilocks house.

It was four thousand square feet and sat on half an acre, with a pool designed for parties. There were bar stools in the pool which faced a barbeque pit, with a waterfall, two built-in bars and a wine area. This was a beautiful party house and I watched Reed's devious intentions wind viciously in his brain. I was looking for places to shoot and it had a casita the previous owner used as his workshop. This was going to be my studio and I would use the spare bedrooms as shooting rooms as well. This was late 2005, when the Vegas housing market was booming. The asking price: $840,000.

While out of my range as a sole buyer, with Reed as my partner my liability would have been less than $420,000 after the down payment. Back then, lenders were giving mortgages away, with only ten percent down, which was doable if I worked my ass off the next few months. The only sticking point was I had to be the sole name on the mortgage because Reed already owned property in LA. I worried what would happen if our partnership deteriorated, but with Vegas housing prices on the upswing, we could sell for a profit if things fell through.

I MEAN... WHAT COULD POSSIBLY GO WRONG?

The Senator was leery about only my name being on the mortgage while this dude Reed would be joint owner on the deed. Before signing paperwork, he advised we hammer out a contract outlining the terms should the partnership fail. Reed flipped the fuck out.

"Since when did I become the guy who was going to fuck you over?" were his exact words. "Maybe we shouldn't do this."

I had started to pull up stakes and was in go mode. Turning back now would upend everything. I did my best to placate Reed and assured him I didn't think he would fuck me over. All businesses have risk and if things went south, we needed to protect ourselves. The conversation ended with him refusing to sign any sort of agreement. If I was going to do this, I had to take all of the risk. The tingling in my ball bag kept me moving forward, despite logic and a strong gut feeling. No matter what happened, I reasoned, I could work my way through anything.

HEY, AT LEAST IT'S AN ETHOS.

My final interactions with Joy were unpleasant. She labeled me as a "dog thief" and a "piece of shit," overlooking the fact I had been taking care of the cats she abandoned for the past fifteen months since she left, on my own dime. I sent her the personal items she left behind, also on my own dime, but I was still a "piece of shit." I made one last attempt to deliver her cats and was willing to drive halfway between Florida and her to do so. Moving them with me to Vegas in a moving truck with a German shepherd who chased them incessantly was not an option. When the time came to make it happen, she backed out, offering no explanation. When I told her I set aside time to do this while juggling several other things, she yelled "everything isn't about YOU."

Ultimately, I had to give her cats away to someone who told me they would find them a new home. It broke my heart and I will never forgive Joy for putting me in this position. If you decide to own a pet, it is your responsibility to stay with the pet, regardless of your circumstances, until it breathes its last breath. The irresponsibility of some pet owners sickens me to the point where I prefer animals over humans. I never found out the fate of her cats, nor do I want to as I fear for the worst.

I have had no further contact with Joy, although I got reports on her from a mutual friend. She kept at the rap game deep into her forties, still writes and speaks like she was raised in the hood, and still believes I am a piece of shit dog thief who should rot in hell.

By late March of 2006, I traded in my beat-down Jeep for a new Nissan Titan which was being shipped out to Las Vegas, packed up a moving truck, and headed west with Jamie as my co-pilot and eight grand in the bank. Failure was not an option.

5 MOVING IN, CAN YOU REPEAT THAT PLEASE?

As I pulled in, the previous owners were finishing up moving their belongings. I walked through the house, reeling at the sheer size of it. How did I pull this off with eight thousand dollars to my name? Now I was responsible for financing this monstrosity, so it was time to get to work.

While the former owners lugged furniture, I sat on the pool deck with Jamie and searched for a wireless signal and hit up the boys in Canada to strategize.

My contacts were instant messenger screen names. I'd only met one guy face-to-face, a chubby Italian named Bosco who flew to Miami to supervise the first five scenes for their new website named *DoctorAdventures.com*. All I knew was they were happy with my work and their wires always arrived prior to shooting.

My main contact had the screen name 'Brazzer.' He was in charge and during my transition from Florida to Vegas, he verbally committed to giving me at least twenty scenes per month. I had other clients as well, some who had already committed to four scenes a month and others who ordered haphazardly.

Given I was only one man, I would have to drop most of my other clients to produce at this volume for Brazzer. Their sites focused on big titties or oiled-up asses and included *JuggFuckers.com*, *BigWetButts.com*, *BabyGotBoobs.com*, and *MommyGotBoobs.com*. They knew how to drive traffic to other people's content by creating TGP's (thumbnail gallery posts). This was the free porn before the tube sites emerged, only in photo form because photos are smaller in size. Brazzer and company got very good at this and were entering an era of expansion. They were leveling up and their plans were going to be explosive and game-changing.

Brazzer explained he was sending down his partner, Steph, and another guy named Tony to help get me set up. The first evening in my new house, as I was unpacking boxes in my kitchen, the phone rang.

"I'm pregnant," Meridiana said.

"Can you repeat that, please?" I asked as a million thoughts swirled through my mind.

Was it mine? No, I didn't cum in her. Yeah, but this is not foolproof and I didn't wear a condom. So? He probably busted a nut in her even though he insisted he didn't.

"Almost six months," she said.

I did the math. Oh shit.

"Well, it explains why you disappeared. I guess."

She told me she got freaked out, planned on getting an abortion, but couldn't go through with it.

"So, it's either mine or his?"

"Not exactly." She explained the father could have been a variety of other people. Even the other guy in the foursome, or other male performers she did scenes with. Or her ex-boyfriend, whom she had been fucking during our blossoming love affair.

SUCKER!

She was disgusted with herself and called herself "a slut."

WELL, IF THE SHOE FITS.

She'd spent the last few months in Arizona rehabbing her addiction to OxyContin under the watchful eye of her mother. She didn't know what to do, but she was going to have a baby in less than four months. She wanted to know who the father was even though she was leaning toward giving the baby up for adoption. Her ex maintained he was sterile.

Before she sought out her co-performers, she asked me to take a paternity test. I agreed and told her to find a testing place in Las Vegas.

That night, more thoughts swirled. She is telling me this now? She was fucking her ex while she claimed to be falling for me? An OxyContin addiction? Rehab? How do I know she is even telling the truth after all the lies she has already told? How am I going to afford this?

I called Potential Father Candidate Number Two.

"Did Meridiana call you?"

"Yeah, she did. What the fuck are we going to do, man? I swear to God, I didn't nut in her. I pulled out!"

We tried to make sense of it all, both of us feeling duped and discluded. I felt like a guy on Maury. I wanted to be the one who dances on the couch and not the sucker with his hands over his face. We decided if she wanted our DNA, she was going to have to get a court order.

Fear is a powerful emotion. It blinds you. It paralyzes you. It leads you to make cowardly choices. Had I not been blinded by fear and done the right thing, the manly thing, I would have saved myself a few years of grief. Karma came knocking in the years to come. As it should have.

The next day, I told Meridiana I wasn't going to get a paternity test and the rest was up to her. I wished her luck and if she wasn't ready to be a mother, adoption sounded like a sound plan. Then I hung up.

I was a cold dick about it. If I got a paternity test and the baby was mine, not only would I have a huge mortgage, but also monthly child support. I didn't want to be a father. At least not right then with such an uncertain future.

YEAH, BUT YOU'RE BETTER THAN THIS, AREN'T YOU?

These internal debates weighed on my conscience over the next months. Hoping for the best wasn't going to make this go away. As I waited for the inevitable bomb to drop, my guilt skyrocketed, leading me to make even worse decisions my family and I are still scarred from.

BUT, IT DID MAKE FOR GREAT DRAMA.

Reed was awaiting my arrival so he could bring in girls to impress and to shoot. A few days later he showed up alone. Jamie rushed him, cornered him, and barked. I had never seen her do this before.

"Easy, Jamie. He's all right."

She backed off and kept a watchful eye on him. Weird. No, not weird. She knew.

He had been shooting in LA for years and made arrangements to bring in girls. He found local girls and brought them in for 'go sees.' I had to make contacts with local male performers because I was not the star of my productions like he was.

Reed's desk was on the other side of the wall of my toilet and I always heard his conversations while taking a dump. He had a business partner who ran Reed's websites and upcoming DVD lines. This was early 2006, the time to be getting out of the DVD business. What stood out was Reed had a very short fuse and confrontational demeanor. Over the course of the next few months, he would come to town with girls he was hoping to fuck or was fucking off camera. We both used these girls for our productions.

Steph and Tony arrived a week later and by then I had painted and carpeted the casita. It was ready for production. Steph was a young Greek with a large frame who could not have been any older than twenty-five. He liked to talk about bench pressing. Tony was a short, bald Italian roughly the same age. These guys, seven years my junior, were my new bosses.

They gave me an overview of their plan, which was for me to shoot for their existing sites as well as some new ones. The niches were simple: using girls with either big tits and/or big asses, and their concepts were basic. I would shoot unscripted gonzo style with a lot of tease leading up to the sex. It was a simple formula needing colorful sets, colorful couches, and sexy wardrobe. Brazzer, whose real name I learned was Ouissam, understood big tits and big asses were where the money was. Simple, yet effective.

Steph and Tony accompanied me to stores around town where they bought five very colorful couches: orange, red, lime green, blue, and yellow. I was adamant about discretion, so we had to invent ways to inquire about our needs for these purchases. We had a few laughs, like when Steph asked the sales person how sturdy their couches were.

"They're pretty sturdy, sir."

"Yeah, but what if I were to, like, jump on them with all my weight?"

We also purchased a doctor's table for *DoctorAdventures.com*, along with doctor equipment such as stethoscopes, blood pressure gauges, and the like, as well as rugs and colorful fabric. When all was said and done, my house looked like it was furnished by Willy Wonka. For backdrops on the walls, I painted large canvases my crew later dubbed Lagina Originals. Tony thought his kid niece could paint better.

I DIDN'T KNOW HE WAS A FUCKING ART CRITIC.

During their stay, I came across a piece of paper someone left on my kitchen table which read the following:

Purchase furniture which suits the needs of our production.
Inform and instruct Vic on how we need our productions to be shot.
Help Vic schedule and facilitate the first 20 scenes.
█████ ████ ██ ██

This no doubt was a task list ordered by Ouissam. Curious, I wanted to know what this fourth item was. After a closer look, I was able to make out the following:

~~*Become friends with Vic.*~~

A constant analyzer, I tried to interpret the objective and its subsequent crossing out by Tony or Steph:

~~*Become friends with Vic.*~~

The concept resonated until I figured it out. People don't become friends with people based on a mandate. It happens, or it doesn't. The fact it was an objective meant, at the very least, it was hoped I would believe these guys were my friends. Because friends are loyal. Friends work hard for their friends. And friends want to do right by their friends. I have a handful of people I would call my actual friends.

Over the years, I built up walls and made it difficult for people to penetrate my outer shell. I had been burned and disappointed by friends who only wanted something from me. It takes a while for anyone to get close. I enjoyed the camaraderie, but it was clear to me these guys, while friendly, weren't my friends. I was a commodity who could help make them wealthy. In turn, these guys would suit my needs and get me where I wanted to be in life. It was symbiotic. The note set the tone for how I was going to conduct business in the future with the company, and mostly everyone else in the business.

Shortly after, Steph returned to Montreal while Tony stayed the next few weeks to help assist the first twenty scenes. There was a handful of talent in Las Vegas, but the majority of girls were from LA. I needed to form relationships, specifically with LA Direct, which at the time was the largest and most powerful agency.

I had dealt with the owner, Derek Hay, during my final days in LA. I shot a solo scene with one of his girls at his condo where he set up shop. In three short years, he had transformed himself from a home-based business into a venture and represented over a hundred of the biggest girls in porn.

A common complaint about Derek was he put his girls through the financial wringer. He also earned a reputation as tough and confrontational. Derek was a performer going by the name of Ben English, because he's British and I guess because Big Ben is in London.

WOW. DEEP.

Even back then, I thought it was weird an agent was also the talent fucking his clients on camera. But I was a neophyte. I made the call and a guy named Kevin answered the phone. I introduced myself only as 'Vic' and told him I needed girls.

"Vic? Vic Lagina?" he asked.

"Um, yeah?"

"This is Kevin! You shot me and my wife's first scenes! How are ya?!?"

Kevin and Kelly Kline were now working as agents at LA Direct. I was in, just like that. Tony was impressed. The first batch of LA talent was on their way. In an effort to save money on hotels, Tony suggested I ask the agents if the girls could stay at the house. I was uncomfortable with this since I did not want to come off as a creeper. But I did it for Tony. I called LA Direct, hoping for Kevin. Instead, I got Lisa Ann.

I remember jerking off to Lisa Ann during my early Florida years, before I got my Masters in 1998. Reed told me she was a "fucking cunt." He shot with her once and it did not go well. Now she worked for Derek as a booking agent. Tony wanted to book a girl named Naomi for several shoots over a two-day period. She was an anal girl and did interracial, so she would be perfect for *buttsandblacks.com* and *bigwetbutts.com*. I secured back-to-back days with her, then closed my eyes, gritted my teeth, and asked about talent staying at the house.

"No. Absolutely not." My head was barely left intact.

After we hung up, I sarcastically thanked Tony. He had a good chuckle on my account.

Tony's initial visit to Vegas set the stage for what would become the biggest and most successful company in porn. You would never know it based on how little we put into the production. The girls provided their own wardrobe and makeup, which at times left a lot to be desired. I was shooting two scenes a day, including still photos, to maximize their time in Las Vegas. We were dealing with two hundred dollar per-scene male performers and you get what you pay for: small dicks and having to wait at times for them to get their dick hard. Even with Viagra and Cialis, wood was never guaranteed.

After a few days of production, Tony realized I needed an assistant. I was picking up the models from the airport, building sets, shopping, taking photos, shooting video, backing up content, and then dropping them back at the airport at the end of the day. Enter Jodi.

Jodi had more ink on her body than a phonebook. She was referred by a local performer/madam whom she met as a makeup artist on a shoot. Having makeup credentials would come in handy. After a brief conversation, I hired her on the spot. She had a sweet demeanor, a nervous laugh, and was married to a chef. Perfect. There was no risk of inter-work penetration.

After a few weeks, Tony returned to Canada, and Jodi and I were left on our own to output twenty scenes a month for the Brazzers.

AND NOW, A WORD FROM JODI:

Walking in to meet Vic for the first time you would first notice his appearance and overall energy. His features are strong, his mane is long, almost a German shepherd in human form. Then you would notice how organized, quick and intelligent he is. This would make working for and with Vic one of the most fun and productive jobs I ever had.

Of course the subject matter was never boring, but it could have gone haywire at any moment that control slipped. These are not your normal people that show up to work every morning. Since the airport was between my house and the studio, picking up the talent on my way in just made sense. That would start the tone of the day. Vic and I were great with our silent text alerting one another on what kind of times we were about to have. Was the talent at the pickup area? Did they miss their flight? Did they maybe party too much the night before and are a complete train wreck? Or 'please dear god be that smiling, moisturized, hydrated and shiny person waiting with a carry on, ready to jump in my little beetle and zoom away.' Whichever one you were, you can bet I let Vic know what we were in for.

In the beginning it was just Vic and I and we ran a well-oiled machine. Pick the talent up, get them in hair and makeup, while Vic got started shooting photos and filming I would go grab lunch and whatever else supplies needed. Have you ever walked into a Walgreens to ask for a box of anal douches? Not a little box of enemas, a giant brown box filled with enemas. What reason could you possibly have to need such a thing? I had a long story about working at a nursing home cooked up that I luckily never had to tell. Amazon would have been such a face-saver then.

Rest in Porn

I always had an issue with people sharing memories and stories about people on Twitter shortly after they died. This never made sense to me. Shouldn't they have told the person all of this nice, mushy stuff when they were alive? Putting it on Twitter after the fact made it about them.

Do they really have all of these wonderful memories of them? What about when they were assholes or when they showed their shortcomings? Shouldn't this be part of what made them unique, what showed their humanity, the good and the bad? So, I decided to do this with whom I knew in the industry, both on and off set. Some of these will not be your typical remembrances. I am certain some people will hate me for being this forthcoming. I can see how some could be viewed lacking class and dignity. However, painting a truthful picture lead me to some realizations.

I found in these recaps, like me, a lot of them were secretly in pain and doing what they could to numb themselves. I feel fortunate I made it out alive and was able to write about it. Who knows, perhaps it may save someone else's life.

IN MEMORIUM:

Billy Glide, 7/25/70 - 5/24/14

When I first shot Billy, it was around 2006 and I liked him right away. He was only three years older than me, but he looked like a guy who spent a lot of time at the beach on a surfboard and had aged, tan skin.

He had a big gap between his front two teeth, which accentuated his goofy aura. He was klutzy, falling down a lot and knocking things over with his animated limbs. When we were shooting at the eventual Gilespie House, Billy would stay over a few days to shoot multiple scenes and during after hours, he loved to drink red wine. One could find Billy by following the trail of spilled red wine.

Billy's biggest asset was his thick, girthy penis.

This was before Danny D and Dredd. Back then, Billy Glide had the thickest dick in porn. I watched and heard Tory Lane moan "Billllllllllllyyyyy Glid-ddddeeeee" as he entered her anus after several failed attempts. While I had a lot of strong, successful shoots with him, he did hit a rough patch where he could not contain his orgasm. There were a lot of short bursts of humping followed by the inevitable pull out where he had to slap his dick on the female talent's leg or ass to keep himself from cumming. During one scene with Savanah Gold and Candy Manson (both RIP), he came four times. On one hand, this is impressive, but on the other, they weren't usable pop shots as he pulled out onto his hand.

Eventually, members turned on Billy and requested he not appear in Brazzers productions. The head office abided and I saw less and less of him. This was when he slid into his dark patch. He started dating a Russian performer named Olga around 2008 and I then saw the other side of him. I hosted a NYE party at my house. At one point, she asked me to talk to him because he was getting dark and negative. I was rolling on ecstasy, but even so, what could I do? They continued to date over the next few years. The last time I saw them, it looked like things had gotten worse. He would keep checking on her, wherever she was.

On May 24, 2014, he died in his sleep. An initial report by Alana Evans stated he was bitten by a rattlesnake and did not go to the hospital. This report was later debunked. The official autopsy report on *findagrave.com* says he died of accidental ethanol intoxication, with an enlarged heart and fatty liver as 'other significant causes.' He was forty-three years old.

6 BUILDING AN EMPIRE, THE G HOLE, AND THE PHANTOM SPIDER

The next six months were a whirlwind. Mondays were prep days and Tuesday through Friday were production days. Typically, a girl would land at eight in the morning and Jodi would put her through makeup and wardrobe using the spare bedroom and bathroom. I would shoot photos and video for the first scene, we would break for lunch, shoot the second scene, and then she would head to the airport to fly back to LA. Afterwards, I would back up the content, process and burn the photos to DVD, and build the set for the following day. I was an animal. By Friday night, all I wanted to and could do was soak in my bathtub and wash the bodily pain away.

LATHER. RINSE. REPEAT.

There were the usual production problems which plague a director who is limited on budget for male talent. When their dicks were hard, it was difficult to see good penetration due to their small size. A lot of times I would shoot in two-minute intervals and cut while the talent went into a corner to jerk himself hard again. This went on until we made it to the pop shot, which wasn't always a cake walk either.

Sometimes it took thirty minutes for the guy to pop, but it's better than popping too soon. We'd have to wait for him to regain wood and finish the scene, if he even could. Stunt pops were a solution, but not on my sets. Perhaps it sounds like fun, but I preferred hiring proper male talent as discussed in Lesson Seven of *Vic Lagina's School of Porn.*

A lot of the scenes involved baby oil. They wanted baby oil on the tits, on the ass, and as a result, I had baby oil all over my floors and Willy Wonka furniture. I tried to shoot those scenes first so I could mop up during lunch.

I grew to hate baby oil. I hated the stench of it and finding traces throughout my house. The worst was the toilet seat.

YOUR BUTTCHEEKS MIXING WITH THEIR OILY DNA.

You would have to flip a coin to decide whether this is better or worse than grabbing a door knob full of lube. I hired cleaners to detox my house every Saturday, but I had to live amongst filth during the week. I created an invisible line off limits to talent which included my office and bedroom.

As a result of my hard work, I developed a good reputation with Los Angeles agents and talent. I wanted to be different than my first day in porn. This was not a crack filled condo in the Valley.

Agents liked me because they were making double the money with two scenes in one day in Vegas. Girls would typically only work one scene a day in LA unless they were put through the meat grinder by their agent. The talent liked it because they were making double the money, but perhaps more importantly, I was running this thing like a business. I wasn't the guy fucking them while I held a camera. They got paid the same day and their checks never bounced.

Jodi told me which girls were intrigued by my disinterest. I wanted to avoid a bad reputation by not becoming another scumbag pornographer. My best bet was not to sleep with anyone unless we had a genuine connection.

HEY DUMMY, THE ONLY CONNECTION IN PORN THAT MATTERS IS BETWEEN YOUR JOHNSON AND HER VAGINA.

AND NOW, A WORD FROM JODI…

Even though Vic was like my brother I have no qualms in saying he is very attractive from the outside in. Lots of the starlets were always trying to get the details on how to get his attention. This was always a fun game of love connection. There was a core group of just really fun good hearted people that came through. Not what I expected at all when I first started. In fact I met my best friend to this day in that fateful makeup chair.

Needless to say, the after-hours of "making the donuts" was some very fun debauchery. Admittedly I would encourage him to bring back starlets that he had interest in that were funny and intelligent to hang and party with. That led to some hazy but very fond memories. Like tripping on mushrooms, looking at the sky full of eyeballs only to look over to inform my friends of this alarming situation to find them fully fucking in the hot tub. Time to go inside.

When you think about dating and courtship in the real world, it's the opposite of what my world had become. When you date someone, you are supposed to get to know them first. If you jell with their personality, you hope for the best when you see them naked. Then you hope for competence in bed. Otherwise, you have wasted weeks or months of your life.

In porn, you see what the girl looks like without makeup when they first roll in. You see them naked immediately and gauge whether you like their vagina and the amount of pubic hair. You determine whether they have a full booty or a flat ass. You know if they have nice natural boobs or manufactured bolt-ons.

Then, you get to see how they have sex! Personality was secondary. I could only spend a few hours with the majority of these girls. We had nothing in common except for a physical attraction and desire to bust our mutual nuts.

Reality check: I am aware the majority of the girls were fucking me because they believed it could benefit their porn careers. Fucking to them was like shaking a hand. In turn, I was having fun, dirty, marathon sex with porn stars. These were the other symbiotic relationships I was forming which rarely caused me personal drama. Mostly it seemed whatever stories the girls were spreading lead to more opportunities in the bedroom.

Reed came out every three to four weeks and was soldiering his half of the bills. He was heavily invested in the DVD game. DVD's were on the decline due to the rise of the internet, but he seemed positive about his prospects. Because we only put ten percent down on the house, I had two mortgages at high interest rates. The payments were low for a house this size and we paid the minimum each month and split the bills.

Early on, things were smooth, but a storm was brewing.

Around Memorial Day, Reed brought his business partner Manny to Vegas with two LA girls in tow. Manny and Reed were also shooting scenes for Brazzers.

I greeted Manny in my driveway and saw his truck was all keyed up.

"Wow, someone really fucked up your car, huh?"

"Yeah, it was my ex-girlfriend, but I slapped the shit out of her for doing it."

LOVELY.

I had been hanging out with the madam who led me to Jodi and we had a dysfunctional couples' Memorial Day weekend. The madam invited a few local shooters (cameramen) over to the house.

This was my first encounter with Huggy. Down the road I would employ him as a director for the better part of six years. It seemed as if Huggy and his partner wanted to conquer the Vegas porn scene but were not advancing.

The characters gravitating toward me were an eclectic bunch who had their own agendas and motivations – and very demented perspectives on life.

The madam was running her girls and working her phone as she dispatched them to their jobs. Manny and Reed talked about their porn conquests and performers of interest. Having them watch me get blown by both the madam and one of the weekend ladies in the jacuzzi didn't bother me. Them discussing how I looked like the male porn star Julian and how I could have a good career as male talent, did.

"You can make so much more money!"

"Yeah, but at what cost?"

I heard this from female performers as well.

"Girls would love working with you!"

WELL, HIS FATHER WOULD NOT APPROVE.

This side of my life should be mine, even if occasionally other people watched. Was I being recruited? It all seemed so weird. It was not a particularly settling energy to be around and I was glad when the weekend ended.

A few weeks later, I hosted The Senator's younger brother's bachelor party. I invited Reed so The Senator could meet the man he was uncertain about.

I met people at this party who would become some of my best friends. They spawned like gremlins and their presence has resulted in the best times in my life. They have also helped me maintain my sanity during the insanity. Unfortunately, Reed had his first of what would be a series of meltdowns which would jeopardize our house partnership. I cannot recall the exact reason for this episode, but I believe it had something to do with a girl not paying attention to him.

Fueled by copious intoxicants, everyone was in good spirits and having a good time. Except Reed. Reed was screaming and slamming doors. One of my friends thought he was ready to throw a stool out of the window.

NOT IN OUR FUCKING HOUSE.

I confronted Reed and asked him what his problem was, but he was drunk and could not articulate his words. I played buddy with him and brought him to his room to lay down. The madam threw a Xanax down his throat. I watched his face melt into mush until he was fast asleep.

The next afternoon, Reed emerged from his bedroom and went out to the pool to work on his tan. We never discussed the incident, so this was his free pass. The Senator was now certain my house partner was a spectacular train wreck and warned me the impending crash was imminent.

Reed's next visit to the house would seal our fate.

A vast array of strange things happened during year one in the big leagues of porn, but one in particular stands out.

Over a two-day stint, I shot a girl named Felicia for four scenes. This girl did everything, including interracial and anal. On day two, the wheels came off. It was another dreaded baby oil scene and it was the last scene of the day. Jodi had already gone home, so it was just me, Felicia and the male performer Nik. I rolled camera when something odd happened.

Felicia ignored my direction, leaned up against the wall, giggled, and then slowly slid down to the floor. Then she stopped reacting to us.

Neither of us knew what to do. Call the cops? Paramedics? She was breathing and wasn't turning blue, so we held off. Nik, who had been in the military, grabbed her slippery oily body and managed to drag her into the hall shower and turned on the water. I heard her screech. Nik later told me she began lapping up the water like a thirsty dog. After the shower, Nik laid her on the floor on her stomach, covered her up with a towel, and stood watch while I called her agent. I felt like John Travolta calling his drug dealer when Uma Thurman overdosed on his high-powered heroin in *Pulp Fiction*. The agent was a lot calmer than Eric Stoltz.

"Is she still breathing?" he asked. I said she was. "Well, just keep an eye on her in case she stops. I am sure you don't want police and paramedics coming to your house unless absolutely necessary."

GOOD POINT.

Having an ambulance and cop cars at the end of my driveway while a slippery porn star was rolled out on a gurney would not impress my already suspicious neighbors.

I hung up and peered into the bathroom, watching Felicia snore soundly on the tile.

"Guess we're not doing the scene, huh?" Nik joked... I think.

This was an overreaction, but something in my brain reminded me we were two guys alone with a passed-out chick. This is the kind of thing rape stories are made of. I called Jodi and asked her to come back. If needed, she could serve as a witness that me and Nik conducted ourselves as gentlemen. I ordered both her and Nik dinner for their troubles while Felicia slept for the next hour-and-a-half as we discussed what the fuck just happened. Obviously, it was drugs of some kind, but which? I wasn't the walking pharmacist I am today, so I was clueless. Nik didn't do drugs, so he was of no help.

Then it occurred to me: Felicia fell into a G-hole.

GHB, also known as gamma-Hydroxybutanoic acid, is a naturally-occurring substance found in the human central nervous system, as well as in wine, beef, small citrus fruits, and in small amounts in most animals. GHB is a central nervous system depressant used as an intoxicant. Its effects are comparable with ethanol and MDMA use, such as euphoria, disinhibition, enhanced sensuality and empathogenic states. At higher doses, GHB may induce nausea, dizziness, drowsiness, agitation, visual disturbances, depressed breathing, amnesia, unconsciousness, and death. The effects of GHB can last from one and a half to three hours or longer.

BINGO!

JODI'S RECOLLECTION:

After lunch, I would usually get the talent ready for the second shoot and would go home. Unless I would get an after hour text from Vic. One such text came in one night. This particular starlet was troublesome all day. I could tell she would be a bit high drama, but no one could predict what happened next.

The text read something like this:

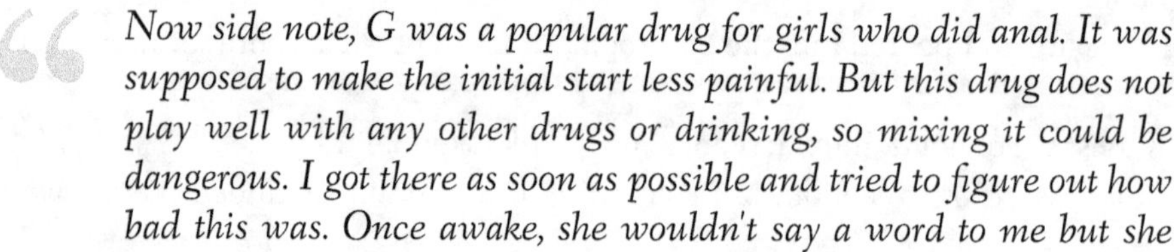

She passed out during the photos and slid down the
wall, I think she G'd out.

Now side note, G was a popular drug for girls who did anal. It was supposed to make the initial start less painful. But this drug does not play well with any other drugs or drinking, so mixing it could be dangerous. I got there as soon as possible and tried to figure out how bad this was. Once awake, she wouldn't say a word to me but she

was aware and walking around so I got her into the shower. Time passed, I went to look in on her and saw she was just kind of frozen in the shower. My instincts told me she was trying to plan an escape. I told her if she got dressed and got her things I would be happy to take her back to the airport and she could still catch her flight. This did get her moving and I did as promised, though she never ever said one word to me. Not even a peep when she left my car.

Since this incident, I have experimented with GHB on myself a number of times. The result is the most passionate and euphoric sexual experience imaginable.

My guess is Felicia took it without telling us so her anal scene would be more pleasant. Regardless, I wanted this passed out poohbah off my floor, recovered, and out of my house.

All three of us peered into the bathroom while Felicia awoke. Jodi took control. Felicia sprung up like a kid who realizes she is about to miss the bus and packed her stuff. In five minutes she was out my door and headed to the airport.

Five years later, the head office requested Felicia be shot for MilfsLikeItBlack.com. I reminded them she G'd out on one of their shoots, but pickings were slim and she was booked with Huggy. 'The incident' was never discussed. I wonder if she even remembered. That shoot went smoothly, but this was the last time she worked for me.

Bye, Felicia.

The Senator advised me to find local counsel in case this happened again. I mandated a drug and alcohol policy. Word got around these things were not allowed on Brazzers sets. It didn't happen again until 2011 when Jennifer White passed out with an anal plug inserted during a live show.

I tried to keep things as professional as possible. I heard countless stories about producers in LA blowing lines and creating a party atmosphere on their sets. To me this was a liability that could end my livelihood.

I was four months into my new surroundings and was lonely. Jamie was a solid companion and as much as I despised most humans, I pined for an emotional connection. I created an online profile and was forthcoming about my occupation.

After several dates with a few 'civilians' (as we called people outside of the industry), I came to the harsh conclusion as a pornographer, a normal relationship was not going to happen. Some girls were intrigued and asked a lot of questions, but ultimately I was a novelty, someone they could talk about with their friends.

Others got freaked out and we never progressed past the first date. I was relegated to dating in the industry, otherwise destined to be alone. Surely there was a porn chick out there with a heart of gold and a good head on their shoulders.

OF COURSE THERE IS AN AWESOME GIRL OUT THERE WHO ALSO TAKES LOADS ALL OVER HER FACE FOR MONEY ON A DAILY BASIS. IT'S GOING TO GO SWIMMINGLY. HAVE FUN, FUCKTARD.

Along came Nikki, a girl Reed found and brought out to Vegas. I also had a girl staying with me for a few days before named Charity. We'd hooked up the night before Reed and Nikki arrived. She was eager to impress and easy enough on the eyes, so I went with it, even if there was no challenge to it. The plan was for both of us to shoot Nikki while Reed worked Charity into a few of his shoots.

It derailed the very first night, when all four of us went out to dinner.

Like Meridiana before her, I was smitten with Nikki. She was cool, funny, had the most splendid, voluptuous ass and a picture-perfect vagina. She was also an extremely dirty performer which turned me on. She gravitated toward me and it was obvious she was not vibing with Reed.

While we were shooting pool, Reed asked which girl I was interested in and I had to disappoint him.

The following day, Reed wanted to shoot a boy/girl scene with Charity. The next seven words she uttered would be the beginning of the end for he and I.

"I'd rather do the scene with Vic."

I don't think Charity meant much by what she said or knew the reason why she said it. I wasn't male talent. But we watched Reed's demeanor change from pleasant to putrefied in a nanosecond. It was already clear Reed could not handle rejection. However, watching me be more attractive to the opposite sex was too much to bear.

Was it my fault? Of course not. But tell this to a fractured ego. Even if I explained how he came across as creepy and aggressive, would it have made a difference?

Nikki and I bonded during her stay. She was in a bad relationship with a guy in Arizona and in no rush to get home. Our oasis in Las Vegas provided the perfect sanctuary. On the first night, I showed her the various places she could sleep, including my bedroom, Reed's bedroom, and the couch. She chose the couch. On night two, she slept in my bed and aside from a lot of talking and some kissing, we slept. On day three we had sex and it was amazing. Day four was her twenty-second birthday and I treated her to a fun night out. I didn't think leaving Charity and Reed alone would be a problem.

Wrong again.

I took Nikki to the Wynn, where the plan was to have drinks and check out the club XS. Instead, I started receiving text messages from Reed.

> "Maybe we should end this house partnership so you can be the King of Vegas."

I stared at the screen. My knee jerk reaction was to calm him down and attempt to keep everything together. Instead, I pondered what it would mean to fully take on the house. I told him we'd discuss it later. Shortly after, Charity called saying she was locked in the bathroom and Reed was pounding on the door, berating her. Nikki's fun night out was cut short and we went home.

When we arrived, Reed's position was he wanted to brush his teeth, but she locked herself in the bathroom and this angered him. It was obvious Reed was still pissed she rejected him.

Nikki found out Charity was bulimic, which is why she locked herself in the bathroom, presumably to vomit. Shortly after, she had me drive both of them to a treatment center where Nikki hoped to steer her in a helpful direction. Watching Nikki help someone she didn't know made me believe I'd found the porn chick with the heart of gold.

I fell hard, which would lead to our undoing.

AND NOW A WORD FROM NIKKI...

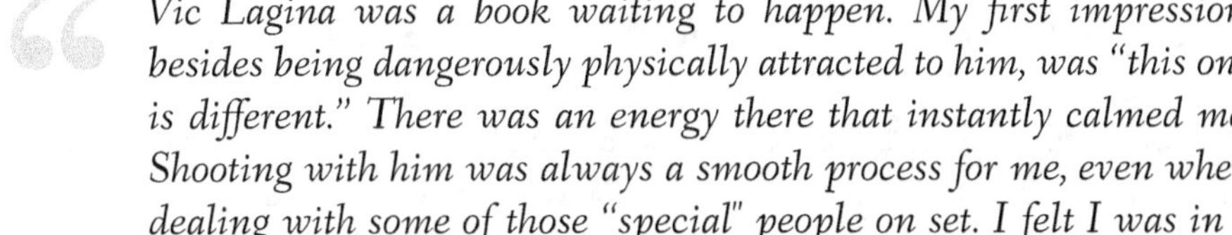

> *Vic Lagina was a book waiting to happen. My first impression, besides being dangerously physically attracted to him, was "this one is different." There was an energy there that instantly calmed me. Shooting with him was always a smooth process for me, even when dealing with some of those "special" people on set. I felt I was in a safe and professional environment.*

Around this time, Meridiana was giving birth somewhere to what could have been my child. Meanwhile, I had other pressing things to handle.

How was I going to handle Reed and our upcoming house divorce? Once Nikki and Charity left, we discussed terms. My tactic? Guilt. As a Jew, I knew how to use it well. Guilt is our Kryptonite, but a powerful weapon.

"This is exactly why I asked for a contract with you six months ago. Now, I am going to be responsible for a very substantial mortgage. Thanks."

After a brief pause he said, "I'll get back to you soon on terms. But I'll make this easy since I feel terrible about it."

GOOD. I HOPE IT KEEPS YOU UP AT NIGHT.

It only took four months for the house agreement to fall apart which was very disconcerting, but not as much as the notices from my mortgage company. This 'good' mortgage had a balance beyond what we initially borrowed. We had to make much higher payments or be in default.

The mortgage was designed for failure. The low payments were alluring for a naïve buyer wanting a house beyond his income bracket. Interest was accruing faster than the minimum payments. Loans like these caused the housing bubble to burst in 2008 and sent the real estate market into turmoil. Las Vegas would become the worst hit city in the country and I was worried I would be stuck with a house I grossly overpaid for. Many people in this situation, even if they were gainfully employed, would have failed and lost everything. I am not like many people and I had an expanding business. I became one of the few who battled back and kept what he worked for. Honoring my debts was my problem and I'd muscle through it. I do my best work when my back is up against the wall.

Reed's first settlement offer was to structure a system where he would also benefit from an eventual sale of the house, even though he was no longer making payments. I would also owe him his fifty thousand dollar down payment over the course of a year, plus the mortgage payments he already contributed. After a year, I would be subjected to eight percent interest on the balance. The Senator rejected these terms.

"He wants to reap the benefits from profits made from a sale. But you reap the benefits when you stick with a property, not when you bail out in less than six months. Tell him to come up with something better."

This may be the one time I took The Senator's advice.

I laid the guilt on thicker, resulting in an outstanding deal. He would get his down payment within six months, otherwise I would owe interest. In turn, he would have to sign a quit claim deed removing his name from the title. Upon execution, I would give him a fifteen thousand dollar check. He agreed and the house became my sole responsibility. Except I didn't give him a check for fifteen grand, I gave him a check for twenty five grand. My plan was not to pay him another dollar until the six months were up, after which I would present him with the full balance, with no additional money owed. I doubt he saw this coming.

A few months later, cash strapped, he sweetened the deal to get the balance sooner.

During this time, I learned firsthand of the evasive, infectious vermin known as the dreaded Phantom Spider. On occasion, I would encounter performers who had sores on their bodies covered by band-aids. They had been bitten by a spider, one they never saw.

My birthday was coming up and I took the week off to spend with Nikki. She was supposed to drive up to Las Vegas for a week of sex and amazing cooking, but her phone soon went to voicemail and she stopped answering texts. All the plans I made, including presenting her with a painting I made for her, were in jeopardy. I even went out and bought gift-wrapped lingerie sets from Victoria's Secret.

OY VEY, DUDE. IS THIS A PORN PARODY CALLED "ROMANCING THE WHORE WHO HAS A BOYFRIEND"?

After a few days, she got in contact. Her relationship had come to a head, he stole her phone, and she had to move all of her belongings into storage. Being Captain Save-a-ho, on the spur of the moment, I drove to Arizona with her painting to salvage what was left of my birthday week.

BIRTHDAY WEEK? WHAT ARE YOU, SIX?

After a day in Arizona, we drove back to Vegas where I gave her the lingerie and asked her to cook for me. She was over it and her crush was all but gone. Her agent, fucking Derek Hay, had work for her and she needed to go to LA. This prick yelled at me months prior for banging his talent.

"I'm not running a dating service, Vic!"

"Yeah, but your talent wants to hang out with me in Vegas."

"I don't care! If I have her marked available, then she must be available to work and not hanging out with you in Las Vegas."

"Yeah, but this is something she wants to do."

Pause. "If you want to spend personal time with my talent then you must clear it with me ahead of time."

"OK, I'll do that, Derek."

GO FUCK YOUR FACE, YOU LITTLE BALD PRICK.

I was surprised he didn't try to shake me down or mandate a fee whenever I hung out with an LA Direct model. I still had sex with his talent, we just had to plan around their off days. Still, I didn't want to get another earful from this dickhead, so I got her a plane ticket and off she went.

A grim realization fell over me. There were no porn stars with hearts of gold.

They were dysfunctional hustlers with a vast array of problems: drugs, materialism, loser boyfriends, needy, ailing parents, or all of the above. There were obvious life occurrences and trauma which made sex work seem like the best (and only) option. Instead of taking on a 9-to-5 job, they fucked on camera to solve these problems. A handful were savvy, brand-growing businesswomen. The majority were not and were living cock to mouth, scene to scene.

One of them left me with a parting gift.

All the content I'd been shooting for Brazzers resulted in their unprecedented growth. Their next step was to follow the footsteps of one of their competitors, Naughty America, and start shooting more scripted series. Naughty America's formula was simple and effective: they shot basic scenes playing into young male fantasies.

What would it be like to fuck my teacher?

Or my sister's friend?

Or my best friend's mom?

Or the hot chick at the office?

Brazzers wanted to follow this format, but do it better and incorporate the key element for success: big tits.

They placed a ten-scene order for the site which would change everything: *BigTitsAtWork.com.* After those scenes were completed, they invited me out to LA for a party at the Playboy Mansion. My knee had been hurting and was swelling up. It looked like I had been bitten. It must have been a spider! A spider I never saw. A PHANTOM SPIDER!!!!

The swelling became so severe I headed to the ER after I returned from LA and the Playboy Mansion, an experience I would not enjoy based on the pain I was in. They gave me antibiotics, a tetanus shot, and opened the wound. Once the antibiotics kicked in, the infection started to drain. I went into the shower to facilitate the drainage, but it was painful to touch. The discharge from the wound looked like ketchup and mayonnaise and seemed to never end.

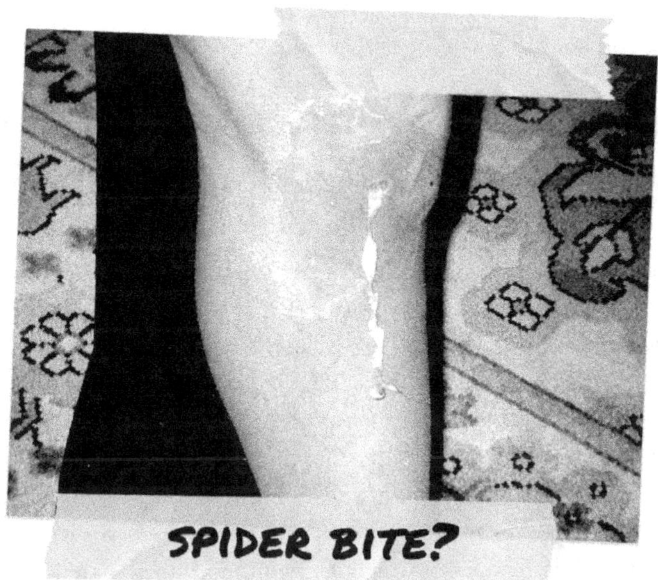

Thanksgiving was coming up and I was due to fly back to Philadelphia. I managed to hop on the plane but the spider bite was not healing properly. I made a second trip to the ER where the nurses drained the wound until no discharge remained. I almost passed out. They packed the wound with what looked like a shoelace.

Eventually, the wound healed... but it wasn't a spider bite.

VIC LAGINA'S SCHOOL OF PORN

LESSON TWO: WHEN SHE'S ON HER PERIOD

So, the talent you booked is having a visit from Aunt Flow. No problem!

THERE ARE NO PROBLEMS, ONLY SOLUTIONS.

While it might have made more sense for the performer to cancel, she did not want to lose out on the money. The solution? A triangular makeup sponge. Or two. Performers would shove these inside themselves and nine times out of ten, it did the trick.

Male talent complained the sponge was chafing the head of their penis. Johnny Sins and Xander Corvus would show me said chafing. Granted, these guys are packing seven-plus inches. These sponges absorb the performer's natural juices, so a lot of additional lubrication is needed. With some male talent preferring to shoot without sponges, there was lots of cutting camera and wiping off during the scene. Just another day at the office.

After most of these shoots, it was not uncommon for female talent to ask male talent or crew to help them remove the sponges because they tended to get pounded deep within the performer's cervix. If they cannot be removed, a trip to the ER might be in order, so the first plan of action was the all hands on deck approach.

It's very important to make sure all sponges are removed, otherwise infection and a malodorous stench will set in. The first performer to ask me to help her remove her sponge was Bree Olson.

This was around 2007 when I was still shooting in my house. Bree was a busy performer and booked out months in advance. I shot two or three scenes of her in a day and they had to be rushed because we only had so many hours before her flight back to LA.

As I type this, I am having flashbacks to when I shot her with Johnny Sins in what is now my unused dining room. She wore a cheerleading outfit and threw up on my wood floor after deep throating Johnny. It happens in porn. I recall cleaning up her vomit and thinking "wow, this is the first human vomit I have ever cleaned up."

On this particular day with Bree, we had two scenes scheduled and she was on her period, so up went the sponges. The second scene was for *SexProAdventures.com* with Bree and Alec Knight. The scene went smoothly as it always does with Bree and Alec. Alec headed for the shower and Bree asked if I could help her remove her sponge. I told her this was my first time and she giggled.

I washed my hands thoroughly and kneeled before her while she sat up on a desk.

AND HERE. WE. GO.

I looked off to the side, inserted both fingers and searched for sponges. I was really trying to visualize the interior of her vagina. After a few seconds, I hit pay dirt and felt the spongy apparatus which minutes before was pounded in deeper by Alec. I widened my fingers and tried to grasp it. Slippery sucker. I squinted again, as if trying to drop the metal claw to win the stuffed animal. I looked up at Bree. She was staring down at me, giving me the cutest smile.

"I almost got it," I said.

"You're doing great, Vic."

I widened my fingers again and removed the Goaltender of Periods, its once white color now a rosy pink. She thanked me and off she went. Wonderful woman. Very fond of her.

I got to know her bodily fluids very well on our shoots. While this was not the last sponge I removed, it was the most memorable.

YOU NEVER FORGET YOUR FIRST.

7 GAME CHANGER – WHAT DO YOU NEED?

BigTitsAtWork.com launched to monumental success, taking the idea of Naughty America's site, *NaughtyOffice.com* and doing it better. Brazzers was now on the map.

The guys were ecstatic and not only wanted more scenes for BTAW, but for their next site, *BigTitsAtSchool.com*, a direct copy of Naughty America's *MyFirstSexTeacher.com*. They wanted me to improve upon Naughty America's shortcomings. They were doing one-take intros where the talent was making up the script on the fly before tearing all of their clothes off and fucking. I received detailed scripts from a writer named Bramm Stroker (great name) and made them a reality. Bramm always ended his scripted sections with *and the rest writes itself*...

Ouissam sent me a graph detailing the site's traffic before and after BTAW launched. Thousands of unique views a day turned into over a million. But I didn't need a chart to measure their success.

Instead of providing me only with what they could afford, it became, "What do you need?"

My first answer was more money for male talent.

WE NEED BETTER COCKS.

The two-hundred-dollar locals weren't cutting it. I needed guys with bigger dicks who could fuck without losing wood. Professional cocks for a professional operation.

There was more money for wardrobe and props and I hired another employee. Enter Teenah, my other large assistant. I cannot be sure where Jodi found Teenah, but she was a model in the Big Beautiful Woman (BBW) niche. I became known as the producer with the two fat chicks.

My father and his wife visited me and my new digs in Las Vegas. I did a poor job convincing them I was shooting corporate videos and explained client confidentiality forbade me from talking about specifics.

This was my cover story. Not only with him but anyone who asked. Even though my father knew I dabbled in porn while living in LA, I told him I stopped. If you want to keep something a secret, you can't tell anyone. Even if someone promises they won't tell anyone, they do.

You are then left sometimes in socially-awkward situations where you are being judged. It was nobody's business. The Senator knew, but as my attorney, he was bound by confidentiality.

It didn't matter since everyone assumed I was in Vegas shooting porn anyway. They just couldn't prove it. The lying became exhausting at times based on how nosy said asker was. My father's wife was among the most curious.

They were impressed with the house, which only piqued their interest in my murky career. They asked pointed questions about my purchase price and the ballooning Vegas market.

In an attempt to halt the inquisition, I mentioned I had a house partner. This foreign reasoning only made the questions multiply. I explained the situation with Reed. I got the sense they suspected Reed was more than a business partner and I can understand why.

SOUNDS PRETTY GAY, DUDE.

In their generation, people got married in their twenties and reproduced. My brother did and he now had two kids. I never desired to live in the normal world and always went against the grain. This life path made no sense to them.

They saw a man who had little success in relationships and never married, so maybe he's gay? When my brother told them I had been dating here and there, their first response was, "Girls?" I found the humor in it. So my options were: be considered gay or come out as a porn producer.

NOT EXACTLY THE STEREOTYPICAL CLOSET CASE.

It didn't help when they saw the Willy Wonka furniture. Pretty sure I went from *probably gay* to *probably gay pornographer*. It didn't help when I declined to show them the secret room where my client's 'top secret products' were stashed. Had they peered in, they would have found a doctor's table, student desks, and other props. After four days, they returned to Philadelphia bewildered.

Meanwhile, the bosses saw me as their workhorse and took care of me. I flew to Montreal to meet everyone, dine on extravagant dinners, and enjoy nights of debauchery at Montreal's finest strip clubs. They would not allow me to pay for anything. The Brazzers team were all fraternity brothers in Montreal and said I too was their *brazzer,* which they said is the Arabic term for brother. Or, it's a vulgar Irish word for 'female prostitute.'

Ouissam was Lebanese and a lot of the Brazzers team was of either Greek, Italian, or Middle Eastern descent. Salam was heavy set with some sort of Middle Eastern affluence. He suffered from alopecia, which causes loss of hair, and he resembled Uncle Fester. Frank, or Franco as he was called, was Sicilian. Yancee was a heavy set black guy. These were the guys I would interact with the most.

Ouissam and Salam were partners in the enterprise, along with Stephan. If there were additional partners, I don't remember them. Their mission was not to be the biggest porn company, but the *only* porn company.

WORLD DOMINATION, MUH HAH HAH. WHAT COULD POSSIBLY GO WRONG?

Upon returning home, I wanted more than ever to achieve their lofty objective. They were keeping me busy and providing the means to maintain my lofty overhead. Those years, despite the grind, were the ones I look back at with the most fondness. It was fun building this company with these frat guys, well before the big expansion and corporate culture took over.

MrBigDicksHotChicks.com was a popular website and the next target of the Brazzers. Their MILF sites were doing well, so they created a hybrid niche site called *MILFsLikeItBig.com.* Another large order came in and these scripts were much more involved. The bosses wanted guerilla-style intros: on golf courses, tennis courts, and shopping malls, all on the fly and without permission. I occasionally ran into trouble with mall cops and groundskeepers, but I didn't care. The Brazzers were so happy with my initiative, Ouissam gave me a ten-thousand-dollar bonus.

Meridiana had been on my mind and guilt and uncertainty kept weighing me down. I was curious if she had a boy or a girl and whether she kept it, so I reached out.

Nine months to the date of our sexual romp in Florida, she gave birth to a girl named Bliss. She decided to keep her. She still had no idea who the father was, but based on the delivery date, she narrowed it down to three people: me, the other male performer, and her ex, who also refused to take a paternity test.

A REAL CAST OF CHARACTERS.

Meridiana was fine with not knowing who the father was, because she feared for the worst. If it was either her ex or the male performer, having to explain this to her daughter later in life was too much for her to bear. In a demented way, I was flattered she thought a pornographer was the best parental option.

Did I leave things at that? Too simple. I was lonely and if I was the father, this could fill my void. I allowed my Kryptonite of a guilty conscience to take over and began rebuilding the relationship with Meridiana.

We talked for hours, night after night. She didn't want a career in porn and returned to stripping to support Bliss. She was hesitant to visit me. We made plans, but for one reason or another, they always fell through.

Based on my prior porn relationships, my feeling was I was destined to be single. Porn stars were unaccountable on a personal basis and motivated by their next paying gig. It is a sex business after all. If I were to have a relationship with anyone while a pornographer, I would have to make compromises. This led to a series of bad decisions.

RAISE A KID WHO MIGHT NOT BE YOURS? HELLUVA COMPROMISE, DUDE.

March was approaching and Reed's interest-free grace period was ending. We had a few exchanges since he received his first check, one of which was a nasty email he sent me late at night while he was drunk.

At the time I was shooting interracial scenes for Brazzers, but having a difficult time finding reliable black performers. Early morning flights seemed problematic for them and the locals rarely showed up on time, nor could they seem to keep their dicks hard.

Manny (Reed's partner), shot a lot of interracial scenes in LA and was a perfect candidate. Several months later, Reed caught wind and accused me of fucking up his business. Manny had stopped working for him and took on more and more Brazzers work. Reed grew nastier until I told him we would no longer correspond, except when I sent him checks.

Things were unraveling for Reed. He was no longer producing for Brazzers and his DVD business was going downhill. DVDs were going the way of the dinosaur as the business shifted to the internet. I still owed him twenty-five thousand and he was desperate for cash. He was under the assumption I'd pay him over time, with interest, but he had no idea come March I would be free from his debt. He needed money now, so he said if I paid him on a faster schedule, he would shave the balance by eight thousand.

I did the math and kept falling short. I explained the situation to Ouissam. He had dealings with Reed and knew of his Jekyll and Hyde persona.

"How much do you need?" he asked.

"About five thousand."

"OK. Invoice for it and I'll give it to you so you can be out from under his thumb."

HOT DAMN. SHOULDA ASKED FOR MORE, I GUESS.

These guys were my salvation. Ouissam came through and I sent Reed a check. The buyout was complete, with Reed getting less than his down payment in return. My next order of business was to refinance my mortgages for a better interest rate and free myself from the current mortgage which was eating away at my ass. My quest for financial stability was taking shape.

A few final words about Reed: he showed me ropes and with his advice, I morphed into something successful. He deserves credit for helping buy a house I had no ability to buy. It's unfortunate how things went, but you can't partner with someone so volatile. He represented everything in the business I did not want to become: angry, lonely, negative, drug dependent (in his case, alcohol), and bitter.

People in porn like to gossip and I would hear bad stories about his behavior, temper, and business tactics.

TELL THAT BITCH TO CHILL! TELL THAT BITCH TO BE COOL!

We did not speak for another five years until we buried the hatchet at the AVN 2013 convention. He was opening a talent agency and was going to be an agent. The venture was short-lived. Reed isn't a bad person, but he is the result of what happens when the claws of this business sink too deep. I hope he lands softly. He is still administering facials for his websites, well into his sixties.

WELCOME TO JURASSIC COCK.

Funny enough, the longer I remained in the business, the more I became bitter, negative, and drug dependent.

8 A Brilliant Decision

After many cancellations, Meridiana agreed to visit me. It was time to gauge whether she could be a proper life partner.

I had just gotten my second dog, Joker, mainly to give Jamie and me a much-needed companion. I underestimated what it would be like to work out of a house with a puppy, but everyone adored him and he naturally developed a keen interest in women's undergarments.

You would think having protected sex with Meridiana would have been paramount to me, but your beloved author had a bad judgment problem. Especially when it came to sex with beautiful women. In my early years, I always used a condom, but I had an extreme distaste for the smell.

LATEX RUBBER MIXED WITH VAGINAL ORIFICE JUICE AND THE REQUIRED MANUFACTURED LUBRICATION EQUALS UNFAIR PUSSY FUNK.

Smell is the most powerful of the senses, so when I huffed a foul stench during sex, it was hard to maintain interest. Women would often complain condoms made them dry and would burn. No condom not only alleviated the stench of latex, it felt amazing.

SALIVA IS ALSO A PERFECTLY SUITABLE LUBRICANT IN PORNLANDIA.

Since I was not having sex with civilians, I had the benefit of knowing they were tested because industry protocol circa 2007 was every performer had to have a thirty-day test for HIV, chlamydia, and gonorrhea.

BAR WAS NOT SET HIGH BACK THEN. BUT IT WAS BETTER THAN NOTHING.

Performer testing did not become more reasonable and stringent for at least another six years. Two hours into her visit, Meridiana and I were having sweet, amazing, mind-blowing, unprotected sex. She scrambled my network and introduced a nasty virus into its system, one which would take a few years to eradicate.

MERIDIANA WAS HERPES IN THE HUMAN FORM.

Keeping my options open, after she left to head back to the Midwest, I reconnected with Nikki and brought her in for several scenes. These would be the last scenes she would shoot for me and some of the last in her career. I still had a major crush on her, beyond the mind-blowing sex.

I flashed on the selfless gestures Nikki showed the bulimic Charity when Reed went mental. She had a solid core, her emotional disconnect notwithstanding. She knew she needed a life plan.

During the day, she would have sex with two different guys for two scenes I shot and at night, I had their leftovers. I was mindful she showered and brushed her teeth before we had sex and neither of them creampied her. One must be able to look past traditional definitions of cleanliness to fuck adult performers. At one point I got so lost in the moment I came inside her.

PEDESTRIAN MOVE, DUDE.

Nikki was not pleased. My bad all the way. I had been under the unconfirmed assumption she was on birth control because this would make sense if your job entails having unprotected sex. Surprisingly, birth control seemed a rarity in the porn world. I get it. I would not want hormones fucking up my body either.

The next morning, after our steamy encounter in the outside hot tub, she saw what looked like a bite on her elbow. To be fair, there was a spider in the vicinity we both saw. A spider bite! But, did she feel a bite? I don't remember a scream of pain. After a day or two, I had what looked like bites on my chest. They were similar, but not like my knee six months prior. The pain was the same, as was the ketchup-and-mayonnaise discharge. I visited the dermatologist after Nikki left. Doctors are supposed to be nonjudgmental in their diagnosis, but there was no mistaking the disgust in my doctor's eyes.

"This looks like a staph infection. We see it a lot in meth addicts."

"Doc, I don't smoke meth."

DUDE DID A LOTTA DRUGS BUT HE NEVER CONSUMED METH INTENTIONALLY.

Staph, he explained, is a small bacteria living on the skin of all of us. If it gets below your skin, and if your immune system is not robust like a drug addict's, it develops into a painful and nasty infection that can be difficult to treat. It's easy to transmit with skin-to-skin contact, which is why seeing them on performers was common. And I was fucking these women on the regular.

YOU FILTHY DIRTY BASTARD.

The sore looks like a boil and the scarring afterward is permanent and rough. He took a culture, put me on two sets of antibiotics for thirty days, and gave me cream to place under my fingernails. A few days later, he called to confirm it was a staph infection. This time he had a more concerned and less judgmental tone. Thankfully, the meds worked and my staph infection was cured, but it left what resembled stab wounds and bullet-hole scars on my torso. They are my reminders of what can happen when you rub skin with dirty women. The mystery of the dreaded, feared, and elusive *Staph* Spider was solved.

With Nikki moving on from her career in porn and my desire to avoid staph, I gave Meridiana my full attention, concessions and compromises be damned. I was ready to be with one woman.

If a test confirmed it, I would also be a father to Bliss. Meridiana and I danced around me getting a paternity test, but she wanted to wait. She did not want to confuse Bliss if me and Meridiana did not work out. These rationalizations would lead to the biggest mind fuck of my life. She was tired of being a stripper, so I offered to find her a job in my business which would help support her daughter. This was my first attempt at repenting. Meridiana agreed to move to Vegas, but Bliss would stay in the Midwest with her family while we tested the waters.

The Brazzers wanted me to sign an exclusive producing contract with them. I did not want to commit myself to a grind that was taking its toll on me physically. Toward the end of my career, I had a crew with a production manager, a makeup artist, a wardrobe girl, a photographer, a set builder, and a PA, and they did all the heavy lifting. Back then, me and my two production assistants were still doing it all. We would revisit the conversation again about nine months later.

Meridiana would serve as my production manager.

Scripts were getting more ambitious and we needed different locations than my house and paid extras in the scenes to shoot non-sex parts. Reality Kings and Bang Bros. were our direct competitors as we took a large chunk of Naughty America and Mr. Big Dick's Hot Chicks customers. Now they set sights on these two biggest whales in internet porn. I needed more hands and there was talk they were sending some Canadians to assist. The first was the writer Bramm Stroker, who had assisted with Manny's shoots. Now they wanted to send him to me.

Bramm shadowed me and I taught him the basics. Becoming a solid shooter takes practice and motivation. Bramm became my first still photographer. Eventually, he would move up to director.

AND NOW, A WORD FROM BRAMM STROKER...

My time in the industry was relatively short, but memorable. At 19 I started working in the Mansef head office as an editor and script writer. A year later, I traveled to Vegas for weeks at a time to shoot photos and help Vic on set wherever I could. Mostly I was there to learn from the one producer we all felt would be the best influence on me. Not before long, I directed my first scene just shy of my 21st birthday under Vic's guidance and mentorship.

Vic was always a great support system. When I started shooting, I was inexperienced, so being sent to a strange city to shoot porn was like a crash course, but Vic was there to help me navigate the various degrees of crazy that I would encounter in Vegas and the industry.

Shooting was stressful at times, but we usually kept things fun and light. I followed his lead and learned a lot from him. We had a similar sense of humor, respected each other's opinions and suggestions, most of all, Vic always had my back and defended me with any issues that came our way.

I have fond memories of discussing, and quoting The Big Lebowski, trips in his pickup truck to various shooting locations, listening to Stern on the radio, and the various wacky misadventures and partying out in Vegas.

The need to move production out of my house could not have come at a better time. We painted the rooms and the guys even paid to have two of the bedrooms and the casita tiled. They added trees to the perimeter of the yard and reinforced the side metal gate doors so you could not see through them. Now I could shoot more scenes outside.

We split the costs of nice rugs and furniture, but the scenes all looked the same. I ran into issues with the county when my neighbors complained I was running a business outside of my house. I rectified this by getting a home-based photography license. This worked up to a point, but it's not exactly legal to shoot porn in a house. Moving operations became necessary. More importantly, I needed to have my own personal space if I was going to settle down with Meridiana.

Meridiana was disgusted by porn because she made the "horrible mistake" of shooting scenes during her six-week stint and couldn't get over it. Her life back home changed forever when she found out she was pregnant. Someone she knew came across the work she did during her brief stint in the industry.

Her family was mortified. People mocked and laughed at her. She maintained she was addicted to OxyContin during her time and it clouded her judgment. All in all, she hated the thought of it, yet she was getting into a relationship with me.

I thought she would be the perfect civilian companion because she met me while I was in porn. It was a gross miscalculation and whenever it drew her ire, I held it was the price a pornographer had to pay to be in a relationship. I also fucked Meridiana when I met her as a pornographer, so setting a solid foundation for trust was not easy. This foundation was made of sugar on a swamp on a fault line.

I contacted Brian, who helped find my house, and told him I was looking for another house to operate out of. He also was in the dark about the nature of my job. He found us temporary daily rentals until we found something longer-term.

I had refinanced my mortgage for more favorable terms and the house was appraised for eighty thousand more than the purchase price. It looked like my house was only going to increase in value but four months later, the Vegas housing market burst and prices saw their sharpest decline. Vegas took years to rebound.

Porn was recession-proof. Money was coming in and business was booming. I had all the money I needed to power through the snap decisions.

Another of Meridiana's mind fucks was telling me she was okay with my fucking other girls as long as she knew. She mentioned on more than one occasion having read books with words like 'Sex' and 'Power' and 'Ethics' in them. It seemed she had an open and realistic perspective about sex and the absurdities of monogamy. She said she wasn't interested in other partners.

OK, DUMB-DUMB.

Meridiana told me just don't lie to her. I vibed an elaborate trap, but I put it to the test early on. The Brazzers were in LA and invited me out. There was a performer I had sex with in the past who invited me to stay at her place and we all met for drinks. This is when I met Blake.

Blake was a fraternity brother of Ouissam, Salam, and Frank. He was a black guy from New Jersey whose Canadian visa was running out and he needed to return to the United States. They wanted to give him a job and they were sizing up his options.

When the Big Boom happened, more spending and employees were required and I wanted to step away and only be responsible for my income. I also did not want to put my name or business on any leases.

This is where Blake fits in. They were willing to open business accounts under his name as well as any long-term lease. I was to be the man behind the man who, if shit happened, would be absolved of any responsibility. He was the quintessential fall guy, but the Brazzers had bigger plans for him.

The house next to mine was in distress and became available to rent. Blake signed a one-year lease for the property, applied for a photography license, and a convenient new location materialized. It would also house Blake, Bramm, and two newcomers.

With my house cleared of any remnants of porn, Meridiana brought Bliss.

Awhile back, someone gave me a very potent pot brownie, and the morning of, I had incorrectly dosed it. The girls were due to arrive at 6 p.m., but by 10 a.m., I was paralyzed by this brownie and there was no escaping it.

My paranoia zeroed in on the biggest fucking question of them all: "Is Bliss my daughter?"

I had to face this, in every manner, for the next eight hours while high as a kite. I was now resembling an upstanding member of society when I headed to the airport to pick them up. This would be the first moment I looked into the eyes of my possible child.

The weed helped because I was more in tune with my senses and perception. When Meridiana wheeled around the corner, I got my first glimpse of this adorable and happy child. She came to a standstill, we locked eyes, and Meridiana whispered in her ear.

There was happiness in her gaze. Or maybe I was still baked out of my skull and overthinking things. My first thought was I don't think she is my daughter, but I would try to act as a father figure. We were locked and loaded and there was no turning back. I didn't want our sordid history to affect her impressionable young psyche. This was Meridiana's main concern, so I made it mine as well.

HOW IS TRYING TO BE A GOOD DUDE WORKING OUT FOR YOU, DUDE?

9 THE CANADIAN INVASION

On day one, I pegged Blake as a buffoon.

He was a nice buffoon, fun to party with, but not one I would trust with money or responsibility. He was good to send out for sandwiches, but he had zero production experience. He was titled a production assistant but he was sent there to observe and report on me. He was Brazzers' eyes and ears. A buffoon. A buffoon who would leave a wake of destruction in LA, Vegas, and Miami.

Jodi and her husband moved to Portland, but I convinced the guys to allow me to bring her to Vegas for a few weeks at a time. In her absence, I hired local artists. Eventually, the bosses were unhappy with her work and disapproved of her marijuana use close to set. We said our goodbyes. I still had Teenah, but her days were numbered. Meridiana didn't like her, which sealed her fate. Enter Stephanie who would ride it out with me until the very end.

One day I was shooting Cody Lane who didn't look well. Over the years a pretty, healthy-looking girl diminished into a thin and vacant soul. The second time I shot her, she told me she was addicted to OxyContin. On our last shoot, I couldn't finish the scenes because she thought she was going to pass out. Having flashbacks of the G-hole, I killed the day while Teenah and Meridiana looked for a hospital. Upset she was not making any money to feed her habit and her trip to Vegas was a waste, all the while withdrawing from OxyContin, things turned nasty.

Cody accused Teenah of trying to give her meth, at my request, so she could complete the scene. She claimed she had the bottle cap with the substance and was going to have its contents run at a lab. Worse, she was demanding twenty thousand from the Brazzers, otherwise, she would sue. Blake told me the Brazzers were suggesting I settle and they would reimburse me.

"Fuck. That," I said. "If she wants to sue me, tell her to go for it. I did nothing wrong and you are not to give her a dime. Watch what happens next."

Nothing ever came of it and Cody vanished. She later spent time in jail.

But could I trust Teenah? Did she offer her meth? I confronted her in my office while recording the conversation and she held her innocence. Still, Blake and I did not trust her.

The times Teenah watched my house, I found things a little off. My hot tub was partially drained because someone incorrectly positioned the levers required to circulate the water just through the jacuzzi. I also had been keeping a stash of Xanax in my drawer which magically disappeared.

We just needed a reason to fire her, because she was the kind of person who would claim unlawful termination or other litigious nonsense. I was overthinking things and giving her too much credit. Blake fired her and she got three month's severance. We never heard from her again.

I had a brilliant idea for a new assistant. Hailey was a performer friend of mine from my Miami days. She traveled to LA a lot to shoot and often stayed with me. We never had an emotional connection, but we liked each other's body parts.

Often, she came out with girlfriends and brought them into the bedroom. She gave me blowjobs to relax me when I was stressed out.

Hailey was wonderful like this. She had talked about wanting to shoot less and be more involved in production, so we kicked around the idea of her becoming an assistant. Meridiana knew about our history and reiterated she didn't care if I had sex with other women. I flat-out asked her if she would have any kind of problem with Hailey working for me and she said no. I asked her several times if she had a problem to let me know.

She waited until after Hailey arrived.

Morty was another Canadian sent by Montreal. He was a young black kid in his early twenties who served as an editor. He was from Zimbabwe and on his way to being a foreign exchange student in *Vic Lagina's School of Porn.*

The company would not sponsor them so neither Bramm nor Morty applied for visas to work in the United States. They would make two to three-month visits before they had to go back to Canada. A few weeks later, they were back for another stint. This could only be stretched so far. Montreal did not want to take the proper steps in getting them visas, because they were assessing whether they would transform into viable directors. Also, they worked cheaply because Montreal paid them their salaries directly. All Blake had to do was make sure they had a roof over their heads and money to live. Both Morty and Hailey lived in the house next door along with Bramm and Blake. Blake enjoyed expensive dinners and going to clubs, events which we all attended. Montreal footed the entire bill.

Most couples enjoy a honeymoon phase, but Meridiana and I were never afforded this luxury. Things were tough from the jump.

COUGH. COUGH. JOY.

She was supposed to be my employee, but she not only undermined my authority, she rarely completed tasks to my satisfaction. As an employer, you don't care about your tone while delegating tasks to your employees. A girlfriend deems her boyfriend is just being an asshole. Countless fights resulted from my giving Meridiana a hard time for not completing the job I was paying her for.

YOU LET THIS STRUMP WALK ALL OVER YOU. AND THE BOYS IN MONTREAL WERE BEING FED BUFFOON BLAKE'S OBSERVATIONS.

Meridiana did not want our colleagues to know we were a couple. She rationalized people would not take her seriously if they knew she was the boss's girlfriend.

BUT YOU ARE LIVING TOGETHER, YOU CRAZY BITCH.

She failed to realize people will take you seriously if you do your job well and take initiative while delegating tasks with confidence. Maybe I was giving a twenty-one-year-old too much credit and too much responsibility.

MAYBE? HA!

When I fired Meridiana and made Hailey my production manager, I never heard the end of it.

Sometime in late 2007, at around 9 p.m., Metro paid me a visit under the suspicion I was operating an illegal brothel. Thankfully, I was no longer shooting out of my house, but a larger problem existed: Blake and company's house was across the street from my racist neighbor. I am convinced she was the one who called County on me when I landed in Las Vegas in 2006.

Blake and Morty piqued her interest. As Blake recapped it, she said to him, "I see you going in and out of that house. What's going on?"

"Well, I'm moving in here with a few other people for the year."

After looking him up and down, she replied, "Interesting," before walking away. I knew where the heat was coming from. I hired a production assistant named Derrick who sported a nice afro. He dropped off women with suitcases at the house on a daily basis. We also shot a loud scene in the backyard.

The Vice cops knocked on my door and the dogs went nuts. I opened the door to find two Vice with their yellow and blue jackets on, backed up by two Metro officers in police cruisers.

Fortunately, Meridiana wasn't home, otherwise, I imagine she would have gotten vocal with them and the situation would have escalated. I stepped onto my porch, in my jammies, and asked how I could be of service. I could tell right away they knew this was a bunk bust.

"We got a report this residence is running an illegal brothel within Clark County."

"I see. Do I look like a guy who is running a brothel out of my house? As you can see, nothing is going on right now except soon-to-be bedtime."

They asked about the house next to mine and if I was affiliated with it. I debated whether to throw out the lawyer card, but we were packing up shop, so I might as well diffuse the situation.

All my lawyer friends advised me to never do this again. However, it worked. They had photos of license plates of Derrick's car and of him, and ok, I could see how this man may look like a pimp to them.

"Do you know this man?"

"Oh, I've seen him around and I wave to him, but I just assumed he was buddies with the new neighbor over there."

"Do you know what your new neighbor does by chance?"

"He said he was a businessman. Seemed like a nice enough fellow."

This went on for about ten minutes, but at the end, the Vice cops' dicks went limp and they sulked their way back to their cruisers. Getting porn away from my cul-de-sac became all-important to me. Regardless, shooting in houses would always be risky.

YOU'RE ONLY AS STRONG AS YOUR BIGGEST ASSHOLE NEIGHBOR, DUDE.

2007 was ending and I was having dinner with Meridiana and her friend Herschel, who later became my accountant. I received a text message from Penny Flame telling me Brett Brando, the director for Naughty America, wanted to jump ship and shoot for Brazzers.

This was big news and something the company could benefit from.

Me being a company man and only wanting to do right by the people who were paying me a lot of money, I decided to bring it to the Brazzers. It would forever change the dynamic of the company. It was one of a few instances where I vouched for others and they received a lot of work and money as a result. This was money that could have stayed in my corner.

The harder reality to face is when the people you helped turn on you and try to take what's yours. For the next several years I would have to protect what I built because a recession and free porn were coming and those without work were all trying to get a piece of the Brazzers pie.

IN MEMORIUM:

Cody Lane, 11/28/86 - 1/9/21

The first time I shot Cody was a few months after I moved to Vegas. I booked her through her agent Tim whom I never met, but who people described as a "little gnome."

From what I remember, she shot and stayed with a director named Chico Wang (who died by methadone suicide in 2008 while also being implicated in the murder of his wife, performer Haley Page). Wang shot a lot of extreme hardcore scenes and Cody was featured in a few of them. She entered the industry at eighteen or nineteen years old and did most sex acts on camera, so she was very popular.

She hailed from Louisville, Kentucky, and had the accent to match. She also walked around barefoot a lot, so I would have to tell her to wipe her dirty Kentucky feet whenever she went shoeless on camera. Although I was in a steamy love affair with Nikki at the time I met Cody, I was attracted to her and would have acted upon it if she gave me the go-ahead.

I was rarely a first-move type of person because I feared rejection. A side product of this was the appearance of being gentlemanly and non-creepy. In this business, it was a good thing. About six months later, Cody was requested by Montreal to shoot a few scenes, but she was taking a break from anal, which disappointed them. After all, she was known as an anal performer with a big booty, but maybe she just needed a break. We found a few scenes for her to make it worthwhile to fly to Vegas from Kentucky.

My South Florida soldier, Jordan Ash, made it in for one of the shoots, his first for me in Vegas. I was still shooting out of my house and Cody crashed in one of the guest bedrooms. Everything was laid back.

In the evening, we both ended up naked in my jacuzzi and talked about life. OxyContin had been wrecking the country and Cody fell victim to it in Kentucky. She seemed like she was in a great headspace when we shot those scenes, but was worried about relapsing when she returned home.

It sounded as if she was hoping she could stay in Vegas so she wouldn't relapse. Odd to think of Vegas as a safe space, but it was my sanctuary through all of this.

She mentioned she was hooked on Oxy and I was astounded to hear pills on the street cost eighty dollars *per pill*.

EXPENSIVE HABIT, DUDE.

Throughout history, there never has been a happy ending to a heroin story and this is the reason why I never fucked with opioids. Their grasp is too strong and knowing this going in made it easy to steer clear of them. If you're wondering at what point two naked people in a jacuzzi start having sex in this story, I am here to disappoint you.

Her gnome had warned her I fuck all the girls.

She didn't want to be just another porn chick I banged in my hot tub, despite my charm. Fair enough and all valid points, especially since I was trying to rekindle things with Meridiana. I remained a gentleman for the duration of her stay.

FUCK YOU, GNOME!

This would be one of the times where I wish I had a *Sliding Doors* moment to see what would have happened if I let her stay in Vegas. If I put those goggles on, I would most likely be trading one train wreck for another.

Regardless, it's interesting to ponder the 'what if's'. On one hand, she had a pretty intense stretch of scenes in LA for several months before heading back to Kentucky. Lots of anal and double penetration, sometimes multiple times a day which was normal back then. I can see how this would be murder on a butthole, hence the painkillers.

I'm speculating, but maybe this was where her addiction started. Or, she got into porn to support the habit. She returned to Kentucky and I booked her for a few more scenes the following month. The signs of a relapse were all there, starting with missing flights. We had multiple shoots booked for her, but those scenes never got off the ground and there was the subsequent fallout.

I kept track of Cody over the following years to justify my stance on the day that went sideways and her later attempt to extort me and the company. She had stopped shooting but stayed in the private sector, aka escorting, in Kentucky.

She was arrested not long after and a quick search of her legal name on the internet produced several mugshots and arrest records ending in 2020. Her crimes ranged from

DUI to drug possession (methamphetamines, marijuana), to carrying a concealed weapon, to third-degree terrorist threats, to fourth-degree assault. Some of the mugshots are downright sad. I assumed she would have been another casualty of drug overdose.

Not the case.

On December 16, 2020, Cody was hit by a drunk driver and remained hospitalized before succumbing to her injuries on January 9, 2021. She was with a long-time partner and had a daughter. The photos I saw showed a happy mother and wife. Her partner looked like a nice guy who loved her. I can imagine it not being easy for him at times. Online records show she was on probation and I would like to believe Cody was turning a corner in life with motherhood and staying sober.

She was thirty-five.

10 ENTER HAWKMAN

2008 turned out to be my best year financially. The Brazzers doubled my scene rate, regardless of whether I was directing or producing. With Bramm and Morty moving up to direct, I was producing close to thirty scenes a month. I coordinated two shoots a day for me and Bramm to direct so we could be twice as efficient. Soon I would have another director under my supervision for the next few months.

I heard about Brett through performers who mentioned we both ran our sets efficiently.

The Brazzers wanted me to get a feel for Naughty America's work so I could improve upon it for *BigTitsAtWork.com*. They gave me a password for their site so I could do research. I saw 'Directed by Brett Brando' before every scene. Brazzers never gave me credit and I didn't ask. Production credit didn't interest me. My bank account did.

Brett wanted to discuss joining the Brazzers team and offered to take me to dinner. Ouissam was hesitant because he didn't want to get sued by Naughty America for taking its director. Still, it was worth looking into because he was a good shooter and it would elevate the product. He conducted business above board, which was a problem the Brazzers were encountering with other directors.

Rumor had it Manny, Brazzers' main director in LA, did not operate in a professional atmosphere. Girls talked about open drug use during shoots and how Manny often tried to get the talent to blow him for his POV line.

The most egregious allegation was he would overcharge the Brazzers for female talent and pocket the difference. If true, here was a guy making north of thirty grand a month and scheming for more. Girls tend to be vocal when someone fucks with their money, so the rumor was likely true.

The Brazzers also asked me my opinion of Blake. The exact question was, "Is Blake helpful to you?"

I answered "yes" but I should have followed up with, "As in getting lunch for our shoots kind of helpful." This was pretty much what he was doing. And observing. And being a frontman. Saying Blake was helpful was a mistake that would lead to future headaches.

I liked having Blake around. He was fun, and the dinners he was taking us out to were delicious. I hate clubs, except when the Brazzers were picking up the tab.

One night, we partied after a MILF group scene and got a center table next to the cast of *ER*. John Stamos was there and I have to tell you, he's a handsome dude. I never talked to him, but when one of our MILFs said she wanted to fuck him in the bathroom, he smiled and said, "No thanks."

ALOOF. DISINTERESTED. WELL PLAYED, SIR.

I'll never forget the club night with Blake before the first Giants/Patriots Super Bowl. We had just arrived at our table and an older guy with salt and pepper hair grabbed one of our bottles and poured himself a drink.

"Whoa buddy, those are ours," I told him.

He apologized and walked over to a different area and poured himself a drink. I wondered what the hell it was all about. Then I noticed he was licking his lips and teeth. I had seen this before.

It was Gary Dell'Abate, Howard Stern's producer!

Artie Lange was in town doing stand-up and he and a lot of the Stern guys were there, along with about four or five little people dressed as Oompa Loompas. JD Harmeyer was there, but I didn't talk to him.

Years later, I would become friendly with JD and he stayed at my house in Vegas. I told Gary I was a big fan and I felt like an asshole for not letting him have a drink, to which he replied, "I was the asshole. Do you want a beer?" It made my night.

The first time I heard Howard Stern was in seventh grade on WYSP-FM. My father drove me to school sometimes because he knew I hated taking the bus. Getting bullied and berated for being Jewish was standard, even when I stuck up for myself. We listened to Stern in silence and I loved what I was hearing on free radio in 1985. I became hooked over the years and in an odd way, he became Uncle Howard. Howard influenced me to remain in porn even though it was unsatisfying to my soul. Whenever he bashed an actor leaving a hit show they were being paid millions for because they were unfulfilled resonated with me.

WORK IS A FOUR-LETTER WORD, DUDE.

Brett took me to Pink Taco at the Hard Rock Hotel. Like me, he was in shape, but ten years older. He had a hawk-like beak and was a fan of Michael Scott particularly "that's what she said" jokes. He told me Naughty America's days were over and he wasn't happy with how things were being run. He was ready for a change. We talked about running things like a business and keeping quality high by setting high standards. On paper, Brett could be an ideal partner, though our alpha male ways might not be able to coexist.

The Brazzers agreed for me to train Brando on how we shot scenes differently than Naughty America. He would shoot for three months in Vegas under my supervision as his producer before operating on his own.

He brought in two guys from LA, Kory, his photographer, and Derwood, his assistant. We rented two houses where we would shoot and where Brando and his crew would lodge. Brando stayed by himself in one house while his crew stayed in the other. With everyone shooting together, I was responsible for thirty-five shoots a month. So much money was coming in. However, tensions with Meridiana were mounting daily. We fought all the time and she always suspected me of cheating, even though I wasn't.

WHAT HAPPENED TO FREE LOVE? OHHHHHH, IT WAS BULLSHIT.

She didn't trust Hailey, because I fucked her in the past. She held a never-ending grudge against me for replacing her with Hailey as my production manager. I explained it was a busy time and I needed a competent manager. She set her sights on getting rid of Hailey. For a six-month stretch, Hailey did a great job. She was a delicate flower and the pressure of thirty-five scenes a month weighed on her. She also had a fondness for Xanax and other pills prescribed to her by her doctor.

Meridiana was still getting paid for a job, but I can't say what the job was. She wrote checks for talent. Yet, I had to go home from location to pick up the checks since she was unwilling to be on set. She said she didn't want to be around porn and was sickened by it.

She claimed to be suffering from depression, never wanted to get out of bed, slept all day, and was up all night. I would find her on my computer searching for wrongdoing. The questions mounted and she was always suspicious. She tried to trick me into giving her information that didn't exist. If I received a text, she'd pry. If I wrote a text, she asked to whom. I told her she made me feel like an innocent man on death row. No matter how many times she was unable to find anything, there was no changing her mind. I was guilty.

This soon made me angrier, because there were beautiful women who wanted to fuck. I refused in the spirit of monogamy, even though my girlfriend believed otherwise. I asked myself:

IF YOU'RE GETTING BLAMED FOR IT, WHY NOT JUST ENJOY IT?

If you are asking where her daughter was in all of this, you aren't alone.

Bliss was mostly being cared for by her uncle, whom Meridiana referred to as her dad. He was the only member of Meridiana's family I met. She had a bad relationship with her folks. If the stories were true, I can see why Meridiana turned into the fucked-up person she was. But I never met her mother or father during the entire relationship.

I suggested she needed to be a more involved mother and to be around her daughter more, so she would have to move here. Meridiana wanted reassurance. She feared her daughter was going to bond with me, only to get confused later if we broke up.

I was all about the well-being of her daughter, who could still be my daughter. Meridiana was worried about what if I wasn't the father. It didn't matter, the whole situation was snowballing into a shit show of gargantuan proportions.

The elephant in the room we both failed to address was my family didn't know Meridiana had a child. I could be her father and they might have had a granddaughter and niece unbeknownst to them for the past two years.

The one time I dropped my specimen at the service, Meridiana forgot to bring Bliss and the test never happened.

With each day the pressure to explain my fucked up life to my family mounted, but it was too mortifying. When I finally broke the seal, it was as nauseating as it sounds.

To get me to agree to an exclusive production agreement, the Brazzers offered me a signing bonus. The Senator hammered out the details, upping their initial signing bonus of thirty thousand to fifty and offering a guarantee of twenty-five scenes a month for two years. Shortly after, Brando was contracted as well.

With the signing bonus, I put in wood flooring at the house, solar heating for the pool, and turned my old production studio into a private suite for guests staying at *LaginaLand*. It was time to find a more permanent pad, so Blake, Brian, and I found The Gilespie House.

LET'S. FUCKING. GO.

IN MEMORIUM:

Shyla Stylez, 9/23/82 - 11/9/17

I met Shyla in 2006 when she fucked Jack Venice in my kitchen for *BigTitsAtWork.com*. Friends have told me they recognized my kitchen because of her scene.

Shyla was a bombshell. Her explosive energy was contagious and she brought it every time she performed. Her energy and willingness to do A-N-Y-T-H-I-N-G made her so popular. She was all gas and zero brakes in her personal life as well, like she craved intensity every waking minute. She lived her life in sixth gear.

When we started to hang out, she drank a lot. Straight vodka. The sex was amazing, but because she was so hot, let's just say I didn't last as long as I wished.

MULLIGAN, PLEASE!!!

She invited me to a Christmas Party in Vegas she was hosting and I became part of her entourage, looking out for Shyla. Her drug dealer, who looked like a young Gregg Allman, showed up carrying a metallic briefcase.

VERY MIAMI VICE, SIR.

The cocaine came out and stayed out. It did little for me. I had not yet given in to the white devil. Shyla became distant, with an evil glint when she stared at me. I was hoping to fuck her at some point, however, everyone in her entourage was content with blowing lines until the sun came up, except me. I said my goodbyes and went home, getting the sense they were relieved the awkward outsider was leaving.

Then I got into my relationship with Meridiana and this acted as a buffer. Meridiana was jealous of Shyla because Shyla and I fucked a few times.

I always joked Shyla could wear a potato sack and she would still sell. But make no mistake, she devolved into a train wreck. It was no secret within the industry she was a full-blown alcoholic. Everybody knew from the head office (she shot over fifty times for Brazzers) to producers to the talent.

She might have been sneaking drinks in the bathroom, so I told the head office we needed less scripted, more visual scenarios for Shyla. The faster the better. I wanted to make sure we got a compliant scene.

Sometimes they would listen. On other days we would have to cut dialogue and rush the intros, which pissed off the head office. She was a disaster, but boy did she have some memorable scenes.

One of the wildest live shows (*Brazzers Live 5*) was a contest between Shyla, Phoenix Marie, Bridgette B (who had a personal beef with her, unbeknownst to anyone until the night before the show), Nikki Sexx (who never made it because she had some sort of mental break), and Trina Michaels, one of the sweetest people I met in the business. Phoenix and Bridgette got into a fight after Bridgette threw water on Phoenix. Phoenix yanked her to the floor by her extensions. While it made for great live television, in hindsight it was a huge liability. The fans determined the winner by online voting and it was a photo finish between Shyla and Phoenix, with Shyla being the ultimate champion. Her prize money was five thousand dollars. In a generous gesture, Shyla split her prize money with her competitors. Despite her hard-living lifestyle, she had a good heart.

During a scene with Xander Corvus for *BigTitsAtSchool.com*, it was apparent during the lengthy dialogue Shyla had been drinking. During the stills, she told me she didn't like him while Xander was trying to stay hard so he could fuck her in the ass. I had to call the day. Shyla felt I shouldn't pair her with "C-grade" talent. Keep in mind, C-grade talent Xander Corvus became a contract performer for Brazzers. He was a certified cocksman, even if he was highly emotional.

A few years later, I checked in on her. She sent me a few photos of herself in a shower, covering her nipples and it looked like she had bruises on her arms and legs. This wasn't uncommon for her as she enjoyed rough sex. But she was hiding something.

My suspicions were a botched boob job. It could explain why she stopped shooting. We discussed getting together. Shyla said she'd fly herself out to Vegas, which I did not lend much likelihood to.

Lo and behold, she made it to Vegas, with some drama leading up to her departure. As I interpreted it, she was too drunk to fly. She called it a misunderstanding.

OBVIOUSLY.

A day later, she landed in Vegas. She was wearing sunglasses, a hat, and baggy clothes, in a sad attempt to hide her condition. She was a mess. Her face was puffy to the point she could barely keep her eyes open and kept her glasses on most of the time.

When we got back to my place, I fired up the jacuzzi and we stripped naked. Confirmed the botched boob job. Lots of scarring and damage to the nipples. She was self-conscious about it, a departure from the Blonde Cyclone she was a few years earlier.

It also looked like her liver was distended. I don't know how else to explain it, her midsection looked very bloated. I knew this was a big mistake and I should have left it well enough alone.

THIS IS WHY I NOW EXIST.

Now, what happened next, I am not proud of. We got into my jacuzzi and we started making out while she jerked my dick. Let's be clear: I was repulsed, because I can be shallow. I'm working on it.

Here was a busted-up sex worker with no test. Still, my dick responded, especially after she started blowing me.

YOU DISGUST ME, BUT I LOVE YOU ANYWAY.

Then we fucked in my jacuzzi. I tried to think happy thoughts. I didn't want to offend her since she flew across the country to see me. Was this considered a mercy fuck? Is this what women feel compelled to do to avoid an awkward situation? With all this running through my head, I still came.

BECAUSE YOU ARE A FILTHY PIG.

I was concerned about having to have sex with her again before she left, which I hoped would be soon. I blocked it from memory, but I get the strong sense I did.

FILTH!!! FILTHY!!!!!

Her phone blew up and it was whomever was getting her side gigs. She was adamant she was not going to take any jobs and she was on her personal time.

PLEASE, GO WORK. MAKE YOUR PAPER. HE WILL NOT BE OFFENDED.

In between all of this, I would listen to her ramble. I shortly realized there literally was no need for me to even speak. It would have been a conversation about nothing which went nowhere. She would continue to speak, and giggle, with her eyes closed, sunglasses still on - even if I left the room, which I did frequently.

At some point, I decided to feign sleep, and I heard her leave the room and talk to someone on the phone all night. Later, I would find out it was her friend, also a performer, who shortly after would shoot for me. Shyla left the next day and it was the last time we spoke. After she left, I found she'd drained almost all of the vodka from a bottle in my freezer.

I wish the airlines kept her on the no-fly list so she would have never made it to Vegas. The memory I would have of her is the hot sex pot who shared her prize money. Instead, it's scarred, bruised, and puffy Shyla. An unfortunate trajectory of a retired and chewed-up porn star.

Shyla died in November 2017. I was under the assumption it was from accidental ethanol intoxication. News outlets were reporting she died in her sleep while visiting her mother in British Columbia.

Here's what her friend told me: Shyla was murdered in Texas on a job. She was aware of what everybody, including me, assumed. According to her, Shyla's mother said it happened in a small town in Texas and local law enforcement covered it up. Her mother was scared and this is why the family went with the died-in-her-sleep version.

One detail I found interesting was her body was cremated immediately. If this is true, then the rest of the story may be plausible.

End of the day, who is going to care if a washed-up porn star was possibly murdered in a small town in Texas? Could anything ever be done if Shyla was indeed murdered? I find it odd the story has not been posted anywhere, so maybe this is a start? Maybe one of you true crime podcast fuckers out there can take on the case.

WE DEMAND JUSTICE FOR SHYLA!

Shyla was thirty-five years old when she passed.

11 THE GILESPIE HOUSE, THE BRITISH INVASION, AND THE FIGHT FOR BIG COCK

The rivalry among Brazzers, Reality Kings, and Bang Bros was heating up. Naughty America had effectively been crippled by our superior content and its star director, Brett Brando, defecting to greener pastures.

MILFsLikeItBig.com had expanded to *PornstarsLikeItBig.com*, *TeensLikeItBig.com*, and *BigButtsLikeItBig.com*. There was a need to keep the steady flow of large professional penis in our production rotation. We had our usual guys, but in a preemptive move, Reality Kings began putting them under contract. We were forced to do the same. Brazzers had to win the fight.

This is when MySpace was a thing. I started getting pestered by someone who would be a thorn in my side over the next several years: Keiran Lee. A few girls I had shot went to London and mentioned a young male performer with a huge dick who was looking to come to the United States.

They mentioned my name and Keiran's onslaught of harassment began. This was NFL playoff time and my beloved Eagles were engaged in one of several in a string of heartbreaking losses. Now this Limey prick was bombarding me on MySpace every few minutes. Just to shut him up, I told him I would book him for a scene when he came to town, a promise I carried out a few weeks later.

At first impression, Keiran was a nice guy with questionable fashion sense. He wore a flamboyant scarf and was over-bathed in bad cologne.

The scene was for *DoctorAdventures.com* and we shot in the makeshift doctor's office next door.

One twist: Keiran had to perform the entire scene on crutches, no small feat for any performer, let alone one who is auditioning. When he dropped his pants, I knew we found our contract guy, one Reality Kings knew nothing about. After he fucked on crutches without issue, I told Salam we should contract Keiran. More vouching I'd regret later.

THE FOG OF WAR CAN CRIPPLE DECISION-MAKING.

When Hailey arrived to Las Vegas and was about to work for me, I told her it would not be in her best interests to have sex with Bramm.

COCK-BLOCKER!

I may sound like a cock-blocker, but it was for both their benefit. Bramm was a nice kid, but he had zero game when it came to women. He knew some of the girls in the business I had sex with, and he would frequently come to me and ask what he should say to get said girls to have sex with him. He was a lost cause, but some of the loosest girls in the business threw vagina his way. I sadly watched Bramm turn into a lost puppy, following them around.

FUCKING AMATEUR: DISINTERESTED AND ALOOF. MUCH TO LEARN YOU STILL HAVE, GRASSHOPPER!

Neither listened, and Bramm was now hooked on porn star pussy, living under the same roof as him.

Blake had been spending time in LA with Manny, working on digging up dirt on him. The Brazzers wanted to validate the rumors before firing him. Brando could then take over his workload once he finished my training in Vegas. Unbeknownst to me, Blake was setting things up to start his own production entity in LA. I was so busy managing my own shoots plus shoots for Bramm, Morty, and Brando. Blake was also splitting his time in Las Vegas helping to get my next production house ready.

I met David Dunn through my real estate agent and his house was perfect. It was two houses separated by a pool on an acre of property. The main house was two levels and seven thousand square feet. The casita was two thousand square feet with a bedroom, kitchen, bathroom, and garage. Surrounding it was a dirt trail because David was a professional dirt bike rider.

David was married with two daughters. I could tell he liked to drink, smoke, and party because he was doing all three when we toured his house. His lot had ample privacy with only one neighbor, but their viewpoint fell well below the perimeter fence. To enter the house, you needed to be buzzed in through a gate, so I deemed it secure enough for our productions.

Brando took over retrofitting the house and had Kory and Derwood do his heavy lifting. He had them build a makeup room off the front entry and turn both garages into mini studios.

Blake furnished the rest of the house with fifty thousand dollars, paid for by Brazzers. In less than a month, the house was ready for production and lodging the talent. The house would become a legendary breeding ground for late-night debauchery and bad decisions. I, of course, would partake in none of it. I was in a committed relationship.

"LOOK AT ME AMERICA, I'M MATURE!" DUMBASS.

Blake was spending money cavalierly out of an operating account I used to pay talent. While I submitted meticulous invoices, Blake's looked like a third-grader's math homework. He would complain about the accountant who was pressing him because his numbers were 'round.'

V-E-R-Y round.

"I need six thousand dollars," he said once on the phone. "For the shoots!" Hangs up, shakes his head, looks at me, and goes, "The accountant is really pissing me off, asking me exactly what I need the money for." He said that, for real.

I reiterated the importance of invoicing for whatever he withdrew and to keep track of things, because it was paramount talent checks never bounced. Blake assured me he was aware of the balance and I need not worry.

I THINK YOU SHOULD WORRY, DUDE.

Meridiana and I traveled to Hawaii and got along so swimmingly I believed we could work and be happy. Porn aside, of course.

Hawaii is the happiest place on Earth and in all likelihood would enable both Jews and Arabs to coexist. Production was shut down while we were on vacation and checks were bouncing. Blake's account mismanagement had come to a head.

I never bounced a check in this business. This could tarnish my reputation. Only that buffoon could ruin Hawaii.

Blake conceded and said he'd fix it. So he shifted the blame onto Meridiana, a detail that was hidden from me for months. In the interim, Brazzers replenished the operating account and insisted only Meridiana write checks. Blake was no longer allowed and a new set of eyes was watching the account from Montreal. In truth, I was the only one writing checks and handling all business aspects because Meridiana no longer wanted the responsibility. She claimed to have wrestled her trust fund away from her mother.

Her grandmother left her a sizable amount of money and she sued her mother for control. Details were sketchy, but she was going shopping a lot. My money was no longer needed, which elated me.

While in Hawaii, I started my hockey team without its goalie (aka, didn't pull out) and in a few months Meridiana was pregnant. I was thrilled to be a father, even though Meridiana and I were nowhere close to being on solid footing.

If I was ready to start a family with her, then it didn't matter if Bliss was my daughter. We were building a family and what could be a stronger bond?

SANITY?

Our plan was to tell my father and his wife about Bliss on their next visit, but our pregnancy took over and we effectively put the cart before the horse and never mentioned Bliss in the process.

Blake had pushed out Manny while Brando completed his training with me and moved back to LA. Brando was now Brazzers' #2 director, a title he tried to shed. Brando was always a competitive guy, from bowling or go-kart racing.

LITTLE DICK, MUCH?

By now, I had taken a backseat to directing, focusing on producing Bramm and Morty's scenes. I was burned out on shooting. Two straight years had taken its toll.

My contract stipulated I would get paid the same if I was producing or directing. I exploited this clause to the fullest. Brando hammered home his opinion I should be directing. I could not tell if he was trying to be flattering or if he was prodding Brazzers to make me work as hard as him. Either way, I did not pick up a camera again for another eight months and only for special scenes.

I wasn't lazy, trust me. Business was exploding. My time was better spent in a management role. I was also experiencing severe back pain from working my ass off to build Brazzers over the past two years. The more I visited my applied kinesiologist, the more I realized the psychic toll of my business and personal life was manifesting in physical pain.

APPLIED WHAT? JUST SAY "DOCTOR," DUDE.

After we returned from Hawaii, Meridiana suggested I consider hiring her friend from back home to replace Hailey. The manufactured conflict was at its peak. Hailey was buckling from the pressure and her relationship with Bramm made our work environment uncomfortable. Bramm was always mopey because Hailey stopped fucking him.

I agreed to bring in her friend Moe. (My iron dome of a legal team suggested I change his name. We had a nickname for him, so I adjusted to make it work. Plus, Moe was one of The Three Stooges, although this guy was more of a "Curly" than "Moe.") He was to start as a production assistant while elevating to production manager and then replace Hailey.

Moe was a hard-working bald guy eager to make his mark. Meridiana and I strenuously suggested he not have sex with Hailey. He ignored us within the first three days.

In year one, Moe was a soldier who never rattled. He got more inspired when he took over as production manager. Over time he would unravel, revealing an emotional constitution his subordinates would never respect. In the interim, Meridiana was happy she replaced the girl who replaced her with a loyal friend. It occurred to me I was engaged in a chess match over my business with my girlfriend.

When word hit they gave Blake a significant number of scenes to produce, I was livid. They were diverting work from me, fucking with my ecosystem. I vouched for him as a gopher, not as a producer.

THIS ISN'T GOING TO END WELL.

Blake had no production experience other than watching me and he never held a camera, yet he was the Brazzers' fraternity brother. This was the start of the massive shift from Brazzers being a fledgling company to a corporate-driven entity. The head office had lost its fundamental practice of rewarding its hardest workers, who would in turn work harder for them.

Things got worse when Morty was denied U.S. entry and I was down a director.

But, I had a plan.

Vic Lagina's School of Porn

Lesson Three: Prepping for Anal

You are going to be asked to shoot a BGA scene, a boy/girl/anal scene.

There's a lot to consider when casting any anal scene, none more important than the strength of the talent's anal-taking capability.

It's best to cast performers who enjoy anal sex on and off camera. Believe it or not, those unicorns exist, although not as many as the adult industry would have you believe. It's not every day you find a gem like Ashley Fires. Chances are you may have to shoot someone who is apprehensive.

Ideally, the agent would school their rosters on the how-to's of anal preparation. This was rarely the case.

An inexperienced performer should seek guidance from a grizzled veteran, like Phoenix Marie, on how to prepare for and perform anal scenes. Phoenix proved early on she was a unicorn. I shot her first Brazzers scene in my home studio in 2007 and she is STILL going strong decades later. After that, she was booking BGA's left and right.

In my first studio, I'd roam the halls, bouncing back and forth between my corner office and whatever room we were shooting in. In doing so, I heard bits and pieces of odd conversations. This one was with Phoenix and another performer getting anal tips from Phoenix's expert tutelage. I only know this because all I heard from Phoenix was, "the best way you can really gauge your digestive system is to eat a lot of corn, then you'll know how many hours it takes to come out." If anything, I do miss this type of candid speak which is frowned upon in work places. Porn was the last occupation without an HR department and it was the last bastion of free speech anywhere. *Memories.*

Smooches, Phoenix.

The physical preparation takes many forms. It's not uncommon for a performer to sit in the makeup chair with a butt plug to prepare for the day ahead. Coffee and any other caffeine products are ill-advised as they act as a diuretic and laxative. While most performers knew their bodies pretty well, our practice was to have candy available to ensure their blood sugar remained high.

It's standard for a performer to come in the evening before to start their anal prep regimen. Traveling on the day of anal is not recommended. Having a well-rested anal performer could be the difference between a decent shoot and an excellent shoot.

Always have douches and enemas on hand and a private area for cleaning. Performers will need/want to evacuate themselves at different phases of the day. Between makeup, pretty-girl photos, intro stills, and intro videos, a performer needs ample time to make sure they are clear to shoot.

THE CHUTE IS CLEAR.

Patience is a virtue. Some performers spend an hour in the bathroom doing final preparations. I'm thinking of you, Krissy Lynn, always well over an hour, always clean as a whistle.

Don't forget about the woodsmen. Casting male talent is the second biggest variable in producing a quality BGA scene. Some male performers loathe anal, some love it. For example, Charles Dera and Johnny Sins hated shooting anal scenes.

Ramón Nomar, Mick Blue, and Markus Dupree vigorously enjoyed anal sex. Say what you will about the Eastern Bloc, but they hands-down produce the best anal male talent in the business, and I will die on Mt. Dupree, Mt. Nomar, and Mt. Blue. When you hire the right professional, a turd nugget on their Johnson is no deterrent. He will wipe it off and soldier on.

There's a good reason why Charles Dera dislikes anal scenes. Circa 2007 was the only time I legitimately saw Dera get mad. We were shooting an anal scene in my garage when the female talent's dirty ass juice dripped into his cowboy boots. He loved those boots. As a signature of sorts, while naked, he wore them sockless during his scenes. While I saw the unmistakable rage in his eyes, he remained calm and said "I will be right back. I am going to take a shower." I made awkward chit-chat with the colonically challenged female performer while Dera scrubbed the liquid shit off his legs and boots. The more I think about it, I never saw him wear those boots again.

SOMETIMES ANAL IS JUST IN THEIR DNA.

It's key to keep the female from getting insecure. Jordan Ash's secret was to 'Barry White' her ass. "You gotta be very slow, very smooth. I whisper in her ear everything is going to be all right. Looooooovvvvvvveeeeeee." Sometimes the best-laid plans still won't work. When this happens, try your best.

Or... have the memory of an elephant while taking copious mental notes and write a book about it.

The worst case of poor anal preparation happened during a live show. Given the live aspect, we had a wiping station and trash cans off-set where male talent would use baby wipes to clean off and be camera ready. "Wipe off, get back in the game, kid," was the motto. This story involves a popular porn star who was well-versed in anal sex, having done anal, double penetrations, and gangbangs regularly.

Typically, we would not go live until late afternoon. This is a brutal ask, given the talent will be hungry and losing energy late in the day. This particular star was eating during the day *and* drinking coffee.

When I asked her if this was a good idea, she said, "It's ok. I'm vegan. I'll be fine."

One had nothing to do with the other and I knew full well what a vegan diet consists of: beans, vegetables, fruit... fiber. Plus coffee. Needless to say, we depleted the wiping station that day. My cameramen were on set during these shows while I was in the control room, looking at the live feed and directing Pete on the TriCaster. Her ass juice resembled the meal of a vegan and was spread out all over Jordan Ash's torso. My cameramen did a good job framing out the feces and with a mix of camera cuts, the viewers never knew how disgusting porn can be.

What about anal virgins, dude?

There was a time when getting someone's first anal assigned to your crew was a bit of a feather in your cap, a chance to be braggadocio on the Brazzers forum to show everyone who was a King Shit Brazzers Director. Getting assigned a first anal scene fucking sucks. Why on earth would you want to shoot a nervous female performer who is self-conscious about taking a penis up their anus on camera for the first time, in front of a room full of men? There were a few performers who were outstanding on their first anal (Rachel Roxxx, I am looking at you), but more times than not, it was a tough climb up Mount Bungus. However, we always made it.

There are no problems. Only solutions. Nothing can stop us!

My career is a testament to self-belief, challenges met, competitors bested, but sometimes even the strongest find an insurmountable foe.

For me, it's the prolapsed anus. You will never unsee it and your first will jar you to your core. It never gets easier. For those not in the know, a prolapsed anus is when the anus turns inside out and pokes out of the rectum like a tongue. Or an alien.

Some even have a fascination with the pink sock. In some truly graphic anal scenes, directors encourage the female performers to push it out.

My opinion? If your anus is prolapsing, tone down how much anal sex you have and go see a doctor. It's not supposed to do this and you may have to wear diapers in the future.

DON'T GET UP, CLASS ISN'T OVER YET.

To inch even closer to rock bottom, I have seen performers lick another female performer's prolapsed anus.

CLASS DISMISSED. WHO'S HUNGRY FOR LUNCH?

12 HELLO HUGGY AND THE RISE OF THE TUBES

A few months after I moved to Las Vegas, the madam I was fucking invited a heavy-set Mexican over for a pool party. He and his partner were trying to launch their website and they were getting started in Vegas. The man was a giant grizzly bear, but his calm demeanor inspired the nickname: Huggy Bear.

When the Brazzers visited in 2006, I invited Huggy and his partner out for drinks to gauge their interest in assisting me. I wanted to help people out. Tony was not impressed and labeled Huggy as "fishy."

When I signed my exclusive contract with Brazzers, I gave up my unaffiliated clients. I had one particular client from my Miami days I wanted to leave in good hands, *InnocentHigh.com*.

I threw Huggy and his partner the work and all seemed happy. As a token of appreciation, Huggy handed me an envelope full of cash. More envelopes were forthcoming if I would send more sites. When Morty was held back at the border, I asked the Brazzers if I could audition Huggy and they reluctantly agreed.

Huggy's first shoot for *BigWetButts.com* was a small disaster. He never realized Katja Kassin's oily ass touched the lens and left a distracting smear on the image. He was overwhelmed. Apparently, I had been misled. I thought he was shooting for not only his site but for other sites I brought to him. Knowing what I know about Huggy now, it's clear what happened: Huggy talked up his abilities, but wasn't able to produce at the level he claimed. I witnessed this throughout our six-year relationship.

Despite poor results, I worked with Huggy, because I needed him to work out. I also wanted to believe in him. A few months in, Frank and Salam wanted me to fire him. I convinced them to be patient, especially since Huggy posed no threat of being deported or held up at the border. They went along and he progressed to an acceptable level.

I'm sure Huggy will tell you he is a great director, better than me. In another medium, I might need to defend this. Frankly, to rank one's self in porn is absurd.

FUCK IT, I'LL SAY IT: VIC LAGINA WAS A BETTER DIRECTOR THAN HUGGY.

Speaking of the need for relevance in porn, I butted heads with Brando on this subject. Brazzers had opened up a forum for its members to talk about porn. It would be a never-ending source of tension and drama for the business. Naughty America had its forum, as did Reality Kings and Bang Bros, so Brazzers needed to follow suit.

The forum was an inescapable vortex. I was engaging and being engaged in the drama. I had been on the forum *GoFuckYourself.com* while trolling for work in Miami and I witnessed the keyboard warriors engage in combat. I had a vested interest in the phenomenon called Brazzers I helped create. As an OG, many fans stroked my ego, praised my work, and seemed excited to converse with a porn director.

Like all things internet, there were dozens of trolls poking you to get a reaction. Others just wanted to pit people against each other to see what happened. I guess if you have a lot of time and porn is your world, then baseless harassment seems like a great hobby.

Brando had his own thread where he posted pictures from set. He wanted people to know who he was so they could see he was a big deal in Brazzers World. He also needed everyone to know when his scenes were rated in the top five, despite the fact this changed rapidly, because it was based on the number of scene views.

FUCKING NERD.

Even to this day, my scenes have the most total views on the network, but who cares? While it would have been nice for Brando to acknowledge *how* he got into Brazzers as a nod of appreciation, it never happened. I got asked direct questions about Brando's porn and my thoughts on it and those answers were sent back to Brando.

I got baited by a troll. I don't think I said anything offensive. It was honesty. These were the main points:

I am not a big fan of spending a lot of production time on the intro or story. Most people skip this part and get right to the point. So why waste the money? I also found it laughable when porn stars try to act seriously, or even worse, when a director is trying to be serious. If I want to watch a serious movie, I would watch a good one in a theater with good acting. Not with non-actors who really don't want to be doing it because it's keeping them from fucking and getting paid. Furthermore, if you spend a whole day with acting and other such nonsense, how much energy would the performer have for the actual fucking? I preferred the basics, and so did my talent: brief intro, hot chick, hot outfit, hot sex. Laid, sprayed, fade, and paid, and off you go. Everyone is happy because it was fun, smooth, and efficient. When word got back to Brando, he was livid and whined to Frank.

HOW DID YOU THINK HE WAS GOING TO TAKE IT?

I had to answer to Frank about how it's not professional to "talk shit" about other directors and it needed to stop. I told him I was just answering a question honestly and it's just my opinion. Frank could not argue with any of my points. Those who liked Brando's style of porn could watch Brando's scenes. For those who liked my style, they could watch my scenes. There was no right or wrong, and I applauded them for being able to give the members variety. Truthfully I wasn't sorry for what I said, nor did I think I was in the wrong. The perceived slight was left unresolved until Brando called me directly. He was highly agitated, and he wanted an explanation.

"Brando, let's remember what we are doing for a living. We are shooting porn. We are shooting people fucking on camera, for money. We are not sending people to Mars, we are not curing cancer, we are not changing the world. Let's not take ourselves too seriously."

He was silent and had nothing to say. I finished the conversation by telling him I had no hard feelings, and I still respected him which is why I recommended him to Brazzers in the first place.

SUBTLE, BUT EFFECTIVE - FOR ONCE.

Moving forward, we had mutual understanding. Aside from the occasional business function, I never interacted meaningfully with Brando. Even when he moved back to Las Vegas several years later we maintained our distance (after the election to mandate the use of condoms in porn in LA).

One of the last times he did call me was to inform me Blake was telling people in the business he was the owner of Brazzers.

Blake made enemies out of the gate. Manny was still pissed at Blake for helping get him fired. He was trying to make things difficult for him. Brando had told me he had an interesting conversation with Sean Michaels. It went something like this:

Sean: "Hey Brett. I met your boss the other day."

Brett: "My boss?"
Sean: "Yeah, Blake Brazzers."

STILL NOT A BETTER NAME THAN VIC LAGINA. 'BLAKE BUFFOON' WAS MORE APROPOS.

Blake was living it up in LA and going to all the porn parties. He was making waves and not ones a growing company would prefer.

He was clueless there are no secrets in porn. Porn people love to gossip. There is a lot of time to talk shit when you are waiting in a makeup chair.

TALK SHIT AND FUCK. IT'S WHAT WE DO BEST, DUDE.

After the initial mention, performers started to also meet the 'owner' of Brazzers. I had to break it to them.

It got so bad both Brando and I informed the head office. He was causing a ruckus, making mistakes, and mismanaging funds.

I spoke with Salam and Frank about Blake, and told them Blake was a good bull-shitter and an even greater liability. They insisted he was a great guy, so they kept backing the Blake horse.

FRATERNITY DOUCHE NOZZLES. OH SHIT, I FORGOT YOU WERE IN A FRATERNITY, DUDE. DOUCHE. NOZZLE.

During one of his shoots, LAPD raided him. The location was red-flagged as a porn house.

Blake now had to leave LA. He set his sights on my town.

Subsequently, I was ordered to send my invoices to the new accountant, Nick. Unbeknownst to me, Blake and Nick were good friends. He was nicknamed Tank, short and broad, like Quasimodo.

Nick asked a ton of questions about my invoices and expenses. He was investigating whether I was defrauding the company. I am sure this was after hearing Blake's take on why the operating account was overdrawn.

For example, Blake was saying Meridiana bought her new breast implants with corporate funds. I'd bought her a new set with my own money.

FOOL! BUT YOU DID GET YOUR MONEY'S WORTH.

Over time, Nick gave up his witch hunt because he found zero evidence proving any of Blake's bullshit allegations. Nick and I found a mutual respect. This would prove beneficial during the short time he was elevated to company CEO.

Four more Canadians were sent down: two to me and two to the other Brazzers crew in Las Vegas, spearheaded by Blake and his friend Jake, his production manager and accountant.

Even though Jake never worked in production, he gave Blake a fighting chance. He was smart and contributed to Blake's unfathomable longevity. Overall, Blake was bringing disaster to my turf and soon their fuck-ups would be associated with my well-oiled machine.

With Blake closing the operating account and starting his own offshoot, I needed a solution, which Meridiana presented. Her friend Herschel agreed to handle the accounting for a modest salary. Herschel was a portly Jewish businessman who was also a voice over actor and announcer.

This side gig provided supplementary income while requiring very little time. His most prominent characteristic, aside from not allowing the Vic/Meridiana drama to affect the business relationship, he was a stickler for the rules. I was sure my operation would be above board in all facets. The account was in his name and would be his responsibility.

Herschel was a reliable asset during the forthcoming business and personal turbulence. He benefited from numerous raises over the next eight years until Brazzers deemed him expendable.

Butler and Kyle were younger men who had spent time as editors in the main office. Butler would be the photographer, while Kyle ran camera and directed. Butler reminded me of Napoleon Dynamite, complete with social ineptitude, awkward fashion sense and warped humor. Kyle was more of an athlete with a cocky attitude at a whopping five-feet tall.

Robbie and Chad went to Blake's crew, along with Bramm and Hailey. Bramm requested to be moved to be around Hailey. She was exiled from my crew after Moe's promotion and Meridiana's manipulative plan.

Robbie was a thin, bearded man who looked like a perpetual film student and suffered from digestive issues. Chad was a dull bald guy who specialized in sound. I submitted paperwork to the Canadian government explaining they would train under my guidance. I am not sure if it was legal, but their lawyers signed off and it bought us some time before they could possibly get held up at the border.

Kyle was experienced and needed no training. He was passionate about film and had an enthusiasm I hadn't seen in anyone. He reminded me of myself, even though he was half my size.

When I was his age, I was half as cocky. We developed a disparaging rapport, a lot of it dancing on the line. Moe could not handle Kyle, or his disrespecting Moe's authority as his production manager. Tension brewed. Our product was solid, everyone was making money, but the amount of bullshit with all the infighting was exhausting.

STOP BEING SUCH A WHINER ABOUT FILMING FUCK MOVIES.
WORK WAS A DREAM COMPARED TO HOME.

My hands were full with Meridiana's pregnancy and her ever-changing emotions. Handling her took up wide swaths of my day. I would be outside on the phone, pacing on the dirt track, trying to resolve our issues to no end.

I dreaded coming home and the only solace was when the dogs greeted me. Those dogs kept me sane. Jamie absorbed most of my negative energy, because when I was hurting, so was she. Which was a lot.

In her first trimester, every time I was set to go to an appointment with her, the doctor would cancel and have to reschedule. At least that's what Meridiana said.

She said she attended solo appointments, which were scheduled when I had work conflicts. She told me the reports were good. She also said we were pregnant with twins. I saw proof of none of it, except there definitely was a baby growing inside of her.

COWGIRL WAS THE MOST COMFORTABLE FOR SEX. WHEN HER PREGNANT
BELLY MADE CONTACT WITH HIS, IT WAS WEIRD AND AWKWARD.

Bliss was living with us full time. Meridiana bought her a princess bed set and furnished her room.

I have occasional fond memories, like watching superhero cartoons to help her fall asleep. For the most part, Bliss was undisciplined. She was delightful in the morning, but would deteriorate into a demon after 10 a.m. Meridiana had zero control and allowed a toddler to dictate everything.

Bliss had trouble sleeping through the night and woke up crying. Often, she would sleep with us, which in the early months I tolerated to help her get acclimated. When it turned into a nightly thing, it seemed unhealthy. When I was a child, I would sleep with my parents if I was scared, but they expected me to sleep in my own bed. I wanted to ask my brother about it, but he had no idea Bliss existed.

I was the delegated enforcer. It wasn't too difficult. I probably looked like a giant ogre to her. When she got unruly, I put her in time-out and listened to her scream for mommy.

Meridiana liked to sleep all morning. To assist in her quest to do nothing, she convinced me to hire my cleaners full-time to watch Bliss while I was at work. They would also landscape and clean. Meridiana agreed to cover half the cost.

Even though I was accused of cheating, I never wanted to. It doesn't mean no one caught my eye.

The angel's name was Jackie, a young starlet who got out of bed one day to head to the airport when another girl flaked. She will tell you she doesn't remember seeing me that day, but I will never forget it. She had such a happy smile and a pleasant demeanor. It was refreshing. She left a mark.

FORESHADOWING!

The Brazzers, now operating as Mansef (a combination of Steph and Ouissam's last names), attended a lecture featuring the 'biggest expert in internet porn.' How one gets this title puzzles me, but his message was clear: free porn is coming. Tube sites are coming. Prepare yourself.

Mansef had a plan no one knew about until the damage sent shockwaves through the entire porn industry. They were opening up their own tube site and staying ahead of the curve.

PornHub.com was launched. Content on PornHub was user-uploaded. Any scene on a user's computer could be uploaded onto PornHub. Traffic was in the hundreds of millions per month and could be directed anywhere. This changed the landscape of porn forever, especially when tube sites started multiplying like viruses.

It was genius, but tube sites ended what was once a profitable business for many people. When you turn people from busy to unemployed, from successful to nearly broke, you make a lot of enemies. You also create an environment where people are chomping at the bit to hoard theirs and take yours. My ass would soon have so many sets of teeth marks it nearly broke me.

We were in The Great Recession and now we had to stay on a monthly budget. Up until this point, the sky was the limit. Brazzers would spend money on lavish cars, locations, and props to up the production value and outdo the competition. Brando did an *Eyes Wide Shut* parody which cost north of thirty grand. The returns from the pay sites no longer justified large budgets, so we scaled back production.

Make no mistake, we were still putting decent money into our scenes. With the cutbacks, we were also pushing the boundaries by taking unnecessary risks. Like the time with the rented police car when Huggy, Scott Nails, and Keiran Lee got arrested.

The previous day we'd shot a scene with Keiran as a police officer pulling over two chicks.

GEE, I WONDER WHAT HAPPENED NEXT.

After reviewing the footage, something was lacking. We had rented the police cruiser for a substantial amount of money and we needed to see it more. I should have left it alone.

The next morning I had two shoots. One scene was Scott Nails getting tag teamed by three girls. The other was a boy/girl scene with Keiran Lee, with Kyle and Butler directing in a comic book store. While the girls were in makeup, I suggested Huggy take the police cruiser a few blocks from the house and shoot some fun, *Super Troopers*-type of footage.

STINKS LIKE SEX IN HERE.

The office could edit it into the intro. We had a small window until the rental company came to pick up the car. The task was taking longer than I imagined. Then I heard sirens and police cruisers flew down the street. Then a helicopter.

Scott Nails texted me in handcuffs saying a neighbor called Metro reporting an officer in distress and they were under arrest. Huggy and Keiran were being hauled downtown and I had four girls getting out of makeup with no male talent available. What a predicament.

They were holding Scott at the Boulder City police department. After waiting in the parking lot for about twenty minutes, he came strolling out. He had paid his outstanding tickets and was free to leave.

"Can you do two scenes?" I asked him.

"Yeah. Just let me nap for an hour after the first one." Problem solved.

YOU MEAN 'SOLUTION FOUND.'

I dropped him off at the Gilespie House, where he knocked out the scene with the three girls. I then set my sights on freeing Keiran and Huggy. The officers were trying to find something to charge them with, because they had to call in the cavalry for an officer in distress.

I headed up to the comic book store with Scott, where Butler and Kyle were waiting all day for any male talent to show up and perform. They were ecstatic when I finally arrived with Scott. With the second scene underway, I headed downtown to wait for Keiran and Huggy.

Along the way, I stopped and got Huggy a half dozen hamburgers. The best way to quell an angry bear is to feed him. After waiting outside the station for two hours, Keiran came out still in his police uniform.

Both were seemingly upbeat and jovial. When Huggy opened the door, I expected him to punch me in the face - which in all fairness, I deserved. Instead, they regaled me with their hilarious encounter.

Keiran actually thought the experience was fun. He will also try to convince you he wasn't frightened, even when a few black gentlemen who were also waiting to get processed were fucking with him, telling him impersonating a police officer was twenty years mandatory. He would also tell you being in a holding cell after you swallowed Viagra wasn't exactly an ideal situation. He found humor in the fact Huggy was almost crying at the time of the arrest, especially because the handcuffs were slapped on his thick wrists too tightly by the arresting officer. They also could not get the seatbelt over his large frame after they put him in the backseat.

Huggy will tell you Keiran was in fact shitting in his pants during the whole experience but was not disputing anything else. The cops confiscated our camera and impounded the police car. Apparently, the car had no registration as a functional vehicle or a prop vehicle for film production. I paid an attorney a three thousand dollar retainer to handle whatever charges were going to be filed and to retrieve our camera. Somebody would have to handle the car. Not my problem.

We got the camera back and no charges were filed against either Huggy or Keiran. Apparently, stupidity is not a crime.

The footage never made it into the end product and the scene was pulled from the member's area. (I am not exactly sure why, but as I get into later, it was probably for compliance reasons.) It was all for nothing. I saved our two shoots and everyone made their money.

At the end of the year, Meridiana miscarried our 'twins.'

Vic Lagina's School of Porn

Lesson Four: The Pop Shot

In over eighteen years of shooting porn, I never missed the money shot, also known as the pop shot, also known as the cumshot. I take pride in this streak for some twisted reason.

According to porn lore, a diet consisting of celery and pineapple juice will result in sweet, voluminous pop shots.

I refer to it as the 'pop' because 'money' shot sounds too hokey and 'cumshot' is a little too vile for this classy fellow. Danny D earns top honors for the most voluminous pops during my tenure. There were times I could not believe what I was seeing. He shot seemingly endless geysers of ejaculate, spewing ropes everywhere: her face, her boobs, the couch, the wall.

"Danny, I am trusting you will clean your jizz off the couch and wall once we start striking the set?" was a sentence I used more than once. To his credit, Mr. D always cleaned up after himself.

I could never bring myself to ask how he did it. I suspect if he had a secret recipe, he would keep it to himself.

Legendary bastard.

Regardless of volume, it's important you do *not* miss the pop shot. People have tried to fake them, but a trained eye can spot a fake a mile away. Fake creampies too (and fake squirting, but more on this in *Lesson Six*). The most impressive male performers are those who are able to do two real pop shots in the same scene.

Respect, young man.

Based on the analytics, the most popular and requested pop shots were facials (no surprise there) and creampies. Anal sites requested anal creampies at times, but they were not always popular with performers. Most male talent will claim they can't pop from having anal sex, something to do with a lack of grip, but those who can, we applaud you because it's a big ask.

CAN'T CUM FROM ANAL? DON'T RUIN THE MAGIC, DUDE.

There was a time when Mark Spiegler, porn agent and overall cranky bastard, would not allow his talent to take anal creampies because of a higher STD risk. I have no idea if this is accurate, but Mark never went to medical school.

Every now and again, I got the pop request for the boobs or butt, which is rare. Whenever I read the members' comments on the scenes with boob or butt pops, most thought it was a waste. On the other side, there were members who did not like facials and welcomed any alternative. Feminists say facials are about toxic masculinity, dominance, and misogyny, and women do not enjoy this - and they would be correct... most of the time. There are Facial Unicorns. I know them, they exist.

DON'T GET ALL JUDGY NOW, FEMINISTS. ACCEPT. ACCEPTANCE IS GROWTH.

SET-UP VS. FUCKING TO POP

Depending on the male talent you hire, you will have to ascertain what category your talent falls in. I always preferred male talent who could fuck to pop and members appreciated them as well. If the sex felt good enough and the performers were into it, why break it up by going from a wide shot for the set-up, followed by a high-angle shot for the pop?

I could move from the sex angle to a proper pop angle without disrupting the smoothness of the shot. I credit this to regular shoulder workouts every morning. In the early years, while working with greener performers, sometimes they would drop in front of the male talent with their backs to the camera, which is a big no-no. A well-versed performer knows which way to face, how to hold their bodies, and how to continue to perform until the director calls "cut."

Sometimes they would sit near the female, who would hold patiently on her knees, ready and in position. Everyone in the room is quiet while the male talent is jerking his dick, trying to get there. Sometimes it took several minutes. Meanwhile, I was holding steady at a high angle, waiting to hit record, listening to his breathing, followed by the inevitable, "Ready, Vic?"

HE WAS BORN READY, MOTHERFUCKA!

Then another pop in cinematic porn history was captured.

Some of the nuances were memorable. Mick Blue would be on his knees, rubbing his belly and nipples while his breathing increased. I warned the female talent so they wouldn't be jarred. They thanked me after.

One guy squatted, sticking his fingers in his anus while he stroked himself. Another guy asked the female talent to pinch and suck on his nipples. Some would ask the female talent to suck their balls. This of course was never mandatory, but female talent dug deep to get the job done.

WHAT ABOUT CREAMPIES, DUDE?

You would assume if a girl is okay with creampies, she's on birth control. Well, a lot of them were not. Several porn babies are living proof. One female performer told me she was not on birth control for health reasons and preferring creampies, she used a douche of hydrogen peroxide and tea tree oil to prevent being impregnated. I'm not a gynecologist (yet), but I'm sure this is not legit birth control.

Sometimes you have the opposite problem with your male talent: non-voluminous pops, also known as 'the dribblers.' This can happen when your male talent is dehydrated, on a poor diet, over-sexed, or a frequent user of cocaine. There is not much you can do during production. To fix this, use pop-enhancing software in post-production.

For pop photos, a product called *Spunk* thickens the appearance of the ejaculate. But book a fuck-to-pop male talent who doesn't suffer from the dribblers and you're halfway to a winning scene!

13 STUDIO BOUND

Despite all the fights, stress, and dysfunctionalities with Meridiana, I was excited to be a father. I would be a good father and had the means to provide for a child, or children as she led me to believe. The psychological aftermath of a miscarriage is hardest on the woman and Meridiana went from clinically depressed to having a full-on meltdown.

When she had her dilation and curettage, she told me she saw the fetuses removed from her body. She chose to do this back home for her own reasons. When she returned to Vegas with Bliss, Meridiana was a disaster. She never wanted to get out of bed and my fear was she might be suicidal. Life at home was unbearable. I concocted a grand scheme to solve all of our problems.

Meridiana insisted I wasn't fully committed and this is why we had problems. I bought into this theory and agreed to adopt Bliss even before I had confirmation of being her father.

I planned a trip to Hawaii after the New Year where I would propose. In theory, it could solve the Bliss issue, because I was not only correcting the wrong of deceiving my family, but getting married to prove I was committed.

GENIUS. I WANT TO PUNCH YOU IN YOUR STUPID FACE.

I did minimal research on the four C's when buying a diamond: color, carat, clarity, and cut, and visited a local jeweler to make my purchase. The main diamond was a one-carat brilliant cut set between two half-carat yellow diamonds in white gold, setting me back sixteen thousand dollars.

My plan was to propose in a helicopter over the Big Island's active volcano. The metaphor was intentional. I asked, she said yes, and we were both happy.

I set a long engagement, because my rational side wanted to allow as much time as possible to back out if needed. I chose the date 11-11-11, which felt cosmically significant.

I CAN SMELL THE INCENSE AND PATCHOULI.

Even though we were happy at the moment, when we returned stateside, everything continued to unravel. We tried to have another child to fix our problems, despite that it's a bad idea after a recent miscarriage.

HEY DUDE. WHAT DID THE FIVE FINGERS SAY TO THE FACE?

Meridiana then began guilting me into spending more time with *my* daughter. This was still unconfirmed and even though we had started the adoption process, I told her it was an unnecessary guilt trip. She had a plan to solve the issue.

POPCORN. READY.

My cover story about my occupation morphed from being a corporate video producer to working for the government. Either the inquisitor would gloss over with boredom if they assumed it was a state government job, or they would know not to ask specific questions if they assumed I was a Fed.

When we were on a tour bus in Hawaii with a lot of bible thumpers from the Midwest and were forced to stand up and introduce ourselves, I put the cover story to the test. A former police officer on the tour even asked me which branch of the federal government I worked for and I told him I am not at liberty to say. He did not press any further. Later, he told Meridiana about his experiences as a police officer, saying it wasn't the people who talked a lot you had to watch out for. It was the people who didn't. As he said it, he gestured in my direction as I remained a stone-faced killer.

I needed to know for certain whether I was Bliss's father. I researched anonymous testing centers which took hair and cheek cell samples that claimed to be 99.99997% accurate.

A few days later, Meridiana claimed to have taken hair samples from me while I was sleeping and mailed them to her mother, because this was the method she preferred. A week later, she informed me Bliss was indeed my daughter. I asked to see the results and Meridiana was going to get them from her mother.

LET ME GUESS: THE DOG ATE THE DNA RESULTS.

The problem was, I was set to see my family in a few days and needed to be certain before dropping the bomb. One excuse led to another as to why they failed to materialize, so I made Meridiana swear on everything sacred to her that she and her mother (whom I never met) were being truthful. She insisted she was. I headed back east with a photo of Bliss and a bellyful of butterflies.

I have to hand it to my father for not flipping the fuck out and disowning me. I explained to him and his wife the storied relationship with Meridiana, my initial fears when I arrived in Las Vegas, and our rationales for not telling them sooner.

Both of them acted as if they were very understanding. It was a huge burden off my chest. They were elated to have another grandchild, albeit an insta-grandchild, so they suppressed any disappointment. My father studied the photo of Bliss for what seemed like hours, as if he was analyzing every feature of her face. We made plans to bring Meridiana and Bliss back east so my whole family could meet them.

My brother didn't come down on me hard. He listened and understood we had different life approaches. I am sure he expressed his true feelings to his wife who had her own opinions, but on the surface they were supportive.

When I returned to Las Vegas and got another guilt trip from Meridiana about spending time with my daughter, something snapped. It was time to get a handle on things.

YESSSSSSSS!!! FINALLY, YOU PUSSY MOTHERFUCKER!

I paid for the anonymous paternity test, took my and Bliss's samples, and mailed them in. I told Meridiana afterward and her anxiety was unmistakable. Obviously, she had not seen the alleged results. She always said she didn't trust her mother. Knowing we would soon have our answer scared the shit out of her.

A week later at a friend's wedding in North Carolina, I received the results. It was 99.99997% certain I was not Bliss's father.

GREAT. NOW RUN!

I was disappointed. This situation was already a fucking a mess. When I told Meridiana, we were video conferencing her and I saw the look of sadness on her face. I wanted to make it better. I told her Bliss would always be a daughter to me and I would still adopt her. We were a family.

I considered the repercussions and whether I should tell my family the truth. I had already gotten over the hump of informing them of Bliss's existence. Now I would have to tell them "just kidding?" This was too much to bear. Did it matter if

Bliss was my blood? Would she suffer from a family stigma? Meridiana and I decided it didn't matter and to keep it private.

Bliss met her new cousins, uncle, aunt, and grandparents and everything seemed to be headed in the right direction. They treated her as family. Unbeknownst to all of us at the time, Meridiana was pregnant again. Against my advice, Meridiana sent her ex-boyfriend a court order for his DNA. If he was indeed the father, she wanted him to pay child support. I half-suspected money was her motive all along.

NO ONE EVER ACCUSED YOU OF BEING SMART. YOU HULKING HORSE'S ASS.

The dynamic at work among Moe, Kyle, Butler, and Huggy was contentious and I had to keep the peace. Moe hated Kyle and Butler and the feeling was mutual. They left Huggy alone because he didn't take their shit.

During my time in Philadelphia, Kyle and I fought over instant messenger which otherwise would have resulted in fisticuffs had we been in the same room. I had reports from Moe about how Kyle and Butler were conducting themselves on location. I should have addressed it when I returned.

As usual, it started off in jest, but then got personal when he called Meridiana a "whore." Correct or not, he crossed a line.

Kyle knew it was a source of weakness and decided to exploit it. In a sense, it was better this way because I have no idea what would have happened had he said this to my face. Someone could have gotten hurt and it would have been detrimental to the business.

SHOULD HAVE OPENED UP A CAN OF WHOOP-ASS.

Knowing I was done with him, Kyle tried to plead his case to the head office. He swore I was in the wrong and wanted to move to Blake's crew. Butler wanted to follow. I rescinded my letter to the Canadian government, ending his training.

The brass decided Kyle was to return to Montreal and go back to editing. He soon quit and moved to Costa Rica with his girlfriend.

Butler was forced to stay on my crew, and over time, we smoothed out our differences. Away from Kyle and his manipulations, he was easy to get along with. I picked up Kyle's workload and started to direct again.

Blake had been doing a fine job of fucking up. Word traveled that the Vegas crew from Brazzers was in complete disarray. I had worked for three-plus years to build up a strong and professional reputation and I was being confused with the other Vegas crew.

It got so bad, girls did not want to fly out to Vegas because of the bad experiences they'd had. Bramm was fawning over Hailey, who was barred up on Xanax because of the stress of Blake's operation. Robbie wanted to leave Blake's crew and join mine which the office would not allow. Hailey relayed all the information to me through instant messenger and the conversation of me ripping apart Blake was left open on her laptop. This prompted him to visit me at the Gilespie house. I almost ripped his head off.

We were face to face and I was begging Blake to hit me. He knew he poked a sleeping bear. He now understood he was messing with my reputation.

I told him he was in over his head and had no business running a crew. He played the card the Nazis did after World War II. He was only following orders! I told him he needed to tighten his ship or face the consequences. He apologized and was sad things had sunk to this level.

He didn't want to mess up my operation and my accomplishments. He said I was a mentor and a friend and would talk to the head office about moving elsewhere. After this, I had a reputation for being a hothead and someone with no patience when it came to damaging my productivity or business. The next person to test me in this capacity would be Keiran Lee a few years down the road.

AND THIS WAS PRE-COCAINE ADDICTION. WHAT ON EARTH WAS MAKING HIM SO IRATE? OH YEAH, WHORE.

We were ten months into our lease at the Gilespie House when we could no longer operate under the radar. The amount of traffic coming in and out of the house was noticeable and the neighbors knew what we were up to. It was only a matter of time before someone lodged an official complaint and we had bigger problems to contend with.

I started finding a building for us to shoot in. Seven months later, we relocated to the studio which would house our productions for the next six-and-a-half years.

Moving locations was no easy feat. It took careful planning from getting the building approved, having the tenant improvements made, and county inspections to approve the renovations in a quick enough time frame.

Butler knew an American friend from film school and had him come to Las Vegas to potentially direct. The Ginger Giant's name was Matt and we hired him.

While we were moving into new digs, Blake was packing up and heading to Miami where he would finish out his career in porn.

GODSPEED, BUFFOON.

AND NOW, A WORD FROM BRAMM STROKER…

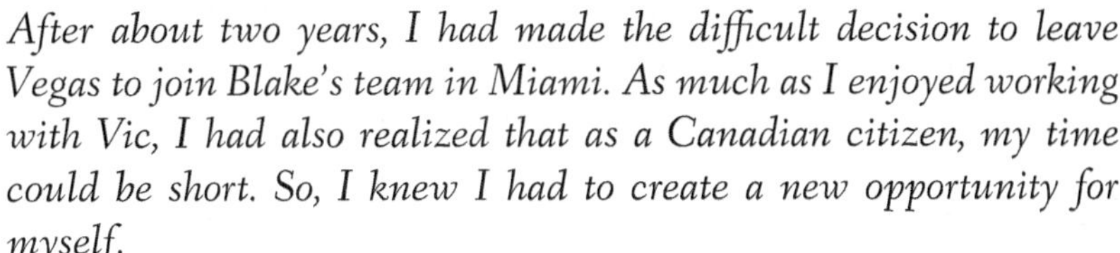

After about two years, I had made the difficult decision to leave Vegas to join Blake's team in Miami. As much as I enjoyed working with Vic, I had also realized that as a Canadian citizen, my time could be short. So, I knew I had to create a new opportunity for myself.

Vegas had also become stale. I found it more and more difficult to live there full time and I wanted to experience somewhere new and exciting, while I still could. It ultimately worked out in my favor, and I was able to obtain a temporary Visa through Blake's contacts. The Visa allowed me to continue living in South Florida for another 3 years, shooting for Blake along with (shooter) Ken Dark.

Outside of work, Blake and I had become very good friends and we had gotten very close. Working with him was a different story. His lack of production experience was obvious and avoidable mistakes were made. His best quality as a producer was hiring good people to work for him, which is arguably the most important part of the job. In the end, I doubt our production in Florida would have lasted as long as it did, had he not had a solid support system around him.

OLIVE BRANCH TO JAYDEN JAMES?

Brando wasn't my only nemesis, because then there was Jayden Jaymes.

Jayden entered the business in 2007. Our first shoot was a boy/girl/girl scene with Nikki Benz. Right away, I disliked her. Sometimes people rub you the wrong way and drain you. After hair and makeup, she was pretty and voluptuous, also a strong performer and reliable. Because of that and her rising popularity (and how her body type was everything Brazzers was at the time), my crew shot Jayden frequently.

But some of the things that would come out of her mouth... and let's talk about that mouth. Jayden was indisputably skilled on camera. However, she couldn't keep a secret. She was loose-lipped, even for porn.

For example, Jayden bragged about blowing Brando. Brando was known for his privacy, so he was miffed. This was a teachable moment for me: keep your dick away from Jayden, unless you want the porn world to know about it.

Once Meridiana was around, banging Jayden became a moot point because their cunt hairs got entangled. To put it a nicer way, they did not like each other. If I am being fair to Jayden, her beef with my girlfriend made it easier to allow her antics to annoy me.

WHAT ANTICS? I AM SO GLAD YOU ASKED!

Porn was thirteenth grade and girls like Jayden were the reason. Petty. Pointless. Mundane.

If Rachel Starr had the best booty in the entire porn industry at the time (she did, hands down), why not be happy for her? Jayden needed to talk shit about Rachel and anyone else she didn't like, whenever possible, to anyone.

No disrespect to Jayden's voluptuous booty in an era preceding butt implants, but Rachel's Ass was created by God. On the seventh day, while he was resting and pondering "what is a divine ass?" he created Rachel Starr.

I give Jayden the benefit of the doubt of being young, under the lights of the porn industry.

My hope is, having been this far removed from the business and now creeping toward her forties, she could acknowledge her...

CUNTINESS?

When I shot Jayden for the last time, the blame fell on Moe as production manager for not informing Jayden of a talent switch. Her original scene partner had a dirty test. Lovely, sweet, and strong performer Charisma Cappelli was the replacement. Unfortunately, all of this was discovered while everyone arrived on set. What to do?

Jayden had a valid point: it was her scene. From Charisma's point of view, because she had nothing to do with this, it was her scene as well. The problem was Jayden did not want to perform with Charisma. The message I got through Moe was it was because Charisma was "a dirty hooker." True or not, her test was clean, and she was more than willing to shoot with Jayden.

Porn rumors claimed Jayden was also working in the private sector. Hypocrite. Perhaps there were hooker hierarchies at play. Jayden bragged to me about all the famous athletes she spent time with.

FIGHTING OVER WHO'S THE BETTER HOOKER. CLASSY.

Complicating things, Charisma had a friend who was local, tested, and eager as a possible replacement if need be. Charisma was a pragmatist while Jayden put forth ultimatums. One option would have been to drop it down somehow to a boy/girl scene while we took a loss for Charisma who was already in Vegas. This seemed wasteful.

My working relationship with Jayden had deteriorated to where I could not be in the same room with her for more than necessary. The misguided entitlement, pettiness, and nonsensical superiority became too much to be around. I respected her wish not to shoot with Charisma and sent Jayden home.

I had to defend my decision to the head office while also covering for Moe's error. I told them it made more sense for Jayden to shoot with other producers she got along with. Jayden was going to let her opinion be known and it soon made it onto the notorious Brazzers Forum.

She had been baiting me on other boards. I shirked it off thinking Jayden would tire herself out. I wasn't going anywhere, nor was I going to respond.

Meridiana and I experienced a miscarriage around this time.

Jayden leaped over the line and said, "His fiancée killed the babies inside of her so she wouldn't have to deal with him for the next eighteen years."

It was haymaker time.

Once her post was written, I told the head office I needed to nuke the Forum. Yancee understood and did not stand in my way.

Sadly, I don't have the exact response. I would love it if any internet sleuth could find my reply because the powers that be deactivated the nasty Forum long ago. I can only remember a few bits and pieces. I named her "Canklesaurus Rex" because of how her thick ankles merged with her thick calves. This caught on. It was mean of me to say she was "hitting the wall faster than Wile E. Coyote on rocket skates."

It seemed like I got a standing ovation from the internet. After, I never heard from Jayden. She stopped shooting for companies, but I don't imply my post had anything to do with it. I imagine she grew tired of the business and figured out a way to capitalize on her brand, and I applaud her for this. I wish her the best in motherhood and hope her world is brighter.

Jayden, as an older and wiser woman, who is now a mother, *Mazel Tov* by the way, how do you feel now reading your words? This is the litmus test as to whether I would consider extending the olive branch to you and wishing you well in the world.

14 THE DEATH OF DAVID DUNN

Before Blake left for Miami, we met for dinner to clear the air. Sporting a Fro-hawk, he reiterated his belief I was a mentor and a friend.

He told me of his plan to relocate and it sounded like a disaster in the making. On paper, Miami was the perfect place for an amateur like Blake because there were amateur girls everywhere. Done right, Miami could be a cost-effective place to operate.

In the coming months, Blake found ways to bleed cash. Instead of hiring local girls, he was still importing talent from LA. Getting talent to travel thousands of miles from home also had disadvantages. There were last-minute changes and drama which would increase their operating costs.

It would take about a year before his frat brothers assigned Blake the proper website, their amateur brand, *Mofos.com*. Still, a lot of resources and funds were wasted. Had I not vouched for him, I could have prevented disasters.

Meridiana had always been a smoker, a disgust I tolerated out of love. Kissing a smoker is like licking an ashtray. Her teeth looked rotted and disgusting, but she claimed it was from her stepbrother punching her in the mouth.

The first time she was pregnant, she said she quit smoking, and I never saw her take a puff.

During *this* pregnancy, she needed to have a lit cigarette in her hand to satiate the fixation and would leave the room to not bother me.

ONLY TWO PEOPLE DO NOT INHALE: BILL CLINTON AND HIS FIANCÉE.

Meridiana said to relax, she liked to drive around by herself. She avoided discussing her suspicious behavior by playing the "you cheated on me" card.

We had loud and angry fights where we screamed at the top of our lungs and she would slam doors. Since we had an impressionable child living with us, I had to leave often before things spiraled.

Some nights I spent on the couch in my new studio, with Jamie trembling at my feet.

I never went to the doctor with her since there would always be a cancellation. But again, there was a baby growing inside her, male twins this time I was told. I had no proof. She did leave the baby's heartbeat on my phone, but I deleted the message not knowing what it was. It sounded like a pocket-dial call and voicemail. Still, I read the baby books and prepared for whatever lie ahead. When she made it past her first trimester, I thought we were in the clear.

Our new studio was sixteen thousand square feet. Custom showers in each bathroom for talent, a washer and dryer, and I transferred the makeup room from the Gilespie House. There was a full room for wardrobe and a prep room. We had ten different spaces to transform into whatever sets Brazzers wanted. We had two thousand square feet of additional space for prop storage and twenty-five hundred square feet of warehouse space for shooting and additional storage. The sky was the limit and we were legally licensed to shoot porn in Clark County.

The safe haven was here. My contract was due to expire a year into the thirty-nine-month lease, so I had financial liability. Rent and fees were north of eleven grand per month and my company was the guarantor. But just as when my plums tingled when I was about to move to Vegas, I was feeling it again.

After we left the Gilespie House, David Dunn was faced with undoing what we did, starting with the garages we make-shifted into studio space. He was sitting on a nine thousand dollar deposit, and as far as I was concerned, he was welcome to all of it. Frank complained about getting a refund, but he needed every cent of it to get his house back into a presentable form. A few months later, David Dunn would not be feeling very well only to find out after a trip to the hospital he had stage four cancer.

Meridiana subpoenaed her ex-boyfriend's DNA and he was Bliss's father. Prior to the confirmation, he had no interest. Now knowing he faced back payments for child support, he wanted to be in Bliss's life.

Meanwhile, the fights were unending and the stress on the baby (babies?) growing inside of her couldn't be helping. Meridiana was perpetually manic with no way to avoid a confrontation, like someone coming off a drug bender.

One afternoon when my parents visited, they were headed out for a bite and Bliss asked to go with them. When they returned, they were exhausted and said Bliss freaked out the entire time and was kicking them.

She became a miniature version of her mother. One day, Meridiana slammed my office door after a mild fight, only to have Bliss repeat the action and then point and tell me, "You're making my mommy upset."

After she slammed the door, I had a wake-up call: this situation was not the 'best for Bliss.' I suggested Bliss return to the Midwest because this was a toxic atmosphere. I spoke to her uncle about it, who agreed and facilitated her return.

The level of dysfunction within my production crew was at an all-time low, because of the new facility. Soon the infighting started, but less so than the year prior.

My production manager Moe would only get emotional if someone disrespected his authority, but he was lonely and wanted a girlfriend. I would see on his open laptop his profile on the dating sites he frequented. Pete was my Korean production assistant and a hard worker. He was unflappable and a reminder the American worker could learn a lot from their Asian counterpart. Huggy was always in a bad mood, but he respected the dollar and gave the operation stability.

AND NOW, A WORD FROM PETE…

The four or five years working alongside Vic at is now all but a blur. When The Dude told me about the book he was putting together, I was naturally excited – because as for the jaw-dropping depiction of events and crazy characters portrayed before the audience, you can't make this shit up.

What is left of my memories can be described as the absolute batshit craziest half decade of my life. We were rock stars. One can argue it was the performers in front of the camera that were the real rock stars, and we were only there to film and bear witness to their 'stardom'. Being in the trenches with Vic, we were the vigilant and dedicated conductors of mayhem and debauchery in its absolute form, holding on at the helm of the train directing the flow of madness for the perverted world to see. On any random afternoon, it would be routinely unremarkable to find Vic and I confined in a hot, crammed, musky film set with some of the world's biggest adult names making smut magic with lights, cameras, and action.

Working as Vic's production manager Vegas came with the expected ebb and flow of any high-intensity, high-stress, high-demand production ecosystem. Throwing porn into the already hair-pulling, nail-biting culture of fast paced film production is like throwing kerosene on a campfire and hoping you don't burn down the campsite by the time you're done.

As the mad conductor of our crazy train, I fought to keep the train on the tracks. During the first few weeks of the Ginger Giant Matt's directing tenure, we predicted his alcohol abuse would be his eventual downfall. He was strong and worked hard, but at night he worked harder at destroying his liver. Matt pissed his pants because he drank too much, once ruining Moe's couch.

Meridiana, now six months pregnant, was back home visiting Bliss when the doctor informed her one of the twins was dead. The other still had a strong heartbeat. Devastated, I hoped the other would survive. A few days later, she said the other baby had died.

Once again, she had her dilation and curettage away from Vegas and watched two dead fetuses leave her body. I reflected the universe was trying to tell me something when really the universe was smacking me in the face with a two-by-four.

IDIOT, HELLO! YOU'VE USED ALL YOUR GET OUT OF JAIL FREE CARDS. GET YOUR MOTHERFUCKING SHIT TOGETHER.

When I heard David Dunn had passed away, Meridiana's fate was sealed. David drank, smoked, and loved cocaine. He was only thirty-nine, two years older than me. He died of lung cancer and was survived by his wife and two little girls. Moe and I attended his funeral and when I peered inside the casket, my exact thoughts were, "That's not going to be me."

When I got home, I shared my experience with Meridiana and told her things had to change. This was no way to live. Knowing she was losing me, she upped her sex game, and despite her begging me to come inside her, I refused.

NO MORE LOADS FOR YOU, DEVIL WOMAN.

She was working on my holiday present, a calendar of photos of her. She brought a photographer to the house who took the photos. His name was Bruno, someone she claimed took photos of girls in *Playboy* and the like.

She said she got a new job with a producer in Las Vegas who was doing a reality show on ultimate fighting. She spent a lot of her time at her job. When I asked to meet her boss, plans always fell through. I had no idea how she was spending her time. After three more months of incessant fighting, I ended it. That's not going to be me!

Three months. Succubus in the black pajamas. Worthy fuckin' adversary.

Bliss had spent five months away with Meridiana, only making occasional visits. Meridiana talked about how her mother left her after she was born and she resented her. Now, she was repeating the same cycle, yet was too focused on trying to keep us together to see it. Because it was 'best for Bliss,' I told her to stop working on us and work on being a good mother.

She wasn't going easy. She laid the sexuality on thick, but I was immune. I had taken my metaphorical Valtrex to suppress the human herpes virus known as Meridiana. Two weeks before she departed, we had a nasty fight and she left. I was wide awake from diet pills and got a text from Nikki. She was in town and hired to party with Michael Bay and Jerry Bruckheimer. She asked me to meet her at the club.

Nikki was also dealing with boyfriend problems back in LA and we compared war stories. She thought it was suspect Meridiana went to her boss's after our fight.

I hopped into a limousine with a dozen women and a guy who was wondering what the fuck I was doing there, and we went to where Michael Bay and Jerry Bruckheimer were partying at XS Nightclub at Encore. That night, Nikki and I had amazing sex at the studio, which would explain my energy when I got home later.

"Where were you? I called a bunch of times. Why are you smiling?"

"Am I smiling?" I asked.

"Where were you?" she insisted.

"You know, after this latest fight, and your latest need to leave the house and go to your boss's, I decided to drive out to the desert and look at the stars and think about life. I turned my phone off. When I was ready to come home, I did. And here I am. And I think you need to figure out when you are leaving."

She did not question me further. I got away with it. So much for her claims she would always be able to tell if I was cheating. She avoided leaving for two weeks. Finally, I got her a ticket and told her to pack a bag.

I did not buckle.

She cried.

I did not care.

She could no longer manipulate me.

Get. The. Fuck. Out.

She threw her engagement ring at me for the twenty-ninth time, and this time I did not give it back. After I dropped her at the airport, I put it in my floor safe, until years later when I gave it to a homeless person.

NO LIE. HE GAVE IT TO A BUM. JAW MEET FLOOR. SIXTEEN GRAND, GONE.

The ring was hexed which was appropriate because Meridiana claimed to be a witch, obviously not the good kind.

AND HE MUST BE A WIZARD OR SOMETHING CHAOTIC GOOD FROM DUNGEONS + DRAGONS. IT'S THE ONLY LOGICAL EXPLANATION FOR HOW HE WITHSTOOD AND DEFLECTED HER LAWFUL EVIL WITCHCRAFT.

A few hours later, Meridiana called me and told me Southwest had to return her to Vegas (translation, she never got on the plane). I suggested she stay at her boss's since he seemed to have an open-door policy. I told her to make a plan to pick up the rest of her stuff and I would coordinate with Herschel to be elsewhere whenever this would occur.

Two weeks later, her stuff was moved out of my house and we were officially broken up. I would like to tell you I never saw her again, but it would not be true. I would like to tell you she never contacted me again, but this also would be untrue. Herpes is incurable. I can tell you with complete certainty she unraveled quite spectacularly over the next year.

None of it would matter because a few weeks later, I would suffer a great heartbreak. It would be a symbolic start for the change which was coming...

A Warm Hello from Oz

You might be wondering what the fuck is up with all the words in the crazy font while Vic blathers on about his existence.

It's just me. OZ. Osmodeus Zpaceball.

Nice to meet you.

So what am I? What are any of us, really, aside from a memory of experiences? A protector? A spirit guide? Ego personified? I see myself every day when he looks in the mirror. In that sense, I am a real, physical entity, named by him.

He's not schizophrenic. At least there has not been an official diagnosis. Watching over him was not always an easy job, but I put in the work over the next ten years as you're about to hear.

Listening to him recap these events over, and over, and over again is starting to make me a little mental. Now I just have to shout out a reaction whenever I want to choke him for being such a pussy. Well, pussy is a bit harsh. He's just naïve sometimes, like a big giant baby, and I have to keep him in line. Today, we have extensive conversations with one another about how to be the best versions of ourselves. We're trying empathy on for size while in self-mandated porn exile and on the 'good' drugs. "Cocaine and alcohol are our enemy" is the current mantra.

Enjoy the rest of the adventure...

PART TWO

DARKNESS WASHED OVER THE DUDE

Sometimes things take so long
But how do I explain
When not too many people
Can see we're all the same
And because of all their tears
Their eyes can't hope to see
The beauty that surrounds them
Isn't it a pity?

–GEORGE HARRISON

15 R.I.P. MY BELOVED JAMIE

My toxic relationship had many victims, both human and canine.

Jamie was absorbing the bulk of my negative energy from dealing with Meridiana. Right before the breakup, she whimpered whenever she jumped up onto the couch to sit next to me. Her automatic response to watching TV was taxing on her. There was a major issue.

Hip dysplasia is common among larger breeds and several vets and dog owners said it was common in German shepherds. Maintaining a healthy weight would help prevent this debilitating condition. I followed the guidance religiously: no human food, proper measurements of expensive food, supplements, and extensive play/exercise.

I even made talent read a set of house rules stating three times: do not feed the dogs. My house sat on a half acre, an ample playground for my beauties. Friends joke they want to come back as one of my dogs in a future life.

I took Jamie to the vet, suspecting she was suffering from the onset of either arthritis or hip dysplasia. The testing was inconclusive. Her hip X-rays looked normal, so they prescribed Jamie pain medication. This initially appeared to remedy the discomfort.

Whenever me and Meridiana fought, I'd cuddle Jamie when she shook. Joker wasn't fazed by our bouts of yelling, but Jamie was terrified and hurting. I would take her with me on the bad nights when I was relegated to the office couch. My pain dissipated when I wrapped my arms around Jamie and told her she was my world.

Two weeks after I showed Meridiana the door, something was terribly wrong with Jamie.

> **WHERE DID MERIDIANA EVEN GO, DUDE? BACK HOME? OR TO THE PHOTOGRAPHER WHO WAS PORKING HER? OH YES, WHO CARES.**

Jamie was walking around like she was drunk. Her balance and motor skills were off, so she stayed in one spot with her head on the ground, whimpering. The only time she would attempt to walk was when I came home because she wanted to greet me at the door.

The following day, we went to the vet to get some answers. After a set of X-rays revealed nothing structurally wrong, we were referred to a CT specialist. The vet was concerned about a possible ruptured disk in her spine, or possibly even a brain tumor.

A back injury would be feasible given how much she and Joker wrestled. Jamie always came out on top, despite the thirty-pound weight difference. I was hopeful this was the case.

HOPEFUL IS A SYNONYM FOR DENIAL, DUDE.

The CT specialist said the problem lay deeper. They wanted to do more extensive testing. The vet prescribed some pain medications and sent us off for what would be our last days together.

All she did was whimper. It didn't matter if she was moving, lying still, or medicated. Every time I heard it, a part of me would die. Her eyes begged me to end her pain. Joker knew there was something wrong, so he would just sniff her ears and let her be.

After the weekend, I took Jamie back to the CT specialist for her full scan. When I picked her up and put her into my truck, Joker flipped out. He did not want me to take her. Until this point, he'd spent every moment with her. She raised him, kicked him around when he got out of line, showed him the ropes, and helped protect his master. He knew this would be the last time he saw her.

I dropped Jamie off and the vet said they would call when the results came in. All day, I feared the worst yet clung to a shred of hope that my six-year-old baby had more life to live. Hope was diminished. She had a deep brain tumor.

There were no good options. The vet believed her chances of surviving the costly surgery were slim. The tumor was too deep. Even if she made it off the operating table, Jamie would face rounds of painful chemotherapy and rehab. The best possible result (however slim) would extend her life twelve to eighteen months, tops.

The decision was obvious. Still, I spoke to friends and family to get a second opinion as most had been through the same thing with their pets.

I had to end her pain and let Jamie go. Following through was easier said than done since losing Jamie would forever destroy a part of me.

The next morning, I headed to the CT specialist to let them know. I couldn't get the words out. They were compassionate and I composed myself enough to fill out the paperwork.

Then, they led me to the waiting room where I had my final moments with my first dog.

The specialist cried when she saw how much pain this was causing me. They see this on a daily basis, which is hard to imagine.

They wheeled Jamie in on a wide cart. She looked comfortable. Her eyes lit up when she saw me and her tail was wagging. The technicians helped her down onto the floor and left quietly so Jamie and I could have our last moments.

I laid beside her and looked into her eyes. I had brought her a few biscuits from home and fed them to her after I kissed each one. I grabbed her paw and thanked her for being the best companion and protector a man could ask for. I thanked her for helping me get through my break up with Joy, for being a good co-pilot during our trip to Las Vegas, for being a good mother to Joker, and for accepting him from the very beginning. And for enduring the painful times with Meridiana.

I apologized for the floods of negative energy. I told her I wanted to end her pain and I was sorry her life was cut short. She should have had more good years ahead. After one last whimper, she licked me on the nose to tell me she was ready.

The technicians came back and explained the process. The first injection would sedate her. When she calmed, they would administer the second injection, stopping her heart.

They asked if I was ready as I put my arms around her body. A dullness crept over her eyes after the first injection and she seemed to finally be free of pain.

After the second injection, her eyes regained her last bit of life. I kissed her nose, told her the pain was about to stop, and how I loved her and would hopefully see her again. I felt her heart stop beating and watched the life leave her body. After sitting beside her alone for a few more minutes, I covered her body with a sheet, left the room, and headed to my truck to weep uncontrollably.

GODDAMMIT, DUDE! NOW I'M CRYING. BUT, THIS WAS THE EXACT MOMENT OZ WAS BORN.

Your responsibility is to stay with your pets until their last breath. Regardless of the agonizing pain you suffer when you have to put your pet to sleep, it's a necessary part of the experience. I will never run from it. The happiness and joy I receive from my dogs is unending and I do not foresee existing without a canine companion.

She is immortalized in my house with a blown-up photo. There was a certificate from the crematorium with a piece of her fur and her paw print, but one of her successors chewed it up seven years later when it fell onto the floor.

Whenever I die, I too will be cremated. My remains and the remains of all my dogs throughout my lifetime will be disbursed in a unique fashion, in specific locations by those important to me.

DEVIL WITCH PUT A CURSE ON JAMIE. NEVER BEEN MORE CERTAIN OF ANYTHING IN MY LIFE.

With a heavy heart, I returned home. Joker did something simple to lighten the mood. My pantry door was open and a bag of microwavable popcorn was torn open. Kernels scattered everywhere. He stared at me pretending to suggest he was innocent. Of all the choices, he went with little pebbles with no snack value. I kissed him on the face and told him it was just the two of us now and he was in charge. I let him outside and watched him pee like a girl, something he learned from Jamie.

The big oaf lived up to his name. He came off as a dummy, but he opened doors with his teeth and was a problem solver although never as keen as Jamie in assessing a situation. His intelligence was relative to his motivation at any given moment. He won the hearts of everyone who experienced his goofy disposition.

After a month, we decided we needed another dog.

I was hoping Joker would step up and assert himself as the Alpha dog, but he was lost. He had the attention span of a five-year-old needing Ritalin. After too much hugging and kissing, Joker would get overwhelmed and run away.

I loved the goofball, but I needed a more emotional companion like Jamie.

Around this time, I was shooting Julia Ann who is a well-known dog lover, rescuer, and advocate. She heard I lost Jamie and suggested I rescue rather than breed a dog as there is a never-ending supply. I found the German Shepherd Rescue of Las Vegas.

The next day, I drove down with Joker to make sure if I brought a dog home they would get along. After a forty-five-minute drive past the brothels in Pahrump, we arrived.

THIS ASSHOLE DIDN'T MAKE A PIT STOP.

The head of the shelter was a fiery woman in her sixties. She instructed me on how the visit was going to proceed. She only lets a potential adopter interact with three dogs. Otherwise, the adopter gets overwhelmed and can't make a decision.

Joker was stressed out when I walked him outside of their cages because they were all barking at him. I led him away from the cages when she brought out the first three candidates. They were all sweet, beautiful creatures who all got along with Joker, but they were missing one important characteristic: a dialed-in, badass bitch.

Breaking protocol, I was allowed to see one more dog.

Enter Jetta.

I walked up to her cage and she jumped and barked at me. Perfect.

Next was the Joker test. They sniffed each other's asses and wagged their tails. No aggression. It was a match. They walked on their leashes and roamed an open containment area. I watched her sit, lie down, and shake on command. She was the one. I signed the adoption papers, paid the adoption fee, got her vaccines, and off we went.

WHAT ABOUT A PIT STOP NOW?

I scheduled a trip to the groomer since rescue dogs have a certain kennel smell. Jetta chewed through her leash but looked happy to be clean and even happier when she saw me come to take her home.

I would soon learn of the different connections rescue dogs have with their owners versus a dog raised from puppyhood. While you can mostly mold and shape a puppy's behavior, a rescue dog is well aware you saved their life and they repay the debt with loyalty. Their baggage is considerable, but with work and love, keen rescue dogs develop a stronger bond with their owner.

Jetta slept by my feet and would not leave my side. She submitted to Joker who was vainly attempting to assert his dominance. This lasted a few weeks once Jetta grew tired of the charade. I took her to work to get her more comfortable around people and it seemed evident she was abused as she feared men. I had a rolled-up script in my hand, and once she saw it, she ran and hid, mistaking it for a newspaper. I told her she never had to worry and she seemed to understand. Oftentimes she seemingly knew what I was asking of her. Julia Ann was right, it was fulfilling to have given this dog another chance. I would reap the rewards in the form of unconditional loyalty and love.

I like to think Jamie had to leave this world to give Jetta that chance. Years later, other dogs would enjoy a life of happiness and paradise at *LaginaLand*. The

German Shepherd Rescue of Las Vegas needed foster homes for their senior dogs. I would one day pay a dog's adoption fee for one of my workers and another one would find their family dog there. With one life lost, four more were given another chance.

Dogs will always be my passion. Every month I donate to the Humane Society to do my small part to advance their noble mission. One day, when this is all over and I have left this business, I hope to build a facility on my next property to rescue dogs.

Dogs are pure.

A dog's life span is tragic and bittersweet. I will be able to save, raise, and love several of these magnificent creatures. This keeps me going most of the time.

I vowed to never subject my dogs to this kind of negative energy in a relationship again.

Now, I needed to inform my family Bliss was not my daughter and the engagement was off.

Vic Lagina's School of Porn

Lesson Five: Hygiene

"Busted toenails equals busted pussy."

- PHOENIX MARIE

If there ever was a topic I am passionate about, it's hygiene.

I learned early on women appreciate fresh breath, clean teeth, and clean-smelling man parts. A healthy dose of man-scaping also goes a long way.

Well ladies, guess what? Men also appreciate these things, despite being animalistic savages.

Wherever you fall on the bush vs. shaved spectrum, we all can agree there are certain parts where less is appreciated. If I had a vagina, there is no way in hell I would let anybody sniff around it unless it was manicured and properly pH-balanced.

Especially if I had a porn pussy!

You would be surprised how many of your favorite porn stars are harboring rotten crotch. In one's professional life, it is possible for a director/producer to distance themselves from stank puss. In one's personal life, it is not so easy and is deeply disappointing. Nothing is worse than building up an attraction, finally closing the deal, and being smacked in the face with the dreaded stench.

Sometimes during sign-out, male talent would tell me about hygiene issues with the female talent. I would relay their feedback in my notes to the head office depending on the severity and frequency of the issue.

Fuck the lawyers, publish the list for humanity's sake!

One particular contract performer's vagina had a notorious reputation for being overtly toxic. After a boy/girl/girl scene, my entire soundstage smelled like a putrid infection. I felt bad for our male performer Jordi, the little Spanish 'kid' who looked like he was fifteen (but really twenty-three).

He had to endure her squatting on his face while giving him what looked and sounded like a toothy, violent blowjob. The other performer said she could still smell rancid box all over the clothing inside her suitcase when she unpacked.

I shared the horror with my superiors in hopes they would tactfully broach the subject with her, but they never did. Because really, how do you tell a woman her pussy stinks? No seriously, I am asking. Despite twenty years in the business, I never could figure out how to tell a performer or sex worker she has a cesspool between her legs. What can I say, I'm a gentleman. Plus, I didn't want to upset them before their scene.

After all these years, I still have so many questions:

How can you be so oblivious your vagina is a sewer?

Seriously, you can't smell it?

Do you have immunity to the stench? If so, share the immunity with the rest of us.

TRANSLATION: FIX YOUR PUSSY FOR FUCK'S SAKE! REPEAT CUSTOMERS ARE THE CORNERSTONE OF ANY SUCCESSFUL BUSINESS!

I learned to pick up signals from male talent when it came to choreographing a scene during the hardcore stills. A quick shake of the head meant, "Please, Vic, don't make me go down there!" Some got satisfaction in taking their dicks out of a stinky pussy and shoving it into the mouth of the host as if to rub their nose in it.

GIVE 'EM A LITTLE SCIENCE, DR. LAGINA.

Vaginosis, vaginitis, and STDs are the most common reasons for an odiferous vagina. When the good bacteria (*Lactobacillus*) of the vagina are outnumbered by the bad bacteria (anaerobes), the balance is upset and results in vaginosis.

There are Catch-22s in the delicate dance of vaginal hygiene, especially in porn. Take douching for example, which most talent does before each scene. Cleaning the vagina via douche makes one temporarily clean, but upsets the balance in the long run.

Having multiple sex partners is also a cause. Furthermore, an STD caused by a microscopic parasite, *Trichomonas vaginalis*, can also cause a foul odor. The talent testing panel tests for this. Ironically, antibiotics, used to treat STDs also cause a disruption of vaginal harmony. If a performer habitually does creampie scenes (or is in a relationship where her partner ejaculates inside her often) there is sometimes a different smell at play: aged semen. So, what is the answer?

WE DEMAND ANSWERS!

Finding balance within the vagina. Natural remedies. Clean living. A diet consisting of prebiotics and probiotics is helpful. But please, find a solid gynecologist and nutritionist if you care to keep your vagina free and welcoming.

And now, a word from Dr. Lagina:

Licensed sex therapists and adult industry veterans recommend boric acid to combat pussy funk. Placing boric acid powder into a capsule and inserting into the vagina as a suppository will remedy the issue within forty-eight hours. Do NOT eat the boric acid as it will kill you.

Ladies, we're all in this together. Poor choices have left me scarred by many sexual encounters. One would think a *Penthouse* Pet would smell better than a Ft. Lauderdale nightclub skank. However, both women, separated by occurrences decades apart, smelled exactly the same: like swamp muck. The following story will put an exclamation point on the topic.

The experience made me consider a life of celibacy, or at the very least, putting my dick on ice for a while.

Any sexual encounter beginning with her saying, "I wouldn't go down there because it's kinda smelly from my period," is a suggestion you should take.

NOT OUR HERO, NOPE, NOT THIS FUCKING GUY.

I would have been happy to engage in other sex acts excluding her stanky twat, but when she said, "Eh, fuck it," it was time to get filthy. Mind you, I have had sex with several women on their period.

In a perverse way, it's like earning your stripes. 'Red Wings' as they are formally known. There have been times when it looked like I slaughtered a buffalo and had bloody war paint all over my torso. Sometimes it was so severe, there were chunks of sloughed-off uterine wall mixed in. (The author would like to commend his team of editors, one of whom foolishly ate lunch immediately prior to reviewing this chapter.) At its worst, the copper/metallic blood smell would singe my nose hairs.

Until this woman.

Very much like the *Penthouse* Pet before her (I'll get to *her* later), as soon as I entered, the odor became unbearable. What to do then? What's the playbook? Leaning all the way forward and smelling either her hair or the pillow is my move. This usually sustains me long enough to climax fast, pull out all over her torso, and run to the bathroom for immediate decontamination. When this didn't work with Ms. Fuck It, I put her in doggie style to save my wood, but the putridity rose into my nostrils and my erection waned into the ether.

"Did you cum inside me?"

Reasonable question, given the circumstantial evidence of a flaccid penis.

"Uh no, I just need to rest on my back a little bit."

"Are you sure you didn't cum inside me?"

NO, YOU FILTHY SKANK. YOUR PUSSY IS RANCID. IT'S WOOD KILLER.

"I swear to God I did not cum inside you."

LET OZ TAKE THE WHEEL HERE, BUDDY.

I laid on my back and she fellated me.

HOW DOES YOUR STINKY PUSSY TASTE? BAD GIRL. BAD GIRL!

This crafty logistical change had her vagina facing away from me, enabling me to get hard again. After a few minutes of concentration, we had liftoff in the form of a mouthful. I ran to the sink, washed profusely, then urinated.

GOT ANY SCALDING HOT BLEACH?

Sleeping alongside her after was super awkward as I pondered what type of savage human could be unaware of the revolting stench. She was twenty-five and pretty. What a shame. I tested shortly thereafter and got a clean bill of health. The point is, she should have known better. She knew it was smelly. Hang up an out-of-order sign across your vagina. Now, all I can smell when I see her name, her tweets, or her photos, is her stanky vagina.

"If I had a major film director like Vic Lagina on set, I'd like to smell nice for the guy and respect him."

- HOWARD STERN, 20TH FEBRUARY 2023

Exactly, Howard. Please ladies, find balance within your vagina.

Whatever the fuck you do with your lives, don't be known as the chick with the stinky pussy.

I said I was passionate about this! Where's the Tylenol?

16 THE BEAST IS OUT OF HIS CAGE

I find it funny to hear people's true opinions about your partner once you have broken up.

"Broken," "immature," "insecure," "jealous," and "pathological liar" were labels my family and friends gave Meridiana, all of which I could not argue with.

She told my parents I worked for the CIA and they already felt manipulated. This cover story was meant for others, not them.

I took my family out to dinner to break the news. All were relieved to learn I was disengaged. They admitted they had sincere doubts the union would last. They went light on me because I was still hurting over Jamie.

Silence ensued during the tale of the fabricated paternity test. I explained how one lie snowballed into the sequence of more lies, how we justified everything for Bliss's well-being, and the entire situation spun out of control. It was humiliating and humbling. I apologized and swore I would never allow my relationships to hurt them again. It was a huge burden to shed. I have lived up to the promise.

LOOK AT YOU, DUDE. GROWTH.

"I never thought she was your daughter," was my father's response. "I studied her picture after you told us and I could not see the resemblance."

Fair enough.

"I am proud of you for being willing to step up and be a father to this child because her mother is a huge fucking mess. But you are better off."

My brother took the news with his usual even-keeled demeanor and tried to understand. His wife's eyes held anger and disappointment, but she held back verbalizing her undiluted thoughts. She was concerned for her children, who were led to believe they had a cousin. Now she would have to explain away their crazy uncle's shenanigans and lifestyle.

Kids are resilient and within six months, the kids (now three of them) made no further mention of Bliss. My oldest niece loves to call me out on all my horrible choices. I only hope she applies such keen wisdom to her own life as it progresses.

Despite my being excited to be a father at the time, I found positives in the miscarriages. Despite the insanity, one thing was crystal clear: the universe was looking out for me and I needed to acknowledge it.

PRETTY SURE THE UNIVERSE WAS MERELY STOPPING THE BIRTH OF THE ANTICHRIST.

About a year prior, my brother surprised with me a phone call asking for "Vic Lagina." He had cracked the code. Despite being meticulous in covering my tracks, the internet is a powerful tool. All it takes is to uncover the right rock to expose the secret. My brother searched an old phone number of mine tied to a webpage Reed created when I was selling his content. From there, he looked up "Vic Lagina" and the rest was easy to piece together.

He understood my discretion and said he was proud of me because he was well aware of how big of an empire I helped create. I asked him to keep it quiet, but over time, the information leaked out bit by bit.

My father also cracked the code around the time I ended things with Meridiana. He read about Brazzers, about my fandom on the forum, and understood his son was a massive porn success. There were no longer any secrets in my life and I was ready for my fresh start.

HEY DUDE, WE'VE NEVER DISCUSSED HOW DAD ENDED UP IN THOSE CHAT ROOMS.

Before I headed back to Las Vegas, I attended a Phillies game with a porn star who was fucking one of the players. He hooked her up with club seats behind home plate. In the top of the eighth, Dan Uggla of the Marlins popped a foul and I caught it. I had been to several baseball games in my life, but a foul ball never landed in my vicinity.

Indeed, times were a changing and I was looking forward to what lay ahead. I didn't know it would be a different kind of crazy.

Back in Vegas, word got out I was single. When you are in a committed relationship, it seems as if girls view this as a sick type of challenge. I had been accused of cheating throughout the entire two-and-a-half-year relationship and the beast within was ready to hunt.

FINALLY, A LITTLE FUN. ABOUT. FUCKING. TIME.

The first girl was a tall, hot blonde who had been in the business for a few years. There had been sexual tension building since the first time I shot her in 2008 at the Gilespie House. A few years later she stood in my studio office and stared at me, her huge triple D's popping out of her top. The visual stayed with me while I had sex with Meridiana.

She was to stay over at my house after a shoot. Nothing about it was natural or organic. It was like, "Finally, here we are! What do we do now?" There was not much in the conversation department. I wanted to fire up the jacuzzi, but there was a lot of dirt and leaves from a windstorm.

I had a bag of mushrooms. It seemed like a great idea to try them, but she was uninterested. I popped a few caps and stems down my guzzle and off I went.

SEE WHY I BECAME NECESSARY? I WOULD'VE TOLD HIM TO PUT THOSE MUSHROOMS AWAY AND OPEN UP A BOTTLE OF WINE. SEE IF SHE WANTS TO TAKE A SHOWER. EVEN BETTER, FIRE UP THE INDOOR JACUZZI. THEN, GET YOUR FIRST NUT OUT QUICKLY SINCE YOU'RE SO DAMN TRIGGER-HAPPY. THEN FUCK HER ALL NIGHT AND GIVE THIS WOMAN MULTIPLE ORGASMS WITH YOUR MOUTH. DAMNIT, MAN! MAKE HER A REPEAT CUSTOMER!

Performing sexually while on drugs never had been an issue and it wasn't the case with Ms. Triple D. The issue was she was transforming into a blonde, doe-eyed giant before my eyes with two bouncy, fleshy balloons on her chest. I was fucking the equivalent of a character who could appear in the porn version of *Lord of the Rings*. I needed help from the fellowship to bring down this beast. Laughing would have been the kiss of death. I couldn't do much except hang on for the short ride.

I had her sleep in another room. The gesture was meant to give her space. I did this to a lot of women over the years because they didn't need to lie with a snoring, farting man while they tried to sleep. I did not consider they may have wanted to.

On the way to McCarran the next morning we filled up the short ride with small talk. I shot her a few times after, but her demeanor was different and aloof. I think about her from time to time and laugh at myself for being such an awkward fucktard. There would be oodles more.

Despite the deep recession, work remained plentiful. Our good fortune should have kept everyone happy, but, rest assured, my crew bitched and moaned. My two-year contract expired and The Senator negotiated a one-year extension. Our scene count remained at twenty-five, but the company got wise and mandated I direct no less than eight scenes a month. Huggy and the Ginger Giant would pick up the remaining scenes and there was no signing bonus or raise.

The Brazzers also wanted to half my rate on scenes exceeding the twenty-five minimum. I was comfortable signing the deal that would get me through year two of the three-year warehouse lease. Perhaps he had contract envy, or maybe because his girlfriend was pregnant, but now Huggy wanted a contract.

The company was not interested in giving him one, because they didn't trust him and preferred he remain under my supervision. They'd received reports from people who met and worked with him: Kyle, Butler, Blake, Chad, Robbie. The consensus: Huggy was an asshole.

DING! DING! DING!

We met for dinner and he was visibly frustrated there were no guarantees. He felt the office was disrespecting him. I pressed hard with the positives: I had kept him busy the past two years, promised him at least thirteen scenes per month, and he wouldn't have to deal with the head office. He had no choice but to accept my terms. I even promised ample notice if the volume needed to drop. It was a promise I kept until we parted four years later. Still, he was scheming for any kind of leverage.

I had eliminated my second mortgage and was hammering down my primary. The house next door remained vacant after the departure by Blake, Bramm, Morty, and Hailey, something my racist neighbor must have been beaming about. Then it went into foreclosure. It was underwater when a family bought it from the bank. My property value was in the red as well. Fortunately, money was flowing in.

During his last visit to Canada, Butler was denied re-entry to the United States. The last of the Canadian dominoes had fallen and I needed to find another photographer. This started the carousel of fucked-up individuals who would pass in and out of my operation. I hired the husband of a local performer who moonlighted as a collector for the casinos and he became quite an asset, later informing me about Huggy's back-dealing ways.

AHHH, MIKE. I LOVE THAT PERVERT. I'VE NEVER MET SOMEONE SO FOND OF LITTLE PEOPLE.

Blake had a production assistant who defected from the dysfunctional Miami crew and wanted a job. At Moe's request, I hired him even though I had enough hands. He worked out fine for the first few months, but soon despised doing the "n***** work" (his words). There were also stories of after-hour altercations with female talent. When he asked for a twenty-five percent raise, he found his exit.

Moe's time in the business had started to show its wear and he was losing focus.

During a location shoot for *MilfsLikeItBlack.com*, which I had delegated to Huggy, the performer, who was Bramm's first sexual conquest in the business, was having a difficult time fitting the male talent's thick girth in her anus. She asked for someone to help loosen her up and Moe stepped up. Had I been on location, I would have advised against it, but I was back at the studio directing. The damage was done and Moe was hooked. After a five-week romance, she proposed, he said yes, and off to the courthouse they went.

The following day, word spread like wildfire and I saw the ring on his finger. We all relayed our concerns.

He knew he made a mistake, but didn't care. His desires were fulfilled with a porn star with no limits on the sex acts she would perform on camera. What could possibly go wrong?

YOU WOULD KNOW.

I understood loneliness in the business, so I focused on keeping my crew from their infighting, enjoying my sexual conquests, and partying.

I was tasked with shooting Brazzers' first live show. The first one was an expensive mess, costing well north of thirty-five grand. Everybody wanted their say. Corporate stressed everyone out with their last-minute changes.

I hired my neighbor to build a permanent stage in one of our shooting rooms, which held a five-thousand-dollar jacuzzi. Two hours before show time, they had us revamp the set. Despite all the insanity leading up to the start time, the show went off without a hitch and I delivered what would be the first of several monthly live shows which would cover all of their eventual brands.

There was a one-year gap between the first and second shows because they were trying to figure out how to monetize them, which they never did. Members loved the shows and the experience allowed them to interact with their favorite porn stars. This kept the shows alive for the next several years.

After the second show, Mansef stepped back and allowed me to do my job. I was the mad conductor of the train wreck live porn show experience. After each show, I held house parties with my crew and talent.

Cocaine entered into my Vegas life. The first gram would start a purchasing pattern of more grams, then eight-balls, and ultimately ounces.

COCAINE'S A HELLUVA DRUG.

Fourth of July, I was invited to a pool party hosted by Lisa Ann and Nikki Benz at Mandalay Bay. I was still playing with ecstasy and hallucinogens, so I brought my Jazz Fest leftovers: LSD, mushrooms, and a pressed pill. I popped the ecstasy before heading down to the pool for what I thought would be a fun day of partying.

I never attended casino pool parties because I had my own pool with its own set of rules. I had no idea security searched your bag, something I would have accounted for had we not been granted immediate entry. Instead of making a last-minute bathroom excuse, I allowed them to search my bag thinking they would not find my hallucinogens. I was wrong and they confiscated them. It seemed they were going to let me off with a warning and allow me to accompany the party hosts to their section. The elevator doors opened and two large security guards escorted me to the casino jail, a room with a lot of CCTV screens.

They sat me down, took my ID, and asked me if I had anything else. Given I had ingested what they didn't find, I denied it and their search came up empty. They ran my ID and saw an upstanding member of society. They let me go and said if I ever brought drugs to their pool or casino again, I would be arrested. When I made it to my house, the ecstasy kicked in. Limitless energy in need of an outlet.

LANDSCAPING MADE PERFECT SENSE.

My cleaners no longer landscaped my house after Meridiana and her money left. My grounds were looking unkempt, so I sawed the palm fronds on the trees in my front hard. Then, I shifted my attention to the backyard. Despite the desert heat, I was unstoppable until after a few swings of a pick axe at a rogue palm tree, my heart felt ready to explode. I took a knee before grabbing a twenty-foot ladder and sawing the palm fronds on the taller trees. When all was said and done, my property looked beautifully manicured. This would now be my method of problem-solving: do drugs, landscape, and find the solution.

Not long after Moe's marriage to the porn star, things unraveled. She spent long periods in LA getting violated in all of her orifices on camera.

Moe was feeling her absence. He needed companionship. They had flirted with getting their marriage annulled but endured another few months before she had enough of his neediness. When she left, Moe spun out.

He did not show up for work or say he was taking time away. Instead, he told Pete who relayed the message. This would have been grounds for termination, but not in my world. Where many employers would fire an employee who wasn't working out, I tried to help them first. Moe's case was no different.

Moe went on a pill bender and when he finally answered my call, I had a long and compassionate conversation with him. I understood his need for companionship and suggested he get a dog instead. I offered to pay the adoption fee and urged him to visit the German Shepherd Rescue of Las Vegas. A few days later, I handed him two hundred dollars and he returned with his new girl, Shady, seeming like a new man. I thought this would fix Moe's problem, but his were greater than a dog could solve and his clock was ticking.

It was around this time my conquests led me to a six-month fling with a single mother named Mason. Another reminder relationships with porn stars were futile.

Mansef ownership was also about to change.

IN MEMORIUM:

Jessica Jaymes, 3/8/79 - 9/17/19

I first shot Jessica in 2009, shortly after moving into the studio. She operated without an agent, so I booked her directly and she was a true professional. Jessica was beautiful, even though she was on the skinny/borderline unhealthy side.

NO MEAT ON THAT ASS. HER COCCYX WAS APPARENT IN DOGGIE STYLE.

She was cool, personable, funny, and a hell of a performer.

She was married and confined by the off-camera rules which bound a lot of married performers. I was engaged to Meridiana and practiced monogamy, so I respected the rules, even if I didn't fully understand them. Once I was single, I sat on a couch with her on the floor of the convention at AVN. We talked about getting to know each other and I got the sense her marriage was on the rocks.

HE ALSO GOT THE SENSE SHE WANTED TO TRY OUT HIS JOHNSON.

A few months later, we had drinks before heading back to my place. The Philadelphia Flyers were making a strong push in the postseason, going as far as the Stanley Cup Finals. Of course, they lost... again.

We had sex a few times during the game and I was a bit taken aback when she *demanded* a facial. This was a finishing move saved for porn, but I acquiesced and we made plans to hang out in the future. She even discussed bringing a friend next time. Being single in porn was turning out to be amazing. Or was it?

YES, IT WAS AMAZING, YOU PUSSY.

The next time Jessica and I hung out was after we shot *Fuck Hard: The Dewey Cocks Story*. This parody came to life when the powers allowed us one 'gimme' shoot each month. In an effort to keep their directors happy, Yancee and Frank allowed us to shoot a concept of our creation. Sometimes I took things in odd directions. See *The Adventures of Wonder Pussy* (with Molly Bennett and Ramón) and an unreleased scene I shot with Angelina Valentine (I'll get to that in a bit).

James Deen was Dewey Cocks, a rock star who fucked a few groupies (Jessica and her performer friend Tiffany) before kicking them out and trashing the hotel room we built at the studio. Deen lit the bed on fire before smashing a tube television and everything else in the room. A reporter was on set doing an expose on Deen which later appeared in *GQ*.[1]

Jessica, Tiffany, and I spent the night in their room at the Luxor. Then things got weird. We had a bunch of drinks and were all either buzzed or drunk. The ladies had an early flight the next morning, so I assumed it wasn't going to be a late night. I was wrong.

In round one, Jessica and Tiffany took turns with me. Jessica was dictatorial and told Tiffany what to do, like how and when to suck my dick. I wasn't sure if Tiffany was into it, which made me uncomfortable.

As the night progressed all Tiffany wanted to do was sleep, which Jessica forbade. She wanted to fuck all night. Jessica was demanding of me, barking orders. She instructed me on how to eat her pussy and how to fuck her. I was a bear caught in a trap and wanted to chew my arm off to escape. Eventually, Tiffany left the room to find somewhere to sleep for a few hours. I escaped soon after. This was the last time Jessica and I hung out, but I did shoot her again. Her last shoot for me was in 2015, before I moved into my second studio.

Like most performers who take a hiatus, I assumed I would see her again. On September 17, 2019, Jessica died at forty. According to the complete County of Los Angeles Department of Medical Examiner-Coroner autopsy, Jessica "had a history of depression, suicidal ideations, and suicide attempts by prescription medication and cutting wrists."

I recalled seeing scars on her wrists and forearms, but it was common to see a cutter from time to time. The coroner investigator, James Cronin, claimed she last attempted suicide in April of 2019 after she cut her wrists, overdosed on Ambien, and left a suicide note. He added she had been hospitalized on an involuntary hold three times in the past. On September 17, 2019, her estranged husband reached out for a wellness check after not hearing from her for six days.

Jessica was found kneeling on her den floor with her head on the couch, wearing a blue robe. Prescription medication bottles and loose pills were found in the bathroom and the investigator noted "in addition to chronic alcohol abuse, she had a history of prescription and medication abuse." The cause of death was listed as 'alcohol abuse and seizure.' She liked to drink, but I had no idea the amount of pain she was in her last several years.

17 RISE OF THE EVIL EMPIRE

Frank called and told me I had to entertain an important individual who was coming to visit the Vegas operation and to be "friendly." Something big was happening.

WE ARE A-L-W-A-Y-S FRIENDLY… DICKHEAD.

Word spread Mansef was the company behind PornHub, where people could view content online for free. The tube site model relied on users to upload content, which meant the site owner did not infringe on copyright. However, the Digital Millennium Copyright Act allowed copyright owners to inform infringing tube sites if their content was being viewed illegally for free. The tube site would then be obligated to remove the content. Constantly eyeballing tube sites was necessary, but smaller companies losing money could not afford to hire someone to do so.

The company I helped create, along with its mostly positive reputation, was no more.

Mansef had developed into an evil corporation people despised. Top performers, like Gianna Michaels whom I shot in 2006 and 2007, were vocal in calling them out. Those making money from Mansef had no moral conflict in cashing their checks. I was in this category, but my job became more difficult. The stalling economy forced a lot of performers to quell their discontent and take money wherever they could. It did not stop them from telling me their true opinion between scenes. Meanwhile, the traffic from PornHub was creating unprecedented growth for a tiny start-up consisting of fraternity brazzers.

Salam had told me Ouissam and the other owners were getting intimidated by a presence in Montreal. They lived close to one another and large black SUV's constantly trolled their neighborhood. So they hired security guards. Most of them were now married and having children. With everything happening, they were ready to cash out and take their fuck you money.

Fabian Thylmann started computer programming when he was seventeen. In the late 1990s, he developed software called NATS (Next-Generation Affiliate

Tracking Software) which enabled website operators to track users' clicks on advertisements and links and get paid a commission. With the money he made with NATS, he was buying Mansef for a rumored forty million.

The man who sat in my office on this rainy day looked like a software developer. I gave him the tour and answered his questions. Frank told me prior to his arrival he was interested in buying the company and was doing his due diligence. I found it reaffirming Fabian was sent to my facility above all others and took it as a sign we were the crown jewel.

HEAR THAT, BRANDO? WHO WAS THE CROWN JEWEL? NOT YOU!

Fabian had big plans including more live shows. After the meeting, I felt very comfortable about my job security. I wasn't wrong, but the company was heading into darker territory.

The first time I shot Mason, I had to do a double-take because it was rare to see a girl in porn with a naturally pretty face. A lot of girls looked like hell coming off the airplane and needed a good two hours in the makeup chair before they became presentable. Not Mason. We had just wrapped a live show and now had to shoot her scene at night.

The IT director in town to run the live show was having his birthday and the bosses wanted us to take him and all the performers out for dinner. It was hard to keep my eyes off her. Later on, she told me she couldn't look up because she felt my stare and was intimidated. The next time I shot her we went out to dinner after. Having a few hours to kill before her flight, we went back to my place and fucked.

BUY THEM DINNER. ACT LIKE A GENTLEMAN. IT GIVES US TIME TO PULL THE RIPCORD IF WE SENSE ANY FUNNY STUFF.

Mason was thin with bolt-ons. Bodily, she had no limits and was game for anything. When a girl gives you a blank check to do whatever you want to her body, it's intimidating if you're not a sadist. Mason was a bonafide masochist and her shoots up until this point were mostly for *Kink.com* and its special brand of BDSM porn.

Being tied up, gagged, and submitting was a normal day of work for her. After our initial fuck, we made plans for a long weekend and I flew her out.

She also liked cocaine. Our weekends were cocaine-fueled fuck romps where we both drew blood, mine in the form of claw marks on my back and hers vaginally. She was happy about this since it meant we did it right. She was carefree, easygoing, and the sex was intense.

We were heading back to my house after a night of clubbing when she mentioned something about an eight-year-old daughter and babbled on.

"Wait, did you say 'your daughter?'"

"Yeah, why?"

"Oh, I had no idea you had one."

"Oh, I thought I told you."

No, you didn't.

No matter. She was enjoying herself and wasn't expecting things to progress. Neither did I. Her casual mention of her daughter was to gauge whether I'd have a strong reaction, which I didn't. She was a weekend fuck. After a few more weekends, this began to change.

HERE WE GO AGAIN. GODDAMMIT, DUDE! YOU'RE FUCKING THIS UP!

In October 2010, the industry shut down for a few weeks when a female performer tested positive for HIV. Industry protocol was to order a mandatory shutdown and everyone was expected to cease production. Patient zero would then be retested while it was determined whom they had sex with both on and off camera.

If they were positive, anyone they performed with would be quarantined and tested for HIV. If any of them tested positive, the shutdown would remain in effect until the next generation who performed with the first generation were tested. Fortunately, in this case, (unlike in 2004 when the same thing resulted in an almost six-week shutdown), no one within the first generation tested positive.

Turned out the transmission occurred off-set as the performer's boyfriend was positive. He was a performer in the gay industry and a gay escort. This was more kindling for the hotly-contested debate about using performers who crossed over from the gay side into straight porn. It was also the start of a long process to revamp the industry standard for talent testing.

Most importantly, it was the official start of the AIDS Healthcare Foundation's movement to make condom use mandatory in porn in California. There had been a mostly silent and unsuccessful movement, but this HIV-positive case was its lightning rod. Most of the industry and performers did not want to use condoms.

"My body, my choice," was their mantra.

I PREFER: IF IT AIN'T SKIN, I DON'T GO IN.

A condom interfered with the wood of almost every male performer I used. Female performers said they burned and were uncomfortable. My earliest shoots in Miami included condoms, but when I entered the big leagues no one requested them. *Wicked.com,* which would eventually fall under Fabian's control, used condoms.

Unless a starlet was a top seller who mandated condom use, I was instructed to avoid these performers because members complained. It ruined their fantasy. While the AIDS Healthcare Foundation made gains over the years, its mandates were mostly ignored. Especially in Las Vegas.

Two years into his contract, Keiran Lee had evolved into a massive diva. His ego was fed by his popularity in the Brazzers Member's Area and his LA lifestyle. He bragged about his friendship with Vinnie Jones and the parties he attended with Jason Statham. He got engaged to Puma Swede. He met her on one of my sets and this was his first attempt to secure a green card.

Puma was Finnish...

HENCE HER NAME MAKING NO SENSE

... and although she had citizenship, he would not be able to get his by marrying her. Undeterred, he conjured up a marriage to another performer, in a ceremony where I was the best man. I signed the certificate "Vic Lagina" because I did not want to be legally on the record for whatever this was.

His contract stipulated he was to shoot nineteen scenes a month and I was forced to split his scenes with other producers. He developed rifts with Brando, director Tony T, Blake's crew, and ours was spawning.

The analogy for Keiran is if I were a teacher and he was my student, he would force me to spend half my time on his needs. He insisted he stay at Palms Place, a sixty-minute round trip drive from my studio, diminishing me of a much-needed set of hands. If we finished the day early and his flight was due to leave three hours later, he would insist I change it, which would cost the company money.

Agreeing with him was easier than arguing with him. Eventually, he would undermine me and weasel his way into a scene slated for someone else. Why? He wanted to fuck her.

"Every hole is a goal," was his philosophy.

COULDN'T HAVE SAID IT BETTER MYSELF. I LIKE THIS KEIRAN TWAT.

If I told him no, he would complain to Yancee. If Yancee said no, he would go to Frank. His batting average was about .500, but his chances of raising my blood pressure were 1.000. Keiran was a nonstop pain in the ass. Yet, he was a true cocksman. Regardless, he was making my life hell and worked on Frank and Fabian to allow him to produce scenes on his own.

My friends were in town for Widespread Panic and I had an extra ticket. I had just shot Mason and she was game for staying the weekend. The first night, my friend Peppers looked down the hallway to my bedroom door to verify the shrieks and screams were sex sounds and not a grisly murder.

Mason was honored our sexcapades kept my buddies awake. After the weekend, Mason admitted she was crushing and we discussed taking things to the next level. Given she lived in California and was also fucking for money on camera presented us with a slew of challenges. I was trying not to take any of it seriously.

TRANSLATION: I KEPT HIM IN LINE.

I liked her, but never thought of her as a practical option. She had all the hallmarks of a broken person: a father she didn't know, an estranged mother, and a baby daddy in jail. We were on a timeline, so instead of putting pressure on anything, I wanted to enjoy her for as long as I could.

The company, which Fabian rebranded to Manwin, was becoming critical of our content, particularly our photos. With Butler gone, the rotation of photographers was not cutting it. I needed someone experienced.

Keiran referred a man named Toad and I now believe this was an act of sabotage. Toad had worked for a lot of different companies in LA, but when pressed as to why he left, the reasons he gave were very vague. He would last about a year before imploding.

We were entering the holiday season, our busiest time of the year. I had to produce a month of scenes in two weeks before shutting down for Christmas and New Year's. We were shooting five days a week, two scenes per day. I needed all hands on deck and the Ginger Giant, who was a production assistant and occasional director, was slipping. His drinking worsened and he was showing up to work drunk.

At the beginning of the month, I gave my crew the usual pep talk. The next day, the Ginger Giant was having difficulty building his set because he was drunk.

Moe and Pete were looking at me for answers, but firing him was only going to make our lives harder. We needed to suck it up for another few weeks and have an honest conversation about his future over break.

When he lost our female talent the morning after they were drinking together, I had no choice but to fire him. She resurfaced a few hours later, hungover. I assumed his directing responsibilities and got the job done. Now also down a production assistant, I hired a husband-and-wife team, performers who had been working as talent agents for Lisa Ann. Lexi handled wardrobe and Ethan would be a PA under Moe and Pete.

We made the quota.

I rented a house in California for a week for New Year's Eve, drove up with Joker and Jetta, and planned on snowboarding the entire time. Mason surprised me with a one-night visit before returning a few days later to ring in 2011 with her sister and friends. During the trip, Meridiana called while I was on a ski lift. Her voice was erratic and she claimed to know about my businesses and said trouble was coming. I asked her to clarify and she gave cryptic answers.

I told her to call my Vegas lawyer. By the time I got to the top of the mountain, he was calling me trying to make sense of it all. He told me to enjoy my vacation since he thought it was nothing to worry about. When I got to the bottom I called her lawyer and got non-disclosing lawyer speak.

Then I asked him to relay one simple message: leave me the fuck alone!

He said he would do his best. When I got back to my rental house, she called again. I went into a Hulk rage and told her I was glad she miscarried and I no longer had ties to a horrible person.

BRUTAL, BUT EFFECTIVE.

Blake called as I was driving back to Vegas. With AVN approaching he wanted to meet up to discuss Meridiana. He informed me of her visit a few months back and suspected she was on drugs. Blake was now married and had a second child with his baby mama. After Meridiana fell out with a friend she was visiting, she had nowhere to stay and imposed herself at Blake's condominium. He said she was talking about sex openly and speaking in tongues.

WITCHCRAFT!

No longer wanting to expose his wife and children to this, Blake kicked her out. She crashed with Bramm. I asked Bramm if he fucked her and he denied it. I wish he had because when I was with her, she talked about how much of a dork he was and how he had no game. I'd be happy to be his Eskimo brother.

I had never attended the Adult Video Network Awards. A silly show where people in my business were rewarded for sex. They made absurd speeches thanking people for their ability to take dick. I had won an AVN in 2008, but not personally. Brazzers never gave me directing credit, but a DVD with all scenes directed by me won 'Best Big Boob-Themed DVD'. Go me. This year, Frank had an extra ticket and asked me to go. I was interested in the Brazzers After Party at Vanity in the Hard Rock, so I accepted.

Lisa Lampinelli was hosting the show and I loved her brand of mean humor. I was hopeful she would justifiably ridicule the industry, but no dice. Lisa was unfunny and boring. Watching the two porn star hosts read the teleprompter and missing the timing of the jokes was excruciating. Listening to porn stars blather during their prolonged acceptance speeches, trying to be funny or introspective, sent us all over the edge, and off we went to Vanity.

The afterparty was a crowded mess and although I got into the VIP section, many of my crew did not. My drug dealer weaseled into the section and Moe would later lament, "Vic had no problem getting his drug dealer into VIP but not his crew." His animosity toward me had begun. Meridiana, unbeknownst to me, was staying with Moe, fueling his contempt.

Now she was on my doorstep. It all started with her texting me in the morning, no longer upset by my miscarriage barb. She needed marijuana and to pick up a chess set I had bought for her.

I didn't have her chess set and I was not going to give her any weed.

She said she was on her way in a cab and I thought she was joking. Michael Vick had just thrown an interception to end the Eagles' playoff run and I was livid. When my doorbell rang, I saw red. I watched her through the door window. Her hair was greasy and partially dyed pink. She looked like she had been up for days. When I told her to get the fuck off my porch, she stared at me. I told her I was calling the cops and she got back in the cab. She texted saying calling the cops was unnecessary. She would leave me alone. If only it were so easy.

It was the last time I would physically see her, but her insanity continued through the next decade.

THIS MAN HAD MORE FRUITCAKES THAN A BAKERY.

18 THE SQUEEZE

Somewhere along the way, Moe almost cut off his hand with a circular saw. I was sitting in my office when I heard it:

"Ow! Oh shit. Oh shit. Oh fuck. Oh fuck," as he ran to the bathroom. I ran toward the door when I saw a trail of blood on the carpet. In the movies, when a character follows a trail of blood, it leads to a corpse. In this case, it was Moe, on his knees with bloody paper towels pressed on the area between his hand and wrist.

"I sliced my wrist with the circular saw."

Instead of asking him why, I told him I needed to see it to determine the damage. Blood never bothered me. One of the coolest things my ex-girlfriend Doctor Blow ever did was tell her chief surgeon I was a resident who had to sit through a veteran's hernia surgery. I was fascinated by how easy it was for a non-qualified individual to make his way into a major hospital's operating room. I watched this crusty vet get cut open with his intestines meshed into his muscle lining. When Moe took off his bandage, I saw bone and muscle.

"Pete. Call 911 and have them send an ambulance."

Pete was the polar opposite. He was turning colors.

"Pete. Keep it together. Don't look at the blood."

After Pete placed the call, Moe got lightheaded, so we each put one of his arms around our shoulders and helped him to a couch to wait for the paramedics.

"May I take a look at it?" one paramedic asked. Although it sounded like a line in one of my movies, he was asking about Moe's wrist. As Moe was about to move the towel:

"Wait. It's not spurting is it?"

Moe shook his head.

"Okay. Let's have a look. Oh yeah. We have to rush you to the hospital. But by the looks of it, you got very lucky and did not sever any veins or ligaments." This caused Pete to gag.

They rolled in a gurney, threw an IV into Moe's arm, tossed his bald ass into the ambulance, and headed to the hospital. Hiring Herschel turned out to be the one good thing resulting from Meridiana's chess game of attempting to control my career. He ran things by the book and we paid heavily for worker's comp insurance. Now we were going to need it.

We covered all the bills. Luckily, he lost no arm function and only had a scar as a reminder of the incident. I am sure he still holds me responsible. I didn't allow him to run heavy machinery for some time, which was wise because he was attempting to get a weed operation off the ground.

Las Vegas did not have dispensaries or delivery services yet, so Moe was distributing weed the traditional way. He enjoyed the product he sold. Day by day, he was caring less about his job and was more focused on other things. Huggy stirred the pot while playing nice to Moe's face.

He threw Moe under the bus in private bitching sessions in my office. I had to address Huggy's complaints directly with Moe and over time could see the burnout in his eyes. Because his subordinates did not respect his opinion or authority, he would turn into Eeeeeee-Moe, a name we called him to his face. It didn't help that my ex was staying with him, unbeknownst to me, buzzing in his ear.

After New Year's, things with Mason cooled. She was conflicted because she had feelings for me. Allegedly, this messed with her head when being fucked on camera. She said it was hard for her to act like the filthy whore she wanted to be viewed as if I was in her brain.

HONEY, GET OUT OF YOUR HEAD, YOU ARE A GREAT FILTHY WHORE.

We were in an open situation. 'Relationship' was not the proper nomenclature for whatever it was we shared. Still, being in a courtship where we both were fucking other people was something I never had experienced. It didn't take me long to figure out it wasn't for me. I told Mason I preferred our 'whatever it was' to remain between us. She didn't seem to think it was a big deal and the rumors circulated. I didn't want my nemeses knowing my business.

LATHER. RINSE. REPEAT.

Fabian was buying other porn companies at a frenzied pace. Soon, *Twistys.com*, *Wicked.com*, and *Babes.com* were under the Manwin umbrella. Manwin was the name synonymous with The Evil Empire.

Fabian was borrowing from banks left and right. With those loans, he would soon purchase Digital Playground and *Men.com,* a variety of tube sites, adult friend finders, webcam sites, and anything else he felt would be profitable. While all this was going on, we were told to cut back spending on production. My contract extension was coming up and The Senator had begun discussions with Frank, none of which seemed optimistic.

Meridiana called nonstop and was threatening litigation. Over what, I have no idea. I needed someone to run legal interference, so I turned to The Senator.

EVERYBODY HATES LAWYERS, UNTIL THEY NEED THEM.

You know who your friends are when they take time out of their civilian work day to help with your crazy ex-fiancée. Especially when they despised her in the first place and told you many times prior.

While he was listening to her rant, he texted me in real-time.

"Now she is venting. I am letting her get it all out."

"Wow. You do great work. She came in damaged, but she has left even more broken and fucked in the head than when she met you. I think I know one other guy who may have surpassed you in this department, but it's a photo finish."

"You know who I feel like right now? Remember the movie Sideways, where Paul Giamatti is running out of the house after retrieving his best friend's wallet which he left there because he was schtupping the fat waitress and her husband comes home? I feel like the Miles character. I am just making it into the car after the naked husband chases me as his schmeckle is pressed up against his car window. Thanks, buddy."

After fifteen minutes, he hung up with her and called me with the rundown.

"One thing I have learned, sometimes you get irate people at the other end of a phone call. What I like to do is sit back, be quiet, and let them let it all out. After she realized I was speaking to her as a friend and not as a legal adversary, she calmed down and we had a very pleasant conversation."

I was stunned. I let him continue.

"Basically, she is saying she is going to have a song on the radio and you are not entitled to any rights."

"Song? What song? What the fuck is she talking about?"

The Senator continued: "Listen, there is no song. But she believes there is a song. But it's not important. What is important is she believes you have no interest in this song, which I relayed to her. I told her you are not against her, you only wish the best things for her, and you want her to be happy. He needs to move on with his life. He wants to be happy as well. He has no interest in your song and is doing just fine with his business. I wished her well, I told her I was rooting for her, and if she needs me, she can call me. I, of course, will not be picking up those phone calls, but she doesn't need to know this."

"That's it?"

"That's it."

I told him he was the Crazy Whisperer and he should think about writing a book. The incident came to be known as 'Firing Meridiana.' With him being a Steelers fan, I got him an authenticated autographed Troy Polamalu jersey for his troubles.

FUCK THE STEELERS. FLY EAGLES, FLY.

Over the next decade, she tried to get in touch, leaving texts and voicemails from various phone numbers. Her methods to penetrate my fierce defenses have been creative yet ambiguous. In 2019, she was arrested twice and spent a year in prison for domestic disturbance, assaulting a police officer, and passing bad checks. Whenever she reached out, the standard operating procedure was simple.

YOU'RE BLOCKED, BITCH! BE GONE!

Mason was in Las Vegas on a mother-daughter bonding adventure. She was staying at New York-New York with her for a few days. We discussed them staying at my house later in their trip. At night, she asked if I would come by the casino for a drink. Wondering how the logistics of this would work, she explained she would leave the room after her daughter fell asleep. We would have thirty to forty-five minutes. It seemed like bad parenting, but I agreed. She told me she was entertaining the idea of becoming an escort.

"It's sort of the same thing, right?" she asked.

"No, not really." I explained porn is tested and controlled. Escorting wasn't.

"But it's a pretty fine line."

She was rationalizing, but I could not correlate how taking money and slinging your vagina to the paying public was close to having sex with a tested male performer in a safe environment. Who was I to argue? It was her business if she wanted to rent herself out to the paying public.

It was Super Bowl weekend and I agreed to have them stay at my house for the evening. She repeatedly asked if I was ok with it. After a half dozen yesses, I picked them up and brought them home. She was a nice girl with manners and a passion for video games. I had an Xbox 360, a PS3, and a Wii, so I knew how we were going to stay busy. She liked *Call of Duty*, especially killing zombies.

I took breaks to blow lines with Mason in my bathroom while she gave me a blow job then resumed playing. After a few more hours, I left her alone while I ravaged her mother's privates at her request in my bathroom. Nevertheless, it seemed like bad parenting to leave a child playing a violent video game while we went off to fuck and do cocaine.

I ONLY SPEAK UP WHEN I DISAGREE WITH OUR HERO'S DECISION-MAKING.

The following day, while her mother was making appetizers and food for the Super Bowl, we tossed a football across my pool. She was a good kid, and I thought about what it was going to be like for her in five years when her horny little schoolmates found her mom searching the internet for porn. It would be enough to destroy a child if not handled properly.

Perhaps it would take years of psychotherapy for her to unsee what she might see. What about the teasing she might have to endure? Mason's method was to avoid the issue for as long as possible. Hoping for the best is one approach. After the game, I dropped them off at the airport and planned to see her a month later at her place in California.

I had been calling and texting a memorable performer, Jackie for an entire summer after I became single. I sent her photos of me with my dogs when I was outside in my jacuzzi, but they yielded no response. Around the time I was doing rails off Mason's ass in my bathroom, Jackie texted she had moved to Vegas. Although no longer performing, she needed work as an extra. Being a humanitarian, I helped her.

She showed up on set and I watched her freeze as she saw me.

"You're Vic?" she asked.

"Yes. I met you before."

"I don't remember."

FEMALE SCOTT NAILS. THAT DUDE NEVER REMEMBERS THE OWNER OF THE VAGINA HE PENETRATES.

"You shot for me awhile back. Bramm directed, you helped us all make money by coming in last minute, so thank you."

I left it there because there was no longer a need to chase her. She wasn't going anywhere. She stopped performing because she had psoriasis and it had spread all over her body. She had gained thirty pounds and didn't feel comfortable with her body, so any extra work would be appreciated. Her positive energy around my infighting crew was welcome, so I hired her a few more times before inviting her over.

She was in the house for about a minute before I stripped and jumped into the hot tub. She clammed up, so I reassured her I didn't care about her skin or her weight. She got naked and into the water with me. Within a few minutes, we were having sex. She told me later if I had sent a better picture of myself the previous summer, we would have been fucking sooner. The timing was better now because I was about to wrap up my whathaveyou with Mason.

Mason picked me up at the airport to spend the weekend while her daughter stayed with the mother of her baby daddy whom she was close with. Every weekend, her daughter stayed with her while Mason traveled to fuck me, someone else, or for the camera.

It was an uneventful weekend with only one session of sex and one long night of cocaine abuse with some of her friends. She was distant and I felt like she needed space. Things ran out of steam. She took me to the airport with her daughter, which was the last time I saw the child. We started fighting on the phone and hung up on each other a lot. She called me arrogant.

OKAY, HOOKER.

We decided to call it quits. Soon we stopped talking.

Shortly after, I searched the internet and saw she was renting her vagina to the paying public for fifteen hundred dollars an hour.

I'M GONNA GO FIND A CASH MACHINE.

A year and a half later I shot her again and we smoothed out any weirdness.

She found a new boyfriend, stopped shooting, got married, and had a baby. A divorce and custody battle soon followed, as did her return to porn.

Frank and The Senator reached an impasse on negotiations when he wanted me to sign a one-year extension acknowledging a drop in scene count from twenty-five to nineteen. Frank explained times had changed and there wasn't enough work to go around.

There was, but Keiran Lee had effectively taken it from me. They were also trying out new directors who worked for less money. Frank tried to convince The Senator the quality of our work had diminished and he could tell which scenes from which producers were selling based on an algorithm.

BULLSHIT. FUCK YOU, FRANK. AND YOUR ALGORITHM.

Frank was dressing me down to make me feel lower than my value. I refused to cheapen myself and reminded him the premium he was paying kept Manwin out of trouble. It was me on the front line. Any problems were mine to deal with. Security comes at a price. In the previous negotiation, Frank got me to direct more scenes and take half my rate on scenes over twenty-five. Now he wanted me to agree to fewer scenes. If I agreed, the chiseling would never end. We ended talks and I operated off-contract.

COCAINE MADE OUR BOY'S BALLS BIGGER.

When word leaked I was off-contract, talk of my impending demise circulated.

Frank's short-sightedness circled back when his fraternity brother Blake was at the center of the next porn HIV crisis.

Vic Lagina's School of Porn

Lesson Six:
Squirt or Piss?

There have been endless debates on this topic and though I am well-versed and have seen a lot in this lifetime, I can't give you a definitive answer.

Yes, I have been with squirters in my personal life and the discharge I cleaned off my tile did not smell like or resemble urine. I have shot scenes where it clearly was urine coming out of her urethra. Certain skilled performers, like Ramón and Markus Dupree, had a technique I named 'the squirt claw,' which resulted in gushers of clear liquid.

Performers drank a lot of Pedialyte (unofficial sponsor of squirting scenes in porn) on the days squirting was required. There was one scene in particular with Kissa Sins and Blair Williams where they consumed at least four liters of Pedialyte and it really showed on screen. In this case, there was a lot of clit rubbing leading to gushers from what I assumed was the urethra. These women were doing very filthy things with these liquids, on their faces, and in their mouths. Afterward, I asked Kissa how Pedialyte helped with the taste.

"It tastes sweet, like candy."

So, in conclusion, here's my analysis: if a woman drinks two liters of Pedialyte, her kidneys then serve as a candy factory transforming the urine in her bladder into liquid candy which then passes through her urethra.

As for the clear liquid the Squirt Claw garnered, the jury is still out. Real-life squirters, like Veronica Avluv, attest it is not urine and she would know. The debate rages on. Perhaps until now.

An article in the International Journal of Urology[1] discussing a study to elucidate the mechanism of squirting concludes:

Methods:

The subjects in the current study were women who were able to squirt. They were not sex workers. A urethral catheter was inserted before sexual stimulation and the bladder was emptied. Then, a mixture of indigo carmine (10 ml) and saline (40 ml) was injected into the bladder. Sexual stimulation was provided to facilitate squirting, which was videotaped and verified. The secretions were collected in sterile cups, and prostate-specific antigen (PSA) and glucose levels were measured.

Results:

Five women (2 in their 30s, 2 in their 40s, and 1 in her 50s) participated in this study. All women were able to squirt; three squirted only with manual sexual stimulation and two with penetrative sexual stimulation. The discharged fluid was blue in all cases, confirming the bladder as the source. The fluid was PSA-positive in four patients.

Conclusions:

The main component of squirt fluid is urine, but may also contain fluid from Skene's glands (female prostate). This is the first report in which visualization of squirting was enhanced.

I GUESS WE CAN CLOSE THE CASE ON THAT ONE!

As for memorable occurrences, I have a few. One girl was given the gift of targeted urinary projection. Once the analytics told Manwin squirting was a popular search on PornHub, we shot her quite often. During a live show, she hit a target on the wall from ten feet away. I have a photo of this because it was flabbergasting. My first studio had four-by-six-foot-wide panes of glass separating the rooms. We used this when we shot police interrogations or science experiments. While I cannot recall the specifics of the scene, it was a science experiment of sorts for *DoctorAdventures.com.* Said performer was to squirt all over the glass from eight feet away. We were to record multiple angles, from inside of the room hitting the glass and from outside of the room, also hitting the glass. This meant someone had to clean the glass in between takes.

His name was Paul and he wore boots and a yellow rain jacket with a yellow hat while cleaning. This also meant our talent had to deliver two geysers, not just one. I recall her drinking a lot of water. She nailed it on each take, but the tiny room smelled like a subway.

I made the biggest *faux pas* a versed pornographer can make when shooting a squirting scene. I blocked it from memory until now.

The aforementioned performer was booked with Johnny Sins. Again, details are sketchy, but I believe she was playing a security guard, busting Johnny Sins breaking into the building. Naturally, he has to fuck his way out of trouble. I remember they were having sex in a control room outfitted with security monitors.

There was a structurally-sound office chair with no wheels and armrests. Johnny put her into a position we called 'The Johnny Pile.' With these chairs, Johnny could do a unique pile driver position without the performer's shoulders touching the ground while her vagina faced the ceiling. Johnny accomplished this with her shoulders on the seat cushion while he maintained sustainable downward thrusts without uncomfortable dick bendage. Hence, The Johnny Pile.

The flip side to the coin, it brings a squirting vagina a lot closer to the camera. The proper way to shoot a pile driver scene is from two angles, low and high. This way the penetration is visible from more than one angle for editing purposes. Perhaps I figured because I was shooting from the high angle and therefore my camera would be in direct fire, she would have known not to squirt. I was wrong. As soon as Johnny took his dick out, after pounding downward for a minute straight, I was in trouble.

Warm piss shot out of her urethra, all over my camera and my face, which fortunately was sporting a big, thick beard. Otherwise, it would have been a direct hit on my chin and left cheek. I calmly put my camera down…

"I'll be right back."

… and left the room. My wardrobe girl was walking down the hallway and saw the look of disgust.

"What happened?"

Grumbling, I managed, "She pissed… on my face."

I scrubbed my face and beard with soap and hot water. Back in the room, I cleaned my camera with baby wipes and the lens with lens cleaner while she begged for forgiveness.

"It's my fault," I conceded. "I should have known better. Let's finish the day, shall we?"

THAT'S RIGHT, BUB. RUB SOME DIRT ON IT AND GET BACK IN THE GAME.

After Johnny came all over her face, I cut camera and thanked her for a good shoot.

"And you should know, this was a first for me."

YOU NEVER FORGET YOUR FIRST. UNLESS YOU BLOCK IT FROM MEMORY.

19 THIRTY DAYS BECOMES THIRTY MINUTES

Before the testing system was revamped, Adult Industry Medical (AIM) regulated the porn industry. A producer only needed login credentials to access the performer's legal name, stage name and testing status, whether clear or infected. Everyone borrowed someone's password so vital information was not as secure as it should have been.

Performers paid one hundred and fifty dollars for an STD test covering HIV, chlamydia, and gonorrhea and they were free to perform for thirty days. The protocol left a lot of room for error and a performer wide open to contract other diseases in the interim.

Mansef wanted me to shoot Dr. Evil for a sequel to their James Bond parody in which he was the star. I hated the idea, but when he told me during a phone conversation in September 2009 he had to decline, the head office wanted to know why. When pressed, he told me in his nasally, whiny voice his injected medication had stopped working and he could not give a performance up to industry standards. I was relieved as was the rest of the industry.

Agents were vehemently against more rigid protocols. The main opponent was Derek Hay of LA Direct Models.

HENCEFORTH! YOU SHALL BE KNOWN AS DR. EVIL!

For him, it was too costly for a performer to have to pay this fee twice a month. He had to retire Ben English[1], his stage name, when his Caverject dick injection stopped working. Dr. Evil now no longer had testing woes as a performer. Some concerned performers like Audrey Bitoni requested a three-day test from their scene partner. The understanding was the requesting performer would pay for the other performer's test. Whenever a performer tested positive for HIV, a press release was issued and everyone was supposed to shut down production.

Typical in cases like these, an industry-wide witch hunt ensued to identify the performer who tested positive. Performers concerned for their well-being wanted to know the name of the infected to follow the genealogy and whether there was an HIV risk to them. It was even expected that said performer out themselves for the 'greater good.' This was standard industry protocol.

Therein lies the dilemma: medical records are protected by HIPAA, the Health Insurance Portability and Accountability Act to protect patient confidentiality. The witch hunts blatantly disregarded this law.

AIM shut down after an exiled ex-performer posted every performer's information on *PornWikiLeaks.com*. There was no longer a governing body for testing and mass confusion ensued. So, with the backing of Montreal and Fabian, the Free Speech Coalition formed with Diana Duke as its spokesman. The FSC took over AIM's role, but they were also to counter the momentum of the AIDS Healthcare Foundation condom mandate in California. After the 2010 HIV case, its cause was bolstered, even though the male talent who contracted the virus said he got it from oral sex with an infected gay male performer.

Another shutdown came in August 2011 after a performer had tested positive. The rumor mill began and news broke it was a male performer out of Miami, working with the Miami Brazzers crew. And... Blake had authorized the male performer to perform after the performer convinced him it had to be a false positive. This was not true. According to Bramm Stroker, who was his crew member, agents and many in the industry were putting screws to Blake to reveal the name of the performer. Despite being told by Manwin to keep his mouth shut, Blake went on a press tour in LA and outed the performer, thinking he was doing the right thing. Those with axes to grind decided to use Blake's misstep to make things difficult for Manwin.

Tests confirmed it was indeed a false positive and production resumed, but the damage was done. The identity of the performer had been released, thus violating HIPAA, and it created a legal matter for Frank and Manwin. This episode led to new testing protocols and a new viewing system for producers which excluded the performer's confidential information.

**BLAKE'S BUFFOONERY ACTUALLY DID GOOD FOR THE INDUSTRY.
WILL WONDERS NEVER CEASE?**

While it seemed like a rational system, because it was coming from the Evil Empire, everyone was rejecting it. The assumption was Fabian had devised a plan to make more money. I cannot tell you if this was correct, but it would not be until the infamous syphilis outbreak of 2012 that testing became more rigid.

Rumors swirled of Manwin wanting to close my studio. They did not see a point in operating in Nevada when the porn industry was in Los Angeles. Agents were telling performers my days were numbered. They in turn told my staff to look for new jobs. Nefarious forces were afoot. My crew was looking to me for answers and all I could tell them was to not listen to the bullshit.

The rumors made no sense. We were shooting four live shows a month and no other crew was equipped to handle them. Regardless of where the porn mecca was, shooting in Las Vegas was cheaper than in LA. My only additional expense was for plane tickets. Where we spent on travel, we made up in cheaper locations, props, and labor. As the work kept coming in, my crew settled down, except for Moe. He thought he was on a sinking ship and Meridiana fueling his misconceptions made him more complacent.

Things with Jackie were heating up. She loved my dogs, loved sex, and treated me well. I began to enjoy her company.

Oh and don't forget, she wasn't getting gangbanged for money.

YOU BEAT ME TO IT. NICE CHANGE OF PACE, DUDE.

Jackie was unhappy with her body and seemed done with the business. The allure of the quick money remained, but she was gathering what a vacant business she was in.

Jackie got into the business at eighteen. She was a high school dropout dating a twenty-two-year-old guy and she supported both of them by stripping. Once they broke up, she entered porn for the next two and a half years.

Her skin issues began and she stopped shooting. When the psoriasis worsened, she had to stop stripping as well. This was when we met. After a few months, her skin improved, she lost weight, and she mentioned shooting a comeback scene.

I didn't trust her fully so she didn't get to know my real name and still referred to me as 'Vic.' She clearly trusted me. I took her anal virginity.

THAT'S ONE HELLUVA TRUST FALL.

I was headed to New Orleans again for my annual Jazz Fest pilgrimage and invited her. At the airport bar, while she was eating her pepperoni pizza slice and having a beer, she saw my boarding pass. When she asked why it didn't say 'Vic' on it, her face reddened. Busted. I thought she was going to leave on the spot.

Perhaps she thought 'Vic Lagina' was his Christian name.

I made an analogy using her pizza slice. Everyone important to me was on the inside of one of the pepperoni slices. Everyone else was on the outside on the rest of the slice. She was now part of the pepperoni. It wasn't brilliant, but it worked. Off we went to Jazz Fest, and after, we were an item.

This is where he says, "I didn't want a relationship." Blah blah. You invited her to Jazz Fest, dude. Pack a pocket pussy next time.

Being in another relationship was the last thing on my mind. I told her we would have fun for a little while before the honeymoon phase wore off. Then she would start to hate my job out of fear I was fucking the female performers and ultimately accuse me of doing so. Then we would break up. Did she really want to endure this?

Ladies and Gents: aloof and disinterested has left the building.

She was young and in way over her head. I should not have expected her to comprehend the challenge of dating me. Still, I gave it a shot. I had the faintest hope she would understand my world since she had worked in the industry.

Hope in one hand and shit in the other and see what fills up first.

You might be asking why I would involve myself with yet another porn girl and expect different results. Simple: no woman with looks, brains, and self-confidence would put up with me and the world I worked in. My choice was to either be alone or date broken women. I was lying to myself that I could handle being alone. Until you become comfortable with it, being alone sucks.

So, we started dating. The only issue was I had her return scene scheduled in a few weeks. I didn't want to cancel because we were dating. I tried to give myself the pep talk.

Suck it up, bitch. You've done this before.

This wouldn't be the first time I had feelings for a girl and had to run camera while she was getting fucked. It may seem unthinkable to the civilian, but I was wired differently.

IT TOOK YEARS OF REWIRING, DUDE. YOU'RE WELCOME.

I compartmentalized the situation and reiterated it was just work. I told myself the looks and sounds of pleasure were an act and both of us were happy when it was over.

OVER A DECADE LATER, A DEVILISH SMILE APPEARED ON JACKIE'S FACE WHEN ASKED ABOUT THAT SCENE. "MMM. JOHNNY SINS." IT WAS NO ACT.

When the topic came up of her shooting more scenes for other companies, I did not try to dissuade her. Meridiana had been giving me a bag of shit about my job for years. I was not going to tell others how to earn a living.

However, there would be rules. If Jackie was going to be fucking other people, then it worked both ways. It was only fair. Like most porn stars, she justified it as work. I didn't care. She further tried to justify it by saying she didn't enjoy it. I still didn't care. Fucking is fucking and the only way I could be fine knowing she was getting fucked was if I was doing some fucking on my own. The conversation ended and she never shot another boy/girl scene again.

HANDJOB OR BLOWJOB SCENES, WELL, THOSE WERE NEVER MENTIONED. CREATIVE LOOPHOLE, JACKIE. YOU SHOULD HAVE BEEN A LAWYER.

I didn't trust a former porn star who made money having sex and now worked at a strip club to be monogamous. Call me jaded or a realist, it was my mindset. The honeymoon phase ended in six months, right on schedule.

On a beautiful day at the beginning of October, Moe gave his thirty-day notice. I was relieved. I didn't have to fire him and we would not be obligated to pay him unemployment. I didn't care about his reason. I started our production meeting. I got the feeling Moe was going to treat the next thirty days as a vacation and I was not going to allow it. Gradually, I prodded him.

When I first saw him zoning out during a production meeting, I went right after him.

"Moe, are you going to work at an appropriate level or are you going to phone it in as you have been the past several months?"

He stared at me with contempt. The rest of my staff could hardly breathe because this was a long time coming. They now had a front-row seat.

"No, I plan on working for the next thirty days, *boss*." His sarcasm only fueled me.

"I just have to question it since, and I think everyone in this room would agree with me, you have been an emotional mess for the past year since your breakup with, uh, what's her name. We all have been carrying your weight which isn't fair. But, if you say so. Let's move onto the next script."

"You know what the problem is? I can't work for *you* anymore."

"Oh yeah? And why is that?"

"Because you undermine me all the time. You tell me to do one thing and you tell the crew to do the exact opposite. How can I do my job?"

"I think you are making excuses for your shortcomings and your ineffective leadership. It's your way. It alienated your co-workers and had them question your logic. I was wrong giving someone like you this much responsibility."

"Like me?"

"Yeah. Someone with emotional issues who does not use logic. Let's not forget, you didn't show up for work for three days after your wife left you. I could have fired you then, but I adopted a dog for you. When you needed money to buy a truck, I loaned it to you without strings. I helped you any way I could. And I won't bring up the issue you caused with my neighbor either."

He had no idea I knew about this. Moe hired my neighbor to build the first live set and also construct walls in our warehouse along with a lighting grid. He failed to mention he would be 1099'ed for the job, which would become another issue altogether in the 2012 tax year. This wasn't the real problem.

My neighbor was sitting on an unused prescription for opioids and Moe made a deal to unload them for a specified dollar amount. However, he needed the neighbor to front the pills. Then Moe's wife left him and he went on a pill bender. My neighbor never received the money and asked me how to handle it. He had no recourse and I told him I wanted no part of it. Between the pill theft and Moe failing to tell my neighbor he was going to be taxed for the contracting job, Moe caused a rift between me and the man living next door.

"Yeah, and why do you think I can't get past my emotions?"

I thought he was asking me a psychological question, so I gave him a psychological response. "I don't know. It's a question for your parents."

His thirty-day notice turned into thirty minutes. Mentioning his parents touched a nerve, one I had not intended. This wasn't a schoolyard argument where we were trading barbs about each other's moms. I brought them up because his emotional behavior was a result of his upbringing.

"That's it, I am fucking out of here." On his way out he added, "Why don't you have Pete escort me out so I don't steal anything!"

"Good idea. Pete, escort Moe out so he doesn't steal anything."

HE CAN BE A COCKSUCKER WHEN HE'S REACHED HIS LIMIT.

Moe was never to be seen again. Occasionally, rumors circulated about his life after porn. Maybe he moved back home and blew glass for a living. Or he was the curator of a museum of street art opened by – wait for it – Meridiana.

WHAT A FUCKING LOSER.

He thought we were going out of business. The factory churned more efficiently after his grand exit.

I had a game plan to elevate Pete to production manager as he'd earned it. Toad had other ideas.

We took a short recess to gather ourselves after an awkward and uncomfortable start. Toad took to pen and paper in another room to sharpen his argument to be my new production manager. Prior, Toad was known for falling asleep on a studio couch until it was time to take his photos.

UNTIL OUR HERO AWAKENED HIM WITH A MEGAPHONE.
FUTURE NAP TIME CEASED.

Now he believed he was qualified for the second most important job in my operation. Pete and Toad were friends, and Pete - bless his heart - was willing to share responsibilities with him on a two-week trial period. I gave it a try. If Toad didn't work out, I could reverse course.

YOU FORGOT TO MENTION TOAD WAS A RUMORED METH HEAD.

Toad's jilted ex-girlfriend (also a performer) told me he smoked meth while surfing the internet all night. She made other serious allegations, but I chalked this up to porn horseshit until I had further proof.

Issues with the head office would accompany his promotion. Frank heard Pete and Toad were doing drugs on the set. I learned the information came from Keiran. I was livid.

Keiran's best friend Danny Mountain had been male talent for the scene, so it didn't take long to figure it all out. Danny saw Toad sweating profusely and acting manic but didn't see any drug use. Instead of bringing me this information, Danny told Keiran, which he admitted was a mistake.

Pete was pissed at Keiran to be accused of Toad's shenanigans. Toad also denied the allegations, even volunteering to take a drug test. We ordered them online and they tested for everything. After his first test, he showed me the strip and it was clean. That said, I didn't watch him piss.

The second time, I followed Toad into the bathroom like a parole officer as he struggled to pee. The test was positive for cocaine and weed. It wasn't meth, but I couldn't exactly use that to exonerate him. I decided to let it be forgotten, which it was due to a lack of evidence. Regardless, I needed to protect myself.

DON'T HIRE RUMORED TWEAKERS WITH SKETCHY EMPLOYMENT HISTORY.

While Toad was daydreaming about a promotion, he still took photos. Pretty soon, he began to piss off my crew with his power trip. Ethan almost knocked him out after an argument. Pete no longer wanted to share responsibilities with him. After two tumultuous weeks, Toad recused himself as a candidate for production manager and continued to alienate himself. Even Huggy didn't want him around anymore. Toad sandbagged a set of photos by taking them from only one angle. Huggy flipped out and banned him from set.

A few days later, Toad quit on his own accord, after some attempted sabotage. On the way out he deleted the bulk of our talent IDs and scripts from our work Dropbox. Or so he thought. I had everything backed up on my laptop.

WAS THAT THE BEST YOU COULD DO?

We had shed two pieces of dead weight. Ironically, our next photographer would weigh over three hundred pounds. Huggy suggested him.

Vic Lagina's School of Porn

Lesson Seven: Hiring and Directing Your Talent

Selective hiring of talent is a key to thriving in this industry. It's also essential to keeping your sanity. All guys think they can fuck hot women for money. Rest assured, they can't. Not everybody was Jordan Ash.

In the early Florida years, there were two online choices to find talent: *Adult-Staffing.com* and *One Model Place*, but agents in South Florida represented adult talent. They were one step higher than a suitcase pimp, although I met plenty of those in the cheap hotel rooms. I encountered other South Florida producers when I needed to rent studio space. They linked me with local talent and solid male performers. This is how I met Jordan.

Back then, Jordan could knock out two or sometimes three scenes in a day, all ending in voluminous loads. At two hundred per shoot, I was keeping him busy. Later on, Jordan would be making nine hundred per scene, but in the Grapefruit League of South Florida porn, two was the going rate for a solid stud.

The other option was using unproven talent. This netted mixed results. One site I was shooting for, *CuteCouples.com,* required me to find a new couple for every scene. In reality, it was two people who had never met. We conjured up a fake story and then recorded their love on camera if the guy could stay hard.

When you are waiting for a dude to regain an erection, you have time to examine your wrong turns in life. I shudder at the hundreds of hours I've spent waiting for some D-grade male talent to get hard. Building a stable of competent male talent is the key to a long career in porn.

FIND A SMORGASBORD OF HARD, RELIABLE COCKS.
GOTCHA. WILL THIS BE ON THE TEST?

However, when you find a male talent with promise, they become your go-to guy for most of your projects. This is where Jordan and I put our time in the trenches. We learned the nature of female talent and the best way to balance professionalism while keeping the clients happy with their specific requests.

Direct communication is important and was my *modus operandi*. No matter how graphic the discussion, it was best to say things without embarrassment. Very much how a doctor might phrase things, just without all the technical nomenclature. With honest communication, your days will be smoother and your career longer. I see a hand. Yes, you with the sparkles?

PROFESSOR LAGINA, HOW DO YOU PASS TIME WHILE WAITING FOR WOOD?

If a male talent was struggling to keep his dick hard or needed a break, to kill time we tried shooting a scene for *BrutalDildos.com*. My client had big asks for the big toys. Some of these toys were five or six inches in diameter and over twelve inches long. For a successful shoot, said toy would have to be inserted at least five inches. Not surprisingly, women who had children were better equipped for success. If we shot this after a boy/girl scene, her parts would be properly loosened.

While house hunting in Vegas, I packed six brutal dildos in my luggage with plans to shoot a few women with deep-seated uteruses. I stashed them in the lining of my suitcase to avoid any embarrassing luggage checks. No matter, TSA found them and acknowledged their search with a notice.

SO WHEN TRAVELING WITH A BRUTAL DILDO, FLY YOUR FREAK FLAG HIGH!

I treated these scenes as add-ons, especially if I had a male and female talent for the entire day. We might as well make as much money as possible. Having a candid conversation with female talent while simultaneously checking the brutal dildo's vaginal depth was part of the job.

I SEE. SO WHILE WAITING FOR WOOD, EITHER PACK A LUNCH OR A BRUTAL DILDO. GOT IT.

After I moved to Vegas and started dealing more with agents and less with talent, the message remained the same: keep everyone informed, which I did via email so there was a record of everything. Accountability needed to be obvious, especially when production dollars were on the line. But therein lies the dilemma: if I am giving information to the agent, I am assuming the agent will convey it. This happened less than I appreciated or needed.

It was also helpful to relay information directly to talent so there were no surprises. This was standard operating procedure. Still, with all of these safeguards, details would sometimes fall through the cracks. Talent showed up neither prepared nor informed. It became apparent where the blame should fall, but holding performers accountable, especially if they were popular, was not enforceable. Not hiring them would only hurt the company not profiting from their popularity.

The bigger the star, the bigger the headache.

Missed flights, possible intoxication on set, and not reading the script were common headaches. Yet, the requests kept coming. If I passed on them, another producer would pick up the scene. Knowing I had a problematic performer on the schedule, I left buffer time in case there was overage. I had to thread the needle timewise before talent lost energy and focus, making sure my crew was there to assist me in delivering this porn baby. It worked out most of the time.

My A-plus rotation of male talent was James Deen (until he was canceled by most studios), Jordan Ash, Scott Nails, Xander Corvus, Mick Blue, Ramón Nomar (until he was blacklisted by the company for reasons explained shortly), Charles Dera, Markus Dupree (when I was allowed), and Johnny Sins. For live shows, we used John Strong, Tommy Gunn, and Marco Banderas. Ramón eventually got the same implant and it extended his career.

I loved shooting Ramón. He had the best attitude and was unflinching when I needed him to wear a sparkly blue leotard and attempt figure skating with Jessica Nyx. "No worries" was his motto.

In 2016, Stoya Tweeted during her relationship with James Deen that he raped her. This was explosive and rocked the industry. He had been riding high, going so far as being cast against Lindsay Lohan in a mainstream film directed by Paul Shrader. Overnight, everything changed for him. More claims rolled in. He was the first porn #MeToo. I asked him why he never chose to fight it in court and his lawyers told him it was a lost cause. Rolling the dice with a jury who may be anti-porn seemed a bad move, despite his version of events. *Why put any of it on official court record?* While his career continued, it was never the same. I was no longer allowed to book him. It was odd since he was one of the first solid male talent I hired once Mansef had money and he became a fixture in a lot of my productions. He was trained under Chico Wang at eighteen. Wang was a twisted porn Pai Mei. Because he was dominant on camera, Deen was heavily requested by Manwin for *PornStarPunishment.com* and hired often by *Kink.com.* He voiced his concerns he was getting uncomfortable with PSP and eventually rejected those shoots. He didn't want to be known for it, and this was in 2011.

All I wanted were guys who knew angles and positions. The more you shoot someone, you get to know their nuances. Sometimes there are preferred positions based on how their cock is curved. Sometimes they need to set up the pop by rubbing their belly like Aladdin's Lamp.

I tried to give performers the sense I was looking out for them so we could find middle ground. If a tough position was requested, they would try it before we told the head office they were out of their minds, which we all knew they were. This was the common thread bonding all performers and producers.

I always appreciated the professionals who built up their brands and made bosses of themselves, but also asked questions and raised any points of concern. They showed up on time and smiled when I said "good morning" and handed them paperwork.

AND NOW, A WORD FROM PETE...

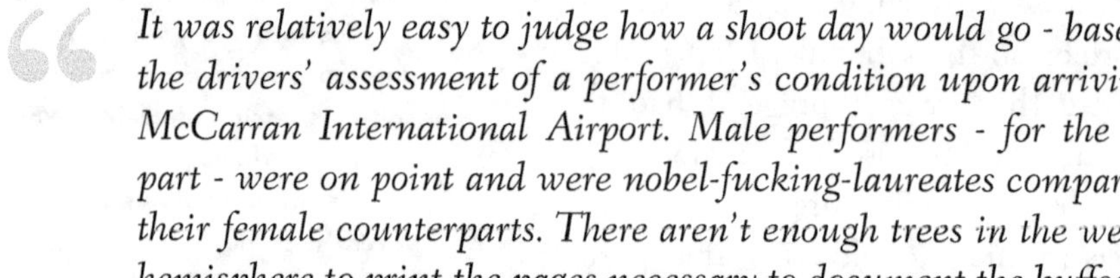

> *It was relatively easy to judge how a shoot day would go - based on the drivers' assessment of a performer's condition upon arriving at McCarran International Airport. Male performers - for the most part - were on point and were nobel-fucking-laureates compared to their female counterparts. There aren't enough trees in the western hemisphere to print the pages necessary to document the buffoonery and pure shit-shows (pun intended) we crew would have to endure with some of these whores.*

Unless I got to know a performer, they were an independent contractor on the other side of my desk, hired through an agent. Aside from general pleasantries, I knew nothing about them. We would discuss what they liked and didn't with their scene partners. If there was a problematic request, we discussed alternatives.

The best course was to be as accommodating as possible, within reason. If talent had specific dietary needs, we considered this when ordering lunch. When a popular performer, who had extreme plastic surgery in the form of fillers, lip enhancements, rhinoplasty, breast implants, butt implants, and liposuction, demanded BPA-free water bottles, we got them. When Katrina Jade, after arriving at the studio, asked to take an hour nap because she was tired from the night before, I refused. I said *within reason.* At times I felt like Mr. Hand from *Fast Times at Ridgemont High*: "Sleep will be had on your time!"

JUST LIKE YOU WOULDN'T WANT HIM TAKING A NAP AFTER YOU HAVE GOTTEN OUT OF HAIR, MAKEUP, AND ANAL PREP AND ARE READY TO GET FUCKED IN THE ASS, WOULD YOU?

The head office put problematic performers in time-out. They will deny this. If a performer missed something important such as a big shoot or event, they withheld bookings for months to spank their bottom. If one ever publicly griped against or challenged the company, they were blacklisted. My friend Sara Jay and Tasha Reign come to mind. I am getting ahead of the narrative, but when the pendulum shifted after the advent of social media and talent platforms, the company needed the performers and their traffic. They started enabling divas, much like the Hollywood system.

PROFESSOR LAGINA... CAN WE GO NOW? CLASS ENDED FIVE MINUTES AGO.

Sorry, went on a tangent there. Hire reliable cocks, use direct communication, keep a light-hearted atmosphere, and be reasonably accommodating.

Class dismissed.

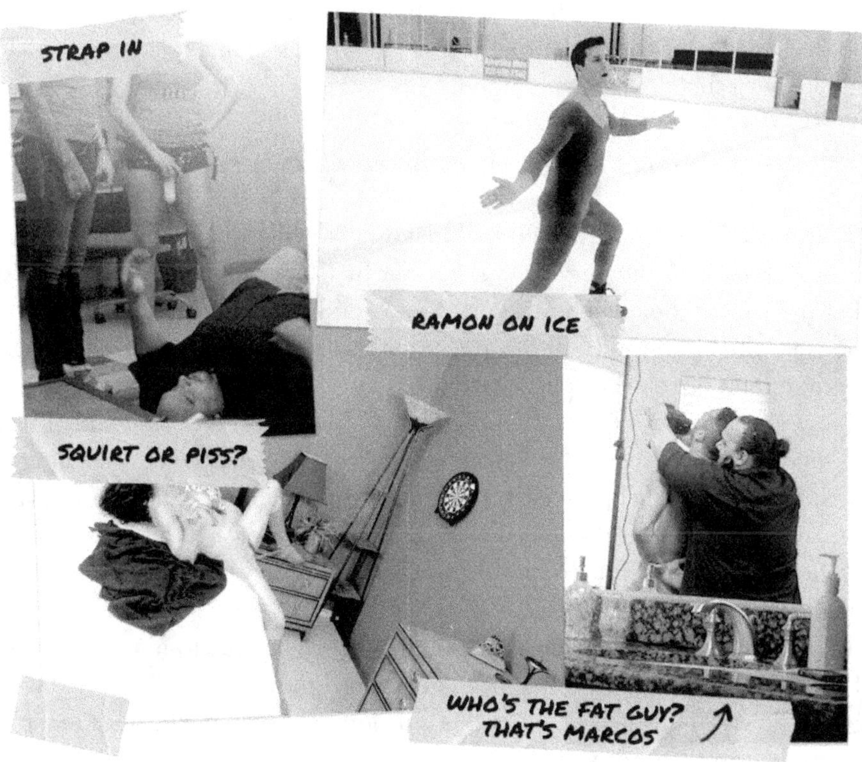

20 MY TWENTIETH HIGH SCHOOL REUNION

Huggy's referral was Marcos, a heavy-set Puerto Rican. Oddly, the two of them looked alike. They got mistaken for one another.

THE TALENTED FAT GUY WAS MARCOS. HUGGY WAS THE OTHER ONE.

Marcos was talented as a photographer and I don't just mean in comparison to my former drug-addled picture taker. I met Marcos several years prior, but he wouldn't work for the two hundred bucks Montreal offered him per shoot. When Toad quit, I was able to cobble a respectable rate. I was stoked about the hire, having never seen a fat meth head. His inaugural assignment was my old fuck buddy Hailey's first double penetration.

OPENING DAY DP. THAT'S GOING ON YOUR PERMANENT RECORD.

I reconciled with Hailey after my breakup with Meridiana. I extended her an olive branch by bringing her out to shoot her first DP, like a true gentleman. We buried the past as I explained the pressure Meridiana had me under back then. Aside from the opportunity to reconnect with an old friend, she needed money, likely to support her obvious pill addiction.

Now, she was about to be penetrated by two penises at the same time. I would shoot more inaugural scenes for Hailey over the years: her first anal gangbang and her first interracial gangbang. With each shoot, she declined in the manageability of her fragile mind. Marcos' first shoot was the beginning. He soldiered through. Over the years, Marcos proved his adaptability to whomever we shot and whatever baggage they brought.

Marcos was not the first employee Huggy convinced me to hire. First was his girlfriend Francesca followed by her conniving brother, Frankie. As a favor to Huggy (who was doing it as a favor to his girlfriend), I gave Frankie a PA job. It was short-lived after he abruptly quit.

After moving into the studio, Francesca quit as my wardrobe assistant. Later she was hired as a secondary makeup artist, which she and Huggy plotted to make a more permanent position. This pissed off my primary makeup artist Stephanie to no end. Before Marcos' footing was secured, Huggy did his best to make Marcos feel he owed him for getting him in the door.

My twentieth high school reunion was coming up. I had attended my fifteenth shortly after I suffered my first staph infection. My cover story then was selling real estate in Vegas. After all, the market was booming and it seemed plausible. Several of my classmates never left town, married and reproduced. They looked fat and miserable. When I spun my tales of bachelorhood in Vegas, envy burned in their eyes. Those looks magnified at the twentieth reunion when I brought my twenty-two-year-old girlfriend.

YEP, OUR HERO IS THAT ASSHOLE.

My virginity taker, Nali, encouraged me to go stag like her. Uninterested in reliving the glory days, I figured Jackie would be the perfect buffer. Nali's job had sent her out to Vegas a few times over the years and she always insisted we meet up. I felt a strange sense of obligation.

The second time Nali came to Vegas, she left a panicked voicemail as her money was stolen and she needed a ride to the airport. I picked her up. She had been dancing with a guy in a club and he must have pickpocketed her. I sensed a different story. I envisioned her bringing him back to her room where he robbed her after fucking her all night. Knowing Nali, this made more sense.

Nali was ice-cold to Jackie at the reunion, unlike the assholes in my class. Several made attempts to get Jackie to go elsewhere with them. It didn't matter that they were married. I found it funny, even more so when she shot them down. It was the ultimate fuck you from both of us.

GRANDPARENTS WOULD'VE BEEN PROUD: DANCE WITH WHO BROUGHT YOU.

The rest of the night was a blur. I pounded a bottle of Jameson on an empty stomach, Jackie almost got in a fight, and our late-night cheesesteak run ended with me vomiting all over the hotel room bathroom.

A RESOUNDING SUCCESS, I SAY.

In 2012, I hired another of Huggy's recommendations: Paul. A single father, he was eager and willing to work hard, driven by the fear of being homeless with a child. Paul was one of the hardest working employees I ever hired (he was the one in the yellow raincoat and galoshes, squeegeeing piss). Huggy thought he was now controlling three of my crew. Besides the two recent hires, the fat bastard also believed Pete was in his corner. Quick origin story on Pete:

On a busy day at the Gilespie house after his girlfriend's brother quit, Huggy called a fraternity brother to help us out: Pete. He was a hard worker and we shared our first awkward moment as employer and employee when we saw the Clint Eastwood-directed *Gran Torino.*

Pete is Korean, and in the movie, Clint Eastwood used every Asian slur imaginable: swamp rat, zipperhead, gook, you name it, he said it. I probably laughed one too many times. I couldn't help it. It wasn't the slurs I found hilarious, it was the ludicrous statements uttered by the grizzled Eastwood. I am certain Pete thought his new boss was a racist. Thankfully, we developed a strong respect for one another. I still consider him one of the best employees I ever had. While he had immense respect for me, Pete got wise to Huggy's backstabbing ways. This was Huggy's major miscalculation.

AND NOW, A WORD FROM PETE...

> *The difference between a project's success and inevitable derailment was always dictated by the man at the helm, Vic. Not many people I've come across in my life have exhibited the ability to keep calm and push forward amidst imminent disaster quite like the Vic-meister. Being the big-nosed, yarmulke-wearing Jew that he is, Vic was always inherently frugal by nature and motivated by cutting costs when possible. For the record, I never saw him put that thing on his head – I always assumed they put it on before bed or something like that.*

After Moe almost cut off his hand with a circular saw, we filed a claim with worker's comp and the matter appeared resolved. However, Moe wanted to throw a dick punch before he moved on.

We were about to shoot a prison gangbang scene with Lisa Ann when two OSHA inspectors knocked on the door. They asked for the manager and I spoke with them outside while I told my staff to continue working. They flashed their badges and informed me an unnamed person who had worked for me filed a complaint. I could either let them in so they could do a quick inspection or, if I denied their entrance, the next step was to get a court order.

QUICKLY PLEASE, OFFICER, WE'RE TRYING TO SHOOT A GANGBANG.

Both of them were pleasant and seemed intrigued about our nature of work. I thought they were going to cite me for not using condoms, which was what Cal-OSHA was up to in Los Angeles. Instead, the complaint referenced debris blocking exit doors, electrical panel issues, and issues with our mounted lighting. Hosting a gangbang is not a workplace safety violation.

MOE, YOU BALD WORTHLESS PRICK.

They allowed me to vent about my disgruntled former employee. Then I told them I needed to notify my staff. While they sat in my office, I told Ethan and Pete to clear out the debris and to check how our lights were mounted. While they scrambled toward the back of the studio where our exits and panels were, I had the agents start their inspection at the front of the huge sixteen-thousand-square-foot studio. They found Moe's claims to be invalid.

But, I was cited for the capital crime of not having a face plate on an electrical socket. Prior to us hosting porn shoots, a major casino used the facility to monitor progressive slots. There were hundreds of electrical outlets throughout the building. Any time we had to change the color of paint in a room, which was frequent, those plates were removed and sometimes cracked or broken. Protocol was to have several on hand just in case.

They dismissed the other charges in the claim, but I was fined a few thousand dollars for this serious offense. My lawyer negotiated the fine down. We now understood the life-saving importance of proper wall plate maintenance. Until the next one broke and was forgotten about.

I told my crew I was given a warning. I didn't want it to get back to Moe that he had cost the company money. No way that douche nozzle was getting any satisfaction.

WE EVEN FINISHED THE LISA ANN JAILHOUSE GANGBANG. BRAVO.

It took six months before my honeymoon phase with Jackie ended after she started to accuse me of cheating. She had no basis for her claims except having "bad feelings in her gut" and bad dreams about it.

HERE WE GO AGAIN.

It was the same cycle of her returning back to her normal, happy self before succumbing to bouts of depression, worthlessness, and more accusations.

I resolved to not miss out on any opportunities. Under a mounting addiction to cocaine, I could justify everything. Eight months into the relationship, I cheated on her.

COCAINE OR NOT, IT'S ABOUT FUCKING TIME WE GOT SOME STRANGE.

The first girl was a beautiful Eastern European with huge boobs. She was staying in town awaiting her shoot the next day. After Jackie headed to work the night shift at her club, I went over to the hotel.

This interlude wasn't my best performance since it was a new and strange vagina and her breath was bad. I enjoyed several hours of toying with her love balloons. Then I slinked back home to shower off the filth. A tinge of cocaine washed the guilt away.

IF YOU'RE ACCUSED, YOU MIGHT AS WELL DO IT. THAT EASTERN EURO LADY WITH THE MAGNIFICENT RACK IS FOREVER BURNED INTO OUR SPANK BANK.

I resolved to not pine over missed opportunities like I had in previous relationships. This rationalization was easy as I imagined Jackie giving handjobs in the VIP room at her strip club.

HANDJOBS ARE UNDERRATED. ESPECIALLY HERS. TOP DOLLAR HEEJES.

Jackie also did bachelor parties in hotel rooms. Given I was once one of those guys, I knew what was going on, despite her reassurances. She even claimed she would only shoot nonsexual videos when visiting her porn producer friend in Los Angeles.

SORRY, WAS I LAUGHING OUT LOUD?

She said these were clothed degradation videos where she would insult the viewer, a hot trend at the moment.

YOU KNOW WHAT ELSE IS TRENDING? VIDEOS OF YOUR GIRLFRIEND GIVING HANDJOBS.

She flew to different cities with her friend whom she did girl/girl videos with for bachelor parties but swore they weren't escorting.

SHE REVEALED A DECADE LATER THEY EACH SUCKED A TESTICLE OF A MEMBER OF A VERY RICH AND FAMOUS FAMILY. BUT NO ESCORTING.

All of it stunk like horseshit, but she swore up and down.

CHOP. CHOP. CHOP. LINE. LINE. LINE. SNORT. SNORT. SNORT.

When things were good, they were great. The sex was still zesty and plentiful, but the fun times skidded to a halt when she would go dark. She would drone on about her self-loathing, daddy issues, and dreams of being more than a stripper.

IT SURELY WASN'T THE PHILANDERING/COKE SNORTING/PORNOGRAPHER BOYFRIEND THAT CAUSED HER ANY ISSUES. THAT MUCH I'M SURE OF!

She asked me to help with her bills. Nope. I was done supporting people who lacked ambition. The things I had to endure to earn my paycheck forbade me. I saw an expiration date on this relationship, but wouldn't do the right thing and end it. I was resigned to being selfish.

I'M SORRY, WHAT'S THE ISSUE? WOW, THIS COKE IS FIRE!

The Eastern European would be the first of several late-night trysts in hotels. My path to self-indulgence and decadence was in hyperdrive.

Civilians just wouldn't understand.

IN MEMORIUM:
Raven Bay, 12/22/89 - 10/2/21

Raven Bay came onto the scene in 2011, appearing on Dr. Evil's website.

She was tall and thin with long black hair and tattoos. The plastic surgeon who did her first boob job should be tarred and feathered for leaving two distinct scars under each breast. She was self-conscious, especially when members voiced their boob scar displeasure in her scene comments. I solved this by keeping her bra on the entire scene, but pulled down to show boob while covering her scars.

This limited how often she was booked. Furthermore, she told me she was at odds with Dr. Evil after refusing his advances on a vacation. According to her, he yelled, berated, and called her awful names because she didn't want to sleep with him. She left LA Direct for another agency, 101 Modeling. It didn't help her career much.

In one scene, she was paired with Audrey Bitoni, also with 101 Modeling. Audrey was picky and insisted her talent retest at least three days before the shoot. She was willing to pay for it. She also had male talent wash their mouths out with a salt solution before each scene. She had her elixirs and potions, which allegedly kept her health in check. Weird as she was, I admired this about Audrey. I hope she's doing well and has discovered more breakthroughs in hygienic health in the porn industry.

This was supposed to be a boy/girl/girl scene, which was news to Audrey even though her agent had all the details. Raven took it in stride, unlike Aletta Ocean who did not like Audrey when they shot together. As a compromise, we agreed the male talent would fuck Raven first. After we cut, he cleaned off his dick, and then fucked Audrey. The script made no sense and it was a general clusterfuck.

SHOOTING PORN IS NOT ALWAYS BLOWJOBS AND RAINBOWS.

After this scene, Raven and I went back to her hotel room at South Point Casino and made it a night. She wanted to date, but I told her I had a girlfriend who would fly into a rage if she knew we were hanging out.

She said if she were my girlfriend, she would let me sleep with anyone I wished, even bring other women into the bedroom. It sounded nice and I kept it in mind, but Jackie and I had to let our thing run its course. Raven got mixed up with the wrong guys who latched on and took advantage. Still, we would hang out whenever she was in town. One morning I found her sleeping outside because my coke-filled nostrils were not allowing me to breathe. My open-mouth throat snores echoed throughout my house. Eventually, she got larger implants which helped cover the scars, but since they did not fit her frame, she also got huge butt implants. This made her oddly proportioned, yet it was what the head office was seeking, so I shot more scenes with her.

Some of them were great, such as the *BigTitsAtSchool.com* with Danny D. Others, less so. While she seemed all there mentally, she struggled to remember dialogue. In a scene with Markus Dupree, she had trouble taking him in her ass, even with quite a few anal scenes under her belt.

"Just fuck my ass, I don't care if it hurts."

To his credit, Markus was concerned about continuing to shoot with her. The compromise was a mostly boy/girl scene with some anal mixed in. It was the last time I shot her. I got the sense she needed a break and shared those thoughts with the company.

Years later, she texted me out of the blue telling me she was sober and had been in rehab for several months. She had twenty-seven days left, but she was detoxing to get off of fentanyl and Xanax. She reached out because, in her own words:

> "u were always such a good positive person and I'm only associating with people I like. I gave up everything after being in a bad relationship and denying my addiction for long. When Jessica (Jaymes) died I was a mess as we hung out a lot. It was so different being able to feel after numbing and being a zombie."

She wanted to get back into shooting, but she had to start from scratch because her ex took her phone and she had no passwords. She was twenty pounds overweight. It seemed like she had a lot more to overcome.

I checked back with her on April 3, 2021, when she was at Sober Living. I asked if she was staying positive and she said "a little," before admitting she was depressed and disliking herself, and was "in the using mood." The conversation dwindled and I told her to stay positive and avoid old and destructive patterns.

On October 2, 2021, a year to the day after she entered rehab, she passed at the age of thirty-one. My guess is fentanyl was to blame.

21 THE MAIN EVENT: HUGGY BEAR VERSUS VIC LAGINA

Huggy remained committed to his ambitious takeover plans. Fortunately, he was unaware everybody saw through his bullshit and was exhausted by his nonsense.

People knew he was a sham no matter how much he talked himself up or when he made baseless promises to try to impress. In his mission to be taken seriously, he was a failure.

LADIES AND GENTLEMEN! WELCOME TO THE MAIN EVENT!
MICHAEL BOOFER HERE GIVING THE TALE OF THE TAPE...

MILFsLikeItBlack.com was his baby. The casting involved three pimps with a stable of black male escorts. The pimps would then sell their services to older women yearning for black dick. The scenes were shot on the fly, reality style. No meaningful script, just loose concepts the three pimps brainstormed: D, Bugsi, and Direct. They were hilarious and the true backbone of the website. This setup was ideal for Huggy since it required no finesse, patience, or grooming. These scenes were devoid of the need for real acting or directing, even by porn standards.

IN THE RED CORNER, STANDING FIVE FOOT SIX INCHES TALL, WEIGHING TWO HUNDRED AND EIGHTY POUNDS, HAILING FROM THE DRIVE-THROUGH LINE AT MCDONALD'S, HUGGY BEAR!

His lead photographer was Mike, (aka 'The Commodore'), the moonlighting collector for the casinos. When we met, the Commodore couldn't read me and wasn't sure I could be trusted. Coke paranoia had me suspicious of everyone. Even so, we became solid friends and confidantes. Until his eventual move to the Midwest, the Commodore was on Huggy's crew.

IN THE BLUE CORNER, STANDING SIX FOOT THREE INCHES TALL, WEIGHING

TWO HUNDRED AND FIFTEEN POUNDS, HAILING FROM THE SUBURBS OF PHILADELPHIA, VIC LAGINA!

Huggy had few ties to the head office and worked hard to conceal this. A running joke was Huggy's shoots took longer because he droned on to everybody about how important he was. He, and not Vic Lagina, could get his people whatever they needed. The pimps got wise to who was running the show and chided Huggy to keep the day moving. Bugsi was an aspiring rapper and Huggy told him he was going to convince the head office to shoot a music video for him and use his tunes in scenes for *MilfsLikeItBlack.com.* I was producing and Huggy was taking credit. After one frustrating day, the Commodore said to watch my back. Huggy was plotting.

After I failed to receive a contract extension, I sized up my options outside of Manwin. Manwin now owned most of the major porn sites and the majority of production came from them. They had massive leverage and it emboldened them with a bully mentality.

Manwin was the pig at the strip club making it rain during the recession. All of us were grabbing whatever we could. Nick, the former CEO, and ex-accountant trying to prove I was embezzling money a few years prior, had left the company. I reached out to him and he said he was considering making another run in the business. He hinted he was affiliated with a whale who wanted to compete with Manwin.

Nick's idea sounded intriguing. I lost interest when he told me this whale was involved in the real sex business (human trafficking). I reached out to Ouissam as well, but he was done with the porn industry, having started a private investment firm. They had no use for me.

My options were limited. While I did not disclose my exact plans, I mentioned to Huggy we were free to seek out supplementary income. I never made any other moves to work outside of the company. I waited to see how Huggy would react.

LAGINA ON THE DEFENSIVE, SLIPPING THE JAB...

Huggy seized this opportunity to prove my disloyalty to the company. Dissatisfied with his income dropping, he vented like a bad James Bond villain and revealed his elaborate plan. The Commodore heard and relayed all the details.

Huggy claimed he got me my business license and Vegas was *his town.* If anyone wanted to make any moves in porn, they had to go through him. To reiterate: I hired the head counsel of the ACLU of Nevada to make sure my license was secured in 2009. He knew the county commissioners and navigated through the red tape. If I ever had run-ins with law enforcement while in production, dropping his name would most likely diffuse any situation.

HUGGY BEAR IS THROWING GORILLA PUNCHES! LAGINA IS TRYING TO WITHSTAND THE ONSLAUGHT.

Huggy claimed the head office was pushing me out. Why else would they renew both Keiran and Brando's contracts and not mine? With all of the talk of condoms in porn in LA, Brando was moving back to Las Vegas. He was seeking Huggy's help to get the proper permits. Sensing an opportunity to make some quick cash, Huggy thought he could jump ship and become an equal partner in Brando's operation. He ranted he was going to take over my workload once Brando made his move.

I had to ponder mine.

The first order of business was to contact Frank and be proactive to counter Huggy's plan and blunt the effect of Brando's move to Vegas. Huggy's scheme to help Brando was not a secret and was birthed during AVN a few months prior. Frank was concerned I would have an issue with Brando being in my backyard as I had been with Blake. I assured him there wouldn't be a problem. Brando knew how to operate a crew.

As long as Brando respected my 'live and let live' mantra we could coexist. I confided to Frank that Huggy was considering going out on his own since our work volume had dropped. I told him I had no problem with it. His quality of work had diminished over time as he struggled with being assigned less work.

LAGINA CONNECTS WITH A BODY BLOW! LEFT. LEFT. LEFT. BODY BLOW! HUGGY BEAR IS DAZED.

Huggy was going to put forth even less effort in the future. Now was the time to work harder, not let petty grudges prevail. Quality was now all-important, so it might make more sense for me to shoot all the scenes and relieve Huggy of his duties.

Frank thanked me for my candor and told me to think it over. It was my decision to make. Frank reminded me they wanted to fire Huggy four years earlier, but I saved his job and it worked out well for everyone. Now was my chance.

LAGINA HAS HUGGY BEAR ON THE ROPES BUT IS NOT FINISHING HIM OFF.

I decided to keep him around. I made sure my core crew knew he couldn't be trusted, but I couldn't stomach having to replace a guy responsible for over half my shoots and revenue. Plus, he would have been a liability elsewhere. So the fat bastard dodged a bullet, again.

Huggy was less than enthused that I remained the sole controller of his career with Manwin. He had thought he had a chance with Brando to usurp my standing. Unfortunately for him, Brando simply used Huggy to help get his studio license. I was Huggy's only option.

DING! DING! HOW IS HUGGY BEAR STILL STANDING?

Brando posed his own potential issues. I had to secure my crew from being poached. I made it clear my work took priority, no matter what. We were in an era of self-preservation. Break the rules and pay the price. Brando was a self-serving opportunist and needed to be treated as such. My employees knew where they stood with me.

Transparency in this business is a rarity my people appreciated. Work kept coming in and their checks cleared. Why fuck with it?

A few of my people moonlighted for Brando until figuring out his sets were not as efficient. Huggy won a small battle by ousting the Commodore as photographer and doing the job himself. I was unable to stop him and his power play netted him a little extra money.

Around this time, Manwin brought the Vegas producers up to Montreal for a weekend-long producers' workshop.

The Manwin building was eight stories and within walking distance of our hotel. The front lobby was protected by three large security guards. The company had ballooned to over eight hundred employees working on different floors and in different departments consisting of tube sites, webcams, gay sites, straight sites, dating sites, and whatever else. It struck me as excessive, overstaffed, and costly.

The overall goal of the week was to improve quality. Then we discussed all sorts of technical stuff: different cameras, lighting configurations, makeup issues, posing issues, and the relative merits of certain sexual positions.

BOARD MEETINGS ABOUT REVERSE COWGIRL. WHAT A BUSINESS.

We also addressed our dear friend: compliance. Every time we met we had to review the ever-changing list of what we could and couldn't shoot.

Credit card companies were the real judge and jury as to what was acceptable. They had rules and if we did not abide, they'd bar Manwin's sites from their payment processing.

The list was long and mostly understandable. In the early days of PornHub, there was a demand for us to shoot darker porn, determined by PornHub searches. A site idea called *Shame On Her* was scrapped because producers like me refused to shoot it. It involved forced sex acts on performers where they looked like they were in pain.

Essentially, rape.

The site devolved into *PornStarPunishment.com.* We circumvented the rape aspect and danced the fine line between consensual and nonconsensual sex through performances. Everything was discussed prior to shooting and girls who were into this type of sex (a considerable number) were booked. Much like *Kink.com*, after our scenes the performer discussed the scene, how much they enjoyed it, how it was their personal kink, and they had a great time.

In 2017, around the start of #MeToo, Dana brought this matter up on Twitter. She claimed Huggy and I told Nacho Vidal to punch her in the face because she was a Kink girl and could handle it. I reviewed the footage. I was directing my own scene on this date with Julia Ann and Toni Ribas for *BigTitsInSports.com* and was not on set for Dana's shoot, nor was giving direction to anyone except Julia and Toni. While I am not sure why Dana roped me into things, I assume it was because the shoot occurred under my roof. I witnessed Huggy trying to explain the nature of the shoot during sign-in and she asked if he was fucking with her. I watched the hardcore and while rough, when she needed to call "cut", Huggy cut. He checked back with her before proceeding and she gave the thumbs up. I did note a big change in demeanor during her sign-out and perhaps this is after she recapped everything in her head. Regardless, she shot for me again a year later for a Wicked Live show. I last saw her with blonde hair introducing herself to me at the Brazzers' AVN party in 2020 where she acted like nothing ever happened.

Shooting these scenes never sat well with me, but I was placated when some of the girls admitted to having rape fantasies. They would engage in them on a personal level with their sex partners. Here was just another safe and controlled environment to practice this kink.

I delegated most of these shoots to Huggy because I did not want to touch them. They seemed to be a ticking time bomb. Some of these shoots did not go smoothly. In August of 2013, Dana Dearmond tweeted she had a bad shoot for

PSP. Her agent told her to delete the tweet and nothing further progressed. Soon after, PSP was under fire, deemed noncompliant, and removed from *Brazzers.com*.

Feigned forced sex was no longer compliant. Even if they wanted to, girls could not be choked, gagged, slapped, spit on, fish-hooked, restrained, have their breathing restricted, or portrayed in any way as having non consensual sex.

GIVE ME FISH HOOKS OR GIVE ME DEATH.

Many performers were upset about this. While these rules made sense to me, others didn't:

- No sex while dressed in an animal costume – bestiality.
- No sex while dressed as an alien: interspecies intercourse.
- No sex with zombies: necrophilia.

While those rules seemed absurd, it was paramount we respected them. We were in a new era of porn.

There was a company picnic in a park for all eight hundred employees and the producers and directors visiting from the United States. Fabian and his CFO Feras Antoon parked their two hundred-thousand-dollar sportscars amongst modest and humble transport vessels. It rubbed me as obnoxious. Further perplexing was watching Fabian sit alone under a tree eating a bag of potato chips.

THAT ASPIE IS A MULTI-MILLIONAIRE. HOW IN THE FUCK?

The last night in Montreal featured a lavish dinner followed by a night of excess and alcohol. Fabian looked like an eighties relic with his collar turned upwards. Huggy leached on and grabbed a seat next to him. I was across the table watching the bumbling fuck-face try his pitch.

Huggy's grand plan was to shoot a documentary about women's empowerment in porn, an idea he stole from Marcos. He believed this was a ticket to fortune and glory. Non-decision-makers intimated Fabian was interested. Huggy pounced.

Huggy leaned in to deliver his grand speech. Fabian waited two confused seconds before shrugging his shoulders and turning his back to him.

CRUSH HIS SOUL, DARTH THYLMANN!

Huggy's grand plans were demolished in seconds. We returned to Las Vegas with the reality of his place within the company finally sinking in.

Back in Vegas, I got a third dog. It started with the German Shepherd Rescue of Las Vegas looking for foster homes for their older dogs. I loaded up Joker and Jetta and we made the drive to Pahrump.

DID WE STOP AT THE WORLD-FAMOUS CHICKEN RANCH BROTHEL? NOPE.

Upon arrival, Jetta started shaking. She had bad memories and the poor girl must have thought the worst. I wanted to make sure my foster dog got along with the kids.

After two candidates showed aggression, a sweet old lady named Roxy played nice with Joker and Jetta on the leash. We isolated them in the same containment area where Joker and Jetta ran the ritual two years prior. Jetta never took her eyes off me and when I left to fill out paperwork, she scaled the six-foot high chain link fence back to me. Loyalty.

At home, Roxy got comfortable. It took a day of her beaming smile to know she wasn't going anywhere. No one could give this dog a better life than me. Despite her lacking bladder control at night and occasionally fighting with Jetta, she was a sweet, naïve, and happy girl. An annoying aunt to Joker and Jetta. They accepted her presence without engaging her or including her in the pack. Still, Roxy loved me for rescuing her and anytime I saw her smile, my heart melted.

THANK YOU, ROXY.

When the German Shepherd Rescue called months later wanting Roxy to attend an adoption event, we made it official. I foster failed.

AND NOW, A FEW WORDS FROM THE COMMODORE...

I first met Vic in the parking lot of the swingers club The Green Door. *He and Moe were unloading gear for a shoot. I approached him about shooting my ex-wife, who was a porn star. He dismissed me like shit on his shoe and said he only booked from agents. I guess he assumed I was her suitcase pimp.*

He rubbed me as an arrogant wannabe porn director, the kind who thought they were the shit and every girl wanted to be with. I could have had that motherfucker killed. He gave me a total of ten seconds before pushing me to Moe who got me my first shoot for Manwin. Moe was a super nice guy infatuated with industry girls. We gave him shit because everyone banged his wife. Vic later gave me more work but initially would not let me shoot with him. Only Huggy.

At first, I respected Huggy. He showed me the ropes. When I began shooting for both of them, I saw the real Huggy. He was too busy flirting with the girls and thought he was the Don Juan of Porn. Girls put up with him because they believed his empty promises.

Huggy was a true piece of shit, always acting like he had money. He had nothing. I worked for a loan shark and lent Huggy money all the time at thirty percent. He paid it back knowing where it could land him. He was constantly plotting how he could ruin Vic or sabotage him. Vic was smarter than that dumb motherfucker and knew what Huggy was up to. Huggy had no idea what he was doing. When he told talent, "... don't listen to Vic, I run the show, I'm the producer, I'm the best they have here," I would laugh. Cocksucker stole my job. He was after everyone's job.

Vic is an awesome dude. Sometimes things went poorly: sad girls were fucked up, sets weren't ready, pictures came out like shit, scripts were abandoned, and Vic would go off the deep end. Vic was a man of details. He knew what it took to make money. Some days I felt like stabbing him.

Yes, I have a strange love for midgets even though they smell like cabbage. I wondered if their pussies were the same size as a normal pussy. Turns out, they were. Midgets are an odd fetish of mine. They're strange little creatures.

A LESSON ON COMPLIANCE:
ANGELINA VALENTINE AND THE INFAMOUS UNRELEASED SCENE

On a hot July day in 2013, I booked Angelina Valentine for a double penetration.

It wasn't her first DP and Angelina was not stoked to be deemed an anal girl. She gave up her anal porn virginity the year before after relentless requests from fans.

The first time I shot her was in 2006 when she started out. Back then, she was all natural with a few tattoos. She was perfect the way she was and a strong performer out of the gate. Sure, I detected some crazy, but more of the fuck-with-me-and-die sort.

Cut to a few years later, the tattoos migrated to most of her body and she underwent a few boob jobs plus lip injections. While her second boob job was too much and despite all the enhancements, she was hot in a trashy way. By late 2011, something was definitely wrong with Angelina.

Previously, she had been in a shaky relationship with a performer with a head full of rocks named Criss Strokes. When Blake was my intern in 2007, we nearly put Strokes under contract because he had a big dick. However, he let men suck his dick on gay websites, a huge no-no back then. There was a time when Angelina would only work with Strokes, so we tolerated him until they broke up.

The last time Strokes worked for me was around 2014. The scene prior, I cast him as Lloyd Christmas in a Dumb and Dumber *parody. He also played* Forrest Gump *in a Brazzers porn parody. So, there is a logical pattern at play. While he killed it playing an idiot, during the most important part, he struggled. While his scene partner Mark Wood (playing Harry) carried the scene, it was a dud and bummed me out. I gave every male talent a pass on days like these. We all have off days and I could not let one mediocre performance outshine all the others. About a year later, he was requested for a boy/girl/girl/anal scene with Phoenix Marie and Carter Cruise. I didn't think twice considering I had seen Phoenix arise many a Johnson. She reassured me everything will be fine. "He loves working with me." The intro and everything about the scene looked beautiful, particularly the set, which my crew transformed into a 1950s living room. But, Strokes could not keep his dick hard for more than a few minutes. We finished, but the scene was so choppy it was garbage. In the past, several stand-up performers instructed me to cut their rate to save face when this happened. It was the proper gesture. I was expecting Strokes to do the same, but instead he said "this is why I don't come to Vegas" while collecting his full eight-hundred-dollar rate. At an AVN party in 2018 he looked terrible. His eyes were sunken and his skin was wrinkly. He acted like nothing happened and suggested I book him again. He could tell I was uninterested. It did not stop him from trying to contact me again, and again, and again in unanswered messages. I figured he would get the memo, then I remembered he has rocks for brains. A few top performers dated Strokes. I guess a big dick can get you further in life.*

Post-breakup was the healthiest and happiest I ever saw Angelina. She was crushing it at the gym and looked fantastic. We spent an amazing night together.

"AMAZING" MEANING LOTS OF ANGELINA-STYLE SLOPPY DEEPTHROATING AND WATCHING HER SMOKE ALL OF HIS WEED.

Her mental state declined. During a boy/girl/girl/anal scene in 2011 with Tory Lane I wasn't sure if they were going to fuck or fight. They had similar competitive personalities and Tory balled up her fist at one point before reeling herself in. I was waiting on any of them to call "cut", but no one did. Ramón, the male talent, never wavered.

I had a thing for hot tattooed messes in the peak of my cocaine frenzy. Angelina and I had a relationship where I checked on her via text. Her responses were all the gauge I needed. If no trouble was indicated, I took the booking.

When shooting performers in questionable states of mind, there was a line between intoxication versus something else. Our directives were simple: no drugs or alcohol (weed notwithstanding). Any violations could end the day.

The concept I created in this case was for *BigTitsAtSchool.com*. Angelina played a female student obsessed with death and much looking forward to a field trip to the county morgue.

Perhaps this was in bad taste, but porn was the last bastion of the First Amendment in an increasingly uptight world and a small opportunity to exercise my rights as an American.

At the morgue, she gets DP'd by James Deen and Danny Wylde. Deen was a pro, even if he was entitled and akin to wrangling a kitten. I had heard good things about Danny and did my best to make him feel at ease. His sense of security did not last long. My guess is a lot of male performers were afraid to shoot a DP with Angelina.

I told Angelina to play it as a she-devil sex bomb who gets turned on at the morgue. She ran with it, intensely. No further direction needed.

After, Angelina went into her zone. One could argue she was acting. She was an outstanding performer, both in the dialogue and during the sex, except in anal. Regardless, the head office had teams reviewing and flagging anything suspect. It was rare for them to shelve something since it would mean a financial loss. As time went on, the head office erred on the side of caution more often.

Unless I saw something, I continued shooting. Days after a scene, performers cashed their checks and continued booking with other companies. If any red flags appeared on my viewfinder, I canceled the scene. My crew would try to salvage the day with local talent and a few additional hours at the office. If we had to cancel a day, the office trusted my judgment. This is how it went until the end of my career.

With this scene, it wasn't Angelina's state of mind vs. performance, but the *tone* and the necrophilia aspect of my concept. When I heard the word "necrophilia," I also heard skidding tires.

"She didn't fuck a corpse, Frank," was how I believe I responded.

"Vic, we went back and forth with this and it's the idea she gets turned on by death which makes it necrophilia."

"No, fucking a corpse makes it necrophilia. I'm not a psychologist, but I'm sure there is a condition where death and morbidity are turn-ons. Are you telling me it's not compliant?"

"It doesn't matter. We're not releasing the scene."

A verbal reprimand and mandate followed to keep 'gimme-scripts' compliant. Brand teams in Montreal wrote the scripts. They conjured up their cockamamie ideas, passed them down to the producers, and we had to make sense of them. Over time, concepts became more and more bizarre. Gimmes helped boost morale and allowed for lighter days on set. Eventually they were phased out, further demoralizing the directors and making our job less fun and more corporate.

I re-watched the scene, a few years removed from the industry. Having taken time to review every clip from beginning to end, here's my conclusion: the head office were a bunch of pussies. This could have been the first step in their pussification. The scene is entertaining as hell. The sex, if edited down, is hot, regardless of when Angelina told Danny she was going to shit all over his dick. It was obvious why Danny never came back: Angelina scared him. The sex was made difficult at times because the anal and DP segments were causing her pain. So, we adjusted accordingly.

Watching the footage was reminiscent of every morning while working for the company. I heavily scrutinized Huggy's scenes because I was not present during his shoots.

People must have thought I loved watching porn, but it was quality control. If I was asked about specifics, I was well-versed enough to back it up with examples. Preparation and organization were my forte. One of my previous wardrobe girls used to say I cared too much. This is why she didn't last long on the job. I did care, and I expected my staff to follow suit.

To keep everyone happy without losing my mind, I needed PEDs (performance-enhancing drugs) so the details were dialed in and the quality remained as high as possible. Some people choose Adderall. Hearing how nasally I was while giving general direction makes it painfully obvious I did a fat rail before work.

When I watched Angelina's sign-in, I saw a hot, hot mess. She was otherwise cognizant and ready to shoot. With Marcos leering in the background, I remembered the day was running long and sensed his impatience. This was validated when I watched Deen's sign-in, where we recorded the time at 1:57 p.m. Production was officially underway close to 2:30 p.m., which I considered behind schedule. 7:50 p.m. was my cutoff time to get people back to the airport for their flights. On days with a difficult DP, I booked later flights sensing inevitable delays. When days went smoothly, talent would complain about having to wait at the Las Vegas airport for five hours after their scenes.

SOMETIMES LIFE GIVES YOU LEMONS, DOESN'T IT?

We started the intro video, where I was fine with her making it her own.

"Just get the point across you're stoked while talking about your field trip to the morgue and then start masturbating."

Her bedroom is designed with skulls and spiderwebs, with heavy accents on the reds and blacks. Pete did an excellent job decorating the set, per usual. I needed her dialogue to be sensical, so I cut a few times because she would say "tomorrow" instead of "today." Her lips were deep red and with all her curves and tattoos (especially her sleeve of a trashy naked lady on this particular trashy naked lady), she looked hot, if you're into this sort of thing.

I AM.

After her initial flub, she pulled it together and delivered a very Angelina-esque intro, slowly getting turned on thinking about the cold bodies, toe-tags, and "watching the other students get grossed out." There was genuine excitement when she said "city morgue."

Before starting her masturbation sequence, I directed her to mix in the turn-on element throughout to which she replied, "Oh I will, honey." And she did. I stopped her once she mentioned jumping on the bodies, citing its non-compliance as actual necrophilia.

I told her to do it again, but to focus on having an orgasm, with no talk about the field trip. They could use this and cut out whatever they had issues with. When I zoomed in, her red lipstick was running onto her chin. Then she climaxed, hair disheveled, before rushing out the door.

HOT. MESS.

The next shot opened with the freezer doors, small stainless-steel doors mounted to a wall. For effect, we added masking tape with most of my crew member's names (including mine) labeled. We loved adding Easter eggs.

Angelina and everyone in the scene, from the medical examiner, to the teacher, to the fellow students, and Deen, who was a great actor, killed it.

We did nine takes, changing it up when needed. Take after take, we were all laughing, but mostly me. I shot it like any other scene, with multiple angles, while keeping the day moving along. It took me sixty minutes to shoot the intro.

We staged an outro with fake jizz since I had to cut my extras loose. Based on how the actual sex scene happened, there's no way Angelina's makeup would match. And, in typical porno magic, the 'corpse' Angelina pushes off the slab (to provide a fuck surface) disappeared. In its place was an ottoman covered with shiny silver material, no doubt stapled in place by Pete.

In the first few minutes of the sex act, aside from some weird noises from Angelina, I saw porn stars performing. Deen helped me out by cueing Angelina on how to max out both dicks during blowjob. Danny stayed strong despite it being his first shoot with this train wreck in an admittedly odd concept. He liked it when Angelina spit in his mouth. The first time I cut was eight minutes in when Danny started fucking her ass. Her legs were flailing and she mentioned the need to let it "soak in there a bit." So, we cut while it soaked.

Once things were well-marinated, I resumed filming the next five-minute segment and she let out a huge belch before we started. Danny fucked her ass, but I could tell she was uncomfortable when she kept giving him the Heisman. On camera, Deen tells him to move her to the shiny surface where he starts to stick it in her ass. She let out a "no" and then apologized to me because she needed to slow it down.

This is where having strong talent helped. Deen, on camera, Barry Whited her ass and slowly started back up. She was more into Deen than Danny. I zoomed to a wide shot where everything was getting into sync. This was the sweet spot I tried to find during every hardcore scene, where everyone got comfortable and could just fuck while I captured it. Sometimes it was immediate. Sometimes it took longer. Deen was the glue while Danny held on for the ride. Toward the end of the clip, she asked for lube when spit was no longer cutting it.

The next clip resumed with Deen in her ass while Danny tried getting a blowjob before progressing into her vagina. Once we started the DP, Deen continued to Barry White by talking her through it. The sex did not match the bitch in heat she played in the intro, but this was the reality of porn. Angelina never dug anal or DP's, yet she (or her agent) booked them frequently. Despite Angelina's eyelashes falling off, we kept going.

We had three minutes of quality DP footage before transferring back to blowjobs and vaginal sex. In total, eighteen minutes of footage, not enough to please Frank. Scenes no less than thirty minutes after editing were the requirement. Angelina started losing steam ten minutes in. Deen calmed her while giving her direction so I did not cut until we had to reset.

Deen told her how to stay in position so he could resume anal. It worked for a minute until she painfully called "cut". I mixed in extreme close-ups to give the editor options, but when she said the lube was burning, I cut.

Each clip was short-lived. She was trying and even suggested pouring cold water to wash off the lube. Along the way, Angelina warmed up to Danny, until he spanked her a few times. She retaliated by spitting on him and his cock. He reached for her head to move it to his dick, but she backed away and mumbled something about shitting all over him. I told her she can't say things like this.

SKAT. THAT AIN'T LEGAL.

I backed up to the transition by picking up on blowjob before having her ride Danny in anal reverse cowgirl. While moving into the second DP position, it got awkward between Deen and Angelina while discussing the best way to hold her legs. It didn't sound organic for a sex scene.

We finished by resuming the second DP position and she sustained for a few minutes. It was time to wrap things up.

We set up the double pop shot and I was right. To the trained eye, the fake pop I set up with the medical examiner before hardcore did not match. Her hair and makeup were destroyed. No matter, since they never released the scene. Like some days, it was a battle. The good, the bad, and the ugly were all beating up on each other to create the artform of hardcore pornography.

Both men covered Angelina. I tried to decipher what she said as I was zooming in on her cum splattered mess of a face, but even after multiple rewinds, all I made out was how she loved their cocks. Before I called "cut", I commented it was the most politically correct pop shot I had ever heard. After another viewing I realized she said she loved *Jewish* cock while smiling at Deen. She then looked at Danny and said she liked his cock, "... but I don't know what nationality you are."

While I walked back to my office, I hit record and apologized to the editor for the choppy scene. I blamed it on shooting someone who was "bat shit nuts." Despite its choppiness, looking at it as an editor, it's salvageable, even when pared down. During sign-outs, Deen was in a happy mood, no doubt because he was done, one-thousand-dollar check in hand and about to hit the shower. Angelina also was in great spirits after being paid seventeen hundred dollars. Despite all of it, I still found her attractive.

FLY YOUR FREAK FLAG!

It was the last time I saw Angelina. I would love to know where she is now and I hope she is doing better.

Danny was all smiles and laughs. He answered all the questions properly while Angelina was bent over behind him looking through her bag. Was he going through the motions? Perhaps, but he collected his seven-hundred-dollar check and I never saw him again.

Was the scene tasteful? No. Was it compliant? Yes. I am tempted to edit and leak it to the world and let the people decide.

ANGELINA! GIVE US A CALL. OUR NUMBER IS STILL THE SAME.

22 THE INFAMOUS SYPHILIS OUTBREAK OF 2012

Brazzers wanted to do a massive live show to kick off the summer. The idea was to have a celebrity type to host the event. I caught wind they were looking at Coolio or Dave Navarro. I saw a different path.

NO DISRESPECT TO COOLIO. RIP.

I first heard Howard Stern in seventh grade while on my way to school with my father on 94.1 WYSP-FM. Over the years, I became an avid fan and when he made the jump to satellite radio in 2006, I jumped with him. This was my chance to do a legitimate business deal with a Stern show staffer.

Our best shot was to get the writing team of Sal Governale and Richard Christy, who were porn fanatics. Plus, both were known to travel for side work while working for Howard.

Sal's website had no means for direct contact, but Richard's did and I shot off a complimentary email. He swiftly responded and turned down the gig because (in his slow Kansas drawl), "I think my wife would divorce me for doing something like this."

HAPPY WIFE, HAPPY LIFE. ESPECIALLY WHEN SHE IS AN EAGLES FAN.

Richard passed the idea to Sal who only asked about the pay. He was surprised there was a legitimate dollar amount attached.

MAYBE THIS CORPORATE PORN THING ISN'T SO BAD AFTER ALL.

We ironed out the specifics. It included an ample fee and extensive marketing support by Sal and the Stern universe. We got on-air plugs, discussions and mentions on the wrap-up show, and plugs on Sal's Twitter feed. Although he was initially a bit abrupt, Sal conducted himself professionally.

I picked Sal up at the airport and took him to his hotel. He was friendly and excited to get to work. The first day was prep. Sal wanted to make the show a success. His wife didn't have a problem with the live orgy as she planned to fly out a day later. His wife being present during a live sex show her husband was hosting was enough to get the Stern engine excited. They discussed the show on the air and The Howard 100 News Department called me for an interview. Portions of the interview were segments before and after the show which aired during commercials. My father was quite proud.

THE BUCKET LIST GOT ONE ITEM SHORTER.

I picked up his wife Christine and we all headed to the set. I did my best to put her at ease before she witnessed a live orgy.

The show was a massive success.

I admired Sal's work ethic. He wanted us all to be happy with his work. As for Christine, she sat off camera reading a book. What does one read while Katja Kassin is getting penetrated in multiple holes mere feet away? *Fifty Shades of Grey*, of course. Occasionally she glanced up and shook her head at her husband's on-screen antics.

For instance, a performer flaked on the show. Members were demanding to know where she was. When Katja had a fist inside of her, I buzzed to Sal, "Ask her if (missing performer) is up there." Without missing a beat, Sal complied.

TEAM WORK MAKES THE DREAM WORK.

When the show was over Jackie joined us and I treated everyone to a nice Italian dinner with copious amounts of red wine. We hugged and Sal said to contact him when I was on the East Coast. A friendship was blossoming.

While visiting family in Philly, I caught the train to New York City to meet Sal. He wanted to sit down with some investors for a new app he'd cooked up. Something to do with finding massage spas in whatever town you were in. He felt it was ideal for porn and asked me to take it to Manwin.

HOW DO I DOWNLOAD THIS APP?

After lunch, he gave me a tour of the studio at SiriusXM. I saw where Howard interviewed the greatest talents in the entertainment business as well as the members of the whack pack. The whirlwind day ended with us promising to stay in touch about the app and other opportunities.

Although the app did not make it to any initial meetings or non-disclosures, Sal invited me to Ronnie the Limo Driver's short-lived *Block Party* in Vegas.

With Jackie in tow, we met Ronnie and although he was a loudmouth on the air, he was very nice, and very short. Richard was there with his wife, pounding beers. Yucko the Clown introduced himself sans makeup as Roger and attempted to seduce Jackie. Eric the Actor (RIP, ack ack) was there with his assistant Yan who steered Eric's wheelchair into trash cans and other obstacles. JD Harmeyer was co-MC. He was as awkward as he sounded on the radio, and prior to the show, he paced around nervously. In a bikini contest earlier in the day, JD, Ronnie, and Eric the Actor voted Jackie the winner and crowned her "Hot Chick of the Week."

SHE BEAT ASS NAPKIN ED'S GIRLFRIEND/CONTESTANT JASMINE TAME.

The show wasn't great for the audience as it was slapped together and lacked upper-echelon production value. I didn't care. We had free access and admission to the backstage green room. After the show, I tried to engage JD in conversation, but it was futile. We were two socially awkward people sitting next to each other. We exchanged numbers and he was easier to communicate with over text, but not much.

With summer winding down, another shutdown was mandated, but this time it was not due to HIV.

The blame fell on a performer named Mr. Marcus and his selfish actions. He was branded with possibly the worst nickname of all time: Mr. Syphilis.

The industry was adopting new testing standards and two facilities fought for superiority. One was Cutting Edge Testing. The other, Talent Testing Service, started operations before Adult Industry Medical shut down, so it became the default laboratory for performer testing.

Unsubstantiated rumors were flying: Manwin owned CET; TTS was owned and operated by Shy Love, a former performer turned agent. There were ongoing fights over the testing mandates between Manwin and LATATA, the Licensed Adult Talent Agency Trade Association. Shy, Dr. Evil and other agents of LATATA wanted to be the governing body of performer testing whereas Manwin were more concerned about HIPAA laws and performer's privacy.

The fight seemed more about vested interests than performer's safety and confidentiality. All that performers wanted to know was which facility to visit so they could work. I pushed Manwin's mandates to keep the factory churning. At times it was maddening and distracted me from providing the highest quality porn to the consumer.

In the event of an outbreak, agents wanted to be informed of the identity of patient zero, although this was unlawful. To gain an edge, TTS included syphilis on its testing panel. According to news outlets, Mr. Marcus tested positive for syphilis, took a penicillin shot, and retested days later. Still positive for syphilis, he then doctored the results on his initial test and returned to work. The version I heard was he went to CET, which was not testing for it yet. He was 'clean,' so he returned to work. Eventually he was arrested and spent thirty days in jail[1]. Chaos ensued.

When Manwin greenlit the shutdown, anyone operating under a brand they owned (aka me) had to cease production. Those outside of the Manwin umbrella could abide, or not.

Many argued syphilis was treatable and not shutdown-worthy. The decision-makers weren't swayed and the shutdown continued. There was a massive uproar due to all the lost revenue. A lot of performers lived shoot-to-shoot.

THEY GOTTA FEED THE MONKEY, YOU KNOW?

The rage intensified when a photograph emerged of Mr. Syphilis receiving a blowjob from Lylith Lavey. Something was clearly wrong with his penis. His black shaft had white bumps all over it. Luckily, Lylith tested clean, but her reputation suffered by association. She sued Mr. Syphilis and settled.[2]

IN THE CASE OF PORN STARLET V. MR. SYPHILIS...

The syphilis outbreak had long-lasting ramifications. It became a lightning rod for more stringent testing standards, as well as further ammunition for supporters of the condom mandate. Measure B was on the ballot in California with voters deciding whether condoms should be required in porn and it passed.

Testing protocols changed drastically when production resumed a few weeks later. The competing testing labs now tested for HIV, Syphilis, Chlamydia, Gonorrhea, Hepatitis B/C and *Trichomonas vaginalis* (a parasite causing frothy/green vaginal discharge with a musty malodorous smell). Manwin also mandated fourteen-day testing. This was poorly received by the industry. Agents and performers cried foul, citing the cost and hassle of more frequent testing. Some agents charged producers an additional fee in defiance. Other outfits still accepted thirty-day testing. Secretly, I applauded more stringent testing standards. Let's be real: the previous standards were absurd.

DUDE, I'M ACTUALLY AMAZED WE DIDN'T CATCH MORE STDS.

On a selfish level, I liked the new testing protocols because I was having unprotected sex with performers behind my girlfriend's back. Access to this history was a wonderful perk. Much like the talent, I subjected myself to the same risks and rarely wore protection. On the eve of my fortieth birthday, my full panel showed no signs of any STDs.

NOT A DRIP. SHOCKING. DUDE MUST BE SUPERMAN.

Huggy was about to lose his last ally after an incident during one of our live shows. This one was a doozy.

When asked "who is the biggest whore in the industry?" only one name comes to mind: Ava Divine. I met Ava in my first six months in Las Vegas. I booked her for several scenes. She spun tales of her whoredom, claiming to suck off drive-thru workers, trans, little people, you name it. She discriminated against no penis, no matter the color, the age, or the size of the individual bearing it. Ava is the cause of one of the most ridiculous memories I have in the business:

Mansef wanted me to pair Ava up with her friend Sexy Vanessa for a boy/girl/girl scene. Their schedules were not syncing up because Ava had a client in town.

Her compromise was for me to allow said client to sit in during the scene. Male talent was turned off by the idea. After a few turned us down, I found a Hungarian performer who accepted.

"No problem. I will just fuck her harder," was his solution. This dude never lost his cool when Anthony Rossano's jizz landed on his arm during a boy/boy/girl scene.

HA! EASTERN EUROS LEAVE THEIR AMERICAN COUNTERPARTS IN THE DUST.

On the day of the shoot, Ava pulled in with what looked like a grandfather in the passenger seat. The man was not well. She introduced him as Chuck and when I went to shake his hand, his shaking hand was balled into a gnarled-up fist. I shook his normal hand and welcomed him. He was recently widowed and found companionship in Ava. He was thankful and appreciative to be here, so much you'd think I was granting him his wish from the Make-A-Wish Foundation. She referred to him as Chuckles.

"Why do you call him Chuckles, Ava?" I asked.

"It's my nickname for him. I call him Chuckles McKnuckles, because he fists my asshole with his bad fist."

FIND ME A SINK.

Chuckles wore an ashamed smile. I saw it again an hour later.

We started shooting, with Chuckles sitting behind me. Whenever I cut, Ava walked behind me and interacted with him. I was too frightened to turn around. When my camera battery died, I left the room to retrieve a new one. I was gone less than two minutes and when I entered my casita studio there was Ava, her hands up and facing me, covered in old man goo.

"Look, Vic, Chuckles came!"

Chuckles had an embarrassed smile and a big wet stain on his yellow pants.

DUDE, CAN WE FAST FORWARD TO THE PART WHERE PAUL GETS FIRED.

Cut to five years later, Ava was participating again in one of our live shows and we messed with Paul's head a bit. We told him Ava was going to chase down our fresh meat and devour him. While this was all in jest, sadly it was the case.

Huggy was running camera during our post show where performers could continue having sex in the showers, if they wished. Ava was baiting Paul into taking out his dick so she could blow him and in a momentary lapse of reason, he complied. Huggy shot it live, capturing Paul's untested penis in Ava's mouth while his hands grabbed her head. It was a three-second blow job.

Pete, who was operating the switching board, asked if he could show it, but I didn't allow it. I knew what the repercussions would be from the head office. However, there was no hiding the act in the raw footage. Later, when an editor was cutting the show, he notified Frank. Given the testing climate and the fire the company had come under, they ordered me to terminate a hardworking single father.

I defended Paul and although Frank was aware of Ava's antics, it was over once

Paul placed his hands on the back of her head. Had he not touched her, it might have saved his job. The morning he arrived at work, I called him into my office.

Seeing a grown man cry over the loss of his job from something so unfulfilling as a brief, flaccid blowjob was painful. Paul had to worry about providing for his daughter nine months after relocating from North Carolina. He moved back and found odd jobs to support them. Huggy blamed Ava for the incident. Now, we needed another PA. Out of all the bad hires I had made in previous years, the next one would surpass them all.

ENTER FUCKTARD.

HOT CHICK OF THE WEEK COMPETITION

ME AND JD

ME AND ERIC THE ACTOR

ME AND RONNIE

23 TURNING PRIMAL

Fucktard had been an extra for us in the past. His illustrious acting career was highlighted when he backed a rented RV into our dumpster during a scene costing a thousand dollars in damage. I take full blame. Even cocaine abuse cannot excuse replacing Paul with this dumb bastard.

FUCKTARD, YOU WERE THE WORST OF THE WORST.
LOWEST IN PORN STANDARDS. THAT'S PRETTY FUCKING LOW.

The porn industry attracts a certain type, some of whose motivation of monetary gain is secondary. They want to be close to the seedier benefits. Fucktard was from this camp. He wanted to be around pussy all day. He was a recipe for disaster given one of his jobs included driving talent.

When Fucktard heard of Paul's departure, he petitioned for the PA job. We needed a fresh set of hands so I gave him a three-month probationary period. Fucktard's performance during that time was stellar and we hired him officially.

Marijuana's proliferation forced me to adopt a more lax drug policy. Weed helped the disposition of a lot of performers and crew, including me. After sign-in, I allowed those in need to take their medicine off premises. Fucktard became ever-baked and complacent.

My relationship with Jackie continued with fun times, offset by her falls into despair.

LATHER. RINSE. REPEAT.

I encouraged her to get help, but she resisted, mainly because she didn't have insurance. When she did, she was relegated to cash-only doctors. Side note: cash-only doctors usually have legal trouble in their past.

They threw around 'bipolar' and 'border personality disorder,' and gave her sample packs of antidepressants. She wanted out of stripping, but didn't even have a high school diploma. I saw promise and believed she could better herself.

No one besides me encouraged her. She loved me for it and said so on a daily basis.

I didn't say it back. I had to be sure I meant it. I could have lied, but that's an awful thing to do. Jackie needed love. She felt Meridiana ruined me and she was bearing the brunt of that failed relationship.

SHE'S NOT WRONG, WALTER. YOU'RE JUST AN ASSHOLE.

My caution resulted from wanting to learn from my mistakes and break the patterns of the past. My inability to love her caused intense arguments. The fighting would spiral her deeper into self-loathing. It was a Catch-22 and I expected a break-up soon. So I continued cheating, like a lying piece of shit.

LIKE A BOSS.

Most never asked nor cared, but if they did, I said I was single. Only a handful of girls knew. Many were receptive if they weren't in a relationship. The majority of exchanges were fun and primal, leading to little personal turmoil. Except one.

THERE'S ALWAYS ONE.

A certain girl/girl-only *Penthouse* Pet we shot for Twistys Live had been on the books but there was always a subsequent cancellation. When she actually made it to a shoot, she looked prettier than her photos, warm and friendly. After the show, the manager of Twistys told me she wanted him to pass on her phone number. We started chatting.

Less than six months later, she was booked again. It was on. After the show, she bought an eight-ball. I had an early flight, so this was my excuse for not making it a late night. I brought her back to my house where we (mostly her) made a dent in the eight-ball. She lined up and snorted rails like an ant-eater.

HENCEFORTH! YOU SHALL BE KNOWN AS ANT-EATER!

I had to stop as my heart pounded.

We yakked it up for hours and I learned a lot about her, namely her love for cocaine. She had a psychologically intense upbringing with two educated and analytical parents. She engaged in intelligent conversation and hours flew by with no time left for what we'd intended. Something told me to wait, so I drove her back to her hotel.

NOT MY BEST ADVICE. IN HINDSIGHT, HIT AND RUN WAS THE RIGHT PLAY.

In the parking lot she climbed into my lap to make out and I declined her invitation upstairs. We agreed to set aside time on her next visit. She partied all night in Las Vegas while I tried to sleep before my early flight. I knew she was a disaster and should have let it go. Instead, my resistance to a quickie only hardened her resolve.

My financial outlook was improving, even with my womanizing and cocaine abuse. I paid down my mortgage and was socking away tens of thousands a year with my financial advisor.

Fabian had been acquiring more companies and his next bite would be his biggest: Reality Kings. The owner of Reality Kings, "Icy" Mike Imber, remained a shareholder, but for all intents and purposes, they were acquired. With this behemoth under the Manwin umbrella, it had become the undisputed king of porn. The monster was everywhere.

My production manager Pete was frustrated with some of our team, namely Ethan the PA. Ethan's motivation sucked and Pete was sick of it. Pete had a difficult time delegating and often did Ethan's job himself. Ethan had been in the business longer than Pete as a former agent and performer in LA before moving to Vegas. He was eleven years older than Pete, so taking his direction was deflating.

Fucktard still portrayed himself as a go-getter, so Pete wanted me to fire Ethan and promote Fucktard. Not listening to Pete and working with Ethan to elevate him was one of my smarter decisions. Ethan figured out he was close to termination and stepped up his game. This coincided with Fucktard decaying into a lazy-eyed pothead motivated by his dick. Whispers of Fucktard being the creepy driver spread. In one instance, an agent called me asking why my driver asked to stay in their talent's hotel room one evening. I gave him a warning and told him this cannot happen again. In another instance, he was forthcoming about sending nasty text messages to a performer who didn't want to play video games with him.

YOUR FAULT FOR NOT TERMINATING HIM THEN AND THERE, WITH CAUSE.

Thank you, Captain Obvious. Jackie had nightmares that I was cheating. When we weren't having sex, she (correctly) assumed the worst. She was a monster to deal with. We got kicked out of a club on my birthday after Jackie started a fight with a girl one table over for talking to me.

HOW ABOUT WE JUST CHEAT MORE, THAT'LL DO THE TRICK.

Then she became friends with a high-end Vegas hooker, a plastic-looking, tattooed knockoff of Megan Fox. She had a boyfriend in Texas, a married sugar daddy in California, and charged three thousand dollars *per session* for her services.

HENCEFORTH! YOU SHALL BE KNOWN AS 3K!

3K admitted, on some nights, she roofied johns and took their money after they passed out. She had a car the boyfriend paid for, designer clothing, Louis Vuitton handbags, yet she lived in a rented house in Jackie's neighborhood. It was as if laboratory scientists collaborated to create the ultimate hooker, down to the complete lack of any moral fiber or compass. She also loved pills, drinking, and cocaine.

AND? WHAT'S THE PROBLEM? THREESOME!

Jackie had no female friends in Las Vegas, so 3K had to suffice. A sick friendship developed which fed her self-loathing and low self-esteem. Jackie was naturally beautiful, but the more she spent time with 3K, the more she wanted to be like her. She talked about getting Botox, her lips injected, her boobs done, and more tattoos. I told Jackie she was perfect as she was. With all the antidepressants swimming in her head, she added cocaine, pills, and alcohol to the mix. Secretly, we were feeding our own cocaine addictions.

Ant-eater came back for her third Twistys Live show. She wanted to spend the night together. She was adamant and not in a purely sexual way. I was boyfriend material. Ant-eater had no idea I was in a relationship. Cocaine prevented me from seeing the disaster and stage-four clinger she was.

Fucking at my house was out as Jackie could pop in any time or find a rogue hair in my bed and lose her mind. So we grabbed a big bag of blow and retired to a room at the Luxor. I was excited for the new strange, and anxious to take the plunge.

PLUNGE. AS IN HE'S ABOUT TO PLUNGE A TOILET...

We drank and blew rails before getting down to business. Her boobs were uneven and scarred, something I missed while directing the live shows. Frankentitties I could handle. It was the stink wafting into my nostrils after I stuck my penis inside her. I had to focus on staying hard.

IT WAS THE SMELL, NOT THE COCAINE, I SWEAR.

As mentioned, I had encountered overwhelming stench in my travels and had defenses and tactics to complete the mission. But, there was no escaping this cesspool and I did my best to finish fast. Once I got my nut, I ran to the bathroom to scrub my dick. The putrid experience was mitigated by my knowledge of her clean test days prior. This rotten crotch was severe, but not diseased. Now I needed to figure out the least offensive way to escape.

PENTHOUSE PET WITH ROTTEN CROTCH. TRAGIC.

Having to work the next day was the perfect excuse, if you are sane. This did not resonate and she pitched a fit. I placated her with kind words before I stopped caring and left.

Ant-eater found out I had a girlfriend and was livid. She called me a "predator" and said I took advantage of women.

PREDATOR? SHE ASKED FOR YOUR NUMBER, DUDE.
YOU FELL PREY TO HER STINKY BOX. CASE DISMISSED!

For the first time I was concerned my escapades would get back to Jackie. Instead, Ant-eater went for the nuclear option: disruption at work.

She told the Twistys manager I gave her drugs and she performed the live show under the influence. Of course, this was all plausibly denied. I pled my case before it spiraled further. Instead of sleeping, I worried about my girlfriend finding out and messaged the manager who was putting money in my pocket every month.

The Twistys manager knew her and all her craziness. He could not believe she admitted taking drugs before a shoot.

My pleaded case sounded reasonable to him. He sided with me because she sounded manic from blowing lines all night. He surmised she was upset because we had sex and I left. I apologized again for allowing a personal matter to disrupt work and the situation was defused.

Later, she threatened to go public and I told her nothing was stopping her. If she wanted industry peers to know she was a performer who needed drugs to work, go for it. I had no problem publicly countering any claims while explaining the real reason I left. Fortunately, it fizzled out. I was bewildered a few months later when she was in Vegas and asked me to get her cocaine.

This should have been my wake-up call to shake the devil which had sunk its claws and either break up with Jackie or stop cheating. I was on a path of destruction and had not suffered any real loss.

I was indestructible.

My personal life was insane.

Then Fabian got arrested for tax evasion.

COCAINE'S A HELLUVA DRUG

24 DID D-LIST CELEBRITY ███████* ROOFIE MY GIRLFRIEND?

** This was at the very top of the "high risk" issues my publishing lawyer conjured for me. Hauser and Ed agreed the D-List celebrity ███████ should not be "named or easily identified." When three lawyers (one of which is getting paid a substantial amount of my hard-earned smut dollars) unanimously agree on a topic, I acquiesced. However, if anyone encountered a similar incident during the AVN convention in 2013, I would love to hear your story.*

HENCEFORTH! ██████ SHALL BE KNOWN AS THE ROOFIE KING!

News spread like wildfire Fabian was arrested at the Brussels airport and extradited to Germany. He was accused of not paying taxes on nearly $100 million of profits from Manwin's umbrella company[1]. The company made no public statements about his arrest, but his detractors, who had named him Darth Thylmann, reveled in this news. I received anonymous texts from joyous parties:

> "Yeaaaaah! ur boy fabian is in jail… it's going to be fun watching you thieves go down… "

Financial problems had plagued the company. A few years prior, the Secret Service seized $6.4 million[2]. Fabian portrayed himself as a different kind of porn kingpin by playing up his tech aspects. In 2011, he convinced a Wall Street investment firm to give Manwin a nine-figure investment loan explaining how an eight-story building was filled with over eight hundred employees. Now, the future of the company was uncertain. With AVN around the corner, I had the chance to gain intel.

Jackie's jealousy was climaxing as AVN approached. She didn't understand my bosses were attending and this was our annual facetime. She didn't understand how any interaction could be had at loud parties in clubs with porn stars everywhere.

DON'T BE MAD BECAUSE WE HAVE FUN AT WORK.

In a sense, Jackie was correct. She had been out of the industry for a few years, but to counter me going out, she met some of her old porn friends. She wanted to spy on me, but she got roofied. Possibly by The Roofie King.

AVN attracts an interesting blend of D-list celebrities. This year The Roofie King attended. I saw The Roofie King at the Manwin party with arm candy who looked miserable. Afterwards he headed to the White Party at Body English where he intersected with Jackie.

I never saw Jackie at the party, but she called on her way home. She was drunk driving and giddy from meeting The Roofie King. She had a thing for D or F-list celebrities, her greatest conquest a threesome with Corey Feldman and his girlfriend, *The Lost Boys* playing in the background.

GOONIES WOULD HAVE BEEN BETTER. SLOTH LOVE PUSSY.

The Roofie King hit on her, but she was a good girl and came home to me for an aggressive session of anal. We'd engaged in butt play before, though tonight she was an anal freak. I thought it was because she was drunk and horny.

The next morning, I had a meeting where I was pitched about partnering in a potential webcam studio. My facility had a lot of rooms and I lived on uncertain ground after Fabian's arrest, so I explored additional options. I knew little about the webcam business and it seemed like a massive headache. To be profitable, the facility had to run twenty-four hours a day. The business model required round the clock security and IT. The biggest question mark: finding reliable and dependable sex workers to fill the rooms. I switched gears and focused on finding solid footing with post-Fabian Manwin.

After the studio tour, I drove him back to the Hard Rock and my phone started blowing up. It was Jackie, but I sent her to voicemail. She called nineteen times and if I cared about his opinion, I would have been embarrassed. Once I dropped him off, I called back.

"You never came home, you fucking liar!"

"What are you talking about?"

"You told me you were coming home last night and I just woke up and you aren't here. You are a liar!"

"Holy fuck, are you nuts? I fucked you in your ass last night!"

Silence.

"You did?"

She had no recollection, but mentioned her anus was a tad sore. Otherwise, I would have had no proof.

Then I realized.

"I think you were roofied last night."

How else could she have forgotten? The cause of the very welcoming anal was making more sense now.

She said she met The Roofie King and he was very hands-on and friendly. He wanted her to stay the night and gave her his phone number. I asked if she left her drink unattended and she didn't know, nor could she remember if he bought her a drink.

Her last memory was driving home. While I have no proof he roofied her, all signs point to the creepy little marmot doing it. A few months later when he texted her, I told her to ask him if he would be interested in double penetrating her with me. He replied he didn't know she had a boyfriend and was going to leave her alone. She seemed sad the D-lister no longer wanted to interact with her.

DP WITH A D-LISTER, SAD TO MISS OUT ON THAT ONE.

The CFO, Feras Antoon, reassured me the company's future was secure. He was adamant. Fabian's arrest was overblown. It vibed like PR talk, but they were carrying on as if nothing was wrong. Internally, things were unraveling and a massive downsizing was forthcoming.

Fucktard regressed further into being a lazy and useless employee. More stories circulated he was trying to fuck the performers. Legend has it he scored occasionally. He was putting a lot of lines out with only the desperate taking the bait. He even appeared in scenes outside of my operation. On his second attempt, a blowbang/bukkake scene, he failed to perform.

His shy cock did not discourage him from telling girls he was a performer, even suggesting his services on our shoots. My major issue, aside from him failing the scene and wasting our day, was his small dick.

FUCKING LOSER. A SMALL DICK TOO.

Marcos and Pete were renting a house with Fucktard. He was falling short on rent and asked me for an advance, which I granted, blindly enabling his laziness.

Instead of paying rent, he bought a PlayStation. Then, a two-by-four he'd drilled into a wall fell on his head. Urgent Care stitched up the gash.

By summer, Jackie was arrested for DUI after her shift. She spent the night in the tank. I found her an attorney and paid his retainer fee. He could plea the case down. I told Jackie to coordinate with him and do whatever he asked. She said she didn't want to go back to jail as it was a horrible experience.

It's easy to forget about handling life when you are drowning yourself in pills, alcohol, cocaine, and antidepressants. Although her life was about to spiral, she completed her GED and was figuring out what came next.

Her co-dependence made my world hers. She truly loved me, but lived through me only. I tried explaining it was unhealthy and she took it as rejection. I still had not said the three words. She asked if I thought I could ever love her. I said I wasn't sure.

There were too many things wrong with the relationship. We were erratic from having wonderful times I wished would last forever to crashing down into horrible darkness. The stability and consistency I sought eluded me. She had no idea how to feel better about herself, but it was impossible when she was polluting her mind.

LIKE YOU WERE DOING ANY BETTER, ASSHOLE. TWO PEAS IN A POD.

The good times felt really good and I loved how much she loved me. She bought me little gifts because she was thinking about me. She loved my dogs and regardless if she worked all night, she got out of bed and headed to my house to let them out when I was working all day. Occasionally, Joker's stomach turned and he left nice piles on my rug which she cleaned up. Compared to Meridiana, I was willing to look past a lot to chase the Jackie I was crazy about. We reached our breaking point when she hacked my phone.

INFORMATION CONTROL, MY GOOD MAN.

We were at my brother's house, the second night in a week-long trip taking us to my father's house, central Pennsylvania to see The Senator and friends, and ending in Pittsburgh, where we met my financial advisor and saw the Phillies play the Pirates at PNC park. I had been careless punching in my phone code and she saw the numbers.

I had several trysts the previous week. The more Jackie and I fought, the more I did rails of cocaine and planned rendezvous in hotel rooms late at night after a shoot. I was getting sloppy and had an ominous feeling she was going to find out soon. Subconsciously, I *wanted* to get caught since I could have been much more careful and deleted any incriminating evidence. I just didn't think she would ever hack into my phone.

COCAINE.

One time I woke up and saw her, because the lights were on. She was up to something, but I fell back asleep. A few hours later, as soon as my eyes were open, she asked:

"How long have you been cheating on me?"

She rolled off names and conversations, hitting me with metaphorical lefts and rights from which I had no defense because I had just opened my eyes. She had all the validation she needed from my reaction alone, but no hard proof. She had trouble with iPhones, because she was a Samsung girl.

She asked me to take her to the airport, she was breaking up with me, and she wasn't going to cause a scene at my brother's house. I pondered my next move. I hadn't admitted anything yet, so was there still a way to spin this? When she came downstairs, I told her she had it wrong, but I'd still take her. We needed an excuse to give my brother and the kids for her sudden departure.

"I just got a call my dogs got out," was the best she could think of. My brother and his wife didn't buy it, but they deferred and off we went on a forty-five-minute drive to the Philadelphia airport.

"You know, once you get on the plane, we are done, right?"

"Well explain this to me, because you look like a cheater."

"You know how you tell me at the strip club you have to tell customers sex is a possibility in the V.I.P. room so you can get them up there? It's a hustle, right? Well, in order for me to get some of the girls to shoot, I have to hustle. Some of them want to fuck, so I use that to make sure they make it to the shoot."

It was god-awful stinky horseshit and the best I could come up with. The strange part: it was working, or so I thought. When we got to the airport, she changed her mind. When we got back to Las Vegas, she broke up with me. A few days later, she wanted to see me.

IT'S A TRAP!

Sitting before me was a very conflicted girl. She said she had a conversation with one of my conquests who admitted we had sex and she needed to hear it from me. Most men will tell you, admit nothing. Even if there's proof, deny deny deny. When she asked me why I did it, I told her because I was fucked in the head. The love in her eyes diminished, replaced by cold hatred. I will never forget that.

A few days later a box of things I had bought her was sitting on my doorstep. She said it was so I could hold them for her. A glimmer of hope. She was not ready to end things. She admitted to cheating when she was back home in Arizona. She did it for revenge.

Slowly, we had conversations about what would or could come next. We discussed a set of rules where we could enjoy other people. I was entering into an open relationship. We were agreeing under a cocaine haze so things wouldn't end.

The next eight months consisted of bigger lies, intense fights, and more cheating. She and 3K became drug-addled, whoring partners in crime.

One morning, she engaged me in a high-speed chase on I-15 during rush hour after I flipped her the bird. She then threatened suicide and I had to involve her mother who drove up to intervene. She took her to a therapist, but this interlude was a temporary patch to a much larger issue.

HE WAS STUBBORN WITH THIS ONE. AS MANY TIMES AS I TOLD HIM TO LET HER GO, HE REFUSED. LOVE IS STRONGER THAN OZ.

IN HER OWN WORDS
JACKIE ON THE ██████ INCIDENT

<u>Transcription of a recording of Jackie in September 2022:</u>

“I went to go spy on Vic to try to find him and see what bitches he’s with. I thought he would be with some hookers, I don’t know whatever starlets are in town visiting during AVN. It was at... the Hard Rock Casino... ”

“So I went there to go spy on him, of course I dressed up slutty. Didn’t find him and seeing a bunch of girls that I knew and they were going to Body English. So, I was like ‘fuck it, I am already here.’ So I went in and... saw ██████. And of course when you run into a D-list celebrity, you’re like ‘oh, that guy.’ He said I was really cute and he’s like ‘I have a bottle upstairs, you can come up here.’ I was like ‘ok, and I remember going up there and Bree Olson was up there as well. She had a white dress and blond hair and I thought she was so pretty. She’s famous, so I’m like ‘ok, she knows him, so that’s cool.’ Um, he handed me a drink and literally I probably don’t remember more than four minutes after that. I think I was just standing there drinking my drink. I just... I vaguely remember, so it all started coming back to me when I started thinking about it. I woke up at Vic’s house, screaming at him that he didn’t come home. I was furious. I called him maybe twenty-eight times (laughs) probably more than that. But texting ‘you’re a piece of shit’ you know the whole nines. Just thinking he didn’t come home, like I am at his house and he’s not here.”

“Well, then finally he calls me and he’s like ‘you fucking idiot. I have been in meetings with my bosses and I did come home last night.’”

“I said ‘no you fucking didn’t. I am on your couch.’”

“’He goes ‘I fucked you in your ass last night. You told me you met ██████.’”

“I said, ‘oh shit.’ So then I started thinking back. I’m like ‘hold on, I don’t even remember even getting to his home. I just remembered waking up, and I started thinking and I’m like ‘I remember leaving, I don’t remember driving, I remember like finding a back door kind of thing, like it was an exit, I guess? And I remember walking down a lot of stairs. And then waking up on the couch. I don’t remember. But apparently we had anal sex, and he came in my ass, and I am a psycho bitch who thought he didn’t come home.”

“There was semen left over in my anal cavity and my ass fucking hurt! I remember reaching back when he said 'I fucked you in your ass' because I don't do anal, I reached back and was like 'ooh it hurts. Ok,' and then I went to the bathroom and there was semen in my butt."

"I literally just remember having one drink. He poured it from his bottle on his table and handed it to me and then... and then nothing. Like who knows how even long I was there? In my recollection I was there for a few moments after."

Jackie forgot The Roofie King had given her his number.

"Alls I know is if he didn't drug me, he had drugs in his alcohol, you know. Some people take GHB for fun, I know I have taken it before in my early 20's. I didn't taste it though since GHB has a very rusty salty coppery taste. I just remember drinking a vodka cranberry and it tasted very normal. So in my mind, I would have noticed GHB. But who knows, I don't know what's out there."

"I probably ordered a drink at the Circle Bar looking for you. Like, just a beer or something, but that's it. When I say 'oh ████ drugged me' I'm like one hundred percent I am not an alcoholic, but I can drink, you know? I've had a whole bottle to myself before and I can remember the evening and yet I had one fucking cocktail, don't remember leaving, and I don't remember having anal sex which is not something I do."

There will never be proof of Rohypnol in Jackie's system. Maybe some other creeper who is not The Roofie King roofied Jackie earlier in the evening. The immediate effects from one drink are highly suspect, if not circumstantial. Perhaps Ms. Bree Olson has more to say on the matter. She was one of Charlie Sheen's goddesses.

PERHAPS BREE OLSON IS THE CENTER OF YOUR PORN UNIVERSE, DUDE.
SHE KEEPS TURNING UP IN THIS STORY.

APOLOGIES TO AVY SCOTT

The night Jackie hacked my phone, she saw conversations with performers I was fucking, had fucked, and planned on fucking. One was Avy Scott, whom she confronted directly.

I first shot Avy when I moved to Vegas. She was dating performer Anthony Rossano, best known for the website *FartHammer.com*. She was cool, naturally beautiful, and sex to her was like a handshake. She said she would love to shake hands with me, but on camera, otherwise it would be cheating on Anthony.

Raincheck.

STOP. EXPLAIN FARTHAMMER.COM. NOW.

Fine. Anthony would pick up a girl, usually at the beach, bring her back to his apartment, fuck her and then fart in her face. Anthony would not reveal if the farts were real or a sound effect. May I continue my apology please?

YES. PLEASE CONTINUE.

When I shot Avy in 2009, she had broken up with the Fart Hammer, but I was engaged to Meridiana. It was hard to repress our pheromones intoxicating one another. "Raincheck," she said.

When our paths crossed again, I kept my relationship status to myself. I didn't want to regret another missed opportunity. Yet, regrets are all I got. The sex (at least for me) was amazing and fulfilling. It should have been the tip (of the iceberg). Dating her could have made me one of the luckiest men in the world.

HERE WE GO AGAIN.

Instead, I got hacked. Jackie called Avy and introduced herself as my girlfriend.

YIKES. DICK PUNCH.

My chance with Avy was lost, forever. Avy was apologetic and told Jackie she hadn't known. It did not escalate. Jackie asked if Avy was who I wanted and I should have said yes.

Avy texted later, more disappointed than angry. She was getting tested to ensure I didn't give her anything.

HOW DARE YOU! THIS DUDE ALWAYS PISSES CLEAN!

I never heard from her again. My guilt was allayed by more cocaine and focusing on other ways to sabotage my life.

Avy, I don't deserve your forgiveness. I was a coked out, lying, cheating bastard. There is no excuse. Hopefully you can forgive me, but I understand if you don't.

25 PAY YOUR TAXES

Blake's tenure at Manwin ended. He never recovered from the HIPAA misstep while new management saw a cash-hemorrhaging buffoon with no talent masquerading as a producer. His crew, including Bramm, was reassigned and dismantled, and rumors circulated Blake was moving into interior decorating.

My fortieth birthday was around the corner and I planned on celebrating in style. I hired my friend's band to play in my backyard and invited friends from all corners of the country. To absorb costs, I planned a shoot with Lisa Ann and Phoenix Marie around the event, which I shot during a sleep-deprived, cocaine-fueled stupor.

I was looking pretty good for forty. No STD's and the picture of perfect health. I was not about to argue.

The night before everyone was due to arrive, Jackie and I got into a nasty fight and broke up. She went out on an all-night bender with 3K and wrecked her car. Another small detail she revealed at the group dinner: she and 3K had sex.

OOOOOOOOOO. ANY PICS OR VIDEO?

I wasn't going to allow anything to spoil my weekend. Aside from cocaine, my numbing agents included whiskey, weed, LSD, and mushrooms.

A PICTURE OF PERFECT HEALTH.

The party was a blast. I ended things by singing Johnny Cash's *Cocaine Blues* while sitting atop the 1976 Winnebago Chieftain I'd rented to the company for our *Breaking Bad* parody.

A few weeks later, Manwin laid off a quarter of its workforce in an event they called 'M-100.' I guess the moniker sounded impactful. Rumor had it security was ushering people out. Fabian's arrest created ripples and loans were being recalled.

MilfsLikeItBlack.com was the first casualty of budget cuts. Its monthly scene order had dwindled from four a month, to two, to one, and now it was over.

I still had to stomach Fucktard's antics until Pete found a replacement. Meanwhile, Pete was making other career plans.

The next to go were live shows. Instead of once a month, they now wanted to shoot each brand quarterly. Our volume was dropping. The handshake agreement I had made with Huggy four years ago had to end since I no longer could promise him thirteen shoots a month. I encouraged him to seek out additional work. He went on and on about all of his prospects.

I planned on spending Thanksgiving with Jackie, but she was so erratic we could not go more than a few hours without fighting. I gave her a few thousand to buy a new F-150, thinking it would make her happy and more independent. Breakups were common. I headed to Philly alone.

BREAK UP WITH HER FOR FUCK'S SAKE.

Her mania was reaching its ceiling due to her addictions. She was visiting friends in LA, but I suspected otherwise. On her way back from LA, she was pulled over and arrested for outstanding warrants stemming from her last DUI. I was livid. She had learned nothing. I ignored her calls from prison.

LET'S GO GET SOME STRANGE.

3K and her mother asked me to pay a bail bondsman and spring Jackie. Jackie needed time to stew about her life decisions. I let the justice system run its course and she enjoyed an extended stay in the Clark County Detention Center.

TOUGH LOVE. COLD AS ICE!

She spent three days in holding. She drank out of a toilet and ate bland bologna sandwiches. The substances left her body and she learned she never wanted to go back to prison. Of course, she blamed her lawyer. The one I found and paid for.

I'M STARTING TO THINK SHE'LL NEVER LEARN, DUDE.

Pete informed me he was moving on from porn to be back to LA closer to his mother. This was only part of the story. He promised he wouldn't leave until I was in good hands.

I believed this was the beginning of the end. When Huggy told me Pete was really leaving because my friend Jordan Ash offered him a job, it hurt. Hearing it from Huggy was an extra twist of the knife.

ET TU, PETER? ET TU?

Pete was free to choose, but the clandestine nature of his recruitment bothered me. Had the roles been reversed and Jordan had an employee I coveted, I would have reached out first. It's common courtesy.

I had no true friends in the business.

The next logical step was elevating Ethan to production manager. He was more than qualified. Pete helped with the transition and he and Ethan decided Fucktard should go. More accusations were mounting that Fucktard took his dick out during rides to the airport.

If they asked for weed, he asked for head. Two A-list performers told the same story. It's never a good time to fire an employee and he was livid when I did it during our holiday break. While I had reason to terminate him with cause and block his unemployment benefits, why kick a loser when he's down?

YOU'RE TOO NICE, DUDE.

I told him he was a casualty of cutbacks and signed his unemployment request. Herschel, the accountant and the man in full control of the operating entity, disagreed. He disputed the creepy bastard's request. In the coming months, Fucktard pleaded with me to allow him back, thinking he was being punished. I ignored him.

AVN 2014 was underway and despite Jackie's protests, I needed to know the identity of the new bosses. When Fabian stepped down as CEO, several parties bought his shares.

Feras Antoon, the former Syrian CFO of Manwin, was now CEO. I had known Feras since the Mansef days. He reassured me I would not be "too affected" by the cuts. This was of little comfort after I witnessed upper management behave like animals in their VIP area. Feras pointed out the various new partners and suggested I try and speak with them.

One of them was David Tasillo, a manager elevated to CFO. He went by Santana and in the past he'd been encouraging and appreciative.

Feras then pointed out 'Icy' Mike Imber, former owner of Reality Kings. He was wondering who the fuck I was.

VIC FUCKING LAGINA. DAMN GLAD TO MEET YOU.

Feras pointed out a few others, but being in a club, all I heard was that the owner of Red Tube also bought some of Fabian's shares. Feras and company rebranded to Mindgeek, because the Manwin name brought a lot of bad baggage. They were still considered the Evil Empire.

While cost-cutting and ROI was their mantra, they hosted elaborate dinner and club parties. Wall Street had recalled their loans as they feverishly tried to secure new ones.

I watched the new VP of Brazzers, George, dump ice buckets of water on upper management and rip open their dress shirts. The company had devolved and selfish pigs were running the show. These men could not be trusted. That said, if there was still money on the table, I wasn't going to leave it behind.

At work, Frank pushed me to reduce costs. It was a broad mandate with no plan of action since they operated inefficiently. My next plan was to trim the fat and push Huggy out the door. To avoid a future headache, it needed to be his own decision.

I squeezed him, forcing him to find supplementary income, until there was nothing left to give. Once he was gone, I'd take over his shoots and make a deal with Frank to absorb half of his pay, allowing the company to keep the remainder. It was naïve in hindsight.

Around the time Pete was wrapping up his tenure, OSHA paid another visit.

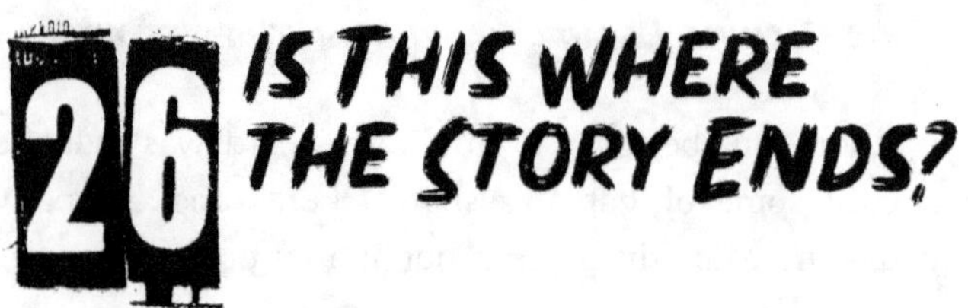

26 IS THIS WHERE THE STORY ENDS?

As I rolled up to the studio, two OSHA agents were waiting outside. I guess it was my lucky day.

They were vague, saying they were investigating a complaint. When they got specific, it was clear who the rat was. Before letting them in, I texted Ethan to sweep for blocked exits, electrical paneling, and of course electrical sockets.

In my office, they laid out five reasons for their visit: exit doors blocked with props, outlet covers missing, blocked electrical paneling, more than twelve employees and lack of an established first aid protocol, and, the dead giveaway, an employee had a board fall on their head and no worker's comp claim was filed.

Fucktard left a trail like a caterpillar.

They asked to inspect the studio from front to back and interview my staff. Despite having a shoot in progress, I put everything on hold to placate them. During their inspection, I texted Fucktard:

"I hope you are aware of the penalties for false claims to OSHA which I will be pursuing aggressively against you."

"I didn't make any claims to anybody."

"Bullshit."

"Whatever Vic. I don't make calls like that. Go ahead. I had nothing to do with it."

"There is a clear item on the list that pertains to you. But I'll let the lawyer handle it."

"But thanks for trying to get my unemployment denied."

So, Herschel's blocking of the claim angered Fucktard. How else could he buy weed while living at his parent's house?

Fucktard added:

"Making false claims to the state of Nevada carries huge penalties."

"So says the stoner."

"Says the cokehead. I didn't call OSHA."

"Time will tell. Get a lawyer."

Empty threat, I know, but I couldn't let him think he got the best of me. The wheels spun on how to exact my revenge.

My staff corroborated he was the numbnuts who screwed the board into the wall which fell on his own head. Since we paid for his urgent care visit, they dismissed the charge. After the inspection, they dismissed all the charges except for the lone electrical socket without a cover. Again. Sonofabitch. The second offense would be costly. In the subsequent months, Fucktard continued to message me and tried to make peace with petty conversation, even offering to buy me and Jackie dinner. I ignored and blocked his number. Fuck him. Once a rat, always a rat.

Pete's departure had arrived and it was nice to send off an employee on amicable terms. Pete brought Ethan up-to-speed so he could manage production. Ethan didn't need much help with his demanding and thankless job, having been a porn agent.

In his first few months, our production reached a new level of efficiency and smoothness. Pete was conflicted. He was taking a huge pay cut to work in LA with Jordan as a marijuana cultivator's assistant. The darkness and stress of the porn industry ate away at him. I respected his choice even though he was leaving a lot of money on the table. Pete's departing joke was convincing me to hire Fucktard's replacement: Pete's fraternity brother Shibby who had been an extra for us before.

AND NOW, A WORD FROM SHIBBY...

"Hey bro, you wanna be an extra in a scene we are shooting in a few days? We'll pay you $100 and some lunch."

Honestly, I'd have done it for free just for the experience, there was no way in hell I'd tell my friend Pete no on this one. I had no idea what to expect, except that it's porn, I'm some background extra, and I'm making $100. So that morning I woke up, smoked a bowl, and drove to the industrial part of town near the airport. Driving past the warehouses hidden away I arrived at the studio and headed to the unmarked front door. I saw Pete's car so I knew I was at the right spot. I walked to the door and tugged, locked. After a minute the buzzer went off and I headed inside just as Pete was walking by. He greeted me and showed me to the director's office that was close by, then he ran off down the hall. I headed into the dimly lit office and saw a few odds and ends of workout equipment, a couch and a large desk. Some hippie-surf bro-stoner sat behind the desk eyeing me blankly for a moment. He introduced himself and I struggled not to laugh at his name. "Vic Lagina" I hadn't heard that nickname since I was a kid, along with Ben Dover and Phil Macrack. He copied my ID and then had me sign a release. I skimmed it without reading and got ready to sign at the bottom when he stopped me and pulled out a camera.

"I gotta film you doing this part."

*After that day, I was hooked. I hit Pete up every chance I got asking if they needed an extra. I'd text him, call him, buy him beers at the bar, I would harass his ass constantly! Luckily they liked me or I brown nosed Pete enough and they invited me back. Then again, and again, and again! I got to do so many fun roles and adventures. EMT, cop, shitty boyfriend, oblivious husband, creepy speed dater, random guy in a restaurant, guy in an arcade mistaken for some woman's son (*I LOVED FLIPPING HER OFF AND BEING MEAN TO HER, *thanks Vic!), Halloween costumes, being a zombie, beating up Santa Claus, I got to live out my acting dreams! Every time I went in as an extra I knew I'd be having fun goofing off and getting paid for it.*

While not a creepy stoner, Shibby was a comic book nerd with no common sense and two left feet. He also sweated a lot. Performers joked I should have received benefits from the state of Nevada for hiring an employee with special needs. Still, I would take a borderline slow adult over Fucktard anytime.

IF CLARK COUNTY ISSUED HIM A DRIVER'S LICENSE AND HE WAS ALLOWED TO OPERATE HEAVY MACHINERY, HE WAS QUALIFIED FOR FUCKTARD'S JOB.

OSHA fined me three thousand dollars for the second offense, which I negotiated down. This was the cost of getting Fucktard out of my life. Fuck. His. Face. He had crossed a line. Firing him took away his dream job and pussy supply.

AND HE STILL HAD TO LIVE WITH HIS SMALL, DYSFUNCTIONAL PENIS.

By March, things with Jackie unraveled. Valentine's Day came and went. She and 3K were heading to a bachelor party in Austin during South by Southwest. I was assured by both that nothing sexual was to occur, only lap dances.

LIES, LIES, HOOKER LIES! THE REALITY, AS REVEALED BY JACKIE IN 2023: 3K NEGOTIATED A JACKIE BLOWJOB FOR THE GROOM. HE WAS UNCIRCUMCISED AND SMELLED LIKE CHEESE. SCHMEGMA!! THE GO-TO PRO-CIRCUMCISION ARGUMENT. OUR HERO IS A JEW. THUS NO SCHMEGMA.

I brought in girls from LA for the weekend. Usually by Sunday I was ready for them to get the fuck out of my personal space. Not Nikki.

We reconnected and once again took comfort in our mutual tales of woe. I flew her in for three days of wonderfulness. We forgot about our problems. We did mushrooms and painted together. It didn't matter that I was blowing rails behind her back; I was finally happy. Timing might at last be on our side. A few days after she went back to her life, Jackie texted hoping I would die. I ignored her.

I flew solo to New Orleans for Jazz Fest. Year after year, I'd experienced culture and great music with my closest friends on Earth. We discovered a pure version of ecstasy called moonrock. The moonies broke the barrier and the music set me free. My soul was touched and my brain was clear, despite all the substances. I vowed to cleanse myself of everything for thirty days to see if I could. If not, rehab loomed. My friends were supportive. Day one was easy. Day two was a little harder. By day three, during serotonin depletion, I needed a comforting voice. Nikki helped talk me through my pain.

For eight years I had numbed myself to deal with the day-to-day life of being a pornographer. I waged a daily internal battle to retain my soul. After eight years, I was feeling something other than the anger from my bad choices, fear of losing everything, and sadness for the pain I caused my family: love for my life. For my family. For my friends. For my dogs. I broke down in tears.

A week into my cleanse I spoke with my father. He and Jackie were friends on Facebook. When I told him my assessment of what she was up to, he asked if I wanted to know the reality of the situation, because she posted it freely.

GODDAMMIT, DAD! DON'T DO IT! NOT RIGHT NOW! HE IS WEAK!

In the month we stopped talking to each other, she found a new boyfriend. He was in the military, had a bunch of muscles and tattoos, and they spoke about how they loved sleeping next to each other. How in love they were, *in four weeks' time.* I processed it and texted her with my best wishes.

I was coming from a pure heart. I experienced this with none of my ex-girlfriends. She called right away, crying hysterically.

FASTEN YOUR SEATBELTS, FOLKS, THE SHIT SHOW IS NOT OVER YET.

She enrolled in college to become an electrical engineer. I applauded Jackie for her efforts to leave stripping. She had difficulty articulating and needed to keep it brief since she was in class. She was still in love with me and was in a relationship to ease the pain of the breakup. It was a rebound with a juiced-up Air Force Ranger she met on Facebook who was suffering from PTSD.

Nikki was getting her life together. Despite our mutual feelings, timing again was not on our side.

ARE YOU KEEPING TRACK OF THIS, DUMMY?

I needed to be alone, but it wasn't easy. Subsequent conversations with Jackie only made things worse. I told her of my transformation. She found it difficult to believe. I explained this person had always existed, buried under a pile of bad emotions and drugs.

She said her new boyfriend loved her in ways I couldn't. I told her I loved her, even if I was afraid to say it. We ended the conversation with a glimmer of hope, but remained on our separate paths.

Did I love her? Or was I trying to get back something I destroyed, discarded, and lost? Despite the insanity, in a lot of ways we were right for each other. We just lost our way.

She was in Arizona with her new boyfriend and her family. After one painful night, at the request of everyone, she told me to stop contacting her. Despite my gizzards being ripped from my body, I avoided drinking and drugs. Pain brings learning and growth. I decided to let her go. She reached out the next morning to check on me. Now, she didn't want to leave. When she returned to Vegas, we would decide our fate.

To regain her trust and confidence, there would be no more secrets. No further need to snoop or hack. I would commit to her if she was willing. My heart was hers if she'd have it. If it didn't work out, I would leave her alone forever. Jackie ended things with her new boyfriend to give us another try.

My cleanse was over. No rehab necessary. Now to show Jackie I could be a model boyfriend. I celebrated with my first beer while 3K smoked pills in her car and my girlfriend sat coldly in the front seat. An uphill battle awaited.

If I saw a dress or a bracelet she would like, I bought it. Even though she was still in school, she relied on the pole. At night I drove her to the strip club so she wouldn't get another DUI. I passed up opportunities to fuck multiple performers.

I HATE YOU FOR THIS. YOU TURNED DOWN AMAZING SEX WITH A-LISTERS. ME AND YOUR JOHNSON STILL DON'T FORGIVE YOU.

During all this, 3K guided Jackie on how to milk me, while pushing her back to the juiced-up soldier.

She was scared to attend her DUI court appearance, so I took off work to go with her. The charges were dropped and she was a free woman. At breakfast, a flurry of bombs exploded. The first bomb? She was in love with the soldier and wanted to go back to him.

I paid the bill and she dropped me at home. Later, she called to say she couldn't live with the secrets she had been keeping. Throughout our relationship, she'd feigned disgust at the mere idea of escorting.

THE TECHNICAL TERM FOR THAT IS 'MISDIRECTION.'

The past six months she had been escorting, but not on the same turbo-hooker level as 3K. It started when a married man paid for her company. He was living a miserable life with a wife he didn't love and kids I hope he did. He helped with her bills and offered to take her around the world. The arrangement was ongoing.

Most recently, I picked her up from work after she was hanging out with a "nice group of guys." They wanted to take her and 3K out to dinner because one of them was getting married. 3K negotiated the fifteen hundred dollar transaction in their hotel room after the dinner.

This was a dagger, because I picked her up and dropped her off, and felt like a chump. She said everything was smooth and they were gentlemen. 3K told her "karma is a bitch" and made her believe being a lying, shallow, traitorous whore was an acceptable way to live.

Now, she needed a change. I had done my fair share of deceiving, but it didn't numb the sting, so I showered her with negative labels and hung up. I could not let go. I still loved the dirty, rotten whore. I still saw the potential.

I said I didn't care about what she did. I asked if we were done hurting each other and if the score was settled. Could we have a fresh start? Every day, I wrote a note of encouragement to help her make better choices. Each note came with a fresh cut rose from my garden.

SO FUCKING ROMANTIC, DUDE. I AM WEEPY.

I encouraged surrounding herself with positive people and taking care of her body and mind.

LOOK AT THE PORNOGRAPHER GIVING SAGE ADVICE.

She stopped with the antidepressants and slowed the cocaine and drinking. We persevered for a bit before the love returned to her eyes. I saw it happen at the Widespread Panic concert, where we were joined by JD Harmeyer from the Howard Stern show.

If someone said to me you can interview President Obama or JD's friend who sets up fun activities for him in Vegas, I'd rather interview your friend in Vegas.

- HOWARD STERN, 14TH JULY 2014

I hope JD doesn't take offense, but I must share the story.

JD had some time off during July 4th weekend and wanted to come to Vegas. I was heading toward a single life and we planned on a memorable weekend. There were aspects of his personality which resonated. He too was from film school ilk and had the sense of film snobbery I once possessed. He reminded me of my awkward, pre-pubescent self. He fascinated me and I loved hearing him every morning on the radio.

Now, he was going to spend a weekend at *LaginaLand*, sans porn stars. Fortunately, he had just entered a relationship, so it worked out.

When I picked him up at the airport, his first request was an In-N-Out burger. He texted with Jon Hein and asked what to order since Jon is a fast food expert. Then we headed to Target to buy him shorts.

It's a hundred and fifteen degrees in Las Vegas and he didn't bring shorts. He wasn't a big swimmer so he sort of waded around my pool. Although I treated him to the VIP experience at the Widespread Panic show with an open bar, he chose to not drink. This made him the perfect designated driver because Jackie and I had heads full of acid and molly.

FULL SOBRIETY IS NOT A PATH WE WERE READY TO TAKE.

JD volunteered to drive. He lived in New York City and who knew when he last drove. Mine was a beast of a truck, but JD white-knuckled it and got us to our next destination.

Next, we went bowling. Although he hadn't had anything to drink yet, he spilled his first beer all over the bowling lane.

HE'S THE SOBER ONE, HUH?

Jackie bowled the best game of her life while tripping on acid. The following night we hit the UFC fights after he scored free tickets. He wanted to get there an hour before the fights. He silently rocked back and forth throughout. He left the next day saying he had a great time, but there was no way of knowing for sure.

A few items on my bucket list were crossed off when I heard Howard Stern, Robin Quivers, Fred Norris, and Gary Dell'Abate say "Vic Lagina" when JD recapped his trip to Vegas on the air. I know it's a silly thing to lend importance to, but this was Howard Stern! How was this even happening?

Years later, JD turned down staying at Jerry O'Connell's house in Los Angeles because he "don't like imposing himself in people's houses." But he stayed at a pornographer's house, sleeping in the exact room which was my former, in-house porn studio in the early days of Brazzers. From that perspective, I am honored.

SUCK IT, JERRY O'CONNELL.

Huggy's workload dissipated to six or seven shoots a month. He told everyone how busy he was and how much he had going on. He worked with Naughty America and despite it falling into irrelevance, the site was still a competitor. Huggy reassured he had cleared it with Yancee, but I was skeptical because it wasn't something Mindgeek would condone. I was correct.

I finally had the ammunition to push Huggy out the door, but the challenge was to make him come to the conclusion on his own. After informing Yancee, Huggy was told to choose. Given Naughty America was providing him with seventy-five percent of his income, his choice was easy. I accepted his decision to move on.

DOWN GOES HUGGY BEAR! TKO! LAGINA RETAINS THE BELT!

We have had pleasant exchanges since then, so in the end, I manipulated the situation without causing any problems thereafter. But make no mistake: he is a motherfucker. My phony veneer of pleasantness was a façade. I forget nothing. I forgive, sometimes.

The harmony within my crew emerged. Naughty America was perfect for Huggy, since their scenes required little time and effort. Nevertheless, his tenure was short-lived.

Jackie was making headway in her battle against her inner demons. Her trust in me suffered a setback when I was wrapping up the most challenging three days of my career shooting the reality series *Brazzers House*.

Mario was the new *macher* for the Brazzers brand. Under him was Ryan, a former writer, and Yancee who was vying to keep his job. *Brazzers House* was Mario's baby. This was the first of its kind and Mario wanted to make a huge splash. We hired a drone operator and multiple cameras captured twelve porn stars competing to make it into a final live show eight months after the competition was edited and released. The winner took home fifteen thousand dollars.

Mario and I agreed he would play bad cop to keep twelve porn stars in line. No one was to leave the house at night and all captured moments would be usable towards the show. We hired security guards to not only make sure everyone was safe, but to also report if anyone left the premises.

Some did to take nighttime escorting jobs and others ratted them out. It really was like porn *Survivor*. When it came time to explain the rules, Mario was nowhere to be found. He claimed his alarm never went off. I had to task-master the biggest project of my career. If I succeeded, I would prove my future worth.

Although I covered for Mario, it got contentious when he wasn't helping me move along production. While I shouldn't have been mad-dogging my new boss, I needed help.

In addition to the monumental shoot, the owner of the house wanted to gain entry during day three of our production. We were caught in the middle of a fight between the owner and a sub-letter who presented himself as the owner and granted us permission to shoot. The owner wanted to know what we were up to and to evict the sub-letter, so we were served a notice twenty-four hours in advance of his intention to enter the premises. Frank blamed Ethan for the gaffe.

I shot longer into the night to get ahead and got up early the next day to finish the job. The raid I'd expected on day three didn't happen.

YOU'RE WELCOME, SAYS TESTICLESE.

After *Brazzers House* was completed, I went home to enjoy the time with my girlfriend. Instead, I had to pick her up on the side of the road because she wanted to walk home from my house. She screamed irrationalities throughout the drive. In her driveway, she threatened to swallow a bunch of pills. When I said I had to call the cops, she ran away and hopped the wall.

Her mother talked her off the ledge, but it was a battle we had to sometimes fight together. Every now and then Jackie questioned my fidelity. I forced myself to remain calm and talk through the issue. Ultimately, she understood both of us had done bad things over the course of the relationship and had reason not to trust each other. I had faith in her and asked for it in return. Could this be enough?

AVN rolled around and this time I included Jackie. I shot a segment for *Mofos* and paid Jackie to be my assistant. No parties, no socializing. I spent all my free time with her. While getting a beer at the day's end, someone tapped my shoulder.

Fucktard looked sad, depressed, and fat. I stared at his hand and then faced the bar. More apologies. He'd called Jackie a few months before hoping to entice her and her friends with a free meal at a casino.

"Hi Jackie, this is Fucktard."

"Fucktard? Fucktard who? The one who called OSHA on my boyfriend?"

OK, I SEE WHY YOU LOVE HER. SHE'D RIDE INTO TOWN ON A HORSE WITH GUNS BLAZING IF IT MEANT SAVING YOUR ASS FROM THE HANGMAN.

"I didn't call OSHA on him!" He hung up and called right back.

"Look, I didn't call OSHA on him, but I might as well have since it was my parents who did."

Like a six-year-old trying to cover up his lies with more nonsensical lies. Years later, I saw him in a public setting and loudly berated him, calling him a rat. He buckled like a bitch. A few hours later, he messaged me on Instagram, not only admitting to calling OSHA, but detailing why. He still believes it was me, and not Herschel, who blocked his unemployment benefits. He also called me a "little bitch" and a "loser."

TALKING TOUGH ON INSTAGRAM. GUESS WHAT? YOU'RE BLOCKED, BITCH!

After AVN, Frank was moved out of the position he held for nine years and the new regime was taking over. Like before, the goal was to further cut costs and be more efficient.

TRANSLATION: THE PIGS WANTED MORE SLOP TO FEAST ON.

Some people fear change, but I wasn't one of them. Evolve or perish.

The first major cut was the live shows. Then we lost the webcam shows.

Now we were pared down to thirteen shoots a month and I was making the least amount of money since first arriving in Las Vegas. Reducing overhead over the years was now paying off. I was forced to live a leaner lifestyle, not a bad thing if you are trying to avoid drugs.

Yancee was let go due to his resistance to change. Ryan was now number two. No one was safe.

With the future unclear, was it time to walk away? The story could not possibly end now, could it?

If a performer was in town, we figured out a way to fit in a 30 or 60-minute webcam show for a company under the Manwin umbrella. This usually took place before the hardcore of a scene for Brazzers. We shot all the non-sex parts, took a break, did the webcam show, and finished up the Brazzers scene. Talk about cramming as much as possible into an already busy day! The funniest thing about webcam shows was Manwin's platform allowed us to see all the other viewers when they turned on their webcams. I'll never forget the fat naked men jerking their dicks on their toilets. I am sure they thought only the webcam model could see them, but it still would not have mattered. It takes a special kind of perv to want a porn star to watch you jerk off. *Jerkoffs.*

PART THREE

STICKING THE LANDING

All things must pass.
All things must pass away.
—GEORGE HARRISON

27 OH NO, WE'RE NOT DONE YET

In the summer of 2015, I ended things with Jackie. I stuck to my word. If I could no longer handle her insecurity, jealousy, and accusations before I cheated again, I would end it. I had to let her go. We were toxic to each other, and having been here before, I wasn't doing it again. Never. Again. After remaining monogamous for the entire one-year reconciliation, I told her it was over. Less than a week later, I was fucking other women.

A WHOLE YEAR WITHOUT STRANGE, THOUGH. BRAVO.

Once Frank was forced out as production manager, the new production regime from Mindgeek took over. Ryan and Mario, under the direction of shirt-ripping George, were tasked with trimming costs and making production more efficient. This was the environment I thrived in.

Ryan was a writer for Brazzers. Mario was his boss who was directly under George, the VP of Brazzers and Digital Playground. Mario was a very short, curly-headed Italian. The textbook definition of a micromanager paired with a Napoleon complex. After *Brazzers House,* he realized he knew nothing about my world and let me do my job.

MARIO HAD HEIGHT ENVY. MADE US TRY POUTINE.
IT WAS DISGUSTING. CANADIANS ARE ODD.

When the new regime took over, as much as I was tentative about my future, I felt a much-needed improvement was coming. Frank was a terrible production manager. I felt too often he was more concerned about winning or being 'right' than being a pragmatist for a collective goal. There were months on end where I received zero feedback, positive or negative, about my crew's content. We took no news as good news.

In general, I always looked for ways to raise the bar, but under Frank's regime, we would only hear about the problems coming from an impulsive Fabian. There were no solutions posed, only "fix it" or "do better." It was very unnerving and frustrating. When he was relinquished of his duties and promoted (to a position I still don't understand), he threw his underlings under the bus in the form of bad reviews to cover up his ineptitude and poor management. I was told he vehemently resisted his transfer. He was hot-headed, hard-headed, and reactionary. He let his fraternity brazzer, Blake, run amok for years. He made me fire Paul. Fuck him. I was happy to be done with him.

Ryan was a pragmatist with a single goal: to make things better and more efficient. All producers were invited to Montreal for a conference of sorts to outline this very objective.

There were seminars about the need to tape over logos so blurring would not be a costly and timely post-production endeavor. We were brought up to speed about the need to create click-worthy ads for their tube sites. Credit card companies had special departments where people viewed our porn to make sure it was compliant.

Where do I apply for this job?

Scenes showing the female as coerced, exploited, or made to look like they were not enjoying themselves were forbidden. In essence, I continued to shoot the same high-quality, vanilla porn. Until the bizarre requests poured in.

In between the meetings, Keiran and I mended fences. He had calmed over the years. He married another performer and had a son. Perhaps with getting older and becoming a father, his priorities changed. Or he realized as a producer, there was only so much one could bite off and chew.

After the seminars, we had one-on-one meetings discussing my pros, strengths, and weaknesses as a producer. Ryan and Mario sat across from me like The Bobs from *Office Space* and outlined their thoughts in their PowerPoint presentation. They noted my organization and loyalty. Areas of improvement were content quality and the need to keep the bar raised. I had my first performance review as a pornographer.

The first step in keeping The Bobs happy was to move into a smaller studio. We had been there for six years and it was time to move on. Easier said than done. We had accumulated wardrobe, props, materials and the like. The studio looked like we were testing missiles. It was time to create a smaller, more efficient studio. I found a seven-thousand-square foot facility, and after a few upgrades, it became the studio of my dreams.

Brando's studio lease was ending and there was talk about Mindgeek opening a Mega Studio for everyone to operate from. Mercifully, the idea lost steam when they considered the logistics of scheduling headstrong producers.

A NOTABLE AND CRUCIAL DECISION.
COULD HAVE BEEN THEIR 'SWEEP THE LEG' MOMENT.

After factoring the necessary tenant improvements, the contractors were at the mercy of Clark County's timeline for issuing building permits. Once permits were issued, it was a matter of completing them and receiving a certificate of occupancy. Simultaneously, my lawyer was again paid to work with the county on issuing me another adult film production permit for this location. The old one was not transferrable. There were a lot of moving parts I had to manage while shooting the entire production slate assigned each month.

Like a quarterback threading the needle from the fifty-yard line into the end zone with time expiring to win the game, we moved out of the old and into the new. It was on time without our schedule missing a beat and costing more money than necessary. Efficient. On a yearly basis, I saved the company sixty-five-thousand dollars a year in rent. This turned some heads.

With so much uncertainty, why would I expose myself to a thirty-nine-month lease? Aside from telling you I had the same tickle in my plums when I wanted to move to Vegas and again when I signed the lease for the first studio, I had no logical reason other than it felt right. Aside from my personal life, this rationale produced great dividends. It was completely reasonable to squeeze more money from this porn sponge for the next three years. It had the makings of a disaster. The kind of story which ends in a brilliant crash and burn far more brilliant than the ascension.

The summer after my break-up with Jackie was a busy one. Once again, the beast was out of his cage, but much wiser. I still hung out with Jackie on occasion, trying the friendship cloak on for size. She did not want to be just friends. I encouraged her to get out more, to make new friends, and to start dating when she was ready. I was having fun and seeking meaningful connections with porn stars.

RESPECTFUL, LIKE A GENTLEMAN.

Short-fused Jackie would see me with someone else, her temper would get the best of her, and a fight would ensue. So, I kept the details to myself and the drama at a minimum.

ZERO DOMESTIC DISTURBANCES ON THIS GUY'S RECORD IN HALF A CENTURY. AND COUNTING.

Eventually, she stopped contacting me as much. Aside from throwing me a fuck here, there, and on my birthday, I could tell she was looking elsewhere to find herself and happiness. That's all I want for her. That's true love.

Around the time I broke up with Jackie, Nikki was newly single and ready to explore something. As much as I wanted to believe her, she lived as a hybrid of a hippie and a gypsy.

HEY DUDE, YOU'RE HER PERPETUAL REBOUND.

Over the years she evolved from a porno-strump to an organic eating and farming conservationist. Her current jobs were setting up music festivals while working as a salesperson for an organic kale chip company. When she visited, she placed five crystals along the ledge of my pool to re-energize. I was reentering the world of hallucinogens and was spending a lot of free time at music festivals. I was attracted to her hippie vibe.

CAN A KITE AND A ROCK WORK IN A RELATIONSHIP?

I visited her on her birthday weekend. She lived in a small unit on a commune and grew her own vegetables. We explored the area and I enjoyed her vibe. Her Aunt Flo was just leaving town, so at Nikki's request, we didn't have sex until the last day I was there. She wanted to wait to see if we had a connection beyond the physical.

Before we did the deed, she consulted her Tarot cards. The cards must have told her we should fuck and off we went. I was pent-up sleeping next to her the previous nights. I should have jerked off during my three-minute allotted, water-saving shower. I spent the entire session trying not to cum, resulting in unsatisfying sex for her.

STILL? WITH THE PREMATURE EJACS? YOU DISGUST ME. YOU'RE SUPPOSED TO BE A PROFESSIONAL BY NOW!

We said our goodbyes and discussed making plans, but summertime was busy for her on the music festival circuit.

There were a lot of sexual encounters with porn stars after the breakup. The white devil maintained her seduction, but not in the depths as before. Cocaine is a deviant drug and fit well with the deviant lifestyle I was leading. I had two sides: the music-loving hippie who used LSD, mushrooms, weed, and moonies to re-energize his soul at music festivals, and the diabolical porn producer who did rails off of porn stars' asses. I grew my hair out along with a beard, resembling Jesus.

A JEWISH PORN JESUS. THERE GOES THE WHITE CHRISTIAN MARKET.

The Viking Warrior look was a hit with the ladies. After all the dysfunctional relationships, the ups and downs in the porn industry, and watching my yearly income dwindle, I grew comfortable in knowing what made me happy. When work took its toll, I moved the needle back to normal by being a weirdo at music festivals and dropping acid. I smoked weed daily. I was painting and spending time with my dogs. Every day, I wanted to make them feel loved to the fullest.

My only encounters with women were from the job. I didn't go to bars. I stayed in my bubble of bliss. I did not care about being in a relationship. I wanted life to be as simple and stress-free as possible. I wanted every day to be a happy and grateful one, surrounded by good energy when I was away from work.

THEN STOP FUCKING PORN STARS WITH ALL OF THEIR 'GOOD' ENERGY.
ACTUALLY, NO, DON'T.

Staying this positive was impossible when cocaine re-entered my life. The occasional deviant detours occurred. These detours turned into benders, sometimes during the work week so I could stay awake and alert. When my nose couldn't inhale anymore and my heart felt like it was going to explode, I took a break. A month or so later, the cycle would restart.

THE DREADED COCAINE TRAIN.

I looked at myself in the mirror and wasn't liking what I saw. However, if a hot porn star asked me to do lines off her tits and ass, who was I to say no? Then I'd be back on the train.

QUICK MATH EQUATION: PORN STAR PLUS COCAINE PLUS SEX EQUALS ROCK

STAR. UNTIL COKE DICK SETS IN UNLESS YOU ACCEPTED THE RISK OF DEATH BY TAKING CIALIS OR VIAGRA WHEN HIGH.

While I enjoyed those absurd rock star moments, the novelty wore off. I enacted a rule where the only acceptable time to use cocaine was off a desirable tit and/or ass.

THAT'S A GOOD RULE TO LIVE BY.

One night on a bender, while pondering my imminent death, I came up with these scenarios:

Either a jilted and jealous lover will shoot me dead, or

My heart explodes after doing cocaine off a porn star's ass, or

I get diagnosed with throat cancer from eating too much pussy.

All three were plausible. Given throat cancer is curable and is the happiest of endings, I was striving for this as opposed to being shot dead by Meridiana in my driveway. Thank you, Michael Douglas[1], for giving me hope. As for being less cavalier about my box chowing, it didn't happen. I enjoyed it too much.

On October 1st, 2015, my second studio opened. Even though we downsized, my crew appreciated the upgrade. Our volume was thirteen to fifteen shoots a month, with me as sole director. Marcos ran stills and proved to be great to work with. We had a good flow and camaraderie that the talent appreciated.

I created the climate-controlled sound stage by sectioning off a portion of the warehouse with a heavily insulated wall. A control room with a window made sense in case they resurrected live events, as well as a large shower for shower scenes and for talent to wash off post-scene filth. The office space held a makeup room, dressing room, wardrobe storage, and Ethan the production manager's office. I had tile installed, giving it a more polished and professional look than the former ragged-out carpet. A second-floor climate-controlled space overlooked the warehouse. This was my new office. I set up a conference table for production meetings and wired surveillance cameras to monitor each room. Now it was time to show Mindgeek what we could do.

We hired a war veteran as our set builder because every set now had to be created using fake walls called flats. In the previous studio, we shot in four-walled rooms which had low drop ceilings making creative lighting difficult. Now, we controlled all the elements.

Shibby annoyed us to no end. He was a hard worker and he sweated a lot, but lacked common sense and pragmatism. We did the thinking for him and it was exhausting. He forgot to bring items to a location shoot, extending our work day. I was grateful he was just a comic book geek with two left feet as opposed to a creep like Fucktard, but my lectures were ongoing.

AND NOW, A WORD FROM SHIBBY:

One day Pete starts telling me about this shitty employee they had, guy was a lazy ass and was hitting on all the talent - poorly - and about to get himself fired. So I kept getting onto Pete - fire him and give me his job! Every time I saw Pete I'd ask him if they fired the guy yet. Soon enough I was in the door, my lazy ass replacing him and without a solid nugget of experience. I was lucky though, Vic's crew were great people. Some days the hours were too long and the pay a little underwhelming, but the memories I took away will last a lifetime. How many other guys can say they worked in porn?! Now I'm building sets, meeting porn stars, hanging out and having fun and still get to be an extra - it was awesome! Except for holding the boom - man I hated doing that! Holding this long ass pole out over a couple people while they fuck? This seems like it that could be clamped onto a pole or something so I can sit in the next room and fuck around on my phone. I did try to be good and hold it steady - almost always. I might have bumped it once or twice when Vic was being a turd nugget.

While I saved Mindgeek money by moving into a smaller studio, they were looking to make more cutbacks. I was an independent contractor, but as usual, all of my employees were run through payroll via Herschel's entity. Now George, Mario, and Ryan were cutting costs further. George declared Herschel unnecessary and they would no longer pay for my accountant. This was an oversimplification of his job title.

George wanted spreadsheets that were easier to track. It was an ongoing headache. I wanted an accounting system covering all the necessary overhead. The proposed system had too much guesswork and my fear was we were not being reimbursed properly to produce the scenes. Herschel seemed more necessary than ever, despite George's opinion, so his job was safe for the time being.

A few months after my visit with Nikki, she told me she was late. She was under a lot of stress from the music festival circuit and her job as a kale chip salesperson was ending. This wasn't the first troubling call. After her trip while I was still with Jackie in 2014, she asked about my last STD test since her plumbing wasn't right. My plumbing was fine as I tested every two months.

It was nothing, but she was a little neurotic. When she was worried about being pregnant, I wasn't concerned. No matter how pent up, I didn't cum inside her. All I asked was to know when she got her period. The idea of fatherhood didn't scare me. If the universe had this in its plans, I would ride it out.

MAYBE TRY CONDOMS. JUST KIDDING, I'D NEVER ASK US TO WEAR CONDOMS. THEY SMELL.

After a few more weeks, I asked her if she was still late. She wasn't, she just forgot to say. She also forgot about exploring a relationship. I learned from my experiences to enjoy whatever moments we had. About a year later, she got pregnant during Burning Man and was expecting. She seemed excited and I wished her well. We were not meant to be.

UNTIL SHE COMES AROUND AGAIN.

During the Mindgeek conference, I had drinks with Bramm. His visa had run out after Blake's crew and business were dismantled and he was now working at a restaurant. He was eager to get back into the game, so I met with Tony. The same little bald man who helped me get set up in Vegas was now running Digital Playground. He said he'd take care of Bramm.

Bramm was hired as a writer. As much as I enjoyed helping him, the favor paid dividends when Bramm asked me to shoot for Digital Playground and to produce and direct their second live show. It was the perfect way to showcase the new studio's abilities in the live format.

The first scene was a *Star Wars* parody that pitted Charles Dera as a Jedi against Kleio Valentien, a Sith apprentice. She was covered in red body paint and wore yellow contacts and a long headdress. We produced it three weeks before *The Force Awakens* was released, so post-production needed to be rushed. I was unprepared for the reaction. It broke company records in advertising clicks and sales.

How in the fuck did that happen? During production, it seemed like a disaster. Charles Dera had been out of porn for years and decided to make a comeback so he could earn money to open a jiu-jitsu studio. Dera was also an MMA fighter nicknamed Pretty Boy because he once was a Chippendale's dancer at the Rio Hotel. He could be my favorite male performer of all time. He was nonstop entertainment on set and always got the job done. He was there to fuck the hole, no matter what energy the day delivered.

He donned Jedi robes, delivered Jedi lines, had a lightsaber battle, and fucked a red-and-black alien. Welcome back, buddy! The red paint rubbed off onto Charles nonstop. The headdress was heavy on Kleio's head, making the performances difficult. I shot the sex first to get it out of the way before the epic lightsaber battle. They were to use The Force to remove each other's clothes. Nothing a little fishing line couldn't handle, right?

When we completed it and handed the raw footage over to post-production, I remember thinking, "Who is going to jerk off to this?" The answer? Nerds. Lots of them. It's why it broke records. To be fair, the end result looked much better than expected due to the post-production team.

Talk began of doing another one down the road. I was now shooting for another brand and took on the expensive and complicated features they were producing. We executed their live show so smoothly Mindgeek had me produce a live Brazzers *Big Game Halftime Sex Show* in case people didn't want to watch Coldplay. Our relationship was on the mend and we developed a mutual respect after reaching our collective goals. In other words, I made Mindgeek a ton of money.

KEEP THE OINKERS HAPPY, DUDE, AND THIS CAN GO AS LONG AS YOU CAN HANDLE.

I watched Jackie graduate as valedictorian of her class and receive her associate's degree in electrical engineering. I was proud of her but her real test was coming: applying what she learned in school to real life. Would she be able to get a job away from the strip clubs and the lifestyle she said she hated? Would she be able to wake up every morning and go to said job? I had my doubts, but I wanted to believe in her.

As valedictorian of her class, she was to give a rose to someone who inspired her, helped her, and whom she looked up to. Her mother was in the audience, as well as her whore friend, 3K. Out of all of them, she chose to give her rose to me.

VIC LAGINA. INSPIRATION TO REFORMED WHORES AND PORN STARS.

A short, bald guy who resembled Charlie Brown was there as well and she introduced him as her friend. Something seemed off. A week later, she told me she was dating him. I revealed I was having sex with porn stars and civilians, ranging from early twenties to mid-thirties. Afterwards, she told me how disgusted she was and called me a "dirty old man."

GUILTY, YOUR HONOR!

I hadn't been fucking civilians but the thought intrigued me. I didn't have much to lose. People are swiping left and right, but it wasn't sex I was after. I had my fill of sex workers with clean tests. This presented an opportunity to meet women without sex as the motivator.

I created a forthcoming profile on a dating site. Women could decide if they wanted to get to know a successful pornographer.

Some dates led to more dates. I met interesting and beautiful regular women. We discussed open relationships without reservations. I met doctors, scientists, single mothers (although I tried to avoid them), students, bartenders, casino dealers, and it was all very casual. I went out on two different dates with two different female bodybuilders. Between the funny voice from the steroids and my assumption I'd be going eyeball-to-eyeball with a clit that resembled a huge baby penis, I pulled the eject lever quickly on those dates.

WHAT A BIG FAT PUSSY. HIM, NOT THEM.

Still, the dating attempts melded well with the other side of my personality which fed off satisfying sexual encounters with sex workers.

Sal Governale reached out asking me to shoot porn stars wishing Howard Stern Happy Birthday while having sex. I turned around the content to Sal, who was pleased. A few days later, the clips aired on the show, with Howard and Robin saying "Vic Lagina" a lot. This fulfilled me in ways many may not understand and opened the door to *The Howard Stern Show*.

I made a second trip to their studio where I met Gary (again) and had another awkward exchange with him, Will Murray, Jason Kaplan, Sal, Richard, and Jon Hein, who stared at me like a serial killer. I was now a friend of the show.

With Jackie no longer speaking to me and therefore not having to hear her complain about AVN, I decided to enjoy myself to the fullest. AVN was similar to hunting three-legged gazelles. There were new and old encounters in hotel rooms and ice machine rooms. On an afternoon when I didn't want to go to the convention, two women came to my house for a proper threesome. One of them returned for seconds. It was effortless.

At night, a performer who was married and in attendance with her husband invited me to her lesbian girlfriend's room so we could have sex while all five of them watched. It was like fucking in front of an Olympic committee. They snickered with every change in nuance. Due to the molly and cocaine swirling around my system, I wasn't fazed. When the hour away from her husband was up, I was not able to nut, so I moved on to another performer in a different room who finished me off. I missed the husband by one minute. This was near the height of my deviance, which peaked two months later when my best friends came out for the beginning of March Madness.

When two girls blew cocaine up each other's assholes on my pool table, also known as *boofing*, I realized how insane my world had become. After, I used sage to cleanse the energy of my personal space and reflected on my life choices and the path they could lead to.

REMEMBER DAVID DUNN?

Unless you are Keith Richards, this path ends in sensational self-destruction. It's not how I wanted to go.

THROAT CANCER, REMEMBER?

Maybe cocaine was no longer for me.

We had a busy and difficult spring, including a Digital Playground feature based on *Ex Machina* entitled *Sex Machina.* This was my first foray into the adult feature realm and I fucking hated it. A typical Brazzers scene was a five minute intro followed by thirty minutes of sex. A Digital Playground feature consisted of five sex scenes with lots of poorly written dialogue in between, shot over four or five days. It was a house of cards. While it was important to make the sets and wardrobe amazing, when my production days extended beyond the usual eight-to-ten-hour sessions to double that, I questioned what the hell I was doing.

I had always made fun of serious porn, yet here I was shooting it. Why was I getting paid the same for working almost twice as hard? Still, I cashed the checks and worked my ass off, sometimes under a cocaine-fueled fury. My temper was shorter and my tolerance for nonsense was at an all-time low. I delegated a lot of tasks to Ethan as a buffer. As time went on, the overall energy at the studio turned negative and self-preserving rather than working as a team. I needed a break from the job and the drugs. I went home to family for ten days. When I returned, I was a new man with a new approach to life.

The desire to do cocaine was gone. I no longer liked the way it made me feel. During the infrequent moments I relapsed (like doing a rail off a tit or ass of a porn star), I regretted it. So, I evolved into a hallucinogen and marijuana user, connecting me to the energies of the universe.

GO WATCH THE SECRET AGAIN AND SHUT THE FUCK UP.

Jordan Ash, Pete's boss and the man who ran the marijuana cultivation operations in LA, was diagnosed with a brain tumor. I was happy we had mended fences over Pete's hiring, but I hadn't stayed in touch with him. He had the tumor removed and was now engaged in a battle for his life. Pete said he was a shell of the giant he once was. He was fortunate to have a hard worker like Pete to run his operation. When Pete left, I thought my time in the business was over. As captain, I would always have to correct course to stay in calm waters.

The last area of improvement was to upgrade my camera. While shooting porn in 4K was in the not-so-distant future, after testing and research, I zeroed in on a pricey Sony FS-7. Now, I was firing on all cylinders while creating the highest-quality scenes of my career.

Bramm was on vacation in Cuba when a writer under him made the case for his job. Her name was Lisa and she convinced her boss Tony she could do Bramm's job better and cheaper. The problem? She had never been on a set, adult or otherwise. As difficult as *Sex Machina* was to pull off, with some days ending at 2:30 a.m., it was further disheartening to hear Lisa pick apart irrelevant things. Mild scratches on plexiglass?

FUCK YOU, WOMAN.

She would pore over spending to save fifty dollars here, twenty-five dollars there. Annoying and time-consuming. I had my usual volume of Brazzers shoots to produce and direct. My staff grew annoyed with her when she chose to micromanage their jobs: jobs my team had been doing for years.

I welcome constructive criticism. Hers was horseshit. Things boiled to a head when they asked me to create their second *Star Wars* parody.

I told Tony their faltering brand was further suffering from this inexperienced person making decisions. He wasn't hearing any of it. Lisa was in over her head. This was why we were having repeated forty-five-minute phone conversations. I looped Ryan in because even though he had nothing to do with Digital Playground, his Brazzers scenes were affected.

Lisa's one scene demanded my attention when we had thirteen Brazzers scenes slated. Tony said she was doing a great job and no one else was having problems with her. I had multiple conversations with Keiran about Lisa, just to make sure it wasn't me. He was having the same issues. Either Tony was in the dark or felt loyal. He replaced Bramm with Lisa while his brand was in shambles, so he had to stick to his guns. Brazzers led all of Mindgeek's brands in sales. Ryan had solid production teams in place, so I was emboldened.

A few months before, I did a four-part parody of *Ghostbusters* for Brazzers to coincide with the theatrical release of the all-female reboot. This series was five women, four men, and four times the budget of our *Star Wars* parody, yet we discussed it for fifteen minutes total. Ryan sat back and let me do my job.

As things with Lisa boiled, our *Ghostbusters* parody was wildly successful. I used it to assert some muscle against her. After several repetitive phone calls and a finalized script, breakdown, and budget, I ceased communication and let my staff do their jobs.

I told Tony it was right to take a break after the next *Star Wars* parody because we were not on the same page. Their system was designed for failure without enough resources to pull off the ambitious shoots they wanted. If the executives were unhappy, I would be the fall guy. As much as I enjoyed taking their money, I was ready to forego the additional income and live even leaner with their brand in such disarray.

The second *Star Wars* parody was ambitious and the budget was not enough to pull it off. We called in some favors. Kleio Valentien again donned the headdress and applied the red-and-black full-body paint while Ramón Nomar looked like a warrior from either Raider Nation or the Kiss Army. We stretched the set budget to create a temple on the sound stage and built a three-step platform for them to have anal sex.

Considering all of the elements, this day was going smoothly. Until Lisa chimed in. She had been bothering Ethan to check the progress of her set. Despite being told we build sets and strike them after the day's completion, Ethan reminded her we had seven sets to build before hers. We would update her two days before the scene. Except we wouldn't because she would no doubt have changes impossible to pull off with little time and money.

On shooting day, Kleio and Ramón started their eight-hour body makeup. When we were close, Ethan, against my advice, took a photo of the set for Lisa. My plan was to send her and Ryan finished photos. Instead, Lisa had a meltdown about how she didn't like the chair. The fucking *chair*. It was a tiny detail. Lisa was determined to make a difficult day unnecessarily more difficult by meddling over pointless issues and stressing everyone out. I told my crew to cease all communication and focus on the task at hand.

FUCK YOU, HAG. WE'RE SHOOTING PORN, NOT CITIZEN KANE.

The shoot took twenty-two hours. Kleio took the brunt of the punishment. She didn't get to shoot her anal scene until fifteen hours after sitting in the makeup chair and not being able to eat because, well, you know. In between segments, both performers needed two hours to retouch their makeup.

Once I got the last shot of the lightsaber duel at 5:30 a.m., Kleio collapsed into a trembling heap. Porn shouldn't be like this. I caught Howard Stern live going into work and live again going home the next day. Ridiculous, brutal, inhumane, and probably fineable if someone lodged a complaint. Still, we completed the scene with better-than-expected results. Like last time, I knew the nerds would help me break records.

The next day I emailed Lisa, annihilating her for her incompetence and inexperience. I didn't care anymore. I didn't plan on shooting for Digital Playground any longer and it needed to be done. Other producers stepped forward and reiterated my claims. The other Digital Playground producers tolerated Lisa's bullshit because they didn't want to cause waves or jeopardize their income. When Ryan took over production, Lisa was demoted back to scriptwriter, with no interaction with producers or budgets.

KICK ROCKS, HAG.

Ryan was the polar opposite of Frank: organized, calm, communicative, and respectful. We talked a lot on the phone. Sometimes he sounded drunk and showered excessive praise. He watched my scenes, some of which he wrote, over the course of his entire tenure and appreciated what I brought to the table. He had seen a lot of producers come and go and respected how I evolved with the times.

He considered me one of their big guns. My only fear was my ally losing his job or moving on, making my status again uncertain.

George took notice of Ryan's success in creating a leading brand and working well with producers. Now he was in charge of all brands for Mindgeek. Brando gave up his studio, making me the only studio-based producer. My footing seemed solid.

Even though he broke things, excessively sweated, and prolonged production days by forgetting his tasks, Shibby retained his job for two years. When he asked for his review at the twelve-month mark, I told him he had reached his ceiling after his first raise. He would have to be happy with the work he was receiving along with the free daily lunches.

Shibby wasn't ambitious. He lived with his mother and loved his two dogs. Everything he did annoyed me but I kept him on because he worked hard. When I realized scolding him for fucking up fixed nothing, I drew up a written warning putting him on probation. Weeks later, he found a job as a veterinary technician.

Yes, he's the guy who holds your dog's tail while the veterinarian takes its rectal temperature.

AND NOW, A WORD FROM SHIBBY...

I was definitely the laziest guy on the crew, but luckily they didn't give me too much hell for it. I got to choreograph a lightsaber duel once. That might have been the most fun I had, nerding out at home with a couple of wooden poles and a friend mapping out combat moves 10 pages long that no one will bother to memorize or do. Looking back, I loved my time in porn.

We left on good terms, so I did not anticipate another bogus OSHA claim as retribution. Years later, Shibby moved from dogs to humans as a first assistant/surgical tech.

SEE, FUCKTARD. THIS IS HOW YOU HANDLE UNEMPLOYMENT.
GO OUT AND ACHIEVE ANYWAY, DEADBEAT!

Shibby's replacement was a former Chippendale dancer friend of Charles

Dera named Juan and an immediate upgrade to my crew. He had production manager written all over him, so Ethan kept his bar set high.

Jackie resurfaced about three months after calling me a "dirty old man." She had broken up with Charlie Brown. In her time away to find herself and happiness she discovered what's really out there. She told me I ruined her because there were no men who could match me and I would always be better.

GOAT STATUS CONFIRMED.

I was happily single, so friendship was the best I could offer because I was not interested in giving us another try.

PROUD OF YOU, DUDE. BESIDES, THERE WAS STILL MORE BOOFING TO DO.

Previously, I had disposable income and could buy anything I wanted. Custom suits, a Corvette, a Raptor, VIP seating at concerts, expensive dinners, and enough cocaine to buy a high-end sports car. Now, I was forced to live lean, which was uncomfortable but put me in the same category of mostly everyone in the world. I was getting to where I needed to be, I just needed to keep the porn train on the tracks for a little bit longer.

Huggy left Naughty America. If you asked him, it was time for him to leave the adult world. If you asked the crew, they were tired of his shenanigans. After Huggy's departure, they poached Marcos, depriving my crew of a talented photographer. He was their next director. The hits kept coming when Herschel got forced out.

SOLID FOOTING WAS AN ILLUSION.

IN MEMORIUM:

Daisy Monroe, 12/10/90 - 9/3/19

About a week after my final breakup with Jackie, I shot Daisy. A few days later, we started hanging out. She weighed maybe a hundred pounds, blonde with blue eyes, hot tattoos, enhanced full C-cup breasts, and was new to the industry.

After she shot for Brazzers, the numbers were such that she never made it further up the porn chain. I was still worried Jackie might show up and cause trouble. So, we hung out at Daisy's apartment near the Palms Casino.

She had one of those hairless cats and it would climb into bed while we were fucking. Usually within ten minutes of nutting, I washed up, hugged goodbye, and left. Daisy did not seem to have any issues with this. She was drawn to my dickish behavior.

Her porn career was stagnating, shifting her toward low-level productions. Daisy supplemented her income in the private sector with bachelor parties, other times outcalls. She was open. I asked her how she fucked someone who was physically repulsive.

"My mind just goes elsewhere," was her reply. It made sense given all she needed was a condom and a bottle of lube. She found success in the private sector, having stashed tens of thousands of dollars in a safe deposit box. I found this pretty gangster.

We spent New Year's Eve together, ushering in 2016 at a concert at the Brooklyn Bowl Las Vegas. After we brought in the new year at my house, she asked if she should go. After eight months of sex, we had never slept in the same bed together. She stayed the night.

ROMANTIC.

Remember boofing on the pool table?

WHO COULD FORGET BOOFING ON THE POOL TABLE?

Daisy was one of the boofees while Austin, a porn star, dominatrix, and former PA played boofer and boofee. Boofing was a new frontier (low) for me and I was unsure what I found more entertaining: watching the act of boofing, or the reactions of my friends during boofing.

After the boofing extravaganza, Daisy found an actual boyfriend. Maybe she needed more than I could give, but we stayed in touch. Despite doing outcalls, her code was if we had sex, it was cheating.

BUMMER, MAN.

Austin told me Daisy's boyfriend was a piece of shit who stole money from her which she allowed. It saddened me because she was engaging in sex acts with often gross men and this dickhead was stealing from her.

They were going to buy a house in Mexico. I asked if it was a good idea with their tumultuous history, but she was on board. She introduced him to her family and they were unsupportive. I checked in with her from time to time and offered my advice. She was set on the relationship, knowing it was toxic. I was there many a time. I hoped she'd figure things out on her own.

I heard about her death after the fact when Marcos casually mentioned it on set. Austin confirmed she swallowed a bunch of pills. I found a memorial from her family online. It read, "She took her own life after the ups and downs of a bad relationship."

She died on September 3, 2019, at the age of twenty-eight.

28 BIZARRO-WORLD

In 2016, the head office had grounds to get rid of my accountant Herschel. Herschel had full control over the operating account and was the sole proprietor of the entity which ran them. This insulated me from any liability and allowed me to focus on directing and producing. Ryan told me an irregularity, an extra twenty grand wired some months ago into Herschel's entity, had been found.

After vouching for Herschel, I had egg on my face. This could be the end. When I asked Herschel about the irregularity, he said he'd mentioned it already. I assumed it was a payment for upcoming scenes and thought nothing of it. Herschel failed to mention it was an additional wire unrelated to any submitted invoices.

"Is it still in the account?" I asked.

"Yes, but I transferred it to a T-Bill so it would make money until it was discovered," was his reply. Gulp.

He insisted he could get it back (which he did) and acknowledged it was a stupid move. My last tie to Meridiana was about to be severed. I tried to save face by explaining it to Ryan, but I knew what needed to be done. Since the money was still there and could count against the month's budget, all hope was not lost. I had already booked a trip to Maui on a shoestring. Maybe when I retired I'd open a bar in Maui. This was a recon trip and the timing could not have been more horrible. Ryan gave me the silent treatment. Mindgeek wanted me to twist. In Maui, I dropped acid, swam with the sea turtles, and awaited my fate.

They wanted me to create a new entity for me to fully control, including accounting. I got the sense the extra twenty grand was a test Herschel failed miserably. They needed a reason to oust him. I was crushing it each month and they were making a ton of money. By porn standards, I had less baggage than others, so Mindgeek tolerated my nonsense.

The transition was smooth and business resumed. Lisa, who was a thorn in my side at Digital Playground, was fired. I was rehired to shoot their features knowing she could no longer annoy me, but Tony left Digital Playground and the company shortly thereafter. Tony was there since the beginning. I had a lot of porn history with that little bald man and he was the last original domino to fall. Then, as proof things were getting stranger, the Cubs won the World Series, ending a one-hundred-and-eight-year drought.

The Digital Playground feature, *The Gang Makes a Porno* (a spoof on *It's Always Sunny in Philadelphia*), was shot in this timeframe and is the work I am most proud of in my entire career.

While the world spun awry, I enjoyed the greatest stretch of work stability of my entire career. Maybe I had a communal experience with those turtles in Maui because my personal and professional worlds finally co-existed harmoniously. The goal was to keep raising the bar. I repeated the mantra to my staff and to the creative team in Montreal. This is what kept us employed.

MAKE THE APPEARANCE OF BEING A TEAM PLAYER. REPEAT THEIR MANTRAS BACK TO THEM. EAT A SHIT SANDWICH ON OCCASION. REPEAT.

PornHub was the crown jewel in the Mindgeek arsenal while Brazzers led profits in pay-sites. While the company never quite shed its Evil Empire moniker, performers were getting contracted left and right. With the economy improving, tube site profit-sharing taking off, and clever PR marketing with PornHub, Mindgeek was going mainstream.

The business model had changed, but a lot of people were making money. The power dynamic shifted when performers created outlets to capitalize on their brand. Now they were able to make more money on talent platforms like Only-Fans, Fan Centro, and SnapChat Premium. Performers promoted these on their social media accounts, some of which had *millions* of followers.

Mindgeek had enough work for everyone. We were all sucking from the teat. As long as you did well by them and stayed loyal, the work poured in. Infighting amongst producers stopped. It was live and let live. Because I shied away from social media, it was easy to not get sucked into the vortex of drama. But in the changing times, it was impossible to avoid getting hit by the collateral stink of social media.

While on vacation and days after a shoot for Mindgeek in Los Angeles, Nikki Benz, who was also Brand Ambassador for Brazzers and Mindgeek, claimed she was raped on one of their sets[1]. Her accusations against the director, Tony T, turned heads and dropped jaws. I shot Benz dozens of times. She was a bad ass bitch who spoke her mind and stuck up for herself.

I met Tony T when I hired him in 2006 as male talent. He was performing in some of the most hardcore porn around. Very rough and demeaning. On our shoot, Mansef thought it would be funny if Tony dressed up like a Sheik. Tony is Egyptian and a practicing Muslim. He told me he already got shot at once because he was in porn and there was no way he was going to wear a robe and headdress. Fair enough. After he left, my house stunk of his cologne. He moved up to producer and director for other companies until Brazzers brought him into the fold. He helped during our live shows in their earliest iterations.

Tony had a reputation for making female talent cry and putting his crew on edge. Numerous female talent told me their stories. He was branded an "asshole." My experiences with him were pleasant. Despite my best efforts, I too have been called an "asshole" repeatedly. If someone showed up ready, prepared, and left their foolishness off my sets, I would not be an asshole. I imagined things being the same for Tony. However, we both dealt with a lot of foolishness.

YOU ASSHOLES!

Still, I couldn't reconcile why Nikki decided to announce this via tweet while on vacation in Fiji with other porn stars.

Mindgeek executives heavily scrutinized Ryan and pored over all the communication he had with Nikki. They decided Nikki failed to indicate this rape occurred immediately after the shoot and Ryan kept his job. Mindgeek publicly severed ties with Tony T and a shitstorm of lawsuits were filed. Tony sued Mindgeek and Nikki Benz[2]. Ramón Nomar, who was male talent on that scene, also sued Nikki[3] but later dropped out[4]. I was no longer allowed to shoot Ramón and he was blacklisted. Nikki then sued Mindgeek and opened Pandora's Box[5]. Tony won a judgment against Nikki[6] therefore exonerating him in a court of law of any wrongdoing. Tony taught me one important lesson: Mindgeek was very litigation adverse. He was crazy enough to take them the distance, legally. Oddly, I understand his insanity.

Social media was now a place where followers became lynch mobs and people were guilty before trial. I was never concerned about having a #MeToo moment. What I feared was getting caught up in a production-related social media controversy that ended my career. These were troubling times, especially when you're paying people to fuck on camera with script demands coming from Montreal. I had to be extra careful in my personal life and at work.

LOTS OF VETTING AND INFORMED CONSENT IN THE FORM OF TEXT MESSAGES. MY BOY KEEPS EVERYTHING.

Trump won the 2016 election. Bruce became Kaitlin. America's Dad was convicted as a serial rapist. Anything was now possible, including Jackie getting married and becoming pregnant. My friends were concerned I would be upset by the news. I wasn't. I was amused. Her wedding photos looked like they were in a rock and roll-themed Vegas chapel.

She looked hot, and he looked short with a lot of tattoos. He had a confounded smile, either wondering what the hell he was doing or what he might be in store for. He managed the bar she drank at daily while figuring out whether the two of us were possible. Off they went. I heard from her after her son was born.

DON'T WORRY. HE ISN'T OURS.

In 2017, I grew close to a performer who had a tragic ending which a freelance journalist later exploited. I was embroiled in this scandal over the coming years.

I first shot August Ames when she was eighteen. She was a funny, goofy Canadian with perfect natural boobs and an acne condition. An LA director sunk his claws in and they were married to help her secure a green card. While I never met Kevin Moore, I heard through talent gossip he was talking shit about me and Mindgeek and what an asshole I was.

THIS AGGRESSION WILL NOT STAND, MAN.

People described him as angry with a serial killer vibe. Over the years, August and I experienced a very professional relationship. I shot her, she got paid, and she went about her way. Sometimes the shoots were mechanical and she was all business. Other times we laughed a lot and had fun. She showed a side that was beautifully dorky. I was taken aback in the spring of 2017 while shooting a Digital Playground feature where she opened up on a personal basis.

She made it clear she had always been attracted, but couldn't act on it because of Kevin. We kept things professional.

"I won't be married forever," she said. I was supposed to shoot her a month later, but her agent (and Kevin) canceled due to medical reasons. Later, she told me she'd tried to "off herself."

After a brief stint at Naughty America, Marcos returned to my crew and was now a director for Mindgeek. August was booked for one of his scenes. According to Fat Chris, her agent at Foxxx Modeling, August often changed travel plans at the last minute. I was tired of the extra expenses, so I coordinated everything directly with August.

She preferred to come in the day before to rest and prepare. Whatever got her here and made her happy. The sexual tension was high on the ride from the airport to her hotel. She said she was conflicted and wanted me to come to her room.

"I cheated on Kevin before and he found out about it and I am paranoid about doing it again."

"I don't want to make things difficult. If you want me to come up, I will be happy to, but I don't want to cause you or me any drama."

"Fuck it. Come upstairs with me. But I need you to turn your phone off."

I'LL MAKE HIM THROW HIS PHONE DOWN THE TOILET IF IT MEANS WE'RE FINALLY FUCKING.

While a little concerned about her paranoia, I turned off my phone and took her upstairs, resulting in a wonderful experience.

I BET IT WAS LIFE-CHANGING.

She confided in me about her inner turmoil and bared her soul. She had been unhappy for a long time with Kevin. He was controlling about her career and paid her little attention otherwise. They had separate rooms in their apartment. After he shot his scenes, he played video games with his cat on his lap. She was alone and in pain. We made plans for future rendezvous.

Whenever I shot her, she stayed for a few days. We watched and laughed during the entire first season of *Big Mouth*. I learned not only did she get her first period during school like one of the characters in the show, but also had a speech impediment in high school. She fucked one of her teachers. She had a major daddy thing going, so I understood.

She suffered from depression, but was in therapy and taking "happy pills." She liked my presence in her life. It gave her hope as she planned on divorcing Kevin after the new year. The last time I shot August was in October 2017, the subject of much contention in the years to come.

As usual, she came in the day before to hang out. Between the wonderful sessions, her loneliness was palpable. She was no longer concerned about our affair getting back to Kevin. We had a lot of sex in twenty-four hours. Intense sex, with a few light bruises here and there. My makeup artist covered them up and we shot around them. She stayed the night and although I figured sex was the last thing on her mind, she initiated and everything *seemed* fine. The next morning, after she returned back to Kevin and he saw her bruises, the shit hit the proverbial fan. Ryan messaged asking me what happened.

Kevin called Ryan and asked if the company endorsed male performers subjecting his wife to an overly rough scene. Sensing another Nikki Benz situation, Ryan needed my take. I relayed it was a normal day without issues which was the truth. Still, I texted August to get clarity.

She told me Kevin saw her bruises, flipped out and she broke down crying.

Her male talent in the scene, the Russian Markus Dupree, could easily be taken as an abrasive asshole. I'd heard he was solid and tried him out a year before his scene with August. Markus had a sense of how he was perceived, but because his "English no good," he relied on performer Veronica Avluv to soften me up ahead of his shoot. She viewed him as one of the best performers she'd ever worked with. And Veronica was a high-intensity performer. Lisa Ann, who is known to be very particular in her choice of scene partners, chose Markus as one of her male talent for her final scenes for Brazzers. Their shoot was smooth and without issue. In fact, she raved about how considerate and professional he was.

Markus wanted every scene he was in to be great. As Veronica explained, if he was moving a female talent around, he was doing it to position her so *she* looks good on camera. This is where he was grossly misunderstood. If he held her leg at a certain angle, it eliminated the ripples of skin on the female talent's midsection.

He treated his body like a workhorse, didn't drink or do drugs, and got plenty of sleep before a scene, so he drove in the night before. It's a work ethic I will never argue with. Initially, he told me he didn't do scripts, but I talked him through it, and over time he enjoyed acting.

He was a crazy Russian. Most times, the mood was high with a lot of laughter. Other times, his loud personality or wrangling him to get through lengthy intros was tiring. On-screen, the guy delivered better than anyone I worked with in my entire career. I doubt Markus had any intention of making someone feel pain during a shoot. He had a green card and could be deported. He understood the importance of calm waters, even more so after all of this.

The day after the shoot, August revealed Markus was a little too much for her. When I asked why she didn't call "cut" or tell me, she said, "I just wanted to get it over with."

I told her I had no idea she felt any of this, especially since we spent the night together after the scene. She told me she really wanted me to hug her and hold her. She said Kevin wasn't mad at me, just at the company and Markus. Shortly after, Kevin texted Markus threatening messages. A few months later at AVN, where Markus won Male Performer of the Year, he and Kevin almost fought. Ryan of all people interjected and tried to defuse the situation.

She did not blame me or Mindgeek and thought it best to put Markus on her *no* list. Brazzers reviewed the scene and while they didn't see any compliance violations, they shelved it to keep the waters calm. Markus had an eye-opening experience, the first of a few. Everything calmed down until August took her life six weeks later.

I was shooting a big scene in a mansion with four female performers when Ryan called. I was speechless. I knew she'd been in pain, but I thought medication and therapy were helping. She was optimistic about getting divorced from Kevin after her green card was finalized. She seemed excited to be out from under him.

In text conversations weeks after *the scene*, she seemed fine. She was tanning, doing laser hair and tattoo removal, and shooting. I was due to shoot her about two weeks prior but she had canceled through her agent. When I reached out, I didn't get a reply. None of it made sense. It still doesn't. Such is depression.

We tried not to talk about it until after the scene was finished. I compartmentalized my pain by focusing on the job. Cold and robotic.

NO. YOU'RE A MANAGER. WHILE THIS WAS TRAGIC, A JOB NEEDED TO BE COMPLETED. AND SO IT WAS.

They found her hanging in a public park early in the morning. Kevin said she was upset about getting trolled and shamed on social media for not working with a male performer who also did gay shoots. She went out to calm down.

It disgusted me to see Kevin play the victim and mourning widower. He held her memorial service, *in the park where she hung herself.*

WHO THE FUCK DOES THAT?

He set his sights on those he felt were to blame for his wife's death. One was Jessica Drake, the director of the aforementioned scene with the gay male performer, who criticized August for backing out. The other was Markus Dupree. After her scene with Markus, Kevin claimed she never shot again. Her texts to me said otherwise.

#MeToo had dropped like a motherfucker as we continued our descent into Upside-Down World. Then, of course, the unlikeliest of all things imaginable happened: my Philadelphia Eagles won the Super Bowl.

A few months later, Mindgeek sent me a Super Bowl LII Commemorative Helmet with over twenty-six signatures from the World Champion Eagles squad including #9, "Big Dick" Nick Foles. This was a token of their appreciation for being a "longtime friend and frontline commander for Brazzers." My mind was blown. I welcomed this healthier and productive dynamic and the gesture showed they knew me on a personal level and thought to buy me something meaningful. It would have been nice to walk into the porn sunset having all these fuzzy feelings.

In 2018, life was truly heavenly. Work was great and my home life was stress-free sans entanglements. Attending music festivals with friends was something to look forward to. Being around such positive people offset work annoyances. Cocaine kept a backseat to LSD and weed. I was getting older so chilling out on the white devil was best for my heart. The resulting positive headspace was tenuous.

I entered into an open relationship with a civilian Dutch girl for nine months before the usual became too much to deal with. She heard me mumbling to myself many times.

"Are you talking to yourself?" she asked in her funny accent.

NO, DUTCHIE. HE'S TALKING TO ME.

Any potential partner was navigating a minefield of red flag tripwires. People close to me held out hope I'd find someone and reproduce. That said, I didn't want to bring another life form into this world as this place has gone crazy, pockets of light notwithstanding. I wouldn't want to leave someone behind in this mess.

While hopes were high for 2019, I had a bad feeling. Years ending in 9 were historically bad for me. In 1989, my mother died. In 1999, I was dating Doctor Blow. In 2009, I was engaged to Meridiana.

The investigative reporter's podcast was supposed to be an objective study into August Ames and why she took her own life. After she committed suicide, a producer working with the reporter contacted me to get my perspective on the Markus Dupree shoot.

I was apprehensive, but they insisted they were pro-porn and pro-sex worker. Given Mindgeek and I were absolved, why not put her text messages on record and let her words tell the story. I gave an anonymous account. The reporter didn't throw many curveballs and respected personal details.

They did extensive interviews with some of my crew and several others in the business close to August. She was painted as likable and in pain. The producer told me Kevin was trying to control the narrative and make it a case against Jessica Drake, cyberbullying, and a horrible scene with Markus Dupree. Kevin came off as a manipulative sociopath and Markus Dupree, who declined the interview, drew the ire of several people.

Mindgeek was bombarded with requests for a statement, which were denied. They were agitated that I spoke to a reporter without informing them, but the shoot was under my supervision so I had to do it. I told Mindgeek within a week the social media mobs will be angry about something else.

This was the new normal. I shot August several times and she never had an issue calling "cut." Now I had to somehow be even more cognizant about female talent's mindset and comfort. However, with so many balls in the air during production, I still relied solely on a performer's words.

WE'RE NOT MIND READERS, DUDE.

Markus signed a lucrative contract with Mindgeek in 2020, which he attributed to me. If I thought Markus Dupree was a woman-hating abuser, he would never have been on my sets. While I understood there was a culture and language barrier, it was my responsibility to make sure everyone was comfortable and knew what details were expected.

Meanwhile, my newest dog, Jordan, came to live with me after a performer friend joined the Navy. Jordan submitted to my other dogs and I now had four mouths to feed. But not for long.

When I rescued Roxy, she was old. She peed herself when she slept and walked slowly. I kept her going for another six years with a considerable amount of pain and anti-inflammatory medications. She slowly declined and needed assistance with everything in her final year. Eventually, she could not move. She cried like she was ready. A vet came over and Roxy left peacefully in my arms with Joker, Jetta, and Jordan surrounding her.

RIP, SWEET ROXY.

It was a three-dog show for a while, with Joker slowing down. After he passed ten, I knew we were on borrowed time because of his size. I treated every day with him as a gift. He developed a thyroid issue a few years prior which required medication. His hearing diminished over the years, so Jetta and Jordan did the hearing for him and Jordan became a wonderful protector and rat assassin. Soon after, he had a heart murmur and Joker was on a path to heart failure. The way of the purebred.

I stopped getting his teeth cleaned when the vet couldn't any longer guarantee he would awaken from the anesthesia. He was showing the same signs with his hips as Roxy and I feared a rough year lay ahead. He was incontinent and on probiotics and then he suffered from gastric dilatation volvulus, where the bloated stomach twists and needs to be tacked to the abdominal wall.

I rushed him to the emergency room at midnight and despite knowing he likely would not survive the procedure, he had the surgery. He succumbed two hours into recovery, eight days shy of his twelfth birthday. As rough as those twenty-four hours were, I am thankful he went quickly as opposed to suffering as Roxy did. I'll always miss him. 2019 was going as expected.

RIP, JOKER, YOU GOOFY BASTARD.

After Roxy passed, I planned to rescue a male puppy. In a weird display of fate and timing, Joker passed two days before his kid brother's arrival.

THEY WOULD HAVE HATED EACH OTHER.

Enter Junior, a six-week-old Siberian Husky and German shepherd mix. With one blue eye and one brown eye, he was born in a litter of eight in the LA ghetto. The next generation of my pack had started.

Junior came to work with me every day, and while he loved all the members of my crew, he hated most of the performers. For instance, he growled and barked incessantly at Xander Corvus, even though he met him at a young age and saw him frequently. While his animosity was directed mostly towards male performers, his ire was focused on a handful of female performers with whom I shared his feelings.

YOU SHOULD ALWAYS TRUST A DOG'S OPINION.

My relationship with my family had never been stronger. They recognized I got my shit together while kicking the porn world's ass and setting myself up.

While smooth and steady, work was never without its annoyances. Mindgeek's creative teams were always in flux, so I worked with a lot of millennials who came and went. The goal was to operate a well-oiled machine from top to bottom. Millennial strangers critiqued and scrutinized my footage. I said I would incorporate their suggestions into my shoots for all of Ryan's team to see.

I TOO AM A TEAM PLAYER. I SMILE WHILE I EAT YOUR SHIT SANDWICH.

They had learned to take my suggestions, but I had to acquiesce, even if I thought their ideas were ludicrous. As long as I cared, delivered, and adjusted to the ever-changing business model, I could do this for as long as I wanted.

Once the tube sites opened and proliferated, our directive was to shoot ludicrous shots to create clickbait advertisements which in turn led to paying customers. They were writing scripts where performers crashed through walls and continued performing. Quality seemed secondary or even tertiary. It was all about marketing. But as their Front Line Commander, I delivered, which gave me and my crew job security.

Mindgeek's demands were ongoing. Brando shot a scene on location that drew the ire of the owner who *somehow* found out his house (or his boat) was used for a Brazzers porn production and sued. As such, we now had to get written permission. They acknowledged their house would be used to shoot filthy, sweaty sex, including but not limited to, the kitchen counter, kitchen floor (very popular), living room couches, master bedroom, master bathroom, and anywhere else. The owner acknowledges any and all square footage may contain porn star DNA. No big deal.

THANKS, BRANDO.

Only mass-produced artwork with a UPC code could be used as wall art. Otherwise, we needed an artist's release. While shooting in my studio made sense, Mindgeek assigned a few location shoots each month. Why? My ads did better when I was on location. To solve this problem, Ethan found a willing luxury vacation rental company. Now there were no cutting deals on location rates. I paid our guy up to a grand depending on the location size. It's not like Mindgeek didn't have the money. They just chose to squeeze wherever they could while demanding more and more.

The next annoyance was the demand to cover up logos of any size. In fact, Christian Louboutin red-bottomed shoes were banned because it became a legal issue. I guess he's not a porn fan. Even fake knock-offs were banned. In previous years, we learned quickly to keep wardrobe simple and without major logos. However, there were company logos everywhere, and with the progression into 4K video, everything was legible on camera and open to litigation. Blurring was required in post. Their next idea was to fine the producer for the editing time.

They gave us ample warning. One was a tiny Ray-Ban logo Raven Bay had on the glasses she wore in her scene. Mind you, we bought several generic pairs of glasses for these scenes, but silly Raven wanted to wear her own glasses and wound up getting us our first strike. After all, who in the blue fuck is going to catch this? I told my crew from wardrobe to makeup to production assistant to photographer to production manager I needed them to keep an eye on the small details. I had the big details covered, but I needed them to catch the small shit.

I was not going to pay the fine out of my pocket. My solution was, should it happen, staff had to pay for their own lunches (which the company paid for anyway) until the fine was paid off. They heeded the warning until the next time when Bridgette B wore tiny Gucci earrings with the letter G throughout her entire scene. A lot of blurring was required and it netted me a seven hundred and fifty dollar fine. Time to brown-bag it, people. It never happened again.

At my age, most girls in their twenties, even if they had daddy issues, would deem me too old. When I hung out with girls in their early twenties, I got the vibe those witnessing were under the assumption the girls were my sugar baby. Or I was their father.

WHO CARES? WOMEN IN THEIR TWENTIES ARE AWESOME.

Maybe I was getting too old for this shit. Seriously, how much longer could this ridiculousness continue?

Vic Lagina's School of Porn

Lesson Eight: A Brief History on Porn Agents and the Porn Union

My first experience with a porn agent was Jim South, in his smoky office in Porn Valley where he showed me Polaroids of his talent. He could have done his talent better by putting their photos on the internet, which existed in 2002.

My next experience was with Dr. Evil. In 2003, he was operating out of a small apartment in the Valley, but he had a website and seemed organized. While I spent the next several years in South Florida growing my business, so did he. He became the biggest agent in the porn industry. His website showcased over one hundred top performers in the business and he was ruthless. If something went wrong with one of his talent on set, he berated the offending party in his high-pitched, whiny British accent. There was a time when he controlled the majority of the talent and could dictate any rules he wanted. Everyone hates Dr. Evil. I often wonder if he is the Antichrist.

More agencies popped up and poached Dr. Evil's talent. The industry got sick of his antics pretty quickly. His talent said he brutally overworked them and withheld pay. Producers like me were tired of his dictatorial approach. A bunch of Dr. Evil's models went on an NBC piece with Lisa Ann[1], who once worked at his agency before starting her own. Dr. Evil's secret to controlling his talent was to keep them hungry. That's the complete antithesis of an agent's job. The State of California revoked his talent license, but the cockroach survives. He's still around and I assume will be for a while.[2]

While most of the newer agents did not have the cunty demeanor of Dr. Evil, some of them were flat-out useless. Plan B was in place if certain agents fucked things up. I never understood why these (or any) agents wanted to be agents. As Lisa Ann and Kendra Lust figured out, being a porn agent is a thankless job. I can't imagine the money justifying the headache. Lisa and Kendra weren't agents for long. Based on how professional and organized they both are, babysitting adults must be maddening.

I can imagine it being precarious to have to sometimes talk a talent off the proverbial ledge when they are on a set for a company and are supposed to be shooting. It's these types of conversations about consent that is now scrutinized on porn sets. "My agent forced me to do it," was a common complaint.

Some talent looked up to their agent as their mommy or daddy to help organize and manage their lives. Most want someone to look out for their best interests and find them work. These *should be* the sole jobs of the agent. However, the primary focus was to ensure talent arrived to set on time and performed what was negotiated.

A lot of the veteran performers did not need an agent, and I loved dealing with talent directly. There was no chance of an agent fucking things up. On the flip side, I was leery if a newcomer contacted me unrepped. In today's climate, hiring off the street is Russian Roulette.

When a newcomer asked me about agents, I told them who to avoid. There were vulture agents, like Dr. Evil, who signed unknown, naïve performers to insane five-year contracts.

THAT AIN'T LEGAL.

The closest to an endorsement would be to Mark Schecter of Adult Talent Managers. His heart is in the right place. If there was a hiccup involving his talent, he always made it right. But, what should a good porn agent really be doing? Informing and educating their roster is paramount.

Some of them tried. Agents called me to work out problems prior to the shoot date or on the day. They saved our asses frequently. This was when the system worked.

My job was to provide a safe and professional atmosphere for sex workers while balancing all the production challenges. If a performer had a problem, they spoke up. I relied on it. It's hard to pinpoint when this stopped. Around 2016, some performers were born in 1995 and beyond. Social media, iPads, and smartphones started to proliferate in 2007. This generation communicated independently of verbal cues. A generation of performers, who got validation and reaffirmation from strangers who merely launched ropes to them, now existed and were also sex workers. This new generation of sex worker did not communicate as their predecessors did.

YOU HAVE A MOUTH, LADY, AND IT'S USED FOR MORE THAN DICK-SUCKING.

Playing Devil's Advocate, a new performer could be intimidated on a big set. They might not speak up out of fear of losing future work. Yet, unless they did speak up, I assumed everything was kosher. This was no longer enough and my job description now included *mind reader*. I'm an old-timer, so the solution to this problem lay within the younger generation seeking longevity in the porn industry. The rules need to be reasonable. A job still needs to get done.

THIS IS WHY UNIONS EXIST.

A porn union could help bridge the divide between a talent's rights and a producer's needs.

During my time in the industry, a union was always discussed. The common belief was porn stars and sex workers were not organized enough to create one. This was true until a few years before I made my exit when Alana Evans helped create APAG, Adult Performance Artists Guild.

They boast they are a federally-listed, nonprofit labor union organizing adult creators. Alana shot for me in October of 2013. I still have her IDs for her § 2257 on my laptop. Otherwise, I do not remember shooting her, possibly because she was shooting for *MILFsLikeItBlack.com*, which Huggy handled.

SORRY, ALANA. YOU WERE ONE OF THREE THOUSAND, EIGHT HUNDRED AND NINETY-TWO.

I have been following APAG on Twitter for the past few years and they fight Instagram when a performer gets suspended. They post codes of conduct, which are excellent and should be implemented more. But, what more can they do? Inform and educate the next generation of sex workers about their on-set rights and exercising those rights with words.

All performers are independent contractors, not employees, so can a porn union really have any teeth?

Will performers ever be held accountable when they don't speak up? In an ideal world, a performer would not enter the talent pool until properly informed. The question is never posed: just because a performer is eighteen and legally allowed to appear in adult films, should they?

The legal age to appear in adult studio productions should be twenty-one while performing on their own platforms at eighteen. Presently it's illegal to smoke a cigarette and drink a beer at eighteen, but it's ok to take a dick in your ass on camera for a company's commercial gain while the content is exploited for decades. All this for a modest, one-time fee.

TELL 'EM, TEACH! BUILD YOUR BRAND, MAKE THE MONEY. YOU CAN DO IT!

If it's legal to perform for one's own brand at eighteen, a performer will have plenty of time to gauge whether the adult business is for them while retaining the bulk of their profit. They will experience a better headspace on this path. If it's a career for them, they can always level up at twenty-one and shoot for companies, a little wiser before entering the meat grinder.

I know women between eighteen and twenty-one who wish they had not shot company porn. (I have heard of this also referred to as 'mainstream porn', but I hate this term. 'Mainstream' is real movies. Call it 'company porn' or 'studio porn.') Nowadays, creators control their own content on OnlyFans whereas company porn lives forever. Sex workers can ask Twitter/X for donations through CashApp. Financial Dominance (FinDom) is a thing. Amazon Wishlists allow fans to buy them anything. It's a performer's world.

HOW TALL IS THAT SOAPBOX, DUDE? VOTE FOR LAGINA.

29 LIFE AFTER BRAZZERS

In the summer of 2020, six months into the pandemic, Mindgeek and I parted ways.

The fuckery started while all of us were trying to make sense of our new lives. With everyone home jerking off, PornHub traffic was astronomical, making Mindgeek even wealthier. The Porn Monopoly was happy whatever competitors and small-timers they didn't own were sidelined in quarantine. We all tried to figure out with the Free Speech Coalition (porn's governing body) the proper protocols to resume production. First, testing was needed.

Leading up to June 2020, performers were working with their quarantine partners and generating home income on OnlyFans and FanCentro like never before. A new era in the porn industry began. About fucking time. Performers and sex workers have always been put through the grinder, socially, criminally, and economically, so it was nice when things shifted in their favor. Before, they risked their health while companies reaped the most profits. Not anymore.

Brazzers was trying to launch its own performer-driven platform called Brazzers+. It was Ryan's baby. When I spoke with him, it sounded like an invite-only venture to the top performers. I asked if there were going to be director lines and he said not at first.

By the accounts of the invited performers, it made little sense for them to spend the amount of time it took to complete Mindgeek's specific content requests, aside from staying in good grace with the company. There were few such rules or specs on their own platforms thus far. Their fans just wanted to be fed. With cellphones and the cameras which evolved with them, it was easy and fast for performers to create their own content. Plus, it made them way more money than Brazzers+ was offering for the amount of time spent on their production.

The line Ryan fed me was we were going to make up for lost time in the back end of 2020. Everything would balance. We all took his words at face value, especially when Mindgeek wired twelve grand to take care of my crew during month one. As the captain, I told them to only worry about my crew. Since they were still paying for the studio and not leaving me hanging with the bill, I considered it a win. It's not like I didn't save money to live in case of an emergency. We all wanted to believe in Ryan. Hell, maybe even he believed his words given how confused we all were with the new *new*.

I worked on eight new paintings, relearned the piano, and finished house projects. I had conversations with a Mindgeek minion named Rachel about what a return to production would look like. I spent a lot of time working with the Free Speech Coalition's COVID Task Force. These discussions were futile due to the great divide in thinking. Some were deathly afraid of COVID, others did not care.

Ten weeks into the pandemic, all Mindgeek producers had a long Zoom phone call with Ryan and Rachel. We discussed the criteria for the areas Brazzers producers operated from (Miami, LA, Vegas, Europe) to be followed in order to resume production. After month one, they were no longer compensating my crew. My production manager, makeup artist, and photographer were bombarding me with questions I relayed to Ryan, who sometimes flat-out ignored me. This had become his *modus operandi* when he had no answers.

Through Ryan, Mindgeek released a bold statement in early May stating if they received word performers were working during quarantine, they would "reexamine their relationship" with said party. Rachel said she was scanning social media and taking copious notes. They were mandating people not to work while making PornHub fuck you money. What were people to do except freak out and get angry? Tension was bubbling on Twitter. In early June, Las Vegas opened back up and it fit Ryan's criteria. When I mentioned this, he said, "We are not going to be pressured into resuming production."

Anything Ryan had said up until then was now suspect. The slumber was over. I had to get back into hustle mode. My goal was saving the studio, as this was always my Life After Brazzers plan. Much like the tickle in my plums when I bought my house, I felt the same way when I decided to *buy* the studio in 2015. Yes, I bought that fucker and kept my hand close to the chest. I knew it would ruffle Mindgeek brass and their minions. My crew had no idea. Things only work when you tell no one, especially in porn.

LOOSE LIPS SINK SHIPS. AND ALSO PROLONG EJACULATION.

Buying the building was my biggest leap of faith so far. I was vulnerable to a spectacular crash. While I hoped the music kept playing, one day it would end along with my porn musical chair. Controlling and owning an industrial-zoned studio would buy me some time. While I hoped me and Mindgeek could part amicably, my sense was there are no golden parachutes in porn. Or are there?

They never asked about lease terms. Instead, they had me sign an agreement between my shell company in Las Vegas with theirs in Cyprus, Greece. This dogshit contract outlined the monetary terms for each scene, as well as automatic extensions every six months. If either party wanted to sever for *whatever reason*, all they had to do was notify the other party in writing within fifteen days.

NOT MUCH OF A CONTRACT.

If it made these people happy and kept the gravy train rolling, fine. If I had an issue with the terms, all remedies would be resolved in Cyprus, Greece.

Why did I sign this toilet paper contract? Because I was only as good as my last scene. Contract or not, things were set up so Mindgeek could cut ties with any producer for any reason. This meant they did not care about lease terms. They assumed they were paying the building mortgage of some Vegas landlord.

**THEREIN LIES THEIR WEAKNESS. HE BECAME THE LANDLORD.
THEY JUST DIDN'T KNOW IT.**

As long as I fed the Mindgeek pigs their slop, I received work. All I had to do was keep them happy for three more years for a return on my investment. We went five more years. Overhead was manageable for a studio this size. Now to figure out what else the place could be.

The levee of anger, pain, and frustration about, well, all of it, burst when the cops murdered George Floyd. The next round of cancellations in the industry began. Perhaps this happened to me, depending on the narrative. Here's mine:

The most notable and immediate casualties within Mindgeek were Brett Brando and Markus Dupree, the performer I still maintain is the best I ever shot. In June of 2020, Phoenix Marie told me she heard from Ryan, Brando, and one of his crew members that a performer accused Brando of raping her after a Brazzers shoot, years after the fact. My experiences with this performer had been unpleasant and despite the company's many requests to book her, I refused due to liability concerns. There had been too many cancellations and she could turn on a dime from being happy and laughing to crying hysterically.

AND SHE'S HAVING SEX. ON CAMERA. FOR MONEY. WHERE SOUND MIND AND CONSENT ARE REQUIRED. KAAAAAAAAA-BOOOOOOOOOM!!!

When I first met this woman, I shot a morning scene involving her while she hung around during my afternoon shoot. She looked at me with goo-goo eyes, but there was an instability which I wanted nothing to do with. Brando, on the other hand, allegedly chose poorly. Whatever happened between them bit him in the ass. However, circumstances and credibility meant nothing in the Age of Cancel Culture. While she never made these claims publicly on social media (unlike other rape allegations she made publicly), nor pursued formal charges, he was told by Montreal he had to prove his innocence through his lawyers if he chose to in a court of law. Until then: canceled!

Tags that had been previously and commonly used on tube sites such as 'interracial,' 'Asian,' and the like were facing harsh scrutiny. Racists! We're all human! Black Lives Matter! And if a white performer previously did not want to work with a black performer, well, they must be racist! Canceled! This is what #Porn Twitter consisted of in June 2020 in the New 'Woke' Porn Industry. I haven't even gotten into the trans discussion yet.

Freedom of choice and freedom of expression were being shamed and people were canceled for not standing with current social virtues. I stayed off social media in an effort to keep my waters as calm as possible. But choppy waters lay ahead.

During my time with Markus Dupree, Ryan twice told me to stop shooting him and changed his mind months later. As discussed in the previous chapter, Markus is Russian and he can rub people the wrong way. He relied on me to communicate his concerns before every shoot. If he was uncomfortable with a potential co-star, he passed on the shoot. Not everyone was comfortable or able to do this, which is disastrous when two people are paid to fuck on camera.

The best approach was to hire performers who either liked or loved working with Markus. There were plenty of them because he was so good at his job. Why leave anything up to chance?

The first time Ryan told me not to book Markus was after on-set abuse claims on non-Mindgeek sets appeared on social media. The second time was because Markus rubbed a higher-up at Mindgeek the wrong way. Yet, they contracted him in January 2020. My guess? Our scenes made money. Then, more claims of abuse arose in June 2020. August Ames came up again. Canceled! Once he was canceled, I got an overwhelming feeling the crosshairs were turning on me since I'd advocated for him.

Shields up, Captain Lagina! Evasive maneuvers engaged!

A Zoom meeting with one of the Mindgeek minions about resuming work was abruptly canceled by Ryan, with no reason given. When pressed, I was told I was going to be informed about it "sometime next week." The tactic of making one squirm can be effective, but I now found it annoying and it angered me. This was the beginning of the end. Fortunately, the business was changing and a new business endeavor was suddenly on the table.

I met Grant when he was an extra on one of my shoots. For instance, when gynecologist Dr. Johnny Sins has sex with the girlfriend of the boyfriend who brought her into the office, he played the boyfriend for a hundred bucks. He was funny and eager to work. He ventured into PA'ing for performer turned-producer Johnny Castle for Naughty America.

Grant was hustling, and coincidentally I hired his wife Mandi a few years earlier to handle wardrobe. She was one of the hardest and most organized workers I ever had, so it came as no surprise when she moved on to greener pastures. Now they were starting their own OnlyFans management company and looking for a studio. Timing was everything. On one hand, I had Mindgeek being noncommittal about the future. On the other, the business was changing and here was someone who was well-positioned in the new market.

I entertained discussions with Grant and Castle, his partner, and bankroll. Johnny was the kingpin in the operation and had been building his management company over the past several years. Grant and Mandi were one of the teams operating within. I was never one to leap blindly. Then, I heard why my return-to-work meeting was canceled.

Ryan emailed me an anonymous post about a bad experience a performer had on one of my sets with Markus Dupree. It read:

> *Hi Vic – We need to address this, as it was brought to our attention and if true, is very concerning and problematic.*
> *Based on the description, it is the scene below:*
> *https://www.brazzers.com/scenes/view/id/2675835/dripping-the-ball/*
> *Let me know your recollection of this, and how the day rolled out.*

August Ames came up again. Here was the unedited claim, posted on the website *anonplace.com* in June 2020.

'I had an Anal shoot for brazzers a few years ago with Marcus Dupree for Vic in Vegas. I was excited because I rarely shoot for Brazzers. I don't consider myself an "anal slut" so anal scenes still make me nervous. When I arrived on set I was confused because I had no dialogue and no wardrobe. So I asked what am I doing today on set and I was told I'd be covered in latex paint. This was a big issue for me because I'm allergic to latex. I expressed my concern right away and it was a big issue. They had two gallons of latex paint ready to pour all over me. Vic came in the makeup room trying to figure out solutions. The makeup artist suggested she knows a different kind of paint that would look better anyway. So she left to get the paint. When she comes back she has some paint you need to mix with alcohol in order to activate it. The paint was a sliver metal looking paint and they wanted to drizzle it all over my body. I kept asking what we're the intentions for the paint and I was told it was just for the intro teaser. I get to the point I start doing the intro and I have a glitter face mask on and I'm supposed to drizzle the paint on myself. So I slowly poured it on myself and as I did it started to burn. I turned away from the camera since we were rolling and said "it's burning". Vic says he only needed a few more min of footage and could I hold on. So I did. As the paint dried it stoped burning and I made sure to communicate what was happening. After the teaser was done I rushed to the shower to wash the paint off the makeup artist helped. She re drizzled the paint down my body away from my vagina. So before the sex I asked several times what was expected! I voiced how I wasn't a extreme anal performer. Vic told me this is a standard anal scene I wouldn't be doing anything extreme. He just needed 4 positions from me just like a regular BG. Vic and Marcus had their own talk off to the side without me about the scene. I was already on defense working with Marcus because he seams more like the director than the director. We started with the stills and in the stills Marcus made every decision pertaining to the poses and positions. He wanted to make sure he looks good regardless of comfort. Meaning in doggie I wanted to place my legs a certain way and Marcus re positioned me in a more comfortable way for him. Once the scene was about to start I asked one more time if Vic wanted the scene just like the stills and everything we

> *discussed. He said yes exactly like that. I still have this silver paint all over my body just away from my vagina and asshole. So we start fucking and Marcus reaches his hand out to Vic and Vic hands him what I thought was lube. It was a bottle of coconut oil that smelled old. Marcus squirts it all over my body causing the dried paint to mix with it. Marcus flips me into another position and again reaches out to Vic. I thought I was lubed up enough for anal but then Marcus is handed a new bottle of oil and this time he squeeze the contents of the bottle up my ass hole. I was shocked because I had never done that in a shoot. They basically gave me a enema. Marcus repeatedly did this to me during the scene. I was offended because I specifically asked who what when where why and how. At that point I was just speechless and wanted to finish the scene. Them adding oil to the scene while I'm anally fucked just put that paint inside me. When the scene was done I had Marcus and the makeup artist were helping me take the paint off. I had a visible rash on my arms and legs which is saying a lot since my skin is extremely dark. I had a flight home that night and I started having extreme diarrhea in between the time I arrived at the airport to the time I boarded I shit 4 times and I was cleaned out beforehand. By the time I got home I was exhausted and dehydrated. The next morning I had to call the poison control center. Ultimately I was upset that Marcus and I were told two different things to do to my body and I wasn't fully informed. It made me not be able to trust both people I had once respected.'*

Based on the description of the scene, we determined it was a performer named Ana Foxxx, whom I shot for the *Ghostbusters* parody.

On set, I remember her being funny, pleasant, and professional. I also was a little taken back when she made jokes about her complexion and skin tone ("can you see me over here if I smile?"). But I welcomed her carefree energy. Finding out how she felt *two years after the fact* was shocking. It hurts me this was her experience and I am truly sorry our production caused her pain. I wish there had been communication during booking, production, after the day was over, or any time during the two years before it was posted anonymously. After reading it, I had some questions:

If Ana deemed herself not an "anal slut", then why did she take a booking with one of the most energetic and intense male anal performers in the business? It was my understanding she had worked with him before and, because there were no issues prior, I incorrectly assumed she knew his style.

At the time of the booking, Ana could and should have said, "Thank you for the offer, Vic, but I am not a strong anal performer and Markus might be too much for me."

I would have replied, "Thank you for your honesty, Ana. I'll get you on the next one."

I struggled with publishing Ana's name but ultimately I felt it was the proper thing to do. I can argue that my porn career ended due to her anonymous post. I don't hide in the shadows and I feel Ana should have handled things directly with me or the company, at the time of the incident. I chose a more direct approach. I'll defend any claims of victim blaming since there were literally eight steps in the process where this could have been prevented. It should be noted *anonplace.com* is now defunct.

Given the experience with August Ames about eight months prior, I made sure Markus and female talent were fine with each other before moving forward. I knew Markus could be too much for certain performers. Markus was vocal about talent he wanted to avoid, so I learned to discuss the bookings with him and the minions in Montreal, before moving forward. Sometimes the creative teams tried to shoehorn a performer with Markus, disregarding my concerns. We learned as we went, but post-August Ames, we had a good system in place.

Mindgeek reviewed scenes for compliance before they headed to post-production and nothing was flagged. The scene was released as compliant and is *still* on their website as of this publishing. I even got a review on the scene that it "wound up looking great overall. Good work!" The story elements "exceeded expectations." All ad moments were "executed as expected." All sex positions were "executed as expected." Obviously it wasn't problematic for them, even after Ana's post, otherwise they would not continue to exploit it for profit.

WELCOME TO THE NEW WORLD, DUDE.

If she was nervous, how come nobody had any idea about it? Seriously. I have zero recollection of her telling me, despite her claims. Otherwise, I would have been even more cognizant of her concerns. We ran into technical issues early on with the difficult paint scenario the geniuses up in Montreal cooked up. Her recap states my crew was trying to find solutions so we could get the job done, as per the specs requested by Mindgeek in their script. It sounded as if we were accommodating due to her allergies and helping her clean the paint off her body.

Lastly, how was she comfortable taking a penis in her anus, on camera, in front of three other people she didn't know, in a scene to be released to the masses, but wasn't comfortable speaking up because she felt her body was disrespected? It was her decision to not speak up "to finish the scene." Her words. The logic still escapes me.

THIS HAPPENED IN 2018. WHO YOU GONNA CALL?
PORN UNION! WE WISH SHE DID.

For the record, coconut oil became the lube of choice over the years because of its natural properties. Synthetic lube or other oils tended to cause issues with skin or other parts. When dealing with ongoing requests for oily scenes from Montreal, coconut oil was the best choice and we went through gallons of it.

Whether it was old as Ana claimed, I cannot say. As for "they basically gave me an enema," I shot Markus squirting oil into a performer's butthole at least a dozen times and the footage was used by Mindgeek for their all-important ad moments and trailers. No performers ever complained or called "cut," otherwise it would have been on my radar for future scenes. I understand it may seem gross, extreme, or unnecessary to some, but this was the nature of the industry at the time. I chalked it up to performers wanting to put on a show for their fans and to impress Mindgeek.

I re-watched the trailer and raw scene footage and there was zero indication from Ana that there was a problem. We relied on verbal cues. How else were we to know? She said gave none during the scene and acknowledges this in her recap. This is actually incorrect. She did call "cut" towards the end of the scene because she needed a break, so I cut. Otherwise, she looked and sounded like she was enjoying having sex with Markus. Clearly, there's a very fine line between performance and reality. As for her sign out, when asked the three compliance questions (How did your shoot go? Were you treated okay? Were you asked to do anything you didn't want to do?) she answered respectively "amazing," "of course," and "not at all" with a big smile on her face and said "thank you" at the end, followed by a giggle.

HAS THE WHOLE WORLD GONE CRAZY?!? AM I THE ONLY ONE AROUND
HERE WHO GIVES A SHIT ABOUT THE RULES?!?

I was sad and confused that a massive breakdown of communication happened on my set and during the entire process. Still, I sought ways to make this better, but it was becoming increasingly difficult with the new generation of sex workers. Had the risk finally outweighed the reward? I had been a liability manager for Mindgeek and they trusted my judgment to not only protect them but to protect myself. Now, my judgment was being questioned, and the topic of a performer "powering through" scenes and not feeling they could call "cut" was becoming a narrative. I let this marinate for a bit before I responded.

I cited the daily challenges Mindgeek's creative teams faced us with. Sometimes things go wrong. We adjusted as we went and we learned from the experience. I expressed my concern they were enabling the behavior of performers keeping concerns bottled up until *after* a scene was complete. I reiterated the scene was released by them without being flagged as non-compliant. Any "side talk" with Markus was to make sure he knew what we needed for the scene, due to his language barrier. She made it sound nefarious. I reminded Mindgeek it seemed like she didn't have any issues with Markus, even after his temporary ban. If a bigger conversation needed to happen, I told Mindgeek to stop keeping me and everyone else in the dark so we all could move forward.

OUT OF THREE THOUSAND SEVEN HUNDRED NINETY TWO SCENES, ONLY A HANDFUL WENT SIDEWAYS IN HIS CAREER. THAT'S ONE HELL OF A RATIO.

How could something working so well through three different ownerships for sixteen years be a fluke? It wasn't, but times were changing and now sex workers felt they could not speak up. The previous system was obsolete.

Ryan told me I shouldn't take anything personally.

EAT A DICK, RYAN.

This was a company I helped build since the beginning. I estimate I made them a healthy nine figures during our sixteen years. Now, were they lining me up for cancellation? He cited my *Week-End Reviews* where I praised male talent for being solid and impressive for not having to cut. I viewed uncut porn as a success and a sign the performers were legitimately comfortable and enjoying one another. We were to talk again on Monday. It was time to speak with my lawyer Ed.

ED HAS A COCK THE SIZE OF AN ELEPHANT.

I got into the habit of writing *Week-End Review* emails to Ryan, Rachel, and the creative teams at Mindgeek to help them understand what I was up against during any particular week. Mindgeek briefly contracted one of the performers, Zac Wild, whom I raved about in my reviews. The reviews were intended to give my account of the problems I encountered while they were fresh in my head. The hope was my product would be better while my shoots were as smooth as possible. Now my words were being used against me. You bet your ass I took it personally and was over their corporate bullshit. I was ready to go to war.

NO MORE EATING OF YOUR SHIT SANDWICHES, RYAN.

Ed had to Phil Jackson me off the ledge and explained times were changing. Mindgeek still wanted to be in business with me. I had to adjust. Fair enough. Evolve or die. I drafted an email outlining how we could do even better.

MAYBE GOING THE WAY OF THE PORNOSAURUS ISN'T SUCH A BAD IDEA.

I relayed all of my points to Ryan, putting my position on record. At the advice of Ed, I dropped the lawyer bomb (sorry, 'Producer's Advocate') during the last two minutes of the conversation.

Ryan stammered while he grappled with my insistence on having a lawyer as my advocate. It was not unlike a 'Talent Advocate.' Talent and producer were being asked to do specific requests at the behest of the company for an adult production they are solely profiting from. We were both independent contractors to their shell company. Why should we both not be afforded the right to an advocate?

WHO YOU GONNA CALL? PORN UNION! NOPE, WE DIDN'T CALL THEM.

This made sense if I was going to move forward with them in this new age. I also asked for an altered contract with Mindgeek. If the company wasn't interested, then they would be fine with me working for others. Ryan never replied to my email. Over instant messenger, he made it clear he was not going to engage with Ed about company business. It was time for me to take a leap of faith with Grant.

ED HAS A HORSE COCK.

Marcos and I had been in contact the entire summer. He was chomping at the bit to work and I confessed I thought the Mindgeek road was coming to an end, for me at least. I also told Ethan and Stephanie to plan for the end. Stephanie had pivoted by creating and selling wardrobe on Etsy, while Ethan's unemployment was running out. I asked him:

"What if it's over? What will you do?"

"I don't know. I hadn't thought about it."

He hadn't thought about it? During all this time? And he has a child. This was the guy who handled the details of all my productions for the last six years. People could now understand why things had gotten so frustrating. There were so many layers of it from top to bottom.

HE MOVED THROUGH LIFE WITH A HEAVY WEIGHT ON HIS SHOULDERS. APPARENT TO ALL BUT HIM.

Grant offered me one percent profit participation on the overall gross of their OnlyFans roster. Their goal was to bring in four-to-five million dollars a month once things got rolling. It sounded juicy to me if he could pull it off. With those numbers, all my overhead would be covered with gravy. There were performers making up to two hundred thousand dollars *a month*. Indeed, times were changing.

I brought Marcos in as a partner for the new studio endeavor and gave him half of my percentage. His job was to shoot whoever was on the roster when they needed the studio. My job would be managing the studio. Perfect. In the grueling heat of Vegas in July, we de-Brazzered the studio by eliminating the clutter. The creative teams in Montreal made odd requests. A huge bin of socks was built for three 'teenage' boys to hide in in a department store. Contract star Jordi popped out of it and had sex with a security guard and contract star Nicolette Shea.

FUCKING CLICKBAIT BULLSHIT.

The creative teams never accounted for storing said bin or anything else needed in their ridiculous scripts after construction.

I wish I had angled for a piece of the soon-to-be Brazzers when I moved to Vegas. Ouissam and I discussed it. My sizable mortgage prevented me from taking less up front and negotiating for a stake in the company. My story would have ended a lot differently when the founders sold it to Fabian for one hundred and forty million dollars in 2009, not the measly (ha) forty million initially leaked to the press.[1] Here was my second chance.

While I had security in the bank, Marcos did not and he was focused on money. I told him about my regrets, but he wasn't hearing it.

HE'S GOTTA FEED THE MONKEY, YOU KNOW?

We both had extensive contacts in the business, so we devised a strategy to shoot company-quality content for performers on their own platforms. This was optimism during a pandemic. Or I was just drunk. I spent many afternoons drinking beer by my pool and reaching out to all the performers I knew. The response was overwhelmingly positive. In the world of porn, that is.

I had been discussing my future with Phoenix Marie. She had been one of my staunchest supporters from the start. Same with Lisa Ann. Both of them counseled me on how to make this business model work without the help, and possibly the wrath, of Mindgeek. I wanted to keep the Mindgeek relationship alive and because Brazzers+ had launched, my studio could help them succeed.

The arrangement I had with Mindgeek was they ordered scenes and I invoiced them through my entity, or Herschel's entity before then. Therefore, everything in the building was technically mine. I controlled who went in and out. If Mindgeek wanted to rent the studio, they would have a COVID safe environment. Even though the majority of the business got back to work, Mindgeek was still halting production. They hadn't paid me in four months.

It's common knowledge if you want information leaked, tell Phoenix Marie. Knowing she would tell my plans to Ryan and Mario, their reaction would influence my next move. I knew they would not go for it, but I had to legally go on record via email. They were invited to be a part of it, especially since they were trying to launch Brazzers+, which was not going well.

In early August 2020, Ryan wrote:

> *'Hey Vic – In speaking to Phoenix the other day, she mentioned you offering to open up the studio to talent to shoot their platform content. Let me know – if so, that would be news to me. Thanks, Ryan'*

I confirmed, telling him my need to be only as transparent with my plans as he had been with Mindgeek's as of late. Given there was no movement in returning to work, I had to move forward. I detailed my cleaning protocols and if he wanted to lay claim to anything in the studio, he needed trucks, manpower, and storage. I invited them to rent the space along with the performer-based productions I was hosting. I never received a reply, which in and of itself was one. Three months later, Mindgeek terminated our relationship via email. So, was I canceled? I'm still not sure.

Marcos and I recruited new girls to the OnlyFans roster. They had Marcos' photo and video services as well as studio use for thirty percent of their revenue going towards Grant and Mandi's management team. Meanwhile, I was responsible for all of the overhead and we were not liquid yet. While Grant and Mandi estimated the roster breaking one million dollars within a few months, at the moment, the studio was bleeding. Marcos was content in taking his cut while using the studio for financial gain. He gave zero fucks about my situation. He also wanted payment at the time of the shoot.

THEN WHY IS HE ALSO GETTING A PERCENTAGE? HIS CHARMING PERSONALITY?

Marcos was moody and vented a lot, but he was a good, creative worker. We had amazing synergy in the past. I attribute a lot of our visual creativity to him. He was content being paid through my entity while shooting for other brands under Mindgeek, but he was ambitious and wanted to be recognized for the talent he believed he was. However, he took a lot of things personally and held grudges. Some thought his antics outweighed his talent. Here I was selling him to people for this new endeavor.

"Yeah, Marcos kind of hates me," a local redheaded performer told me.

I gave him free studio time to showcase his talents and attract business. Performers either wanted to rent him or the studio, but not both.

He took a lot of shoots off-premises, on gigs I sometimes got for him, and was making ends meet. I was chasing studio bookings like a used car salesman, during a pandemic. The ship was not launching as hoped. When I challenged Marcos to bring in five shoots a month before taking money, he handed back his half percent in an emailed response. Instead of it going toward the studio's overhead, Grant and Mandi kept it within their company while I absorbed Marcos' responsibilities.

SO, YOU GAVE THEM MORE THAN WHAT WAS ORIGINALLY NEGOTIATED WHILE TAKING NO ADDITIONAL MONIES. SMOOTH. BUT, TO BE FAIR, YOU WERE DRUNK DURING MOST OF THE PANDEMIC.

Marcos continued to suckle Mindgeek's teat and I was happy he landed more work with them. My only request was to let me know as a consideration. I found out he was shooting for Brazzers and their other brands from a local producer helping him scout locations. Over ten years, I put well north of three-quarters of a million dollars in his pocket. Exactly zero dollars flowed back my way.

The pandemic revealed everyone's true nature, including mine. You could say I was the guy who fucked over Mindgeek, but we live in a fuck or get fucked world. I was about to be cornholed, so I moved first. I played my hand in Porn Survivor and walked away with a cool studio. Now it was time to see who was sincere and believed in themselves and reinvesting in their brands to get wealthier in the changing times.

The biggest pro in working with performers for their OnlyFans was working for them, on their time. I took it personally when talent canceled on my Brazzers shoots.

"How hard is it to get on a plane, have sex, and get paid for it?" I lamented.

Now, I had a different perspective. When talent came to Vegas, they got up at four in the morning to catch a flight from Burbank. From there, they sat in makeup before we started production. Hopefully, they learned their lines. Some did, while some stayed buried in their cell phones.

Then they spent a few hours acting and making crazy faces for the ads which went on PornHub before trying to pull off a passionate sex scene with a partner they may or may not be into. After, they had to catch a flight back to Burbank and get back home late. Hell, I was exhausted at the end of the day and I didn't have to travel or have sex. It was tough, especially if they had a shoot the next day. Maybe they did it because they knew what to expect from me.

Now, the shoots lasted only two to three hours and performers were ecstatic to be there. Most importantly, I was working for *them,* so they were calling the shots. All liability about consent or powering through but saying nothing was gone.

Working for Mindgeek had become frustrating over the years. In hindsight, I grew to hate my job and developed a strong distaste for the head office, from the creatives to the department heads, to the brass. It was evident to all but me. My frustration was apparent in my *Week-End Reviews* and it was clear I struggled to understand the new generation of performers. I had aged out of the industry. Instead of being canceled, they were sending the old man out to porn pasture. I thought I had another five years left in the tank. Way off.

Once word got out I was no longer a Brazzers director, everyone ghosted me. It's an interesting dynamic when you can no longer give things to the takers. Most of the industry did not want to piss off The Porn Monopoly or fall from its good graces. Creators were advised to avoid the studio. They were spanking my bottom as they had done to performers who crossed them.

I had my supporters in Phoenix Marie, Alura Jenson, and a handful of other regulars who hired me. Without my crew, it was on me: building sets, lighting, and photography. Given I had been running video and was still at the top of my game, photography came back quickly. The parallels between being a one-man show fourteen years prior and now doing it all again were not lost on me. Except this time, I had my own studio and toys to play with. This was going to be a surefire success. Right?

Phoenix had been in touch with Brando after his cancellation, and he was shocked his 'friends' Ryan and Rachel were ghosting him. He was a big director and had been shown the door over an allegation. She suggested I reach out and I weighed it for a moment. Then I asked OZ if I were in Brando's position, would he reach out to me?

NO. HE WOULD NOT.

I told Phoenix to remind him none of them were ever his friends and to make peace with his new life. Maybe he has. I wish he had fought back, but perhaps he was as over the business as I was. Maybe he didn't want to spend the time or resources airing out his dirty laundry on public record.

At first, shedding the skin of *Vic Lagina, Brazzers Director* was a struggle. I was done hustling and grinding. I didn't realize how much I would enjoy not having to do it anymore. I grappled with trying to understand why I felt so responsible for people in the industry by giving hall passes to subpar work ethics, late arrivals, and bouts of complaining. I should have fired more people over the years and not allowed such dysfunction within my crew.

When Mindgeek returned to production, it was a shit show. While mired in the muck trying to determine what a safe production day would look like, their main competitors, Tushy, Vixen, and Blacked, resumed immediately. Ethan took a job as a PA for them since he knew their production manager. They implemented an expensive COVID testing system.

Meanwhile, Mindgeek asked the male performers to shoot the scenes themselves on cell phones. It took months before a director and two-person crew were allowed on set together. Their crews were the director/shooter/producer, makeup artist, and talent liaison (my idea). They did away with photos, except on the more ad-heavy shoots. Crews took a big hit because talent now commanded larger scene rates and the majority of scene budgets. They paid rock bottom to producers who would tolerate their mandates.

As working in the industry became a huge, undesirable, clusterfuck, it took a lot of acid for me to emotionally part with a sixteen-year business relationship.

To appear progressive in the changing times, Brazzers started shooting trans scenes. Regardless of how much profit it was generating elsewhere, Mario had been vehemently against it for years. Xander Corvus was the first contracted male performer to work with a trans performer on Brazzers. The trend was if a male performer did not want to work with a trans performer, they must be homophobic or transphobic. It. Was. So. Exhausting.

On the other hand, OnlyFans had transformed from a slow-growing success into a juggernaut overnight when the pandemic hit. It received a fair share of media attention and scrutiny. Anytime something makes people a lot of money, it becomes a target.

Grant tried to persuade me to start an OnlyFans account to build up the Vic Lagina brand. Performers suggested it in my waning years with Mindgeek. It would have been smart to have another revenue stream when it was all over. In the past, performers I slept with asked to borrow my penis for their platforms. Being a compassionate individual who also knew how to run a camera, who was I to say no? Especially since it was putting money in their pocket and helping their cause.

A TRUE HUMANITARIAN.

"Content is king," Grant told me.

With all the uncertainty, did starting my own line make sense? Was owning content money in the bank?

I shot a few POV scenes in content trades with performers I felt comfortable with. While fun, it was work. The thought of spending a lot of time building a brand and social media from the ground up while shooting and editing seemed like an undesirable use of my energy and time. The females were the brand, not my schlong. Once content is released, it loses value as the content gets traded for free. It's a monster needing constant feeding. I would have had to eventually show my face, thus violating my promise to my father.

I had been at the top of Porn Mountain for a long time. This reeked of someone desperately clinging to a business they could not exist without. It felt creepy and sleazy. I feared ending up like my mentor, Reed. Plus, if I didn't trust the new generation of performers, why on earth would I stick my dick in them? So, I decided against being a cock wagon.

PLAY THE INTERNET GAME 'FIND VIC'S JOHNSON'. PERHAPS HE SHOULD HAVE REMAINED A COCK WAGON.

After we parted ways, Mindgeek's house started to burn. On February 5, 2021, they were called out by the Canadian Parliament to be investigated for trafficking.[2] How did this happen? Greed. PornHub had been the crown jewel in Mindgeek's collection, based on the traffic alone.

With unverified content of all kinds available in a few clicks, the *hundreds of millions* of *daily* consumers had access to you name it. If a small percentage of those millions joined Brazzers on a trial basis by clicking on an ad, the business model was successful. This is why shooting click-worthy footage had been my mandate for the last several years. This is also why they didn't have any qualms about paying top dollar. It was mainly feeding PornHub. It all changed when Nicolas Kristof wrote an article in the *New York Times*[3], forcing Visa and Mastercard to permanently move their transactions off PornHub, and temporarily off all of Mindgeek's brands.

Unverified porn such as revenge porn, rape porn, coerced porn, and worse could now be found on PornHub, despite the victims' attempts to have it removed. Once Visa and Mastercard enforced their ban, there was plenty Mindgeek could have done. They purged seventy-five percent of their content from PornHub, an obvious blow to their traffic. Now, after a fifty-two-million class action lawsuit[4] against Mindgeek had been filed, the owners had to answer to the Canadian Parliament.[5] They mandated that only verified content be hosted on their site. But, the damage was done.

Back in 2009, when first ownership was about to sell and make their fuck you money, I was approached by Frank to shoot scenes for a site called *Shame On Her*. (I still have the proposed document for this site. It's pretty awful. But, as early as 2009, they were requesting this.) It was intended to use consenting performers signing releases, but it was rape porn, which I refused to shoot. Eventually, it devolved into *PornStarPunishment.com* until it was phased out a few years later during an image cleanse. What does this tell us? This type of exploitative porn generated traffic and sales. I felt even better about my departure.

Another example of porn heebie-jeebies, Jordi was a 23-year-old contract performer who looked 15. I shot him plenty of times with large in-stature MILFs because it played on a traffic-generating fantasy. It was comical. Another ginger kid looked 12. Was it legal? Yes. Was it protected under freedom of speech? Yes. Was it in good taste? Larry Flynt, rest his soul, would have thought so. It did not sit right with a lot of female performers who didn't need the paycheck. I justified it because at least Jordi had stubble and a visible Adam's Apple.

OnlyFans and other platforms had to revise their user agreements forcing performers to provide proper §2257 documentation on their scene partners. While some performers kept compliant documentation, most, like the ones who showed up on my doorstep to borrow my Johnson, did not. Just as PornHub had to purge its unverified content, so did OnlyFans. Many female talent lost their content. Even though my face never appeared and my voice was never heard, I had a few asking me to send my ID and a release.

YEAH, WE'LL GET RIGHT ON THAT, STRUMP.
THEY'RE DOWN THERE SOMEWHERE. LET ME HAVE ANOTHER LOOK.

I inadvertently got my golden parachute from Mindgeek. We shut down on March 13, 2020. Four days later, inexplicably, the forty thousand dollar balance owed by Mindgeek for the remainder of March hit my bank account. Oops. With ten scenes to go, sixty-five thousand remained in my operating account. What does this tell you? Mindgeek trusted me to complete the scenes when they allowed us to resume production. Except they never did. When they later requested I return the money for unproduced scenes, I forwarded it to Ed.

THE ONE WITH THE ELEPHANT PENIS.
ED GETS PAID IN PRINTED PENILE COMPLIMENTS.

Ed sent Mindgeek's lawyers an offer to pay me an additional seventy-five thousand. In turn, I would sign a non-disclosure, non-disparagement agreement. His rationale was a company that made *half a billion dollars* the year prior would be foolish to refuse its most loyal and informed producer a golden parachute.

"Thanks, Vic, for your loyal service over the years! It truly was a great run!"

"My pleasure, gentlemen. I have nothing but wonderful memories and things to say about all of you!"

Easy, right? Sensible? Except chances are you are not an arrogant, greedy pig. Remember when Manwin laid off most of its workforce and denied the remaining employees their holiday bonuses because they had not reached their goals? A few months later, I was gauging my footing with new ownership during AVN. CEO Feras Antoon told me I would "probably" be alright and took me to a VIP area in the club to meet the new ownership. There I saw executives drinking bottles of Grey Goose with porn stars while VP George ripped open people's dress shirts. A night like this would cost anywhere between eighty to a hundred grand. Yet, they couldn't pay bonuses to employees.

OINK FUCKING OINK.

Mindgeek's shell company sent Ed a letter rejecting settlement and demanding the money. A process server showed up on my doorstep delivering the same letter. It wasn't a lawsuit, yet. We tried to gauge what leverage a shell company in Greece had over one in America, but the road to recouping the money would be expensive and uncertain. It was chump change to them. Easier to call it the cost of a clean split.

STAY OUTTA CYPRUS, DEADBEAT!

Perhaps it was paranoia...

NO, IT WAS ME.

... but I envisioned Mindgeek hiring a Greek goon or hitman to try to intimidate or kill me. However, I do not fear death. I believe it's imperative to not only have a great life, but an even greater death. Given my fondness for the Second Amendment which resulted in a modest but effective arsenal, I was always prepared for a goon's arrival.

Maybe we send each other into the Great Beyond in a *John Wick*-style shootout. Now wouldn't this be the perfect ending to my story?

And yet, I never saw a Greek hitman. Or any more demands for the money. They should have made me sign an NDA. Now the story has been released to the masses. Arrogant. Dummies.

THE TRANS TOPIC

I shot a few trans performers on Grant's roster and it was an odd experience. One of my all-time favorites wanted to shoot with a trans performer also on the roster. Before I go into this experience, allow me to digress:

When I was in the grapefruit leagues of porn in South Florida back in 2004 and 2005, I was offered a lot of money to shoot gay porn and I turned it down. I'm not gay. I don't know what gay men want to see in their porn. I don't watch trans porn either. I cannot imagine the life experience of a trans person. Exclusion, ridicule, and discrimination. We all deserve a life of happiness and inclusion. In a show of solidarity, Grant felt it was my obligation. So, I gave it my best effort.

When it came to boy/girl porn, it was imperative to have a strapping man anchor the scene. I appreciated the likes of Jordan Ash, Ramón Nomar, or Markus Dupree. They were strong enough to hold the entire weight of the female performer in difficult positions such as reverse cowgirl or standing cowgirl. When it came to moving my camera around to another angle, a solid male performer kept female performer's legs open so we could see the all-important penetration. This is why we are here. When it came to shooting a trans performer to *top* (what the 'fucker' is called), most didn't have the upper body strength to be a proper top. Even when I shot a more robust trans performer topping another trans performer, the end product looked like two monkeys trying to fuck a football.

Now, I was watching a trans performer who had the body and finesse of a fifteen-year-old boy, fuck a mature, voluptuous hot MILF porn star. It seemed like a giant waste. And the pop? I don't even know if ejaculate came out of her dick when she finally popped. It took a long time. She was shaking, squirming, and moaning, but I didn't see anything come out. Was it dust? Was it the equivalent of old man dribbles? What the fuck was going on? And during all of this, I was asking myself:

WHY IN THE BLUE FUCK AM I SHOOTING THIS?

Regardless, I am sure the scene was very popular.

IN MEMORIUM:

August Ames, 8/23/94 - 12/5/17

It's been several years since August took her life. I miss her. Being removed from the industry for a few years has given me the chance to dissect her last months. I harbored some guilt since her last shoot with me was the one under much speculation. I have watched the scene. Nothing stands out as dangerous or abusive. Another set of eyes might see something different. Because I could no longer discern, it was another reason to move on.

A few weeks before the scene in question and well into our torrid affair, I shot another scene outside with her and Johnny Sins. At one point, she was hot, needed a break, and called "cut". We gave her some water, she burped, laughed, then snorted while she had cooled off. We looked after her. We resumed the scene and it was a fun day. August was a great performer. She could sell she was enjoying herself, even when things were routine. The point is, in the dozen or so scenes she shot with me, she never had a problem calling "cut."

The only time I saw clear frustration was at the end of the video, after Markus' cumshot got in her eye. She stayed put for the outro, which the writers always annoyingly included. Until she had enough and was done. And so, we were done.

I also reviewed her sign-out clip. While she looked pensive and vulnerable, when asked the three sign-out questions (How did your shoot go? Were you treated ok? Were you asked to do anything you didn't want to do?) while holding her check, she never mentioned anything. She had her reasons.

When she stayed at my house, she wanted me to hold her a bunch. I wish I'd held her harder and longer since it was the last time. Her mother wrote a book about all of this and when I read a certain passage, it drives a dagger into my heart. Her mother mentions the shoot and how she wished someone on set was looking out for her. It hurts just typing this. We were looking out for her. I had thought about reaching out to August's mother. Maybe I will one day.

I know what killed August Ames. It wasn't Markus Dupree or the scene in question. It wasn't Jessica Drake. It wasn't cyberbullying for not wanting to work with a crossover performer. It wasn't a neglectful husband. They may have been triggers, but she was a depressed woman who chose to kill August Ames. People need to stop finding scapegoats to support their narrative. We as humans are responsible for our own actions or inactions.

After I had moved on from Brazzers, I met another local producer who volunteered his own August Ames story. They too had their own torrid affair. When I think about it, all I can do is beam a huge smile. On one hand, I want to believe the time we spent together was mutually fulfilling. On the other, I think August hit her "Fuck It" button: fuck her husband, fuck depression, fuck the industry. Maybe she knew where she was headed. All she wanted was to get some pleasure and happiness whilst on this rock, so she did. And I love this for her.

IF YOU ARE SUFFERING FROM DEPRESSION AND ARE CONTEMPLATING SUICIDE, PLEASE SEEK HELP. YOUR LIFE IS TOO BEAUTIFUL TO LEAVE PREMATURELY.

CODA

Howard Stern: "What we're learning here... is how the sausage is made."

Robin Quivers: "Yeah, Vic Lagina put the period on the end of the sentence."

- THE HOWARD STERN SHOW, 19TH JANUARY 2022

I got through 2020 without losing a dog. In early 2021, Jetta passed away. She had been showing signs of aging. One morning, her balance was off and it looked like she had an episode similar to Roxy's.

Jetta was prescribed meds that made her vomit so she avoided them. She was ready to face her ending with dignity. She passed on her own in my foyer, me by her side, with Jerry and the Grateful Dead serenading her into the great beyond. She called her shot and went out on her own, a new experience for me.

With Jamie, it was too soon. Roxy needed help when her body gave out. Joker's passing was sudden. All of their deaths were sad and painful, as was Jetta's, but she checked all the boxes for a great life. It was an easier pill for me to swallow. I sure miss her.

RIP, BOSS JETTA.

I started volunteering at the Animal Foundation in Las Vegas to help dogs. I said when it was all over, I would. With all my newfound time, it was time to walk the walk.

In June of 2021, Grant ended our business arrangement. If I had been in his shoes, I would not have wanted my studio on his books either. His roster was too unmotivated. The studio remained vacant most of any given month. This summed up the new porn industry: why go to a studio when you can use your phone and a ring light at home?

WE WERE AHEAD OF OUR TIME. OR WE GROSSLY MISSED THE MARK.

It was a shame because the roster was making millions per month. I wondered if I had lost something as a porn producer and felt shunned. Mindgeek succeeded in making things difficult for me. I sensed this was coming, so when the ball dropped, I called my real estate agent. Let's call him Moses. He helped me buy my building. Up until when Grant served me my walking papers, the studio was operational for six years.

I am grateful to Grant, Mandi, and Johnny because our one-year endeavor helped slow the studio's bleeding. Its spectacular failure forced me to rethink the studio's plans. The obstacle became the path.

I was relieved to be done with OnlyFans management, because there is a huge degree of dishonesty in the game. This does not apply to the models and performers who manage their own accounts. Lily Lane for instance. Models like her did not want to scam their fans by having someone else speaking as them. It harmed their brand. True, Berat from Istanbul may not know their favorite porn star they think they're talking to is a stoner dude on his couch in Fort Lauderdale. Anyone with a command of the English language will know they are being catfished. Management will eventually be regulated by OnlyFans to avoid fraud, scamming, and catfishing.

For close to twenty years, all I shot were movies that ended in a facial. Sure, my work had been seen by hundreds of millions (maybe billions?). Yes, my work spiced up a lot of marriages. A close friend played Brazzers porn while making love to his wife. Yes, my movies could have filled a few Olympic-sized swimming pools of men's ejaculate. I am grateful for all of this. But, it would have been a wasted opportunity if I didn't shoot something personal before my studio got leased out to a CBD manufacturing company. So, Nikki and I did just that.

I found it cosmically curious that Nikki, who was working for a company which made low-budget movies, re-entered my life in 2020. Things weren't working out with her baby daddy.

REBOUND TIME!

She apologized for being a shithead years prior. I met her when she was twenty-two. She was now thirty-six. Given she was now older and wiser, I entertained the possibility. Plus, the idea of turning the past twenty years of my life into an actual movie was now possible. I had the money, I had the studio, I had the personnel. I asked Nikki to direct to keep it honest. What was I waiting for? Oh yeah, we needed a script!

I went full on Sylvester Stallone in *Rocky* mode and cranked out a script within a week. First, I jotted notes on what I wanted to portray and weaved the story together. Nikki read the script and felt it didn't need many adjustments, so I fine-tuned it to a lean seventy-pages. I had thirty grand for production and estimated this could buy me six shooting days. Thirteen pages of script per day. It was ambitious, but Nikki was up to the challenge and reassured me this was normal for her LA productions. I handled the majority of pre-production, set building, shot lists, and scheduling. I had done this on porn features for Digital Playground, so it came easy. This is what I trained for.

I used all my resources: studio, props, wardrobe, vehicles, house, and dogs, and I called in favors from any porn star still willing to take my call. Pre-production started in early June, with planned production dates of July 29 through August 6 2021, when it would be one hundred and ten degrees, Delta variant raging. Nikki's boss lent his Black Magic camera for free. Nikki wanted to rent Zeiss lenses and a few other special toys. The plan was to have her drive a rental car with the gear while I put her crew into an AirBnB.

I decided to play a major role in the project, but I would not play me.

I WONDER WHO IT COULD BE?

Nikki thought of James Duval, best known as Frank the Bunny in *Donnie Darko.* She had worked with him before and thought he would be perfect to play Vic Lagina. When I was visiting Nikki in LA on one of her movie sets, I met up with Kush, an old film school buddy-turned-director. Nikki and Kush don't know each other, so when Kush mentioned he'd worked with James, it seemed like kismet. A few months later, I was on a Zoom call with him and sent him the script. About a week later, he signed onto the project. Holy shit! This was happening!

The pieces fell into place. I had done some acting before in film school projects in my twenties. I knew it was important to stay within my range, so I wrote my character accordingly.

TRANSLATION, HE'S NOT A GREAT ACTOR.

I wanted to go for a certain look, like a smacked-out pirate rock star.

IS THIS HOW YOU SEE ME?

To prepare, I did a lot of physical labor clearing out my building in the desert heat. I went on a strict diet of small portions, no sugar, and no alcohol six weeks before cameras started rolling. In my twenties, thirties, and part of my forties, I was around two hundred and fifteen pounds. By the time we started production on the movie now titled *Filthy,* I was one hundred and seventy-eight. While this was somewhat impressive for a forty-seven-year-old man without a Hollywood trainer, it sucked. I felt for actors who did this year-round.

Nikki also took on one of the meatier acting roles. Her part comes toward the end when we cut deep into the onion and find out who this guy is and what makes him tick. I rounded out the porn star roles with Jennifer White (who had come a long way since passing out with a butt plug in her ass during a live show ten years prior), Hazel Moore, London Rose, Spencer Bradley, Tommy Gunn, Marcus London, Jason Toler, and Will Pounder. My first makeup artist, Jodi, came to Vegas to do makeup and act. My former production manager, Pete, also assisted with production and played someone from the head office. It felt great knowing not all of my employees were shitbags. Even better to have people ready to rally for the cause. Our cause. We were not just telling *my* story, we were telling *our* story.

For the most part, production went smoothly. It took us a minute to find our groove on day one. We had to cut corners. A few pages of script had to be cut, shortened, or rewritten due to time constraints, but this was normal. The biggest difference was the set-up time for shots. I ran my own camera and shot to edit. This, however, could not be rushed. In production, there are always things in hindsight you wish you had done differently. I would have loved another production day. Otherwise, we did okay.

Acting with James was an amazing experience. He has seen a lot in Hollywood and when I asked if he had any questions about my script, he told me, "No, you wrote an excellent script." It felt wonderful to hear, although I had a hard time believing it because it's the movie industry. He said he related to my existence and experience. Sometimes he would be headed to set, worried he may not work because his co-stars were train wrecks. The movie industry didn't sound much different than the porn industry aside from our filth happening on camera.

James wound up being stuck on a Hollywood production in LA and got to my house about six hours before production started. But, he made it and he made his call time on day one. I put him in my casita and let him rest up.

I wish I had met James in LA before the shoot. We should have had a beer or three and let him observe all of it. Fortunately, he locked in on me during the production when I was in Vic Mode. At night, after we wrapped and were having drinks, Pete and I reminisced. James listened and put it into his performance. Over the next six days, he captured my spirit on camera.

We shot over five terabytes of footage on twenty-three camera rolls. Nikki rocked it. Production can be a high-pressure, high-stress environment, but she kept her cool even when I pushed back on some of her ideas. Reviewing the footage, I liked what I saw and with the help of a skilled editor, we might have something. Even if it never gets released, it was a fun exercise. The footage was used for the trailer for the book you're now reading.

Names have been changed but the stories are real. They are what *I* experienced. If people feel strongly about what I have written or portrayed, they can make their own movies or write their own books. It's not meant to be anti-sex worker or anti-porn star.

IT'S ANTI-FUCKTARD.

There are fucktards in all lines of work and the sex industry is no different. These were the fucktards I had to deal with. Sex workers contribute a necessary service and all classes of people need them. Yet, they get shit on and discriminated against by banks, law enforcement, and the courts. People need to appreciate sex workers and all they do. But please, don't be a fucktard sex worker, otherwise, I will make fun of you.

Once *Filthy* wrapped, Nikki and I said our goodbyes and she headed back to LA to return the gear. I was expecting to see her within a few months, but that never happened. This is our cycle: hot, warm, cold, warm, hot. I have nothing but love for her, especially since we completed our production. It is clear we are not meant to be.

YOU SAID THIS BEFORE. LAST TIME. AND THE TIME BEFORE.

We may cross paths again. But, seeking a relationship with an absent person no longer interests me. Yet I can't quit her. If we again go from lukewarm to hot and she wants to visit, I'll always say "yes" and endure the inevitable cooling and disappointment. I'll always love her and I forgive her for everything.

JUST ENJOY THE SEX, DUDE. BUT PLEASE, NO MORE PREMATURE EJACS.

AND NOW, A WORD FROM NIKKI…

The reason why Vic and I didn't work out romantically is a longstanding topic. I often wonder about it. I think it boils down to the logistics of location, timing, and messy personal journeys. Having two people tied to sex work in some way can make navigating a successful, consistent relationship a challenge. We've always been connected on a very deep level which leaves me at peace.

After we wrapped, I had three weeks to finish moving out of my building for the CBD manufacturer now leasing my property. I moved all the cool and fun props, wardrobe, and furniture into my house along with all of the lights and production gear. With no fanfare, no ticker-tape parade, no final blowout party, it was now over.

In February of 2022, just before interest rates and inflation ballooned, Moses brought me to the promised land. He nailed the asking price, which was double my purchase price.

HOME. RUN.

It was a quick and painless closing. Of all the risky moves I made since landing in Vegas, this was the biggest. No guarantees, no safety net. If any of it went sideways, it would have ended me. I learned to never be afraid to crash into the mountain, otherwise, you'll never fly. Jimmy Iovine said it best on Howard Stern: "Make fear a tailwind instead of a headwind." I kept it together for just long enough. The timing of the pandemic and the exodus from California created a perfect storm.

So, what did a retired ex-pornographer do to pass the time?

THE WORD 'BUM' COMES TO MIND.

Any desire to be affiliated with the porn industry waned until it was completely gone. I was burned out on production in general. When I begrudgingly agreed to shoot for performers, I phoned it in. I became one of those unmotivated porn chicks with no work ethic who always frustrated me. I have not touched my camera since. Maybe this is how Miles Davis felt when he put down his trumpet for five years.

I woke up every day with zero responsibility. I had nothing but time to reflect.

I'm neither proud nor ashamed. I flourished during the golden years of internet porn. I appreciated producing and directing strong performers who rocked out a great scene. A great performer was actually something talent aspired to be.

Now it's a bunch of easily-triggered influencers willing to play with a penis on camera. There are people who care about and need the business. I am not one of them. It's all theirs now.

I blatantly ignored my promise to not end up in an early grave like David Dunn. Or dark and jaded like Reed, giving girls facials on OnlyFans. Either outcome was possible. David's death was the wake-up call that got me out of a mess of a situation. I was reckless in my relationships and actions. I could have easily derailed my situation with the company and my life. I was reckless with drugs and alcohol. I sometimes wonder who was actually behind the wheel.

AHEM.

Cocaine has exited my life. There are too many fentanyl deaths to ignore, one of which was my friend Poop. Apparently, one needs testing strips and Narcan to feel relaxed enough to do cocaine.

RIP COCAINE. WE HAD A GREAT RUN.

Now I have the occasional acid or mushroom trip and sometimes smoke weed. No more booze because I was a total drunk while the world was collapsing. Yet, had I not been drunk, I never would have taken the leap of faith away from Mindgeek. I never would have found the happiness and peace that escaped me during my tenure as a smut producer. Thank you alcohol for giving me the liquid courage to change directions and find inner peace.

I get asked if I am lonely. It's a fair question because, on the exterior, I am a forty-nine-year-old bachelor living alone with two dogs. But, there is a difference between being lonely and being content with being alone. It may seem sad, but I am at complete peace. This is my choice.

YOU AREN'T ALONE, DUDE.

I look back on my relationships with Doctor Blow, Joy, Meridiana, and Jackie, and it's amazing what I rationalized in order to not be alone. I have special lady friends. They are busy with their lives in other states. It's perfect.

AS LONG AS THAT FROWN IS UPSIDE DOWN, MY MAN.

I was seeking my water from a tainted well, looking for meaningful relationships and friendships within the business. Ample time has passed and now I understand I had virtually no friendships during my almost twenty years in the industry. I talk to a handful of people. It's a terrible ratio when you consider I dealt with thousands of people.

JUNIOR WAS RIGHT. MOST OF THE PERFORMERS WERE OF SUBPAR QUALITY ON A HUMAN LEVEL.

I am still great friends with four of the original five Jew Camp bunkmates from 1981. I was seven when I met them. People from all phases of my personal life, from high school through college and the Miami years have rarely stuck. Only a few. Yet those I bonded with for a few months every year at a young age stayed close. Of the five successful Jews, three became lawyers. One became a doctor. The other found success *in the entertainment industry*. If that isn't an accurate representation of Jewish trajectories, I don't know what is. One of them helped me edit this novel. I see what is special in all of it. Despite my anger and resentment from previous experiences and interactions, this is what makes Jews unique. These relationships stood the test of time, even for a loner like me. Thus, my appreciation for my roots has been reaffirmed. There's enough antisemitism in the world.

THANKS, KANYE, YOU FUCK.

We all can do better in our day-to-day behavior, including the Long Island JAPS who rubbed me the wrong way in summer camp, Hebrew School, and Syracuse.

Toward the end, I got the sense it was frowned upon for directors to have consensual sex with the talent on their own time. A former Spiegler Girl (talent from Mark Spiegler's agency, arguably the top female talent in the biz) hired me to shoot her OnlyFans content. I asked if she heard anything about my departure.

"I just heard they didn't like you were fucking all the girls."

HE WASN'T FUCKING ALLLLLLLL THE GIRLS! JUST THE TOP ONES.

"I thought it was hypocritical because I totally blew one of their VPs in the bathroom during the PornHub awards," she added. Oopsie.

I had sex with less than two percent of the industry, so any claim I was fucking *all the girls* is patently false. What was I supposed to do? Avoid unattached sex with hot porn stars? Seriously? Relationships outside the industry alienated me. This was the alternative. Or be celibate.

THE KIDS TODAY CALL IT BEING ASEXUAL.

Was this another reason I was put out to porn pasture? I could understand claims of harassment or abuse, but there were none.

I don't drink and I rarely do drugs or have sex. A far cry from the drunk, drugged-out man-whore I was a mere three years ago.

HEY! "SEXUALLY DIVERSE," PLEASE. WE WILL NOT BE SLUT-SHAMED!

The situationships which remain from those still in the industry will never pan out. For example, one is married and wants me to impregnate her (prefers my genetics; hubby is on board), but her interest and planning grow then wane during her ovulation and hormone cycle. It has grown ponderous, yet my Johnson will always answer her call. Since I am no longer a filthy pornographer...

JUST FILTHY

... it's best to stay in the tested civilian well. COVID was forgotten in porn by 2022. In the age of gonorrhea+, it's safer than fucking active content creators who, along with their scene partners, may not be vigilant in their testing.

<u>And now, a word from Dr. Lagina:</u>

Ok, it's not called gonorrhea+, but STDs which are antibiotic resistant are on the rise, everywhere. A new testing facility called Clear opened in cities around the country. They offer anal and oral swabs in addition to the full panel at an affordable price to performers. STDs can reside in these orifices while not being detected in urine, hence the rectal swabbing. The latest concern is genital mycoplasma. More shit will pop up in the coming years, so testing will have to keep evolving. When I swam in the porn muck, it was toxic. Now it's radioactive. To up the ick factor even more, performers are getting their tonsils removed. With antibiotic resistant gonorrhea and chlamydia of the throat on the rise, they are suffering symptoms similar to perpetual strep throat. Removing the tonsils reduces the symptoms. Chalk this up to 'New Rules': any performer who previously tested positive for HIV but are on antiviral meds are allowed in the talent pool. The rationale stems from medications that prevent transmission of HIV during sex by dropping the viral count in the bloodstream to 'undetectable.' HIPAA laws prohibit disclosure of a performer who previously tested positive for HIV. I would not be able to maintain chub in this situation. I wonder how male talent feel about performing with someone who previously tested positive for HIV. I am glad I no longer have to have these discussions to make money.

Therein lie the dilemma: fucking porn stars has wrecked me on a sexual level. No civilian will be able to match the skills of a sex worker. How can they compete with a professional who has ten thousand hours of dick mastery under her belt?

BEST SHOOT ROPES YOURSELF UNTIL A UNICORN COMES ALONG. BESIDES, DAILY MAINTENANCE BEATS ARE CRUCIAL FOR A HEALTHY PROSTATE.

I no longer speak to those I employed for over a decade. Marcos moved out the equipment he deserted before I vacated my studio. Shooting for Mindgeek was not the greener pasture he hoped for so he stopped. He was betting on crypto to leapfrog him into retirement.

TRY SCRATCH-OFF TICKETS, MARCOS. THE ODDS ARE BETTER.

As for the rest of them, despite all their annoying antics, we were a solid crew for a long time. We produced our highest-quality work during the last years in my studio. There was a lot left on the table. We were a professional team by porn standards and they deserve credit for elevating me and the company. I could not have done it without them.

I live in a daily state of existential examination since porn ended. I read a lot and take deep dives into philosophical rabbit holes, contemplating the big questions. I understand the pointlessness of our existence and I think about death incessantly. None of it matters, nor will it have an impact on the endless void that is our ancient universe. I am well aware I am on the back nine of life. So, I treat each day like it's my last. Now is all that matters.

HE'S BEEN ALONE WITH HIS DOGS THE LAST FEW YEARS, PEOPLE. HAVE SOME COMPASSION. THIS IS WHAT HAPPENS WHEN PORN ENDS.

Whatever entrepreneurial spirit I once had has been extinguished. Running a business with increased costs, shrinking profit margins, and the thought of managing employees stresses me the fuck out.

WHO WANTS TO DEAL WITH A BUNCH OF WHINY BABIES? TOUGHEN UP, YOU GEN Z FUCKS. YOUR PARENTS ENTITLED YOU TOO MUCH. THE WORLD IS NOT A NICE PLACE AND DOES NOT GIVE A SHIT ABOUT WHAT TRIGGERS YOU. NO WONDER YOU ARE GETTING REPLACED BY AI.

I am great friends with Jackie. She had to get married, pregnant, become a mother, and get divorced. We do not want to get into a relationship again, but we do love each other, as friends. I love our honesty about our infidelity. For instance, I have fruit trees in my backyard that she gave me while we were together. Little did I know she dished out hand jobs to a fan with a nursery in exchange for them. The grapefruit tree only yielded three grapefruits while the lemon trees produce a healthy crop each year.

OBVIOUSLY, SHE PUT MORE HEART INTO THE LEMON TREE HAND JOB.

I am happy she is in my life. I tell her I love her. She gave me a ride to and from my first colonoscopy. She's a good friend who sets me up with her friends. What a wingman. She's a good mother too. Her son loves me. I'm his 'Huncle.' On the morbid side, I have tasked her with discovering my corpse. I live alone and could die in my sleep. It would be days before my corpse is discovered and my dogs are placed in trustworthy hands. If she does not hear from me in the morning, she will know something is wrong.

Friends and family keep me in the loop when my former employer makes the headlines. Feras' mansion burned down.[1] The chubby Syrian built an opulent mansion near Mafia Row in Montreal. Once PornHub was forced by Visa and Mastercard to purge seventy-five percent of all unverified content, their traffic and revenue were greatly reduced. Feras listed his unoccupied mansion for $15.9 million dollars. One evening, neighbors reported intruders, a fire quickly ensued, and the entire estate burned to the ground. Arson was the official ruling. Feras claimed it could have been "extreme religious groups."

REGARDLESS IF HE LIT THE MATCH OR NOT, IT AIN'T A GOOD LOOK.

In June 2022, the *Washington Post* reported[2] Feras and David Tasillo, whom the paper cited as CEO and CFO of Mindgeek, abruptly exited the company. A bigger story was brewing.

The porn rumor mill swirled that Ryan was fired. Based on how he handled things in the early part of the pandemic and with the failure of Brazzers+ this made sense. However, instead of being fired, he was elevated to CEO. This was the dumb fuckery that was Mindgeek. Being their CEO is perfect for someone needing power and recognition, but it's a hot seat I would not wish on anyone.

Ryan did a great job in the first three to four years of his promotion to Production Manager of Paysites, but he made bad decisions toward the end of my tenure. I outmaneuvered him and Mario for years by playing longball, taking risks, and keeping things very close to my chest. I wish Ryan the best of luck as CEO. His missteps helped me find my existential bliss. During AVN 2023, a Brazzers director told me Mario was fired due to improper conduct. He wasn't at the convention and is no longer with the company, so it made sense.

MARIO WAS THE CURLY-HEADED FUCK WE ALL HATED BUT PLAYED NICE TO.

In the real world, people get fired. In porn, as long as a performer was selling, they received a lot of leeway. Some of the most problematic performers were put *under contract* by Mindgeek. They gave Bonnie Rotten a contract years after she left the business. She later got wasted on my set before her sex scene and she could not stand up, *while a representative from Montreal was visiting*. I endured her verbal beratement when I canceled the rest of the scene. Ryan apologized for putting me and my crew in a bad position.

Then he contracted the Shannon Sisters, who both had drinking problems.

One day, while her sober sister was shooting a scene for me, her drunk twin cheered her on behind me before falling asleep on my soundstage floor. I sent a live picture to the six-member creative team for Brazzers, including Ryan.

"Looks like she is passed out on the studio floor. I guess all the directing wore her out," I wrote. The minion Rachel acknowledged the twins were "already on strike three" in regards to drinking on set.

Brazzers is a shell of the brand they once were. They no longer have the budget to support higher production value because the majority of that money goes to performers (as it should). The company needs top performers and their traffic to stay relevant. Hardest hit are the crew members. They are not making what I did because the money is no longer there. Those still shooting for them have not yet passed the bullshit-to dollar-ratio threshold. Settling on directors who fit a company's budget *and* rigid production demands leads to lower-quality product. Those still putting up with Mindgeek need the work, love the perceived notoriety, or both.

My advice to current crews and performers: assume they don't care about you. Once you outlast your usefulness and marketability, they will move on. They claim they reward loyalty. I was a loyal soldier for sixteen years and Brando for eleven and they cut us without hesitation. This is their way. Act like a team player, eat their shit sandwiches with a smile, and try to keep your sanity. But understand, given the fragility of today's performer, every producer and director working in the porn industry is holding a ticking time-bomb.

After our parting, I went through all the emotions. It would have been nice to leave on good terms, but they deem everyone replaceable.

AT LEAST IT'S AN ETHOS.

On March 15, 2023, Netflix released a documentary *Moneyshot: The PornHub Story*. One day later, PornHub and Mindgeek were sold. I knew a bigger story was brewing when Feras Antoon and David Tasillo stepped down from the board. Here's the payoff.

The documentary took the momentum from Nicolas Kristoff's article and continued the narrative, some of which I outlined in this book. The stories of the victims who pleaded with Mindgeek to remove intimate, embarrassing, and in some cases non-consensual content, only to find no recourse, were jarring. Mindgeek dragged their feet because they knew this type of content drew massive traffic. Their marching orders (*Shame on Her, PornStarPunishment.com*) in the early days of PornHub reflect this.

The documentary showed Feras' and David's testimony to the Canadian Parliament and it did not disappoint. That googly-eyed arrogant motherfucker David was now a scared and rattled man. Feras sweat bullets as they grilled him about his net worth and the company's revenue. It was awesome to watch and not nearly enough of the repentance they deserve.

They sold and have their fuck you money. With pending litigation, karma may still be served, although the rich seem to always prevail.

The litigation outlined in the documentary accuses Mindgeek of mafia-like behavior, with capos enforcing their policies. The capos in question were performers like Asa Akira whom they paid as Brand Ambassadors. They wore PornHub gear like walking billboards. Over the years, Mindgeek sent me boxes of Brazzers gear which I never wore and gave to my crew. Wearing it felt corny and I didn't want to be a shill for those arrogant dickheads. But, if Asa Akira is saying Mindgeek is no longer the same monster, who is going to question it?

Was Mindgeek organized crime? No. If you knew these knuckleheads, it's laughable. That said, they were a monopoly and if you did not play by their rules, they'd blacklist you. Instead of breaking legs, they squeezed you financially. If I get whacked, then I was wrong.

The fourth ownership of Mindgeek and PornHub are called Ethical Capital Partners based out of Ottawa, Canada[3]. There are six members. One is a criminal defense lawyer. Another is a former superintendent of the Royal Canadian Mounted Police. Another is an accomplished investor and executive who founded Meta Growth, Canada's largest cannabis retailer. It's an eclectic bunch, with zero experience in the adult industry. Perhaps this is a good thing. The company has been rotten to the core for a while, so perhaps it's best to burn it down and start from scratch. Furthermore, they can pass off all of the company's bad baggage onto prior ownership. ECP states they were built upon a foundation of trust, safety, and compliance. Time will tell.

Still, why purchase such a beleaguered brand, even for pennies on the dollar? Data. Tech. Which leads to the next stage of the business: AI porn.

WAVE OF THE FUTURE, DUDE.

Perhaps porn stars, porn producers, and all of their costs and bullshit will become redundant.

I STILL JERK OFF MANUALLY.

Of course you do, and dinosaurs such as myself will keep it old school.

WHY DON'T YOU OVERSHARE WITH US NOW, PLEASE?

I have a designated porn laptop full of clips of those I have been with and those who remain a fantasy. It's my jerk-off time machine. It gives me the unique ability to tap into my mental Rolodex of actual sexual romps with porn stars. Minus the potential smells, over-the-top performances, and awkward post-coital conversation. At one point I made bad decisions because I feared being alone. Now, I get myself off better than anyone and don't have to consider anyone's feelings.

I don't frequent tube sites. Being a farm-to-table kind of guy, it's best to support your favorite sex worker. Join their OnlyFans. Support them directly.

Mindgeek's fate will be their own doing. They rebranded for the fourth time in seventeen years and are now called Aylo. Whatever they evolve into will work out. We had a great run. There is no reason for either of us to be bitter or angry, regardless of how I outmaneuvered them. Maybe new ownership and I will mend fences.

AYLO SHOULD INDUCT VIC LAGINA INTO THE BRAZZERS HALL OF FAME!

Or not. Who cares? None of it matters.

WE ARE MERELY A COLLECTION OF MEMORIES AND STORIES TO ENTERTAIN THOSE LISTENING. ALSO KNOWN AS EGO.

I bought a camper trailer for my truck. It's equipped with a shitter, shower, queen-sized bed, solar panels, and every creature comfort imaginable. Me, Jordan, and Junior travel and live off the grid on acres of land I own in the middle of nowhere.

I still love Vegas, so I check in from time to time. This town took me in and allowed me to flourish. They respect a weirdo's privacy.

I walk the Earth and get into adventures, meeting new people and civilian women.

I won.

I survived.

I stuck the landing.

IN MEMORIUM:

Jordan Ash, 5/28/78 - 10/19/20

Whatever I say about Jordan in this passage will fall short based on his larger-than-life presence. He was a giant at six-foot-five and had a baby arm for a penis leading to a successful porn career. The dude was fearless and gave zero fucks. He had two different colored eyes which were intense to behold, especially on mushrooms at my fortieth birthday party.

I met Jordan in 2004 while he was an up-and-comer in the Florida porn scene. He fit my budget (two hundred per scene) and shooting him was clockwork. Even if he nutted prematurely (which happened rarely), his rebound time was a matter of minutes. He had been arrested for weed and served out his sentence on weekends. He told me how a large black man tried to take his pudding. Jordan already looked crazy with those two different-colored eyes. He also looked like a dude who would not hesitate to bite off your nose.

"No, you can't have my fucking pudding!" The black man walked off, but not before calling Jordan a "cracker ass cracker!"

Both of us thought we knocked up my ex-fiancée Meridiana. Yes, it was him.

When Vegas came calling, Jordan mentioned he would be out in a few weeks to start working. When it fell through, I was relegated to the $200 per scene mopes Vegas had to offer. After about a year, Jordan made it to the West Coast and it was back to business. It also came with a healthy rate bump which rose over the years. During the Big Dick Wars between Brazzers and Reality Kings, they bid for Jordan's services. Honorable man he was, he told both whichever was higher, he would sign exclusively with them. Reality Kings won and we were without Jordan's services for a year. When his contract was up, he came back to us.

He was tough as nails and unflappable. Even when liquid shit piled up on his torso during a live show due to a performer's poor anal preparation, he wiped it off and went back into battle. He enjoyed the acting side and I had a hard time stifling my laughter when he showcased his antics. When he played Raoul Duke in our porn parody of *Fear and Loathing in Las Vegas*, he shaved the top of his head, showing unrivaled commitment.

The one knock against Jordan was his long legs, making some requested positions unachievable. It was common for him to stay in Vegas for a four or five-day stretch. Once he started illegal marijuana grows throughout LA, he could only commit to two days at a time. He feared a fan or air conditioning unit would break and destroy one of his crops. You wouldn't think a male porn star is Mensa material, but Jordan fit the criteria.

He started multiple illegal grows in LA. Heisenberg-level thinking. While it was a bummer when Pete left me to work with Jordan, I supported Pete however I could. I wish I had heard about it from Jordan, but we patched things up on our last shoot in 2014.

Jordan stayed at my house and we buried the hatchet with a lot of whiskey. The marijuana business weighed on him. He talked about paying off the District Attorney, jaded employees ratting on him and having to instill the fear of God in them, and Russian gangsters. As with Walter White, he had duffel bags of cash with GPS trackers buried on land he owned. I don't believe any of this was embellished.

In 2016, he was diagnosed with a brain tumor. I heard from Pete, Charles Dera, and Danny Mountain, who had visited him in the hospital. They said he was no longer the same person and was losing touch. Jordan texted me a few times asking where his check was for a scene we never shot. I showed him the cashed check image of his last shoot in 2014, but he insisted there was another one after and "Why didn't I remember?" I asked Pete for suggestions on how to handle it, and he said he would squash it, but this was the new normal.

On October 19, 2020, four years after his initial diagnosis and a few months in hospice care, Jordan passed at forty-two. According to Pete, the last few months were not easy because Jordan spiraled. His father laid his ashes to rest in the Pacific. I hope there is a Porn Heaven and Jordan is there fucking all the departed porn stars. Everyone is free and without pain.

AND NOW, A FINAL WORD FROM BRAMM STROKER...

> "*I was shooting a scene for BTAS (Big Tits at School) with the late/great Jordan Ash and the lovely Phoenix Marie. Early in the scene, Phoenix was propped up on top of a desk with her legs in the air, while Jordan went down on her. Phoenix comments "oh wow, you're really good at that!" Without skipping a beat, Jordan replies "Thanks, I've been practicing on the fat girls in my neighborhood." Of course, I had to cut so we can all burst out and spend the next few minutes hysterically laughing. It was one of those classic times Jordan's comedic timing completely halted a scene.*

Vic Lagina's School of Porn

Lesson Nine: So, You Wanna Be In Porn, Do Ya?

A number of times young women asked me, "How do I get into porn?" Plenty of agents and producers licked their chops if asked this question. Not me. I told them to have a seat and the conversation went something like this:

"Why do you want to get into porn?"

The responses were usually about money with little thought about the infamy that comes with being filmed. They liked sex, so why not make money doing it?

"OK, and how is the relationship with your family? Will they be upset when they find out?"

Notice the use of *when*. My ex-fiancée, when she shot for the biggest companies during her six-week stint in porn, believed no one close to her would know. Secrecy was an impossibility. Every scene remained on the internet, *forever*.

Once they contemplated this, assuming they had strong familial bonds, my next question was:

"Are you comfortable knowing you will be exposed to Herpes Simplex Virus-2 and may contract genital herpes, which is treatable but not curable?"

"You don't test for herpes?"

"No. While the industry tests for seven sexually transmitted diseases, it does not test for HSV-2."

"Why not?"

"Because many in the industry would be unable to perform in adult films." The testing centers, the Free Speech Coalition, and sex workers may have a different opinion, but I had dozens of cancellations due to outbreaks. Some would claim it was an ingrown hair. Others would say their "pussy was broken." During my first few years in the industry, when I heard "pussy was broken," I did not pry. This could mean a lot of things when dealing with something as complex as a vagina. Later in my career, talent would simply say "I am having an outbreak" and they were replaced. The dick pics with sores I received justified the cancellation. I could be a doctor at this point.

'Dr. Lagina' has a nice ring to it, does it not?

The prospective talent would be repulsed by now. If they weren't, herpes was not a concern. I mentioned testing positive for gonorrhea or chlamydia was bound to happen, likely multiple times depending on how often they shot.

If they were still eager beavers, we'd discuss the psychological downsides. The internet is a mean place. Trolls are soulless. It takes its toll and I drove this point home.

It's best to hire someone to handle social media. Some cannot afford the expense. I also recommend setting up an entity so any maintenance costs (hair, nails, tanning, gym) could be classified as business expenses and therefore tax deductible.

The importance of paying taxes on the monies made is because both the IRS and the California Franchise Tax Board are generally relentless when they send their demand letters.

**SOMEONE HAS TO PAY FOR THEIR MISMANAGEMENT.
MIGHT AS WELL BE STRUGGLING SEX WORKERS.**

Finally, I stressed the importance of communication and informed consent. They needed to learn to be comfortable saying "no." It's about trust and comfort and people need to be reminded. If you cannot say "no" or call "cut," do not enter the porn industry. Stick to OnlyFans. Otherwise, you are a liability to those shooting you and those performing with you.

For men wanting to enter the business, all of the above applies, with a few more important considerations:

The arrival of performance-enhancing drugs changed porn, but they were never the magic bullet. Pharmaceuticals only do so much when the male talent is in his head. If the big head isn't into it, the little head will follow. I spent many hours giving failing talent a pep talk to get both heads back in the game. This was known as The Phil Jackson.

The first step in TPJ is telling the young man to clear his head and not worry about anything else. Focus your mind on the woman in front of you. If she is cold and standoffish, it's not your concern. Focus on whatever part you're attracted to. Once he finds his rhythm, build on it and allow his confidence to grow to finish the scene. This is The Phil Jackson and often it saved the day.

His rebound time determined whether I shot him again. I needed proper male talent who kept his dick hard under the toughest of circumstances. Otherwise, find something else to do with your life. Don't waste time and money. One time a dude called his parents for words of encouragement. He even took to cuddling the female talent on the couch. It worked, and even after he screamed "Victory!" when we finished, I never booked him again.

NERD!

On the flip side, sometimes the attraction is strong and their parts feel amazing. I can empathize, so I bestowed my techniques to those about to cum prematurely: complicated math problems. What is six thousand and forty times eight hundred and nineteen? It doesn't matter. Computation alone sways your mind from the amazing porn star vagina gripped around your Johnson.

JOHNSON? WHAT ELSE CAN I DO, COACH LAGINA? I HATE MATH.

Imagine your favorite football team (in my case the Philadelphia Eagles) getting ass-reamed by their division rival on national television.

If talent (like Xander Corvus in his younger years) had quick-pop recovery time, assuming the female talent consented, I preferred they pop early on camera. Now they could have sex properly for the duration. Otherwise, there would be a lot of taking the dick out, slapping it on her leg a bit before going back in, and repeating the process. This made for a choppy, subpar porn scene. However, this is risky, especially if your male talent cannot manufacture another load for the finale. I was dubious when Xander suggested it on his first shoot. When he mustered more ejaculate, it became his trademark of sorts.

When it comes to administering a facial, know your lasso. Your counterpart prefers you not jizz in her eye. Aim below her nose. Some men who shall remain nameless deliberately aimed for the eyes to administer retribution for a difficult day.

OVER THE LINE! THIS IS NOT 'NAM. THERE ARE RULES.

When confronted with the possibility of no pop shot (second or otherwise), the solution was a 'FIP,' a fake internal pop. A product like Spunk simulated a creampie. A seasoned porn viewer would know, so I tried hiring male talent who could cum within a few minutes of demand.

We also faked a lot of squirting scenes. A performer took a douche with water and squeezed it up inside of her. Male talent then entered her and they would fuck for a few seconds before he pulled out and she 'squirted.' Again, a porn connoisseur would know this was a *fugazi*, so we aimed to hire legitimate squirters or those who enjoyed Pedialyte.

As for on-set conduct, it's simple: don't be a creep. If you are a fan of the female talent who's now your scene partner, keep it to yourself. You may feel it's flattering, but it isn't. They want to have sex with a professional, not a fan boy.

It's also important to have 'the talk' with your co-star about all the yeses and noes for the scene. You should respect their temple and they should respect yours. Be very clear and don't be ashamed. If you don't like fingers or tongues in your butthole, speak up. If you've made it this far, remember this is your sexuality and there's nothing to be embarrassed about. Even better, have this discussion in front of the director with them in earshot. If they hear it as well, there is less room for confusion.

Whenever someone acted outside of a performer's 'yes' list, I called it out, while the camera was rolling, for everyone to hear in any subsequent reviews. It wouldn't be an issue again. Sometimes people forgot in the heat of passion and need to be reminded without it becoming tense. Sometimes it got uncomfortable and trying to keep things calm was dicey.

WALKING ON PORN EGGSHELLS. ANECDOTE TIME.

Bill Bailey struggled during an office scene with Britney Amber for *BigTitsAtWork.com*. He bent her over a desk to start doggy style. He was holding her leg in what looked like an uncomfortable manner and she moved his hand to another part of her leg. He did it again and so did she. The third time she yelled at him.

"You're hurting my leg when you grab and push it down like that!"

He apologized, but the tension was thick. A break might have been wise, but they did not want to lose momentum. Bill tried to power through and his dick went flaccid after ninety seconds. Scenes like these were maddening, forcing an editor to piece together a choppy scene.

I gave Bill a few breaks to clear his head, but it wasn't helping. He resorted to edging himself as Britney waited in position, frustrated and bored. When he was fully erect, he fucked Britney until he went limp noodle. We rinsed and repeated until we had enough footage for Bill to set up the pop, which did not register on camera because he had the dribblers. I never shot Bill again. He died a few years later falling down some stairs while intoxicated at a resort in Mexico.

Many times talent continued fucking after camera cut. If it was in-between takes during hardcore photos to help maintain a male talent's edge and his partner was not voicing any complaints, I saw no issue. When they kept fucking while we transitioned to the scene's next segment, I intervened. I'd rather capture the passion and mojo on camera. Furthermore, I did not want my male talent punching themselves out before the match. Save it for the screen. I had been called a "cock-blocker" on more than one occasion.

Lastly, don't become known as a shower shark. These are men who get in the shower while a female is still cleaning post-scene hoping to get another round of sex in. It will soil your reputation. Let the woman shower in peace. I am not going to tell you everyone acted accordingly on my sets. Things happened when I was not around or occupied elsewhere. Too often I trusted adults in the adult industry to act like adults. Thirteenth grade, remember? Be professional and a gentleman and you will experience longevity as I did.

MESSAGES FOR MY FORMER CREW

Teenah, I'm still not sure you didn't give Cody methamphetamines. If you did, you got away with it.

Moe, I was a dick and hard to work for, but you were not easy to keep employed. I hope you are no longer mopey and emotional and understand how my ex-fiancée may have manipulated you. I hope you gave Shady a great life.

Hailey, I am glad you turned a corner in life and are still with us. Even though you don't remember much, you were a big part of the journey.

Butler, I still love you, you odd goober. I pray you are keeping your weight down and staying healthy.

Kyle, I saw a lot of myself in you which is why you were a worthy adversary. Yes, my ex-fiancée was a whore, but she thought you were a closeted homosexual. Be as you are, man. Be happy and free.

Morty, I love you man.

Bramm, you were my porn kid brother. You got a raw deal from Mindgeek and what's-her-face who replaced you. I hope you enjoyed the ride.

Blake, I'm sorry I almost punched you in front of the Gilespie House. I am glad we ended things on a positive note. Sorry my ex-fiancée was practicing witchcraft and speaking in tongues at your condo. You were way over your head and should not have been given that much responsibility.

Ginger Giant, I hope you're not an alcoholic.

The Commodore, you'll always be much older than me. Thanks for tipping me off about Huggy and allowing me to stay a few steps ahead of the manipulative dickwad. May you find a steady stable of little people to keep you occupied.

Paul, you were a great worker. Frank was an asshole but it was Huggy's fault for getting you fired. He should have turned the camera elsewhere.

Fucktard, you can still go fuck yourself, you rat bastard.

Toad, ideally you're off the drugs and getting your life together.

Huggy, you manipulative, scheming bag of dogshit. Do you have any idea how exhausting it was fending off your silent attacks while also providing job security to you and your family? Do better, man.

Shibby, I was hard on you, but you had two left feet. Thank you for choreographing those lightsaber battles. The nerds who jerked off to it appreciated it.

Juan, best PA ever and a damn fine haircutter.

Stephanie, you were a dedicated soldier. I wish you were on time more often than you asked me for a raise, but you found a makeup replacement when your appendix was about to explode. This is a work ethic I can get behind.

Ethan, we always got the job done. Be safe on your motorcycle. You have a family who needs you.

Marcos, you are talented and your funny demeanor lightened the mood as much as your emotions dampened it. You bore heavy burdens while working for me. May you be closer to your dreams.

Pete, out of all of this bullshit, I gained a true friend. I dealt with Huggy so it would lead to you. Looking forward to seeing how life plays out for both of us.

Jodi, my playa'. You were there in the beginning. You saw how this shit show was birthed. You have seen all sides of me over the years. You are proof there are wonderful people in porn.

AND NOW, A FINAL WORD FROM PETE...

> "*It wasn't easy staying grounded through all this and keeping a sane view of reality and daily life around the studio. Every one of us in our own way at some point came away jaded during this chapter of our lives. We put on outrageous events at the Lagina Compound over the years that blurred the thin gray line between reality and fiction. Collectively as a team, we overcame strenuous obstacles and impossible demands that head office threw our way with class and swagger.*
>
> *Vic was always the white, sticky, viscous substance that held the organization together from day one, and everyone including myself absolutely respected him for that. I made countless acquaintances during my tenure as Vic's production manager. Over the passing of enough years, people tend to show their true color one way or another. Of the countless people I've come across in the adult industry, Vic is one of very few individuals I still call my brother and stay in touch with – I think that speaks to the man that was, will always be - Vic Lagina.*

Killing Vic Lagina

April 2, 2002 - October 14, 2023

I am going to kill Vic Lagina, right now, to turn the page and start Act III of an egoless existence.

VIC LAGINA'S OBITUARY (TO BE SENT TO AVN, XBIZ, ETC.)

Vic Lagina was murdered by a gunshot to the chest, assailant unknown. Vic had Stage 4 throat cancer, caused by HPV resulting from vast amounts of cunnilingus. Vic sensed he was not long for this world and lived accordingly.

Mr. Lagina started his porn career in April 2002 in Los Angeles under the handle 'Ned Wood'. He met the men who became Brazzers while in Miami. Their relationship blossomed into a profitable and symbiotic marriage lasting over sixteen years. In March of 2006, when Brazzers was about to launch its network, Mr. Lagina set up shop in Las Vegas. He was tasked to direct twenty shoots a month for Mansef, the first ownership's entity.

"I have fond memories of Mansef. They knew how to take care of their workhorse. I worked harder for them because I respected them. Unfortunately, appreciation was lacking in subsequent regimes."

Mr. Lagina was tasked with supervising a whopping thirty-five shoots a month and had to recruit to help lighten the load. Two notable recruits were Brett Brando and Keiran Lee. "In hindsight, it was a mistake bringing them into the fold, but I wanted to help the company that helped my burgeoning career. I did not think how their involvement or ambition would affect my workload. Live and learn, which I did." Mr. Lagina produced and directed until March of 2020 when the pandemic changed the business.

"Saying goodbye to the money was the hardest part, but it was the money that kept me in an unfulfilling and increasingly maddening business. Fortunately, I had a

comfortable and happy retirement waiting with no need to work. The industry served its purpose."

Mr. Lagina made less than a handful of friends in the porn industry, but he kept to himself and his beloved dogs. "I had always been a lone wolf, but I had to insulate myself because of the fucktards everywhere. The porn industry is thirteenth grade. I didn't understand why the industry celebrated itself the way it did. In my entire career, I went to half *of an AVN awards show before leaving to end my pain."*
Mr. Lagina spent his final years enjoying each day and reflecting on the shit show his life was the previous two decades. "It was wild, and I have no regrets."

There will be an invite-only memorial service and shiva *down the line for Mr. Lagina. His memoir,* Filthy! The Rise and (Pending) Death of Vic Lagina, *was published late* 2023.

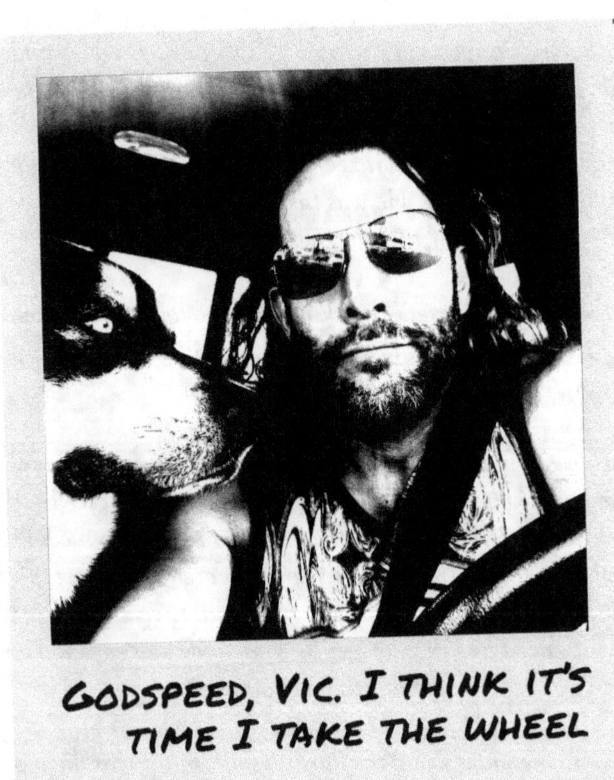

GODSPEED, VIC. I THINK IT'S
TIME I TAKE THE WHEEL

HELLO AGAIN.
EXHAUSTING, ISN'T HE? TRY GUIDING THE BASTARD.
STILL, HE'S COME A LONG WAY. HE IS A TEDDY BEAR AND TERRIBLE IN SOCIAL SITUATIONS. IT'S A WONDER HE GOT LAID SO MUCH.
OR IS IT? I KNOW MOST OF THOSE GIRLS THREW A FUCK AT HIM THINKING IT COULD BENEFIT THEM. WHO CARES IF HE THOUGHT A SEX WORKER COULD LEAD TO A MEANINGFUL CONNECTION? HOW ADORABLE.
LET ME TELL YOU ABOUT THE TIME WHEN A DIGITAL PLAYGROUND CONTRACT STAR ASKED TO STAY AT HIS HOUSE.
WHY ON EARTH WOULD SHE CHOOSE TO STAY AT HIS HOUSE IF SHE DIDN'T WANT TO SMASH?
HE THOUGHT BECAUSE SHE HAD A HUSBAND, SHE WAS JUST LOOKING FOR A COMFORTABLE PLACE TO STAY OFF THE STRIP.
YOU KNOW WHERE THE COMFORTABLE PLACE WAS? IN HER VAGINA, STUPID!
INSTEAD, SHE WAITED AWKWARDLY ON HIM TO MAKE THE FIRST MOVE.

I didn't think a chick as hot as her was interested! Besides, first moves are what get dudes into trouble these days.

QUIET!
I JUST LISTENED TO YOU BLATHER FOR HUNDREDS OF PAGES. IT'S MY TURN.
FIRST MOVES ARE WHAT CONTINUE OUR SPECIES, PUSS CAKE.
WHEN ANOTHER PORN STAR CONFIRMED THE DIGITAL PLAYGROUND WOMAN WAS INTERESTED, IT WAS TOO LATE. THEY TRIED TO MAKE IT HAPPEN ON HER LAST DIGITAL PLAYGROUND FEATURE, BUT SHE GOT A YEAST INFECTION.

I still imagine what her non-yeasty vagina would have tasted like. I am going with fresh watermelon. Instead we have regrets and missing spank bank material.

However, her porn will live on forever.

Before you worry about his mental health, let me assure you, Dr. OZ says he's fine and not schizophrenic. He just whispers to himself sometimes, when he's talking to me.

The hot Dutch woman caught us chatting. She was cool. A civilian anal unicorn. Too bad she only wanted a green card.

Maybe all the LSD has taken its toll.

What would you rather have?

A drug addict pornographer?

A dead drug addict pornographer?

A jaded, mean, soulless asshole?

I think it's wonderful he's an unemployed, financially stable hippie who thinks he resides in a simulation. Now it's time to add NY Times best-selling author to his resume.

With all the women who have asked for his seed, I wouldn't mind seeing a Little Lagina at some point.

After all, he's just helping them conceive, man.

Until then, I hope you folks enjoyed yourselves.

Catch ya later on down the trail.

EPILOGUE
12/8/11 - LAGINA STUDIO ONE

This was the idea (and hope) as outlined in the press release:

LUXEMBOURG—Brazzers members will help determine the next male performers to be signed to Brazzers.com tomorrow at 4 p.m. PST/7 p.m. EST during a live show called *How Hard Can You Give It?*

On a daily basis, Brazzers receives applications from men and women around the world, wishing to star in one of the brands' exclusive scenes.

Always looking to expand on its roster of talent, the Brazzers team has created a one-of-a-kind event geared toward the male applicants. The list was narrowed down, and the chosen individuals were invited to a live audition.

"They will get the opportunity to perform with, and get judged by, some of our industry's most renowned performers," said Frank, Brazzers' vice president of productions. "If these guys want to work in adult, this is the opportunity of a lifetime and the ultimate chance for them to prove themselves."

Brazzers: How Hard Can You Give It? will be hosted by AVN Hall of Famer Julia Ann, while Ava Devine and Hailey Young will take on the male talent, one by one.

The event will include three rounds during which Brazzers members will vote for their favorite male talent. To help members in their decision making, a panel of judges that includes Angelina Valentine, Nicki Hunter and Jordan Ash will provide expert commentary.

The judges will narrow the candidates down to three performers, and the fans will vote for the MVP—Most Valuable Penis. All three will be offered contracts to shoot for Brazzers.

Brazzers: How Hard Can You Give It? will be free for all Brazzers members, while members of Mofos, Twistys and Wicked will be able to watch the event for a minimal fee. —***Courtesy of AVN.com***

The reality: it was a complete and utter failure in its objective yet also happened to be the most intriguing live TV I ever produced. I am not saying it was quality. It wasn't. But it was one of those travesties you can't help but watch.

The event occurred in the chilly month of December of 2011. The holidays forced us to cram twenty-five shoots into a twenty-one-day period, including three live shows. This had to be done before shutting down a few days before Christmas and reconvening a few days after New Year's.

Each day was a battle. When Manwin mentioned the idea in September about trying to pull off a male talent contest before year's end, I said it was ambitious but doable. Their plans were optimistic as they hoped to draw in at least fifty contestants from all corners of the country. My immediate condition: they handle the talent and management search since I had enough on my plate. I didn't need these *meshuganas* emailing me with their bullshit. With fifty contestants, there is a lot of coordinating. While the testing was still archaic, there were plenty of industry-accepted labs in every state. My liaison was Hogan and this was his baby. It was on him to wrangle these puppies.

I never thought fifty guys was going to happen. Idiocy alone would knock it down to at least twenty-five. Operating a twenty-five man gangbang contest was the bar. Still, I needed a few filth buckets who would be down to suck and fuck all of these tested men off the street. We needed competent hosts to act as fluffers and judges. We also needed a personal coach.

Most importantly, we needed security guards keeping an eye on these randos at all times. A lot of horny dicks were going to be around porn stars they beat off to. After Phoenix Marie grabbed and pulled Bridgette B down by her weave during *Brazzers Live 5*, it was all the members could crow about on the forum. While a Jerry Springer atmosphere wasn't encouraged, it wasn't discouraged either. It wasn't until Jynx Maze almost put her heel into Jennifer's White's skull a few live shows later I mandated a Steve (Jerry's security guard) if they wanted Jerry Springer. For this show, we had three Steves, which wasn't enough once Angelina Valentine entered the fray as a fluffer.

This was only a few weeks after Tory Lane nearly punched her during a *DoctorAdventures.com* scene and the clear beginning of her declining mental state. The heads thought this would make great television. They weren't wrong.

Rounding out the "Pussy Panel" were hosts Julia Ann and Nicki Hunter, both fluffers. If a heaven exists, Julia's spot is reserved based on the number of dogs she has saved. In the show's context, I could rely on her to help maintain order. With Angelina in the mix, she had her work cut out for her.

Nicki Hunter. Swoon. Just thinking about her puts a smile on my face. She knew me since the beginning and saw the full evolution. After Joy left me in late 2004, Nicki and her husband invited me over for a holiday party. Her perfume and pheromones intoxicated me on a shoot I did with her weeks prior, so I considered going. My buzz-kill side prevailed when I remembered cameras would be rolling. Footage of me in a porn orgy would live on the internet. I passed and remained infatuated. She was beautiful and sexual with a loving and caring heart. She retired on two hundred acres with a husband and children.

We needed filth buckets to accommodate twenty-five men and I knew who to suggest. Ava Devine, of Chuckles McKnuckles fame and my nominee for Filth Bucket of the Century, first came to mind. She was the only woman I knew who would welcome twenty-five randos into all of her holes live on the internet.

The other potential bucket was my old friend Hailey Young. In her career, she accumulated a handful of bukkake and gangbang shoots. She even swallowed fifty men's ejaculate through a beer bong.

LOOK IT UP. ON AN EMPTY STOMACH.

It was a solid cast to pull this off. We still needed a personal coach and Jordan Ash was my vote. Everything was solidified before Thanksgiving and we started the countdown.

We had about thirty solid applicants amidst the garbage. While I internally gloated about being correct, I let him know this was more than enough. Time for Hogan to focus on testing and making sure they had two forms of identification. He assured me he would handle it.

"The last thing we need is to not have enough guys to fuck Ava and Hailey based on what we're paying them."

Prophetic words come shoot day.

December 8, 2011 arrives and with it comes Hogan from Canada to witness the spectacle. After all, our costs are totaling close to thirty grand. We held our normal morning meeting with the hosts, fluffers, and buckets. This wasn't a typical orgy where we had to go over consent and boundaries with the talent. *They* would tell the contestants what to do, how to do it, training them to handle the pressure of being male talent for Brazzers, the *best* in the business.

It was structured to be porn boot camp. Live for all the world to see. The contestants go through three phases. In the first, all men will line up and be fluffed by Julia Ann, Angelina, and Nicki. Once they achieved liftoff, they are to head to

Hailey's station to get sucked and fucked. If they sustained solid, porn-worthy sex positions showing their general demeanor and prowess, they headed to the final station down a long hallway and through our cold warehouse. There they will have to satisfy an insatiable Ava Devine. Live for *all* the world to see.

Twelve contestants became ten when it became obvious two of them had forged their tests. Now, if they had used Photoshop and added some logos, they might have gotten away with it. Instead, these morons typed out a letter from their doctors who cleared them of HIV, *Chlamidia* (misspelling intentional), and Gonorrhea. I wish I were making this up. On the surface, they looked like a sorry bunch.

"Vic, what are your thoughts here? How is this going to go?"

"Well Hogan, you're not going to find your next Brazzers contract star. However, I promise you are about to see some incredible television."

This was not what he wanted to hear, but I never sugarcoat. I knew some of these guys were going down in flames. But, what could we do at this point? Train is about to leave the station. My crew recruited two more tested locals to fill out this Dysfunctional Dozen.

The contestants are lounging on couches we moved into the studio lobby area. My idea was to keep everyone as close to the front door and bathroom as possible with no room to wander. Some of them won't make it past the first room once the hammer drops. I prayed to Testiclese every day during December because we needed all the help we could get. Doing so also prevented last-minute technical glitches tonight and I cued Julia Ann at the expected start time of 4 pm PST so we could meet the contestants:

#1 – D-Money or Andy Money because he has mush mouth and Julia cannot understand him. He's a handsome black kid, about twenty-five, and his exterior shows potential. Julia tells him to take his shirt off revealing a white tank top with food stains. Angelina reprimands him before tearing it off.

NOT A GREAT START, BUT MAYBE HE IS PACKING SOME HORSE MEAT TO MAKE UP FOR THE FOOD STAINS.

#2 - Travis, who is reeking of confidence and boasting about giving multiple O's and repeat pops. After he calls Angelina "baby," she chokes him with the microphone cable. Angelina rips off his shirt, marks him with the number two in dry-erase pen, and spanks him. He's already off-kilter and intimidated.

THIS ONE IS GOING DOWN IN FLAMES. MARK IT.

#3 – Gianni, but he specifies he is not the gay one. Angelina labels him a "Chippendale" while marking him with the number three. She calls him a liar when he boasts about having done over one hundred scenes.

I'VE NEVER HEARD OF THE GUY EITHER, ANGELINA.

He has a terrible flame tattoo around his navel.

HENCEFORTH! YOU SHALL BE KNOWN AS BADTATTOO!

#4 – Josh, a blond kid in his twenties who sounds like he's been smoking since he was in the cradle. Out of the lot so far, he shows the most promise. He is in shape, but red from the tanning bed.

HENCEFORTH! REDMAN!

Angelina gags and says her pussy has dried up.

I'M PULLING FOR YOU, KID.

#5 – Joe from Jersey, an Asian kid whose biggest claim to fame is being Jessica Jaymes' first *Fuck-a-Fan* participant.

HENCEFORTH! FUCK-A-FAN! YOU MADE IT THROUGH THAT, BUT THIS IS A HORSE OF ANOTHER COLOR.

Upon seeing his hairy chest, Angelina wants to shave him. The ladies ask if he has seen their vagina before and Fuck-a-Fan says he has seen all of their scenes and admits to being perverted.

WHY WE HAVE SECURITY.

#6 – Gavin From Vegas.

NOT A BAD-LOOKING CAT, OH WAIT, NEVER MIND, HE TOOK OFF HIS SHIRT.

Upon seeing his nipple rings Angelina pulls on them until he dances for her, busting out very white dance moves.

HENCEFORTH! YOU SHALL BE KNOWN AS NIPPLERINGS!

#7 – James, who is already sweating, but has swagger and explains it's because he was looking at Angelina for too long, disarming her.

THIS GUY HAS THE LOWEST DOUCHE QUOTIENT IN THE ROOM. GODSPEED.

She rubs up against his sweaty body while he oozes confidence.

HENCEFORTH! SILKYSMOOTH!

#8 – Pong. Angelina has seen him hang upside down and squirt his own cum into his mouth.

HENCEFORTH! JIZZMOUTH!

She found it sexy when he devoured it all. That's marvelous.
#9 –

HENCEFORTH! TWEAKER!

... because he looks like he smoked meth in the parking lot after sucking a dick for it. I am not sure how he made it into this, but it must have been because we needed another body. Angelina is revolted by him and his concaved chest. She demands he lick the bottom of her boot and he declines. She calls him a "pussy" and tells him to sit down.

#10 – Fab from Colorado. Angelina demands he lick the bottom of her boot. They encourage him and he pretends. Julia says, "This would cap a lot of people out of the gate," before she drops spit out of her mouth onto Angelina's boot and licks it. Lost in all of this because he's a foreigner, Fab may now believe this was a mistake.

HENCEFORTH! DASBOOTS!

#11 – Johnny Utah from Vegas licks Angelina's boot and receives a loud cheer from the Pussy Panel. Angelina takes off his glasses and rubs them all over her vagina. This was one of the contestants my crew found within the last two hours.

HENCEFORTH! JOHNNY UTAH!

#12 – Joe sports a V-shaped manscape over his chest and appears to consume steroids like Tic Tacs.

HENCEFORTH! ROIDMONKEYJOE!

I think he was one of the guys who died fighting the Predator. While Angelina takes her tits out and rubs them on his arm, Nicki tells him to flex his pectorals as Angelina takes off her bikini top and puts it over his chest. In the first few months of living in Vegas, I recalled shooting RoidMonkeyJoe with Carmella Bing and her huge boobs. Today he was supposed to be a PA on the shoot, but because he had a clean test and we were short-handed, he agreed to enter the contest.

If you're asking why on earth these guys would subject themselves to this, you would not be alone. Sure, the idea of being a male porn star for Brazzers would be a dream come true for jerkers everywhere wanting to fuck their favorite porn stars. As Jordan is about to explain, this is misguided thinking.

Now this sorry bunch has been introduced, it is time for them to meet their coach. Jordan Ash struts into the center of the room and begins a speech that should have been in a porn parody of *Animal House*.

Staring at DasBoots, he says, "Dude, if you're scared of blood, shit, piss, or cum, you're fucked. Fucking at home is easy. Do you think you can keep your dick hard in a fifty degree warehouse on a concrete floor for two hours? Then you're a porn star, maybe. You gotta dig deep, man. You have to fuck from the bottom of your feet to the top of your head to the tip of your dick."

This is when everyone in the porn parody would get confused looks on their faces. I buzz the cameraman to tell Jordan to move so he can face the camera, prompting him to reach out and tap Jordan. "What!?!?" interrupting Jordan's flow. While he gets the direction, he lets out a "fuck!" before regrouping.

"Your mind must be pure. This is a war. You gotta be focused. Concentrate. You must be point one percent of the best. If you think Viagra will save you, you're fucking dreaming. You're gonna lose wood, but you have to raise that shit back up again. If you can stay focused and ignore all the other dicks in the room trying to fuck the same pussy, then maybe you will have a chance at being a porn star at Brazzers."

He is getting long-winded, so I tell Julia to signal wrap-up. He ignores her. Julia throws a T-shirt at him. He continues to blather.

"It's brought me a good life. Money, more pussy than I even want to think about, but good times too. Beats being an engineer. Forget about everyone else and focus on your dick."

Julia inserts herself into the frame and takes the microphone away while thanking Deepdick Chopra for his thoughts. Everyone claps and I cue them to get the contest underway.

Julia informs the contestants of the rules and has them form three lines, naked. Nicki makes out with RedMan while Julia works on Tommy Utah. RoidMonkeyJoe takes a ferocious deepthroat from Angelina as the rest of the contestants wait their turns while yanking their flaccid penises. Nicki works up RedMan with her mouth as Jordan blurts, "Who has wood? If you do not have wood, you do not step up to the chow line!"

#1 steps up to Julia and she comments on his excessive pubes.

HENCEFORTH! BALLFRO!

"You need to trim those." Tommy Utah is fully erect with RoidMonkeyJoe not far behind. The door opens and Tommy is escorted by security where he finds Hailey waiting for him in an industrial-decorated room with a red hexagon bed as its centerpiece. She's dressed in black fishnet stockings with a shiny black bra and skirt.

I stare at the monitors, my mouth agape at what is unfolding. "Stay on camera one for the live feed. We'll bring up picture in picture when he starts fucking Hailey." After taking him in her mouth, Tommy pounds Hailey from behind as a big smile emanates from her face.

"If the rest of the contestants are this strong, we might actually find our guy," I tell Hogan, whose mouth is also agape. After a few minutes, I send Tommy Utah down to Ava's station. Security escorts him down the long hallway to the warehouse, past the prop room, past the wrestling ring where Ava awaits him. The set has a large white round surface with a chain-linked fence as a backdrop. She sticks his face between her legs.

WHAT WON'T THAT MAN LICK?

Now, I am confused. Do I show sex with RoidMonkeyJoe and Hailey? Or do we go back to the main room and see who is failing? The answer being obvious, I send us back there to witness overconfident #2's micropenis remain limp, despite Julia trying to work her magic.

HENCEFORTH! MICROPENIS!

"You're making me work very hard for a semi. I thought you said you could cum multiple times?"

I tell Brent, my IT guy and board switcher to go into picture in picture.

"Which feed?" he asks.

This is a genuine dilemma. Do I show RoidMonkeyJoe railing tiny Hailey with his huge rhino penis or, do I cut to Ava eating Tommy Utah's ass?

DECISIONS, DECISIONS.

"Ah fuck it, flip back and forth between them." This dilemma remained until we reached the finals. For now, I'm overwhelmed with a plethora of depravity to broadcast.

RedMan achieves lift-off and is sent to Hailey followed by NippleRings. They take turns with Hailey, but they're blocking penetration with their arms. Hailey berates them in her nasally voice and they lose their edge.

THIS ISN'T YOUR BEDROOM, FELLAS.

Nicki is being tender and nurturing to MicroPenis with zero effect. JizzMouth shows up erect, so Nicki goes full porno with her mouth to see how sensitive he is. It turns out, quite. He keeps having to step back and push her hands away, but she tells him to put his mind elsewhere, like baseball. He needs to pound rigorously on camera, so this is a test.

After a few special tricks with her throat and tongue, JizzMouth contains himself and moves on to Hailey. RedMan is back with a rager, while MicroPenis steps up to Angelina with the opposite and goes back to the end of the line. Fuck-A-Fan gets the porno mouth treatment from Nicki, but something tells me we're about to get one of those special live moments. The more he tries to pull away, the more it encourages Nicki. Finally, inevitably, he reaches the point of no return and blows a Danny D-style eruption all over Nicki's left boob and shoulder.

"He's definitely been holding that in for a while. Baby wipes, please?"

BallFro, who advanced out of the viper pit moments before, throws his soon-to-be half-chub in Hailey's mouth. Hailey is undiscerning, so when I see the repulsion on her face, I know there's a bigger story.

"You need to trim those pubes, man. Go to the bathroom and wash up. You're sweaty. Go wash up."

BadTattoo has also progressed into Hailey's hole and sustains a competent rhythm, but resembles a prepubescent rabbit. He gets sent up to Ava who is eating RoidMonkeyJoe's ass.

NO WAIT, THAT'S ACTUALLY A RUSTY TROMBONE.

This is happening while Tommy Utah is turning her anus into mincemeat with his rapid pounding. It's clear who the finalists are going to be, but it will make for a subpar show unless more guys can make it past Hailey. So far, five of the contestants have not made it out of the first room. Tweaker, who has been standing in the background attempting liftoff for the past seven minutes, tries to get fluffed by Angelina who slithers away. SilkySmooth has been silent like a dark horse and is ready to move on after mere seconds with Nicki. Tweaker steps up to Nicki, who brings him into her warm embrace. She even takes Tweaker penis in her mouth, but it has no effect.

BRING ME A BUCKET.

JizzMouth is awkwardly trying to position himself with Hailey while she commands him to open up and not block camera. He finds a sustainable rhythm before Hailey sends him to Ava. Security escorts him down the long hallway, past the linens, past the carpenter's table, past the four rascals aka fat/old people movers. Here he finds RoidMonkeyJoe, wearing nothing but a black baseball hat and Tommy Utah trying to pull off a DP with Ava. She yells at them to tell her "what a dirty cock whore I am!"

WELCOME TO SATAN'S LIAR, PAL.

By the time JizzMouth makes it into the mix, his chub is gone, so he furiously works it back up.

"Go in her ass, bro." suggests RoidMonkeyJoe, so he does, where little penetration is seen nor is there sustainable rhythm. Back down to Hailey. In his place, SilkySmooth enters, having satisfied Hailey moments earlier. RoidMonkeyJoe goes limp and is sent back down. SilkySmooth and Johnny Utah work as a nice tandem when only mouths and vaginas are involved.

"Have them try a DP on Ava, please," I buzz to Huggy, who is manning the camera in her station. After I tell Huggy to frame out SilkySmooth's hairy butthole, they dock successfully. By my porn standards, this would not be an acceptable DP. It's amateur hour with the lack of proper positioning and sustainable rhythm.

TODAY'S WORDS ARE 'SUSTAINABLE RHYTHM'.

RedMan bursts onto the scene, no doubt having to prove to himself he can make it this far. His touch with the atmosphere ends once he is unable to fulfill Ava's demand for anal and down he goes. BadTattoo levels up and begins rabbit-humping in every hole, which Ava enjoys. SilkySmooth lurks in the background, keeping his edge while Tommy Utah and RoidMonkeyJoe remain staples in Ava's room.

RedMan pounds away at Hailey and is showing promise. He's been to Everest and he's lived to tell the tale. But he knows there is more to learn to stay in those heights. He makes a show of the next five minutes by showcasing his skills with Hailey. NippleRings, JizzMouth, and BallFro try to enter the mix. RedMan pulls out and gives Hailey a respectable facial while the contestants try and figure out what to do next. JizzMouth steps up where RedMan left off and takes Hailey into missionary.

"Talk dirty to me!" she demands. JizzMouth continues to fuck her. "Call me a dirty whore!"

"Uhhhhhhhh" SLAP! Hailey gives him one across the face.

"Don't lose your fucking wood now! You got to be able to handle some of the crazy shit your dicks bring out of us." JizzMouth's wood falls forever into the night.

I FEEL YOU, DUDE. SAME THING HAPPENED TO ME THE FIRST TIME I WAS SLAPPED IN BED.

Meanwhile in Mopesville, the doomsday clock ticks on those left behind. MicroPenis, Tweaker, Fuck-A-Fan, NippleRings, and BallFro are desperately seeking erections as Julia and Angelina play with each other. Nicki, feeling generous and sympathy for DasBoots after he munched her vagina for five minutes, is getting pounded in missionary. This is non-scripted and a bonus both for the viewers and DasBoots. It does the trick and he is sent to Hailey. Jordan takes over for DasBoots and slides himself into Nicki, maintaining eye contact with the contestants. "This is how it's done, boys."

"Call me a dirty whore!" Hailey yells at DasBoots as he fucks her. He's all smiles.

"Don't smile! Why are you smiling? Call me a dirty whore! I fucking love it!" He remains silent.

HE DOESN'T UNDERSTAND YOU! HE'S A FOREIGNER!

"I don't know why you're smiling, your dick is getting soft!" After a terrible go of it, he is sent back down to Mopesville.

I drop the axe on MicroPenis, Tweaker, and Fuck-A-Fan. They put their clothes on, no doubt questioning their life choices. Angelina allows BadTattoo to eat her asshole while Julia blows Jordan. MicroPenis watches all of it while still trying to gain an erection, or is he trying to...

"Uggggghhhhhh!"

"Did you just cum on yourself, dude? He did!" Jordan informs the live audience as the cameraman displays the pearl droplets resting on his belly.

THAT MIGHT HAVE BEEN THE GREATEST MOMENT IN THE SHOW. OR THE WORST.

MicroPenis bows his head in shame.

"Go hit the shower, dude," Jordan tells him.

SO. DID THE DAY GO LIKE YOU THOUGHT IT WOULD? WHAT WERE YOU THINKING? YOU DROVE FROM OHIO TO DO THIS???

The Doomsday Clock strikes and the first part of the contest is over. Now, it's time for the members to decide who advances to the finals. Ava is sad only half of the contestants made it to her station and only four went into her asshole. Jordan gathers them one by one and asks what went wrong:

BallFro: "I'm not sure. I didn't do that good."

PERHAPS IT WAS THE PUBES. ELIMINATED!

MicroPenis: "Too many dicks around me. I couldn't get past that."

GO HOME AND FIND SOME MEMORY-ERASING PILLS. ELIMINATED!

BadTattoo: "Far from the best I have ever done."

YOU ARE D-LEVEL TALENT, WORTHY OF BUKKAKE AND AMATEUR VIDEOS. ELIMINATED!

RedMan: "I came twice. I thought I did pretty good, but I know I have ways to go."

WITH WORK, HE COULD HAVE A FUTURE. JUST LAY OFF THE TANNING BED, KID. ELIMINATED!

Fuck-A-Fan: "I was ambushed by superior firepower."

YES, NICKI HUNTER IS A SEMEN ENCHANTRESS. ELIMINATED!

NippleRings (sweating profusely): "It was very hot in there. I was getting overheated."

IT'S DECEMBER, DUDE. ELIMINATED!

SilkySmooth: "I thought I did well." Members agree with him and Jordan knights him with his arm, sending him to the finals.

JizzMouth: "I was doing fine. Those long hallways can be tough when trying to keep wood. But, then Hailey's slap threw me off. I was being a pussy."

YOU ARE A NICHE PERFORMER, JIZZMOUTH. FIND YOUR MARKET. ELIMINATED!

Tweaker: "I can get wood, check out HumptyVis... "

"Go sit down, buddy," Jordan tells him, cutting off Tweaker's shameless self-promotion. As Tweaker sits, he mouths off to Jordan who either does not hear or does not care.

DasBoots: "Is hard to get wood looking at men's asses."

NICKI LET YOU FUCK HER. TAKE THE WIN. ELIMINATED!

Tommy Utah: "I have done scenes with the camera guy's wife, so it was pretty easy for me," he says while still sporting a hard-on. His fate is determined, as is RoidMonkeyJoe's. While the three finalists head down to Ava's station, if the mopes want to get their nut, they may do so on Hailey's face in the final round.

PORN LIMBO, FELLAS.

Quick time out to talk about the camera guy and his wife:

The camera guy was Mike aka the Commodore aka my mole and was married to a performer named Morgan. When Huggy made a play to take over his photo duties and income, the Commodore found greener pastures in Columbus, OH in the form of a strip club and left town after a few years with my crew. Currently, he lives in Florida, is divorced, and has found prosperity. Back to the original point, Tommy Utah was hired by the Commodore and Morgan to shoot content for her website. It is unclear if the Commodore ran camera, but my magic eight ball says: "All Signs Point To Yes." Back to the show.

We stay streaming while Pete and Ethan wrangle Huggy's camera cables. They look spritely compared to the gray-haired production managers they will become under Vic Lagina.

Security babysits the mopes while Angelina eats a piece of fried chicken from the dinner delivered for the cast and crew. RoidMonkeyJoe, SilkySmooth, and Tommy Utah begin the final fuck-a-thon with Ava as Julia, Nicki, Angelina, and Jordan provide commentary while encouraging members to vote.

Meanwhile, all the mopes except MicroPenis, BadTattoo, and DasBoots (who are missing and likely disgusted with themselves) encircle Hailey jerking it as she lies on the sexagon, asking for their cum. Fuck-A-Fan musters another load dump, getting some on her ear.

YOU JUST WANTED TO JIZZ ON PORN STARS, YOU PERVERT.

BallFro is followed by RedMan, now on his third nut.

CONTINUE YOUR TRAINING, GRASSHOPPER.

Last one standing is Tweaker. Hailey sits as the ejaculate of five men rests on her face, seeping into her eyeballs. Tweaker shoots thick, nasty meth droplets onto her face. Security ushers them back into the lobby where they await their participation trophy: a check for five hundred dollars which also purchased their dignity.

The show is derailing and the Pussy Panel is losing steam. Ava is getting fucked by Tommy Utah, RoidMonkeyJoe, and SilkySmooth, but *these are not the droids we are looking for!* Hogan and I are ambivalent. Hogan was hoping for a massive gangbang.

"Yeah, but we saw a man jizz all over himself after not being able to get a hard on around three hot porn chicks. Plus, Angelina's antics were a spectacle unto themselves."

As if on cue, Angelina takes a huge bite of chicken and tosses the bones into the orgy. She then rubs her cell phone against her vagina. Jordan catches SilkySmooth pinching at the base.

"That is not woodsmanship!" Jordan barks. "Angelina, why isn't my penis in your mouth?"

Angelina sits on his lap. He stands up, bends her over the judge's table, pulls down her bottoms, and fucks her doggie. The penetration is facing away from camera, giving members a soft-core angle, but she is enjoying herself. Things derail when RoidMonkeyJoe tries to stick his penis in her mouth. So, she spits chicken at his dick. He backs away and heads toward the orgy. Hailey joins the group, wearing a towel around her clothed body. Her eyes are glazed and red from the sperm swimming in her eyeballs. Angelina breaks free from Jordan as he chases her behind the gangbang. He holds her down by the neck while trying to insert himself.

"Noooooooooo!"

"Tell Jordan to back off! Let's get Angelina out of there, I have hit my crazy limit," I tell my crew. Jordan heads back to the judge's table.

"God? What are we doing now? I am waiting to hear from the voice of God," Julia beckons to the camera.

I had been giving Jordan direction, but his earpiece fell out when he was fucking Angelina. My direction is to pop so we can end this travesty.

"Droppin' loads!" screams Nicki.

"Don't say that. We don't want to be sued by that douchebag Nick Manning!" I tell her over the wireless.[1]

SilkySmooth delivers a precise pop all over Ava's face. It does not come as easily for RoidMonkeyJoe and Tommy Utah, who jerk numb and raw penises. I cut to the camera following Angelina who berates the mopes.

"You think you're cute, don't you? You're props. You're props. And... your dicks are small."

"Get the fuck out of here we don't want to hear your fucking bullshit," Tweaker says defiantly.

"Dude, dude! Clean your fucking teeth, bro. Go clip your fucking toenails... "

"Go fix your fucking tits!"

"You know what? You know what? Can I hit him?" she asks security as she takes off one of her boots.

"Get your fucking ugly meth head out of here, you fucking bitch!" Security starts to move her away while she continues her savagery.

"Get that fucking meth head out of here before I knock you in the fucking grill. Get your concave chest out of this room! Bitch! Fucking lose your teeth, pull them out, get some dentures you fucking meth head. You ugly, trailer trash meth smoking little bitch!" she carries on down the hallway while security stays behind her.

"Thirty seconds!" Jordan announces. RoidMonkeyJoe and Tommy Utah continue to beat their meat to no avail. We have our winner: SilkySmooth aka James Maverick! We wrap for the day. With three shoots scheduled tomorrow we're all physically and mentally drained.

NOTHING A LITTLE COCAINE CAN'T FIX.

THE AFTERMATH

Tweaker wanted to fight Jordan after the show; however, Jordan was completely unaware. He also felt the show was designed to make them look stupid.

"Tell him we can sort it out in the wrestling ring in the warehouse," was Jordan's reply.

"Only if I can broadcast it live," I tell him. Reality is, Jordan would bite off his nose before pummeling all of those rotted teeth out of his skull. Tweaker already had enough of life to work through as it is. No sense in adding to it.

Ava was gracious enough to knock a thousand bucks off her rate due to the lack of volume of contestants. Still, she made over three times her normal rate for a gang-bang, so she was pleased regardless. Eventually, she shed her 'Filth Bucket of the Century' title after settling down and getting married. Not to Chuckles McKnuckles. She shoots girl/girl only for her OnlyFans, a big departure from her previous self.

As for our winner, while he made it through the marathon and pulled out a surprising victory in extremely difficult and challenging circumstances, there was nothing remarkable about him. I shot him a month later for *DoctorAdventures.com* with Bella Reese and Phil Jackson'ed him when necessary, but I sensed his further involvement would produce mediocre Brazzers scenes. It became a moot point as no formal contract was ever offered by Manwin. I never saw James Maverick again as Manwin reneged on the deal for the competition.

HE WENT TO HELL AND BACK AND HAD NOTHING TO SHOW FOR IT. SEEMS FISHY.

A few months later, I needed a replacement for Ramón in a pinch, so a call to Tommy Utah was dispatched. The scene was for *BigTitsInUniform.com* with Emily B, a beautiful import from England. It was a firehouse scene, and she played a sexy firewoman stripper hired to lighten the moods of the firemen who have had a brutal few weeks. Tommy Gunn was one of these firemen. In the *Tale of Two Tommys*, one handled business like a professional while the other maintained a hard-on but could not pop. Minutes turned into ten minutes. Ten minutes turned into thirty minutes. Finally, the solution was for him to watch porn on his cell phone off-set, get close, and then run in and finish off. Another thirty minutes later and after three attempts, we finally got the pop.

PIMPIN' AIN'T EASY.

He was called on one more time, again because we were in a pinch. Again, he had no issue staying hard, but popping was the wait. After, there was no reason to reach out to him.

GODSPEED, TOMMY.

As for RoidMonkeyJoe, I hired him to be a production assistant for a few months to utilize his strength, which came in handy. But his services as a male performer would never be needed for Manwin.

A few months later, I hired Donny, a little person dressed as a leprechaun, to eat out Hailey's ass for a St. Paddy's Day scene. Donny died of an accidental fentanyl, cocaine, and alcohol overdose ten years later. Hailey slid into a worsening state of opioid addiction before finally getting arrested in 2014 and subsequently being placed on probation. She has been clean ever since.

After watching these events unfold on video almost eleven years after the fact, I can't help but feel disturbed by what I was viewing. The problem wasn't the content itself, or that I had been a part of it, but rather I had the ability to wipe it from memory and move onto the next shit show so easily. What were these guys thinking?

While I hope MicroPenis did not jump off a building after his debacle, I do hope he and everyone else in that room now understands what a massive task being a solid woodsman in the porn industry is. I wonder if this breed of male talent is on the verge of extinction given the ever-changing nature of the industry and the reduced demand for such stamina. The last few nights of sleep, I have been haunted by Angelina and Tweaker. It kicked up some dust in the gray matter I needed to process. We really should not have been shooting Angelina over those last few years because her mind was going. But porn enables the broken.

It seems as if I have grown a conscience and developed empathy over the past three years in porn exile. Or I am able to feel again since I'm no longer numb. Maybe I just needed to be reminded of how insane those years were.

STOP BEING SUCH A PUSSY, DUDE.

I appreciate all of you who have taken time to read, listen, and support this endeavor. Whether you loved or hated *Filthy!*, I would enjoy hearing from all of you. Respectfully, of course. I always encourage intelligent exchange of thoughts, even if I may disagree with your viewpoint.

Tweet Vic @viclagina Tweet OZ @zpaceball

R.I.P. 'Poop'

JUNE 1978 - JUNE 2023

This book is also dedicated to Poop.

He died months before publication of this novel from accidental fentanyl overdose through laced cocaine. He was two weeks shy of his 45th birthday.

I am not sure why these dick-less, brainless, soulless, godless drug dealers are intentionally killing their customers. Seems counter-productive, business-wise. If you're dealing both fentanyl and cocaine, here's some advice: use separate equipment when weighing and cutting so you don't kill your clients you fucktards!

I will always miss my friend.

Since cocaine can instantly kill you nowadays, let's be careful out there. I would have suffered Poop's fate had my cocaine-fueled porn journey continued a few years longer. Or maybe I died years ago. Maybe this is the afterlife...

Willy was a noble man
When he lived in Birmingham
But he was losin' his mind
In a world of his own
Willy left on a rainy day
Wings spread and wind in his face
But nobody knew that Willy could fly
Oh, but don't you fly away, boy
Don't you fly away
Don't you fly away, boy

- RAYLAND BAXTER

CORROBORATING EVIDENCE

2. LAYING THE FOUNDATION

1. https://www.independent.co.uk/news/ron-jeremy-ap-los-angeles-harvey-weinstein-danny-masterson-b2264031.html

IN MEMORIAM: JESSICA JAYMES, 3/8/79 - 9/17/19

1. https://www.gq.com/story/james-deen-porn-star-gq-june-2012-interview

VIC LAGINA'S SCHOOL OF PORN LESSON SIX: SQUIRT OR PISS?

1. https://onlinelibrary.wiley.com/doi/10.1111/iju.15004

19. THIRTY DAYS BECOMES THIRTY MINUTES

1. https://pornstarbabylon.wordpress.com/2009/09/27/derek-hay-retires-from-performing-an-industry-rejoices/

22. THE INFAMOUS SYPHILIS OUTBREAK OF 2012

1. https://www.cbsnews.com/news/porn-star-syphilis-case-jesse-spencer-aka-mr-marcus-sentenced-to-jail-for-knowingly-exposing-co-stars-to-disease/
2. https://www.dailynews.com/2015/03/25/porn-star-lylith-lavey-settles-mr-marcus-syphilis-case-with-bangbros/

24. DID D-LIST CELEBRITY █████* ROOFIE MY GIRLFRIEND?

1. https://www.independent.co.uk/news/world/europe/fabian-thylmann-the-ruler-in-the-realms-of-lust-is-arrested-for-alleged-tax-evasion-8411926.html
2. https://www.pressreader.com/canada/national-post-latest-edition/20201021/281921660533755

27. OH NO, WE'RE NOT DONE YET

1. https://uproxx.com/filmdrunk/michael-douglas-blames-throat-cancer-on-cunnilingus/

28. BIZZARO-WORLD

1. https://www.buzzfeed.com/arianelange/nikki-benz-brazzers-sexual-assault-allegations
2. https://casetext.com/case/ismail-v-montchak
3. https://www.xbiz.com/news/216179/tony-t-ramon-nomar-sue-nikki-benz-mindgeek-for-libel
4. https://www.buzzfeednews.com/article/arianelange/nikki-benz-porn-defamation-lawsuit-metoo
5. https://www.scmp.com/news/world/united-states-canada/article/2141167/porn-star-nikki-benz-suing-brazzers-after-she-was
6. https://www.freespeechcoalition.com/blog/2019/07/15/tony-t-wins-court-victory-over-nikki-benz-ynot

VIC LAGINA'S SCHOOL OF PORN: LESSON EIGHT: A BRIEF HISTORY ON PORN AGENTS AND THE PORN UNION

1. https://www.nbcconnecticut.com/news/national-international/porn-actresses-accuse-top-agent-of-fraud-sex-abuse/2050671/
2. https://www.xbiz.com/news/270488/la-directs-derek-hay-indicted-in-pandering-probe (Maybe this will be the nail in Dr. Evil's coffin. Probably not. Cockroach.)

29. LIFE AFTER BRAZZERS

1. https://www.celebritynetworth.com/richest-businessmen/ceos/fabian-thylmann-net-worth/
2. https://www.ourcommons.ca/DocumentViewer/en/43-2/ETHI/meeting-19/evidence
3. https://www.nytimes.com/2020/12/04/opinion/sunday/pornhub-rape-trafficking.html
4. https://www.abc.net.au/news/2020-12-17/pornhub-sued-by-40-girlsdoporn-sex-trafficking-victims/12992798
5. https://www.politico.com/news/2021/06/17/canadian-committee-tough-action-pornhub-495077

30. CODA

1. https://www.independent.co.uk/news/world/americas/pornhub-ceo-feras-antoon-house-attack-b1996359.html
2. https://www.washingtonpost.com/business/2022/06/21/pornhub-mindgeek-leaders-resign/
3. https://www.prnewswire.com/news-releases/ecp-announces-acquisition-of-mindgeek-parent-company-of-pornhub-301774247.html

EPILOGUE

1. https://trademark.trademarkia.com/droppin-loads-77175028.html Fortunately his trademark expired in 2014 and can be repeated for this book.

www.ingramcontent.com/pod-product-compliance
Lightning Source LLC
Chambersburg PA
CBHW071135130626
46553CB00004B/1384
* 9 7 9 8 9 8 9 1 9 8 1 0 8 *